Recent Researches in the
Music of the Middle Ages and
Early Renaissance
Volume 30

EARLY MEDIEVAL CHANTS FROM NONANTOLA

Part I
Ordinary Chants and Tropes

Edited by James Borders

A-R Editions, Inc.

EARLY MEDIEVAL CHANTS FROM NONANTOLA

PART I

RECENT RESEARCHES IN THE MUSIC OF THE MIDDLE AGES AND EARLY RENAISSANCE

Charles M. Atkinson, general editor

A-R Editions, Inc., publishes seven series of musicological editions
that present music brought to light in the course of current research:

Recent Researches in the Music of the Middle Ages and Early Renaissance
Charles M. Atkinson, general editor

Recent Researches in the Music of the Renaissance
James Haar, general editor

Recent Researches in the Music of the Baroque Era
Christoph Wolff, general editor

Recent Researches in the Music of the Classical Era
Eugene K. Wolf, general editor

Recent Researches in the Music of the Nineteenth and Early Twentieth Centuries
Rufus Hallmark, general editor

Recent Researches in American Music
John M. Graziano, general editor

Recent Researches in the Oral Traditions of Music
Philip V. Bohlman, general editor

Each *Recent Researches* edition is devoted to works
by a single composer or to a single genre of composition.
The contents are chosen for their potential interest to scholars
and performers, then prepared for publication according to the
standards that govern the making of all reliable historical editions.

Subscribers to any of these series, as well as patrons of subscribing institutions,
are invited to apply for information about the "Copyright-Sharing Policy"
of A-R Editions, Inc., under which policy any part of an edition
may be reproduced free of charge for study or performance.

Address correspondence to

A-R EDITIONS, INC.
801 Deming Way
Madison, Wisconsin 53717

(608) 836-9000

RECENT RESEARCHES IN THE MUSIC OF THE MIDDLE AGES
AND EARLY RENAISSANCE • VOLUME 30

EARLY MEDIEVAL CHANTS FROM NONANTOLA

Part I
Ordinary Chants and Tropes

Edited by James Borders

A-R Editions, Inc.
Madison

EARLY MEDIEVAL CHANTS FROM NONANTOLA

Edited by
James Borders
and
Lance Brunner

*Recent Researches in the Music
of the Middle Ages and Early Renaissance*

Part I.   Ordinary Chants and Tropes
          Volume 30

Part II. Proper Chants and Tropes
          Volume 31

Part III. Processional Chants
          Volume 32

Part IV. Sequences
          Volume 33

© 1996 by A-R Editions, Inc.
All rights reserved
Printed in the United States of America

ISBN 0-89579-328-8
ISSN 0362-3572

∞ The paper used in this publication meets the minimum requirements of the American National Standard for Information Sciences—Permanence of Paper for Printed Library Materials, ANSI Z39.48-1984.

Contents

PREFACE	vii
Acknowledgments	vii
ABBREVIATIONS	viii
GENERAL INTRODUCTION	ix
Historical Background	ix
The Abbey of Nonantola	x
The Manuscript Sources	xii
Manuscript Inventories	xiv
Notes	xxxii
INTRODUCTION TO THE ORDINARY CHANTS AND TROPES	xxxiv
Kyrie eleison	xxxiv
Gloria in excelsis	xxxv
Sanctus	xxxvi
Agnus Dei	xxxvi
Notes	xxxvii
CRITICAL APPARATUS	xxxviii
List of Manuscript Sigla	xxxviii
List of Works Cited	xxxix
Editorial Methods	xl
Commentaries	xli
PLATES	lxxxiv

Ordinary Chants and Tropes

Kyrie eleison

1. Melnicki 55; Vatican *ad lib.* VI; *Te Christe rex supplices*	1
2. Melnicki 39; Vatican I; *Omnipotens genitor*	3
3. Melnicki 68; Vatican XIV; *Canamus cuncti laudes*	5
4. Melnicki 39; Vatican I; *Lux et origo lucis*	7
5. Melnicki 155; Vatican XV; *Dominator Deus*	9
6. Melnicki 124; *Rex magne domine*	10
7. Melnicki 47; Vatican VI; *Kyrie rex genitor*	12
8. Melnicki 155; Vatican XV	14
9. Melnicki 151; Vatican XVIII	14
10. Melnicki 136	15
11. Melnicki 112 (?)	16
12. Melnicki 217; Vatican XVI	16

Gloria in excelsis

1. Bosse 39; Gloria A	17
2. Bosse 2 (var.); Milan IV	19
3. Bosse 43; Vatican XV	20
4. Bosse 12; Vatican I	21
5. Bosse 11; Vatican XIV	22
6. Bosse 21	23
7. Bosse 51; Vatican XI	24
8a. Bosse 51; Vatican XI; *Pax sempiterna*	24

8b. Bosse 39; Gloria A; *Pax sempiterna*	27
9. Bosse 2 (var.); Milan IV; *Quem patris ad dextram*	30
10. Bosse 43; Vatican XV; *Quem cives caelestes*	32
11a. Bosse 12; Vatican I; *Laus tua Deus*	34
11b. Bosse 39; Gloria A; *Laus tua Deus*	37
12. Bosse 12; Vatican I; *Quem novitate*	40
13a. Bosse 51; Vatican XI; *Cives superni . . . Christus surrexit*	42
13b. Bosse 39; Gloria A; *Cives superni . . . Christus surrexit*	45
14. Bosse 11; Vatican XIV; *Alme mundi hodie de morte*	49
15. Bosse 11; Vatican XIV; *Alme mundi hodie in caelum*	51
16. Bosse 51; Vatican XI; *O laudabilis rex*	51
17. Bosse 51; Vatican XI; *Laudat in excelsis*	54
18. Bosse 12; Vatican I; *Quando regis cunctos*	56
19. Bosse 11; Vatican XIV; *O gloria sanctorum*	59
20. Bosse 12; Vatican I; *Qui caelicolas*	61
21. Bosse 2 (var.); Milan IV; *Hinc laudando patrem*	63

Sanctus

1. Thannabaur 154; Vatican I; *Deus fortis*	65
2. Thannabaur 154; Vatican I; *Pater ingenitus*	66
3. Thannabaur 216 (var.); *Pater lumen aeternum*	67
4. Thannabaur 154; Vatican I; *Deus pater ingenite*	68
5. Thannabaur 223; Vatican XV; *Mundi fabricator*	69
6. Thannabaur 74; *Admirabilis splendor*	70
7. Thannabaur 63; *Quem cherubim*	71
8. Thannabaur 60	72
9. Thannabaur 111 (var.)	72
10. Thannabaur 9	73
11. Thannabaur 10	74
12. Thannabaur 32; Vatican XVII	74
13a. Thannabaur 57	75
13b. Thannabaur 57	76

Agnus Dei

1. Schildbach 226; Vatican II; *Qui sedes ad dexteram patris*	77
2. Schildbach 78; *Omnipotens aeterna Dei*	78
3. Schildbach 209 (var. 2); *Tu Deus et dominus*	79
4. Schildbach 236; *Suscipe deprecationem . . . Dei patris*	79
5. Schildbach 236 (var. 3); *Ad dextram patris*	80
6. Schildbach 87; *Exaudi domine*	81
7. Schildbach 164; Vatican XVI; *Suscipe deprecationem . . . Dei*	82
8. Schildbach 19; *Agnus Dei . . . miserere nobis alleluia alleluia*	83
9. Schildbach 81; *Salus et vita*	83
10. Schildbach 209 (var. 2)	84

Index of First Lines: Ordinary Tropes — 85

Preface

Early Medieval Chants from Nonantola contains all the tropes, prosulae, Ordinary chants, sequences, and processional chants found in three troper-prosers from the northern Italian monastery of San Silvestro di Nonantola: Bologna, Biblioteca Universitaria 2824; Rome, Biblioteca Casanatense 1741; and Rome, Biblioteca Nazionale Centrale 1343. These related manuscripts, which represent the lion's share of complete medieval music books with diastematic Nonantolan notation, were presumably copied in the abbey's scriptorium between the late eleventh and early twelfth centuries. Together they provide a sense of the expanded repertory of chant performed at this northern Italian monastery during the period.

The present work is divided in a way that loosely parallels the organization of the manuscript sources, which is: (1) Ordinary chants by category; (2) fraction antiphons; (3) Proper tropes, prosulae, antiphons *ante evangelium*, and sequences by feast; (4) processional antiphons, responds, hymns, and litanies by occasion. (Complete inventories of the three Nonantolan tropers are found in the general introduction.) The first part of this edition contains all the chants for the Ordinary of the Mass with associated tropes and prosulae. The second contains all tropes and prosulae for the Mass Proper with their associated chants. The third includes *confractoria*, antiphons *ante evangelium*, and processional chants. The fourth contains the forty-one sequences of the Nonantolan repertory, including the earliest readable versions of a number of Notker's compositions. Within each category the chants are arranged according to their use during the yearly liturgical cycle. The reader will note the similarity of this plan to the *Beneventanum Troporum Corpus*, edited by John Boe and Alejandro Planchart, Recent Researches in the Music of the Middle Ages and Early Renaissance, vols. 16–28 (Madison, 1989–).

The general introduction outlines the development of Nonantola's chant repertory and describes the three manuscript sources in detail; it concludes with complete inventories. Each volume contains introductions to the individual repertories along with commentaries on the chants with Latin texts and English translations. Summary lists of manuscript sigla for the sources cited in the edition are found before the commentaries, along with a bibliography of works cited and a discussion of editorial methods. Transcriptions of the texts and music comprise the bulk of each volume. Finally, an alphabetical index of the contents of the volume (individual trope verses or first lines of complete chants) is also included.

This edition is intended to meet the needs of a wide variety of users. Students of Romance philology and of medieval Latin may wish to consult manuscript spellings, which are generally retained. Significant text variants are also reported. Singers and conductors will find the translations supplied in the commentaries to be helpful. Musicologists and scholars of the liturgy can consult the readings and variants to compare them with other versions of the chants and tropes. It is also hoped that specialists will use the commentaries in the first and second volumes in their studies of chant transmission. Most important, the editors hope that these volumes will spark the interest of students, enabling them to study and perform the chants found in this edition.

Acknowledgments

At the outset I wish to express my sincere thanks to those people who contributed to my work on this edition. I owe the greatest debt of gratitude to my friend and fellow Chicagoan F. Joseph Smith, who with supreme patience (both with me and the Nonantolan scribes) vetted the Latin texts, corrected my translations, and offered much encouragement. I am also grateful to John Boe, who guided my early efforts by sharing with me the preface, editorial methods, and selected commentaries from the Kyrie volume of the *Beneventanum Troporum Corpus* prior to its publication. Lance Brunner and Alejandro Planchart encouraged me to undertake this project early in my career, and I remain grateful to them. Some enthusiastic graduate students at the University of Michigan, too numerous to name individually (but you know who you are!), helped me turn my transcriptions and comments into an edition in a memorable seminar some years ago. I also wish to thank Jonathan Besancon, who assisted with the collation of musical variants; David Vayo, who copied a great deal of the music with great accuracy; and Robyn Stilwell, who provided me with a clean text to submit to the publisher. Let me also express my gratitude to the editorial staff of A-R Editions, whose intelligence, editorial skill, and tenacity I have come to admire greatly. Last but certainly not least I thank my wife, Ann Marie Borders, for her patience and love.

James Borders

Abbreviations

AH	*Analecta Hymnica Medii Aevi.* 55 vols. Edited by Clemens Blume, Guido Maria Dreves, and Henry Marriott Bannister. 1886–1922. Reprint. New York, 1961.
Bosse	Bosse, Detlev. *Untersuchung einstimmiger Melodie zum "Gloria in excelsis Deo."* Forschungsbeiträge zur Musikwissenschaft, 2. Regensburg, 1954.
BTC I	*Beneventanum Troporum Corpus I. Tropes of the Proper of the Mass from Southern Italy, A.D. 1000–1250.* Edited by Alejandro Enrique Planchart. Recent Researches in the Music of the Middle Ages and Early Renaissance, vols. 16–18. Madison, 1994.
BTC II	*Beneventanum Troporum Corpus II. Ordinary Chants and Tropes for the Mass from Southern Italy, A.D. 1000–1250.* Edited by John Boe. Recent Researches in the Music of the Middle Ages and Early Renaissance, vols. 19–27. Madison, 1989–. [Part 1: Kyrie eleison. Part 2: Gloria in excelsis. Part 3: Preface Chants and Sanctus. Part 4: Agnus Dei and Ite missa est.]
CT	*Corpus Troporum.* Stockholm, 1975–.
JAMS	*Journal of the American Musicological Society.*
Melnicki	Melnicki, Margareta [Landwehr-]. *Das einstimmige Kyrie des lateinischen Mittelalters.* Regensburg, 1955.
MQ	*The Musical Quarterly.*
New Grove	*The New Grove Dictionary of Music and Musicians.* 20 vols. Edited by Stanley Sadie. London, 1980.
RdCG	*Revue du chant grégorien.*
RISM	Répertoire International des Sources Musicales.
Schildbach	Schildbach, Martin. *Das einstimmige Agnus Dei und seine handschriftliche Überlieferung vom 10. bis zum 16. Jahrhundert.* Erlangen, 1967.
Thannabaur	Thannabaur, Peter Josef. *Das einstimmige Sanctus der römischen Messe in der handschriftliche Überlieferung des 11. bis 16. Jahrhunderts.* Erlanger Arbeiten zur Musikwissenschaft, 1. Munich, 1962.

General Introduction

Historical Background

The Nonantolan tropers contain chants from various geographical regions and historical periods. The earliest state of the abbey's repertory cannot be discerned, but the chants sung there at the time of its founding in the mid-eighth century were probably similar to those of other northern Italian centers, including Milan. A few examples of this early Italic chant have survived in later books, including those copied in Nonantola.[1] One is tempted to label this pre-Gregorian repertory "Lombardic" since some early northern Italian chants have connections with those of Montecassino and Benevento, suggesting an important southern link in the chain of transmission.[2] But a still more important formative influence on the early chant of northern Italy came from across the Alps, from centers where the Gallican liturgy was observed.[3]

There is much to recommend the theory of Gallican influence since worship services in Lombard northern Italy and Merovingian Gaul shared common traits. As far as music is concerned, the Mass rituals of both regions included the singing of a chant during the gospel procession and at the fraction of the host.[4] These have no parallels in the Roman rite. Related chants for these liturgical functions survive in manuscripts from northern Italian centers like Nonantola, Milan, Mantua, Piacenza, and also in the chantbooks of Saint-Denis and other centers of the Gallican liturgy in West Frankland.[5] These add significantly to the possibility of connections between the pre-Gregorian repertories of Gaul and Italy.

The Gallican liturgy was not, however, the only one that likely touched the early chant of Nonantola. Latin translations of Byzantine chants survive in the Nonantolan tropers, as does a single transliterated Greek antiphon, *Ote to stauron*. Although the question of Eastern influence must necessarily remain open for lack of comparable sources, it is probable that Greek chants spread inland to Nonantola from coastal centers like Ravenna.[6] They may also have been transmitted directly by Greek monks who took refuge at Nonantola during the Iconoclastic controversy.[7] It is also likely that the chant repertory that the Franks introduced to northern Italy after Charlemagne's conquest of the region contained antiphons and hymns with Latin translations of Greek texts.

Nonantola's location at the intersection of crossroads linking northern and southern Europe and Eastern and Western branches of Christianity helps explain the foreign elements in its early liturgy. It also accounts for the variety of outside influences to which its chant repertory was later subject. The most important of these came from the Frankish North beginning in the last quarter of the eighth century. Although Charlemagne's annexation of the Italian kingdom coincided with the initiation of liturgical reform, the process of change may have been more gradual than is sometimes assumed. Although Carolingian officials must have exerted pressure on local clergies to bring their liturgies into conformity, we know little about the actual chants that were disseminated in this early phase of transmission. Given the combination of Gallican and Roman elements at such major centers as Saint-Denis, however, the repertory that the Franks brought with them into northern Italy probably included some Gallican remnants. Some putatively Gallican antiphons *ante evangelium* and processional chants, for example, may have been come to Nonantola and other northern Italian centers at this time.[8] Moreover, given northern Italian resistance to the Carolingian liturgical reform best documented in Milan, it seems likely that local cantors would have tried to retain chants from their own repertories to fill the inevitable gaps in the transmitted Franco-Roman corpus.

In the absence of written evidence, the earliest phases in the history of the northern Italian chant cannot be reconstructed with any certainty. Thus, rather than attempting to imagine the shape of this lost repertory, we would do well to focus on the surviving sources of the late tenth and eleventh centuries.[9] It was during this period that the greatest challenge to regional chant dialects was mounted in the form of notated Gregorian chants, which eventually replaced most of what remained of regional Propers (Milan being a notable exception). The transmission of written plainchant thus had an impact similar to the copying of the prayers of the celebrant centuries before; it wiped out improvised formulas and regularized the texts and, in the case of plainchant, the musical settings as well. Notated chants possessed the further advantage of having come from established centers within the Empire, not to mention the spiritual authority of the divinely inspired Pope Gregory the Great.[10] Moreover, the practice of notating chant spread during a period when Benedictine monks throughout Western Europe were actively copying and preserving all types of books. The eagerness with which the Nonantolan monks added to their own collection at this time has been well documented.[11]

Yet even the written Franco-Roman repertory that came to Nonantola in this period was probably not "pure." Rather it already contained accretions, including tropes to what are now called the standard chants of the Proper and Ordinary.[12] Because the origins of the repertory are unknown, the place of the abbey and other Italian centers in the early history of tropes is difficult to assess. Italy may have figured importantly in the origins of troping since MS XC in the Biblioteca Capitolare, Verona, was thought to have been the earliest collection of such accretions.[13] But only a single trope (*Ora est psallite,* fol. 135v) was part of the original ninth-century corpus of this manuscript, which originated in Monza; the other tropes were written by different tenth-century scribes who added their work after the codex had been brought to Verona.[14] Arguments surrounding the surviving manuscript evidence aside—the preservation of which is, after all, fortuitous—it makes little sense to posit that troping originated in northern Italy, far from the region where reform activity was most intense, namely, East and West Frankland. There the suppression of Gallican Propers and other chants would have led to the reassignment of favorite items to new liturgical functions at an early stage. It is difficult to imagine the same level of suppression at Nonantola, where the Franco-Roman repertory spread at a later stage and where non-Gregorian chants like antiphons *ante evangelium* and *confractoria* survived into the twelfth century.

The clergy of northern Italy, however, did not simply adopt the chants of other regions without modifications. Indeed, numerous reworkings of borrowed items are identified below. By way of introduction, it is useful to summarize the findings on transmission as it relates to the repertory of Introit tropes, in which changes are most evident.[15] Comparing trope complexes from one region to another, and from one northern Italian manuscript to the next, one quickly discovers variants. Even in related chantbooks like the Nonantolan tropers and Verona, Biblioteca Capitolare, MS CVII, the same trope verse may be connected with different chants. It may have different introductory verses, its order may change in relation to other verses, and it may be found in a variety of musical settings.

Although much of the Italian trope repertory was borrowed, medieval northern Italian singers also composed new pieces. Italian tropes are found in the earliest notated sources from the region, such as Rome, Biblioteca Angelica, MS 123, an eleventh-century Antiphonale Missarum with tropes that may have resided at Nonantola.[16] About one-third of Nonantolan tropes and sequences are Italian.[17] The emphasis was obviously on making practical collections for liturgical use rather than lengthy anthologies of alternatives.[18]

It should be stressed that, like other chants in the Nonantolan tropers, the tropes, sequences, and prosulae represent different layers of transmission.[19] For example, in the case of sequences there is a particularly close connection between Nonantola and East Frankland. But the transmission of Proper tropes was different; here there is a greater affinity for West Frankish pieces.[20] This connection is particularly evident when comparing Nonantolan and certain northern French manuscripts, especially Paris, Bibliothèque de l'Arsenal, MS 1169. Ties to Aquitaine are also evident, though scholars have suggested that this southern French repertory may itself descend from northern French antecedents.[21] The details of transmission are treated more fully in the individual commentaries.

Interpolations of new texts and music into Ordinary chants demonstrate still different patterns of transmission. They are, for instance, textually and musically more stable than the Proper tropes. Exceptions to this rule may be found among northern Italian versions of Gloria in excelsis tropes, which have been studied extensively by Mark Alan Leach[22] and Keith Falconer,[23] but in general base chants and tropes appear to have been transmitted integrally. This is not to say that the Nonantolan Ordinary was unified in its origins. Indeed, these chants were subject to their own patterns of regional dissemination, meaning that some Ordinary chants widely performed in West Frankland are simply not found in East Frankish sources. In terms of melodic identity, the affinity between Nonantola and centers in northern France is especially clear in the Ordinary, although Aquitaine may have played a more important role in the formation of this repertory at Nonantola than was the case with the Proper.

The Abbey of Nonantola

The former Benedictine abbey of San Silvestro di Nonantola is located about six miles northeast of Modena in the modern Italian province of Emilia. Along with Bobbio and Novalesa, Nonantola was among the most important monastic centers in medieval northern Italy. The abbey and its church were dedicated in 752 and named in honor of the Holy Apostles, but rededicated four years later to St. Sylvester when Pope Stephen II presented the monks with relics of this fourth-century pope.

These relics made the abbey church a site of local religious devotion, but the revenues from the abbey's property insured its early material prosperity. Practically from its institution the monks controlled some four hundred square kilometers of the surrounding countryside, most of it donated by the Lombard king and dukes of Persiceta. The Lombards also granted the monks of Nonantola unusually liberal privileges and immunities.[24] This generosity suggests that the nobility was sympathetic to Benedictine monasticism. Indeed, two years before the abbey's founding, King Rachis had joined the Benedictines after relinquishing the throne to his brother, Aistulf. But the true key to understanding Nonantola's wealth and privilege is kinship. The first abbot, St. Anselm (d. 803), a Lombard duke himself, was the brother-in-law of the abbey's principal benefactor, King Aistulf (d. 756), Rachis's brother. The bond between the two was strong enough to survive the king's death. Desiderius, Aistulf's successor, was so concerned about the abbot's loyalty that he exiled him to Montecassino in 762. Anselm returned to Nonantola only after Charlemagne's conquest of the Lombard kingdom in 774.

Perhaps Aistulf fully supported his brother-in-law's vocation to work, pray, and preserve knowledge, but the site of the monastery suggests a parallel, more pragmatic agenda. Nonantola was strategically valuable to the Lombards in that it overlooked territory they had recently won from the Byzantines. It was also located at the intersection of two major Roman roads, facilitating access to their troops. Thus, although the Lombards considered the abbey a holy place, it also would have been part of a network that included other monastery garrisons constructed in the mid-eighth century.

Nonantola's strategic location has helped us appreciate how the chant of the abbey was subject to so many different outside influences. Because it lay on the frontier between East and West and because its community included Greek and Frankish as well as Lombard monks, the abbey under the Lombards must have been a reasonably cosmopolitan place for its time.[25] Its library was established within a few years of its founding and it continued to grow throughout the Middle Ages.[26] Not the least contribution to this growth was made by St. Anselm, who was reported to have returned from exile at Montecassino with a number of codices from the monastery's famous library.[27]

Nonantola's status was further enhanced when it came under the protection of the Franks in the last quarter of the eighth century, and the monastery enjoyed the continuing support of a succession of Frankish emperors. Lothar, for example, who visited Nonantola in 837, granted the monks the right to elect their own abbot (subject to imperial confirmation).[28] The monastery grew ever more prosperous as the monks began draining the surrounding marshes and digging canals on their lands in the late eighth century. An unintended consequence of this activity was to make Nonantola a prize too rich for the local warlords to ignore. Emboldened by the division of the Empire, nobles vied with one another for the privilege of awarding the monastery and its revenues as a fief. Under Abbot Theuderich (870–87), Nonantola was ceded as a prebend to Bishop Adalhard of Verona, although Pope John VIII strenuously objected to this grant.

These controversies ended abruptly with the reversal of Nonantola's fortunes in the late ninth century. The abbey was destroyed by fire in 890, rebuilt, then sacked and burned again by the Huns in 899. Despite the subsequent rebuilding of the monastery and the nominal support of King Berengar, the surrounding region descended into chaos as local magnates fought intermittent territorial wars. Practically nothing about the life within the cloister from this dark period is known. A complete list of all the late ninth and early tenth-century abbots has not survived.

Although the monastery remained under imperial protection during the tenth century, conditions improved slowly. Eventually, however the monks turned their attention to reforming the community. Their reform may have had more than a local scope; some customs of Cluny are known to have spread to Nonantola at this time in the late tenth century.[29] Assuming that their interests would have extended beyond the abbey walls, it makes sense that the monks of San Silvestro would have borrowed chants from various Frankish centers at this time. It also appears likely that the distinctive Nonantolan style of musical notation had developed in the reinvigorated abbey scriptorium by the early eleventh century.[30] Unfortunately, Nonantolan music books significantly older than the troper-prosers do not survive. A catalogue of the abbey's books compiled in 1464, however, includes twenty-three "very old liturgical music books of no value" (*libri musicale vetustissimi nullius valoris*).[31] Among these items may have been one or two of the manuscripts that form the basis of this edition.

One of the brightest spots in Nonantola's history came in the early eleventh century when Aribert, archbishop of Milan and titular abbot of Nonantola, along with the de facto abbot, Rodulfus (d. 1035), rebuilt the monastery after a fire in 1013. The monastery also acquired thirty-nine codices from a monk named Pietro Ardengo, which Rodulfus himself inventoried.[32] But this period was, as it turns out, only a brief respite from the general decline of the abbey and, by the turn of the twelfth century, the best days of Nonantola were behind it. During the early years of the Investiture controversy, San Silvestro remained an imperial possession with all the advantages this status afforded, but its discipline meanwhile suffered due to interference in the election of abbots. The abbey itself seems to have remained a desirable prize, which helps to explain the papacy's interest in it. In 1077, after the departure of Henry IV, on April 13 Pope Gregory VII celebrated the Holy Thursday liturgy there.[33] The monastery nonetheless remained allied with the emperor until 1083, when Mathilda of Tuscany brought it on the papal side. Nonantola openly declared itself for the pope in 1111.

The later history of the institution sheds no light on the tropers and the repertory they contain, but it does explain why today, when one visits the small town of Nonantola, only the abbey church can still be seen. The modern decline actually dates from the fourteenth century, when the abbey became the object of contestation between the communes of Modena and Bologna. In 1407 it came under the jurisdiction of commendatory abbots; in 1449 only four monks resided there. In 1514 Nonantola came into the possession of the Cistercians, but its decline continued. The abbey was eventually suppressed by Pope Clement XIII in 1769, was restored by Pius VII in 1820, and finally was appropriated by the Italian government in 1866.

The Manuscript Sources

Bologna, Biblioteca Universitaria, MS 2824 [Bu 2824]

It is an incomplete troper-proser comprising thirteen gatherings with 106 folios of medium to poor quality parchment plus two modern paper flyleaves. The manuscript now lacks its opening leaves and the Kyries that would have been copied on them. The first recto leaf, which like the others was furnished with an Arabic number in the upper right corner (a later addition), contains the end of Gloria in excelsis 4. The quire marks run from "iii" on the bottom of fol. 9v to "xv" on 97v; the number "iv" was mistakenly omitted from the series. In its present state, twelve of the thirteen gatherings are quaternia; the first irregular gathering has nine folios. An average leaf measures 17.8 × 12.3 cm. The writing area of a typical page measures 12.8 × 8.9 cm with twenty-eight drypoint lines ruled approximately 4.5 mm apart. The writing space is framed by double lines 4 mm. apart. Prickings are visible in the outer margins and the tops and bottoms of many leaves.

Like the other two Nonantolan tropers, the chant melodies in this manuscript are copied in diastematic Nonantolan neumes, a disjunct almost pointillist type of notation that bears a passing resemblance to the Aquitanian style.[34] (See plate 1.) This type of notation has been adequately described elsewhere and closely studied by Moderini; its most identifiable feature is the characteristic extension of a vertical trait from a given syllable (generally the vowel) to the level of the first note to be sung. The tails of *virgae* and other neumes in Bu 2824 and the other troper-prosers tend to slope only slightly, giving a distinctive verticality to the look of the page. This vertical quality is also apparent in the notation of the Cantatorium of Nonantola, but not in chantbooks employing Nonantolan neumes copied elsewhere.[35] Another characteristic that distinguishes Nonantolan notation is the disjunct *scandicus*, the stepwise ascending three-note ligature, which was written as a single character in other northern Italian styles.

The texts in Bu 2824 are copied in an undisciplined Italian rotunda. The ascending traits of the letters *b*, *h*, and *l* are sometimes wedged, but this feature is inconsistent. Most letters *m* and *n* have finishing strokes to the left. The letters *ct*, *st*, and *et* are not written in ligature; letters *ae* are inconsistently ligated. Pages generally contain seven lines of text and music, both written in the same shade of brown ink. Most folios are the work of the main scribe except for 1r–v, 97r–100r, and 103r–106r, which are done in a smaller hand than the main texts. This scribe employed northern Italian, rather than Nonantolan, notation. One also sees palimpsest additions by a still less expert twelfth-century hand on fols. 8v–9v and 102v in the lower margin.

Despite the uneven quality of penmanship, the manuscript was considered important enough to be decorated, albeit humbly. Five ornamental capitals in red, yellow, and green inks precede three troped Glorias and two Introit tropes: 4v, *L[aus tua deus]*; 5v, *Q[uem novitati syderis]*; 14r, *C[ives superni]*; 15v, *S[ANctissimus namque gregorius]*; and 18r, *V[erbo altissimi patris]*. Small initials and rubrics throughout are done in orange-red ink.

Even in its most complete state, Bu 2824 never contained as many items as the other surviving Nonantolan tropers. It may have been intended for another institution in the region judging from minor discrepancies in its contents compared with the two other sources and by the additions described above. The later history of the manuscript, which is different from the two Nonantolan tropers that now reside in Roman libraries, also suggests that Bu 2824 was not destined for use at the abbey where it was copied. On the inside cover is found the stamp of the library of San Salvatore di Bologna: "2824 | EX BIB. S. SALVATORIS | 768." A note on the recto side of the opening flyleaf reads: "Aut III Appendix Mss. 1237 | Pertinuit ad Monasterium Nonantola." The stamp of the University Library of Bologna has been added on fol. 1r, in the upper right margin. The manuscript is presently bound in parchment-covered paper fastened with three ropes; the title "*Musicae laudes ad Missa*" is handwritten on the spine.[36]

Rome, Biblioteca Casanatense, MS 1741 [Rc 1741]

This troper-proser of the early twelfth century has 192 thick parchment leaves of medium quality; later folios are dark on the hair side compared with the light-brown color of most leaves. A single modern paper flyleaf was added before fol. 1r. The manuscript comprises twenty-five gatherings, all quaternia except the first (four leaves; irregular structure, probably repaired in the course of an undocumented restoration) and the twenty-second (binion). There are no medieval quire marks or catchwords, but on the opening recto leaf of all but two gatherings a modern Arabic number is written in black ink (gatherings 1 and 5 are numbered in pencil). This numbering generally corresponds to the order of the gatherings, though gatherings 20 through 25 are mistakenly numbered "21" through "26." Arabic numbers are stamped in black ink on the lower right margins of every recto leaf (a modern addition). An average leaf measures 18.4 × 12.4 cm. The writing area of a typical page measures 13.95 × 7.8 cm, with thirty-three drypoint lines ruled per folio (4 mm apart); double marginal lines (4.5 mm apart) frame the writing space. Prickings are visible in the outer margins, tops, and bottoms of many leaves. Most leaves contain eight lines of text and music written in the same shade of dark brown ink.

The chant melodies are notated in diastematic Nonantolan neumes. Lines of three different colors of ink differentiate F (red), C (yellow) and, in some chants, B-flat (green). Texts are copied in a rotund Italian script of the twelfth century that verges on Gothic minuscule, suggesting that this is the latest of the three sources. This scribe was more expert than those who copied Rn 1343 and Bu 2824. Ascending traits on the letters *b, d, h,* and *l* are consistently wedged; letters *i, m,* and *n* have pronounced finishing strokes to the left. Tailed *e* (*e caudata*) was written in place of *ae* (in contrast with Rn 1343 and Bu 2824). The letters *et, ct,* and *st* are not written in ligature. The common abbreviations are used for *-bus, per, pro, -que, qui, -us,* and the *nomina sacra*. A superscript stroke shows a missing *m* or *n,* or indicates the suspension of words.

The codex contains nine vinestem initials in red, yellow, and green. These are generally found at the beginnings of major divisions: 5r T[E XPE REX] with a portrait of Christ in a gesture of blessing; 19v P[AX sempiterna xpistus]; 25v C[ives superni]; 35v S[anctus Deus fortis]; 41v A[gnus dei]; 46v S[anctissimus namque gregorius]; 53v N[atus ante secula]; 76v E[cce vicit radix]; 135r V[enite omnes exultemus]. In addition, on fol. 13r the opening G[loria in excelsis] is decorated, but this capital is less than one-third the size of the other initials. As in Rn 1343, the scribe gave some attention to the hierarchy of scripts, so that Rustic capitals generally follow the vinestem initials. Small initials and rubrics throughout are written in red ink.

Whether this manuscript was among those listed in the abbey's inventory of 1464 is unclear, but its resemblance to Rn 1343 and the Cantatorium of Nonantola, both of which can be more securely placed at the medieval abbey, is pronounced. As for its modern provenance the following evidence has survived: the stamp of the Biblioteca Casanatense in the lower margin of fol. 1r and in the upper right corner of the same folio an old shelf number "C IV 2." The spine of the modern binding bears the title "*Liber choralis cum notis musicalibus.*"[37] This manuscript has been published in a facsimile edition by Giuseppe Vecchi, *Troparium Sequentiarium Nonantulanum,* Monumenta Lyrica Medii Aevi Italica, ser. 1, Latina, vol. 1 (Modena, 1955).

Rome, Biblioteca Nazionale, MS 1343 (olim Sessoriano 62) [Rn 1343]

This troper-proser of late eleventh/early twelfth centuries has eleven gatherings of eighty-one leaves, plus four modern paper flyleaves. The parchment is medium to poor quality, with many imperfections; the hair side of some folios is exceptionally dark. All gatherings are quaternia except for the second binion (fols. 9–10) and the eleventh (fols. 75–81), which are irregular. There are no quire marks or catchwords. Leaves are numbered in the upper right corners in modern Arabic numbers (a later addition). The average leaf is 25.6 × 17 cm, making this manuscript the largest of the three tropers. The writing area of a typical page measures 24 × 12 cm; 53 drypoint lines ruled per folio (4 to 4.5 mm apart) with double lines (4.5 mm apart) framing the writing space on either side. Prickings are visible in the outer margins and on the bottoms of some leaves. Most leaves contain thirteen lines of text and music written in the same shade of brown ink.

Chants are notated in diastematic Nonantolan neumes mostly on drypoint lines; red and yellow lines, indicating F and C respectively, are employed. Texts are copied in an uneven rotunda. The letter *a* appears in its closed, uncial form. The ascending traits of the letters *b, h,* and *l* are clubbed; *d* is found mostly in its straight form, but also alongside the curved uncial form. Letters *m* and *n* have finishing strokes to the left. Letters *st* were not written in ligature but *ct* occasional were (see, for example, fols. 8r, 11r, 12r, 13r). The letters *ae* were regularly ligated, though *e-caudata* was used in place of the ligature in rare cases (see fol. 4r "æterne," and fol. 14v "equalis"). In addition to the abbreviations and *nomina sacra* noted above, the scribe sometimes employed superscript *i* (N[i] for *Natali* [fol. 6v]).

As with the other Nonantolan tropers, Rn 1343 is simply decorated with vinestem initials. Five of these are found at the beginnings of major divisions within the manuscript, namely at the first Kyrie (1r: *TE* [*xpiste rex supplices*]), Gloria in excelsis tropes (6v: *P*[*AX sempiterna xpistus*]), Sanctus (14r: *S*[*ANCTUS Deus fortis*]), Proper trope (18r: *S*[*ANctissimus namque gregorius*]), and at the processional antiphon, *Venite omnes exultemus* (52r: *V*). (See plate 2.) Rubrics and small initials throughout are written in red ink, some decorated with yellow highlights. The rubricating scribe occasionally neglected to copy the initials at the beginnings of lines of text; he also made many mistakes in the selection of initial letters. There are also errors in the placement of red and yellow clef lines.

Rn 1343 was copied and presumably used at the abbey of San Silvestro until it was sent to a monastery in Sessoriano. It must have later resided at the Cistercian monastery of Santa Croce in Gerusalemme in Rome, since flyleaf ii bears the stamp of its library as well as the mark of the Biblioteca Nazionale. Flyleaf ii also preserves the *ex libris*: "Codex 211 | Liber Choralis cu<m> Notis qui | antiquis dicebatur Tropanarius." The spine of the parchment-covered paper binding bears the title "TROPARIUS."[38]

Manuscript Inventories

The following inventories of the three Nonantolan manuscripts supplement the brief summaries of contents in Heinrich Husmann, *Tropen-und Sequenzenhandschriften*.[39] Listed are inclusive folio numbers for each chant, along with the text incipit and genre designation. Numbers in square brackets correspond to the place of a chant among pieces of the same category in the edition. Occasionally, a parenthetical remark in the right column designates a piece that is incomplete (fragment), an incipit, or a later addition to the main corpus. Ordinary chants without tropes (*sine tropis*) are also identified as such in parentheses. The assignment of a chant or a group of chants to a given feast or liturgical occasion is indicated where specified in the rubrics of the source; assignments printed in square brackets are supplied from a Nonantolan source other than the one inventoried. Also indicated are chants for which no assignment is specified in the Nonantolan tropers. These might be inferred based on a study of concordants, but this was beyond the scope of this study.

Inventory of Bu 2824

Fol. no.	Text Incipit	Genre [Number] (Remarks)
	[Chant without rubrics designating feast]	
1r–v	Gloria in excelsis	Gloria in excelsis [4] (*sine tropis*; fragment)
	[Christmas]	
2r	Pax sempiterna	Troped Gloria in excelsis [8a]
	St. Stephen	
2r–3r	Quem patris ad dextram	Troped Gloria in excelsis [9]
	St. John Evangelist	
3r–4v	Quem cives caelestes	Troped Gloria in excelsis [10]
	St. Sylvester	
4v–5v	Laus tua Deus	Troped Gloria in excelsis [11]
	Epiphany	
4v–7r	Quem novitate	Troped Gloria in excelsis [12]
	Easter	
7r–8r	Cives superni . . . Christus surrexit	Troped Gloria in excelsis [13a]
	[Chants without rubrics designating feast]	
8v	Qui regis Israel intende	Responsory verse
8v	Potestas eius potestas aeterna	Responsory verse
9r	Sobire et iuste	Responsory verse
9r	A solis ortu et occasum	Responsory verse
9v	Ecce dominator dominus	Responsory verse
9v	Sanctis qui in terra sunt	Responsory verse
	Pentecost	
10r	Laudat in excelsis	Troped Gloria in excelsis [17] (fragment)
	[Chants without rubrics designating feast]	
10r	Deus fortis	Troped Sanctus [1] (fragment)
10r–v	Pater ingenitus	Troped Sanctus [2]
10v–11v	Mundi fabricator	Troped Sanctus [5]
11v	Sanctus	Sanctus [8] (*sine tropis*)

xiv

Inventory of Bu 2824 *cont.*

Fol. no.	Text Incipit	Genre [Number] (Remarks)
11v–12r	Sanctus	Sanctus [11] (*sine tropis*)
12r–v	Sanctus	Sanctus [12] (*sine tropis*)
12v–13r	Qui sedes ad dexteram patris	Troped Agnus Dei [1]
13r–v	Exaudi domine	Troped Agnus Dei [6]
13v	Ad dextram patris	Troped Agnus Dei [5]
14r	Suscipe deprecationem . . . Dei	Troped Agnus Dei [7]
14r	Agnus Dei . . . alleluia alleluia	Troped Agnus Dei [8]
14r	Agnus Dei	Agnus Dei [10] (*sine tropis*)

[Christmas]

14v–15r	Emitte angelum tuum	Confractorium [1]

[Easter]

15r–v	Corpus Christi accepimus	Confractorium [2]

First Sunday of Advent

15v–16v	Sanctissimus namque Gregorius	Introit trope [1]
16v	Almipotens verus Deus	Introit trope [2]
17r–v	Ecce iam Christus	Introit trope [3]
17v	Venturum te cuncti dixerunt	Gradual prosula [1]

Fourth Sunday of Advent

17v–18	A supernis caelorum	Offertory prosula [6]

Christmas I

18r–v	Verbo altissimi patris	Introit trope [4]
18v–20v	Christi hodierne pangamini omnes una	Sequence

Christmas II

20v–21r	Hora est iam nos	Introit trope [5]
21r	Ecce iam venit hora	Introit trope [6]
21v	Iam surgens aurora	Introit trope [7]
21v–22r	Dierum noctuque	Offertory prosula [7]

Christmas III

22r–v	Verbum caro hodi	Processional antiphon [1]
22v–23r	Hodie salvator mundi per virginem	Introit trope [8]
23r–v	Hodie exultent iusti natus est	Introit trope [9]
23v	Hic enim est de quo prophetae	Introit trope [10]
24r	Audi nos te deprecamur	Alleluia prosula [8]
24r–v	Alme caeli rex inmortalis	Alleluia prosula [9]
24v–26r	Natus ante saecula Dei filius	Sequence
26r–v	Hodie natus est Christus	Antiphon *ante evangelium* [2]

St. Stephen

26v–27r	Hodie inclitus martyr Stephanus	Introit trope [11]
27r–v	Qui primus meruit	Introit trope [13]
27v	Grandine lapidum	Introit trope [12]
28r–29r	Hanc concordi famulatu	Sequence
29v	Gloria in excelsis Deo	Antiphon *ante evangelium* [3]

St. John Evangelist

29v–30r	Aeterno genitus genitore	Introit trope [15]
30r	Ille qui dixit	Introit trope [16]
30r–v	Dilectus iste domini	Introit trope [18]
31v–32r	Iste est discipulus	Antiphon *ante evangelium* [4]
32r	Florebit justus ut palma	Offertory trope [19]

Holy Innocents

32r–v	Hodie te domine suggentes	Introit trope [20]
32v–34r	Laus tibi Christe patris optimi	Sequence

St. Sylvester

34r–v	Venite populi ad conlaudandum	Introit trope [21]
34v–35r	Hic est Silvester	Introit trope [22]
35r–36v	Haec sunt sacra festa	Sequence
36v–37r	Usque in saeculum saeculi	Offertory trope [23]

Epiphany

37r–v	Hodie descendit Christus	Introit trope [24]
37v	Forma speciosissimus	Introit trope [25]
38r–39v	Festa Christi omnis christianitas	Sequence
40r	Tribus miraculis	Antiphon *ante evangelium* [6]
40r–42r	Eia recolamus laudibus piis digna	Sequence
42r–43r	Virginis venerande de numero	Sequence

Inventory of Bu 2824 *cont.*

Fol. no.	Text Incipit	Genre [Number] (Remarks)
	Purification	
43r–v	Adest alma virgo	Introit trope [27]
43v–45v	Concentu parili hic te	Sequence
	Sexagesima Sunday	
45v–46r	Sana Christe rex alme	Tract prosula [11]
	Fourth Sunday of Lent	
45v–46r	Mons magnus est	Tract prosula [12]
	Palm Sunday	
46r–v	Ingresso Iesu	Introit trope [29]
46v	Suspensus ligno patri	Introit trope [30]
	Easter Sunday	
47r	Hora est surgite/Quem quaeritis	Introit trope [31]
47r	Christus de sepulchro resurrexit	Introit trope [32]
47v	Hodie resurrexit leo fortis	Introit trope [33]
48r	Iam redeunt gaudia	Alleluia prosula [14]
48r–v	Christe tu vita vera	Alleluia prosula [15]
48v–50v	Ecce vicit radix David	Sequence
50v	Laudate dominum de caelis	Antiphon *ante evangelium* [8]
50v–51r	Ab increpatione et ira	Offertory trope [34]
51r–v	Laus honor virtus	Communion trope [35]
	Easter Monday	
51v–53r	Clara gaudia festa paschalia	Sequence
53r–v	Maria et Maria	Antiphon *ante evangelium* [9]
53v–55r	Dic nobis quibus	Sequence
	Ss. Senesius and Theopontius	
55r–v	Sanguine sacrati Christi	Introit trope [37a]
55v–56r	Cuncti fideles Christi	Introit trope [36]
56r–57r	Laus tibi Christe patris optimi	Sequence
	Ascension	
57r–v	Hodie redemptor mundi ascendit	Introit trope [39]
57v–58r	Quem creditis super astra	Introit trope [38]
58r	Hodie rex gloriae Christus	Introit trope [41]
58r–60r	Summi triumphum regis	Sequence
60v	Hodie secreta caeli	Antiphon *ante evangelium* [12]
	Pentecost	
60v–61r	Hodie spiritus sanctus procedens	Introit trope [42]
61r–v	Hodie spiritus sanctus processit	Introit trope [43]
61v–63v	Sancti spiritus assit nobis gratia	Sequence
63v–64r	Hodie e caelis	Antiphon *ante evangelium* [13]
64r–v	Erant omnes nostri linguis	Alleluia prosula [19]
64v	Pentecosten advenisse	Alleluia prosula [20]
	St. John the Baptist	
65r–v	Hodie exultent iusti . . . Iohannes	Introit trope [45]
65v	Deus pater clamat Iohannem	Introit trope [46]
66r	Audite insulae	Introit trope [47]
66r–67v	Alme mundi rex Christe	Sequence
67v–68r	Lumen quod animi	Antiphon *ante evangelium* [14]
	St. Peter	
68r–v	Beatissimus Petrus catenis	Introit trope [48]
68v	Hodie sanctissimi patroni nostri	Introit trope [49]
68v–69r	Divina beatus Petrus	Introit trope [50]
69r–70v	Pretiosa sollemnitas adest	Sequence
70v–71r	Petre amas me	Antiphon *ante evangelium* [15]
72v	Alme cuncti sator orbis	Alleluia prosula [21]
72v–73v	Serve et amice bone	Alleluia prosula [22]
	St. Lawrence	
73v–74r	Hodie beatus Laurentius levita	Introit trope [53]
74r	Prunas extensa	Introit trope [54]
74v	Qui tibi dedit Laurenti	Introit trope [55]
74v–76r	Laurenti David magni martyr	Sequence
76r	Iustum deduxit dominus	Antiphon *ante evangelium* [16]

Inventory of Bu 2824 *cont.*

Fol. no.	Text Incipit	Genre [Number] (Remarks)
	Assumption	
76r–v	Exaudi virgo virginum	Introit trope [56]
76v	Ave beata Maria	Introit trope [57]
76v–78v	Congaudent angelorum chori	Sequence
78v–79r	Beata es quae	Antiphon *ante evangelium* [17]
79r–80v	Summa stripe genita virgo	Sequence
	Michael Archangel	
80v–81r	Qui patris in caelo	Introit trope [60]
81r	Ante Deum semper gloriae	Alleluia prosula [23]
81r–v	Concussum et percussum	Alleluia prosula [24]
81v–82r	Angele Michael atque Gabriel	Alleluia prosula [25]
82r–83v	Summi regis archangele Michael	Sequence
	Ss. Simon and Jude	
83v–84r	Nobile apostolici admirans	Introit trope [61]
84r	Consortes tuorum effecti	Introit trope [63]
84r–85r	Clare sanctorum senatus	Sequence
	All Saints	
85r	Sanguinis sacrati Christi	Introit trope [37b] (incipit)
85r–86v	Omnes sancti seraphin	Sequence
86v	Gaudent in caelis	Antiphon *ante evangelium* [11] (incipit)
	St. Martin	
86v–87r	Divini fuerat	Introit trope [64]
87r–89r	Sacerdotem Christi Martinum	Sequence
	Common of the Blessed Virgin Mary	
89r–v	Psallat turba devota	Alleluia prosula [26]
	St. Andrew	
89v–90r	Hodie beatissimus Andreas	Introit trope [66]
90r	In dulcedine amoris	Alleluia prosula [27]
90r–91v	Deus in tua virtute	Sequence
	Trinity Sunday	
91v	Salve crux	Antiphon *ante evangelium* [18]
91v–93v	Benedicta semper sancta	Sequence
93v–94r	Alme domine noli claudere	Alleluia prosula [28]
	Sundays after Pentecost	
94r	Laudes debitas vocibus	Alleluia prosula [31]
94r–v	Et ab insurgentibus Deus	Alleluia prosula [32]
94v	Lingua cor simul clamitet	Alleluia prosula [33]
94v–95r	O quam mira sunt Deus tua	Sequence
	Purification	
95v	Ave gracia plena	Processional antiphon [5]
96r–v	Adorna thalamum tuum	Processional antiphon [6]
96v–97r	Responsum accepit Symeon	Processional antiphon [7]
97r–v	Admirabilis splendor	Troped Sanctus (addition) [6]
	[Sundays after Pentecost]	
97v–98v	Alma fulgens lux praeclara	Sequence
98v–99r	Laetamente canamus Deo nostro	Sequence
99r–v	Stans a longe publicanus	Sequence
	[Chant without rubrics designating feast]	
99r–v	Salva nos domine vigilantes	Antiphon (addition)
	[Sundays after Pentecost]	
100r	Semper sonet nostra lingua	Alleluia prosula [34]
	[Chant without rubrics designating feast]	
100r–v	Salus et vita	Troped Agnus Dei [9]
	[Sundays after Pentecost]	
100v	Alma voce canamus	Alleluia prosula [30]
100v–101v	Almiflua caelorum turba	Sequence
	[Chant without rubrics designating feast]	
102r	Sanctus	Sanctus [13] (*sine tropis*)
	[Christmas]	
102r–v	Tu rex gloriae Christi	Antiphon *ante evangelium* [1]

xvii

Inventory of Bu 2824 *cont.*

Fol. no.	Text Incipit	Genre [Number] (Remarks)
	[Chants without rubrics designating feast]	
102r–v	Gloria patri et filio	Lesser doxology (addition)
103r–v	Rex magne domine	Kyrie prosula [6]
104r–v	Kyrie rex genitor	Kyrie prosula [7]
105r–v	Quem cherubim	Troped Sanctus [7]
	[St. Sylvester]	
105v	Dicit dominus	Antiphon *ante evangelium* [5]
	[Chant without rubrics designating feast]	
106r	Hosanna Hagie altissimi	(*AH* 47, no. 363) (fragment)
106v	[blank]	

Inventory of Rc 1741

Fol. no.	Text Incipit	Genre [Number] (Remarks)
	[In Procession with Relics]	
1r–4v	Humili prece et sincera devotione	Hymn [1]
	[Chants without rubrics designating feast]	
5r–6v	Te Christe rex supplices	Kyrie prosula [1]
6v–7r	Omnipotens genitor	Kyrie trope [2]
7r–8v	Canamus (*Kanamus*) cunti laudes	Kyrie prosula [3]
8v–9v	Lux et origo lucis	Kyrie prosula [4]
9v–10r	Rex magne domine	Kyrie prosula [6]
10v–11v	Kyrie rex genitor	Kyrie prosula [7]
12r–v	Dominator Deus	Kyrie prosula [5]
12v	Kyrie eleison	Kyrie [9] (*sine tropis*)
12v	Kyrie eleison	Kyrie [10] (*sine tropis*)
13r	Kyrie eleison	Kyrie [11] (*sine tropis*)
13r–14r	Gloria in excelsis	Gloria in excelsis [1] (*sine tropis*)
14r	Gloria in excelsis	Gloria in excelsis [7] (*sine tropis*)
14v–15r	Gloria in excelsis	Gloria in excelsis [2] (*sine tropis*)
15v–16r	Gloria in excelsis	Gloria in excelsis [3] (*sine tropis*)
16v–17r	Gloria in excelsis	Gloria in excelsis [5] (*sine tropis*)
17v–18r	Gloria in excelsis	Gloria in excelsis [6] (*sine tropis*)
18v–19r	Gloria in excelsis	Gloria in excelsis [4] (*sine tropis*)
	[Christmas]	
19v–21r	Pax sempiterna	Troped Gloria in excelsis [8b]
	St. Stephen	
21r–22r	Quem patris ad dextram	Troped Gloria in excelsis [9]
	St. John Evangelist	
22r–23r	Quem cives caelestes	Troped Gloria in excelsis [10]
	St. Sylvester	
23r–24r	Laus tua Deus	Troped Gloria in excelsis [11]
	Epiphany	
24r–25r	Quem novitate	Troped Gloria in excelsis [12]
	Easter	
25v–27r	Cives superni . . . Christus surrexit	Troped Gloria in excelsis [13b]
	Easter Monday	
27r–v	Alme mundi hodie de morte	Troped Gloria in excelsis [14]
	Ascension	
27v–28r	Alme mundi hodie in caelum	Troped Gloria in excelsis [15]
	Ss. Senesius and Theopontius	
28r–29r	O laudabilis rex	Troped Gloria in excelsis [16]
	[Pentecost]	
29v–30r	Laudat in excelsis	Troped Gloria in excelsis [17]
	St. John the Baptist	
30v–32r	Quando regis cunctus	Troped Gloria in excelsis [18]
	St. Peter	
32r–33v	O gloria sanctorum	Troped Gloria in excelsis [19]
	Assumption	
33v–34v	Hinc laudando patrem	Troped Gloria in excelsis [21]

Inventory of Rc 1741 *cont.*

Fol. no.	Text Incipit	Genre [Number] (Remarks)
	[Chants without rubrics designating feast]	
34v–35v	Qui caelicolas	Troped Gloria in excelsis [20]
35v–36v	Deus fortis	Troped Sanctus [1]
36v–37r	Pater ingenitus	Troped Sanctus [2]
37r	Pater lumen aeternum	Troped Sanctus [3]
37v	Deus pater ingenite	Troped Sanctus [4]
37v–38r	Mundi fabricator	Troped Sanctus [5]
38r–39r	Admirabilis splendor	Troped Sanctus [6]
39r–v	Quem cherubim	Troped Sanctus [7]
39v–40r	Sanctus	Sanctus [8] (*sine tropis*)
40r–v	Sanctus	Sanctus [9] (*sine tropis*)
40v	Sanctus	Sanctus [11] (*sine tropis*)
40v–41r	Sanctus	Sanctus [12] (*sine tropis*)
41r–v	Sanctus	Sanctus [13] (*sine tropis*)
41v	Qui sedes ad dexteram patris	Troped Agnus Dei [1]
42r	Omnipotens aeterna Dei	Troped Agnus Dei [2]
42r–v	Tu Deus et dominus	Troped Agnus Dei [3]
42v	Suscipe deprecationem . . . Dei patris	Troped Agnus Dei [4]
43r	Ad dextram patris	Troped Agnus Dei [5]
43v	Exaudi domine	Troped Agnus Dei [6]
43v–44r	Suscipe deprecationem . . . Dei	Troped Agnus Dei [7]
44r–v	Salus et vita	Troped Agnus Dei [9]
44v	Agnus Dei . . . alleluia alleluia	Troped Agnus Dei [8]
44v	Agnus Dei	Agnus Dei [10] (*sine tropis*)
	Christmas	
44v–45v	Emitte angelum tuum	Confractorium [1]
	Holy Saturday	
45v–46r	Hic est agnus	Confractorium [2]
	Easter	
46r	Corpus Christi accepimus	Confractorium [3]
	St. Sylvester	
46r–v	Angeli circumdederunt altare	Confractorium [4]
	First Sunday of Advent	
46v–47r	Sanctissimus namque Gregorius	Introit trope [1]
47r–v	Almipotens verus Deus	Introit trope [2]
47v–48r	Ecce iam Christus	Introit trope [3]
48r	Venturum te cuncti dixerunt	Gradual prosula [1]
48r–v	Invocavite altissime	Offertory prosula [2]
	Second Sunday of Advent	
48v–49r	Possessor polorum Deus	Offertory prosula [3]
	Third Sunday of Advent	
49r	Qui sedes in alto throno	Gradual prosula [4]
49r–v	Misericors et clemens famulis	Offertory prosula [5]
	Fourth Sunday of Advent	
49r	A supernis caelorum	Offertory prosula [6]
	Christmas I	
49v–50r	Verbo altissimi patris	Introit trope [4]
	Christmas II	
50r–v	Hora est iam nos	Introit trope [5]
50v	Ecce iam venit hora	Introit trope [6]
50v	Iam surgens aurora	Introit trope [7]
50v–51r	Dierum noctuque	Offertory prosula [7]
	Christmas III	
51r–v	Verbum caro hodie	Processional antiphon [1]
51v–52r	Hodie salvator mundi per virginem	Introit trope [8]
52r–v	Hodie exultent iusti natus est	Introit trope [9]
52v–53r	Hic enim est de quo prophetae	Introit trope [10]
53r	Audi nos te deprecamur	Alleluia prosula [8]
53r	Alme caeli rex inmortalis	Alleluia prosula [9]
53v–55r	Natus ante saecula Dei filius	Sequence
55r–v	Tu rex gloriae Christi	Antiphon *ante evangelium* [1]
55v–56r	Hodie natus est Christus	Antiphon *ante evangelium* [2]
56r	Proles virginis matris	Offertory prosula [10]

Inventory of Rc 1741 *cont.*

Fol. no.	Text Incipit	Genre [Number] (Remarks)
	St. Stephen	
56r–v	Hodie inclitus martyr Stephanus	Introit trope [11]
56v	Grandine lapidum	Introit trope [12]
56v–58r	Hanc concordi famulatu	Sequence
58r	Gloria in excelsis Deo	Antiphon *ante evangelium* [3]
58r–v	Magnus et felix	Communion trope [14]
	St. John Evangelist	
58v–59r	Aeterno genitus genitore	Introit trope [15]
59r	Ille qui dixit	Introit trope [16]
59r–v	Amor angelorum et gaudium	Introit trope [17]
59v–60v	Iohannes Iesu Christo multum	Sequence
60v–61r	Iste est discipulus	Antiphon *ante evangelium* [4]
61r	Florebit justus ut palma	Offertory trope [19]
	St. Sylvester	
61r–v	Clementissime Christi confessor	Processional antiphon [2]
61v–62r	Venite populi ad conlaudandum	Introit trope [21]
62r	Hic est Silvester	Introit trope [22]
62r–63v	Haec sunt sacra festa	Sequence
64r	Dicit dominus	Antiphon *ante evangelium* [5]
64r–v	Usque in saeculum saeculi	Offertory trope [23]
64v–66r	Laude mirandum digna	Sequence
	Epiphany	
66r–v	Hodie descendit Christus	Introit trope [24]
66v–67r	Forma speciosissimus	Introit trope [25]
67r–v	Haec est praeclara dies	Introit trope [26]
67v–69r	Festa Christi omnis christianitas	Sequence
69r–v	Tribus miraculis	Antiphon *ante evangelium* [6]
	Purification	
69v–70r	Adest alma virgo	Introit trope [27]
70r	Psallentes legimus	Introit trope [28]
70r–72v	Concentu parili hic te	Sequence
72v–73r	Omnes patriarchae	Antiphon *ante evangelium* [7]
73r–v	Virginis venerandae de numero	Sequence
	Sexagesima Sunday	
73v–74r	Sana Christe rex alme	Tract prosula [11]
	Fourth Sunday of Lent	
73v–74r	Mons magnus est	Tract prosula [12]
	Palm Sunday	
74r	Ingresso Iesu	Introit trope [29]
74v	Suspensus ligno patri	Introit trope [30]
75r	Pater unigenitum tuum	Tract prosula [13]
	Easter Sunday	
75r–v	Hora est surgite . . . Quem quaeritis	Introit trope [31]
75v–76r	Christus de sepulchro resurrexit	Introit trope [32]
76r	Hodie resurrexit leo fortis	Introit trope [33]
76r	Iam redeunt gaudia	Alleluia prosula [14]
76v	Christe tu vita vera	Alleluia prosula [15]
76v–78v	Ecce vicit radix David	Sequence
78v–79r	Laudate dominum de caelis	Antiphon *ante evangelium* [8]
79r	Ab increpatione et ira	Offertory trope [34]
79v	Laus honor virtus	Communion trope [35]
	Easter Monday	
80r–81r	Clara gaudia festa paschalia	Sequence
81r–v	Maria et Maria	Antiphon *ante evangelium* [9]
	Easter Tuesday	
81v–83r	Dic nobis quibus	Sequence
	Octave of Easter	
83r–84v	Eia recolamus laudibus piis digna	Sequence
84v–85r	Christus intravit ianuis	Offertory prosula [16]
	First Sunday after Easter	
85r	Rex Deus omnipotens	Alleluia prosula [17]
85r–v	Sicut tu Christe	Alleluia prosula [18]
85v–86v	Sancte cruci celebremus	Sequence

Inventory of Rc 1741 cont.

Fol. no.	Text Incipit	Genre [Number] (Remarks)
	Ss. Senesius and Theopontius	
86v–87r	Cuncti fideles Christi	Introit trope [36]
87r–v	Sanguine sacrati Christi	Introit trope [37a]
87v–88v	Laus tibi Christe patris optimi	Sequence
88v–89r	Isti sunt qui	Antiphon *ante evangelium* [10]
89r	Gaudent in caelis	Antiphon *ante evangelium* [11] (incipit)
	Ascension	
89r–90r	Quem creditis super astra	Introit trope [38]
90r	Terrigenas summos affatur	Introit trope [40]
90r–v	Hodie redemptor mundi ascendit	Introit trope [39]
90v–92r	Summi triumphum regis	Sequence
92r–v	Hodie secreta caeli	Antiphon *ante evangelium* [12]
	Pentecost	
92v–93r	Hodie spiritus sanctus procedens	Introit trope [42]
93r–v	Cum essent apostoli	Introit trope [44]
93v	Hodie spiritus sanctus processit	Introit trope [43]
93v–95v	Sancti spiritus assit nobis gratia	Sequence
95v	Hodie e caelis	Antiphon *ante evangelium* [13]
95v–96r	Erant omnes nostri linguis	Alleluia prosula [19]
	St. John the Baptist	
96r–v	Hodie exultent iusti . . . Iohannes	Introit trope [45]
96v–97r	Deus pater clamat Iohannem	Introit trope [46]
97r	Audite insulae	Introit trope [47]
97r–98r	Alme mundi rex Christe	Sequence
	St. Peter	
98v	Beatissimus Petrus catenis	Introit trope [48]
98v–99r	Divina beatus Petrus	Introit trope [50]
99r–v	Hodie sanctissimi patroni nostri	Introit trope [49]
99v–100v	Pretiosa sollemnitas adest	Sequence
100v–101r	Petre amas me	Antiphon *ante evangelium* [15]
101r–102r	Petre summe Christi pastor	Sequence
	Translation of St. Benedict	
102v	A domino impletum	Introit trope [51]
102v–103r	In iubilo vocis	Introit trope [52]
103r–105r	Sancti merita Benedicti	Sequence
105r–106v	Candida contio melos	Sequence
	St. Lawrence	
106v–107r	Hodie beatus Laurentius levita	Introit trope [53]
107r	Prunas extensa	Introit trope [54]
107r–v	Qui tibi dedit Laurenti	Introit trope [55]
107v–108v	Laurenti David magni martyr	Sequence
108v–109r	Iustum deduxit dominus	Antiphon *ante evangelium* [16]
	Assumption	
109r–v	Exaudi virgo virginum	Introit trope [56]
109v–110r	Nos sinus ecclesiae	Introit trope [58]
110r	Ave beata Maria	Introit trope [57]
110r–112r	Congaudet angelorum chori	Sequence
112r	Beata es quae	Antiphon *ante evangelium* [17]
	Birth of the Blessed Virgin Mary	
112r–v	O quam clara nitet	Introit trope [59]
112v–114r	Summa stripe genita virgo	Sequence
114–115r	Alma fulgens crux praeclara	Sequence
	Michael Archangel	
115r	Qui patris in caelo	Introit trope [60]
115r–v	Ante Deum semper gloriae	Alleluia prosula [23]
115v–116r	Concussum et percussum	Alleluia prosula [24]
116r	Angele Michael atque Gabriel	Alleluia prosula [25]
116r–117v	Summi regis archangele Michael	Sequence
	Ss. Simon and Jude	
117v–118r	Nobile apostolici admirans	Introit trope [61]
118r	Admirans vates proclamat	Introit trope [62]
118r	Consortes tuorum effecti	Introit trope [63]
118r–119r	Clare sanctorum senatus	Sequence

Inventory of Rc 1741 *cont.*

Fol. no.	Text Incipit	Genre [Number] (Remarks)
	All Saints	
119v	Sanguinis sacrati Christi	Introit trope [37b] (incipit)
119v–120v	Omnes sancti seraphin	Sequence
120v	Gaudent in caelis	Antiphon *ante evangelium* [11] (incipit)
	St. Martin	
120v	Divini fuerat	Introit trope [64]
121r–122v	Sacerdotem Christi Martinum	Sequence
	Common of the Blessed Virgin Mary	
122v–123v	Psallat turba devota	Alleluia prosula [26]
	St. Andrew	
123v	Hodie beatissimus Andreas	Introit trope [66]
123v–124r	Festus nunc in apostolicis	Introit trope [65]
124r	In dulcedine amoris	Alleluia prosula [27]
124r–125r	Deus in tua virtute	Sequence
125r–v	Salve crux	Antiphon *ante evangelium* [18]
	Dedication of a Church	
125v–127r	Ad tempi huius limina	Sequence
	Trinity Sunday	
127r–v	Splendor et imago patris	Introit trope [67]
127v–129r	Benedicta semper sancta	Sequence
129r–v	Alme domine noli claudere	Alleluia prosula [28]
	Sundays after Pentecost	
129v–130r	Arbiter singulorum facta	Alleluia prosula [29]
130r	Alma voce canamus	Alleluia prosula [30]
130r	Laudes debitas vocibus	Alleluia prosula [31]
130v	Et ab insurgentibus Deus	Alleluia prosula [32]
130v–131r	Lingua cor simul clamitet	Alleluia prosula [33]
131r–v	Stans a longe publicanus	Sequence
131v–132r	Laetamente canamus Deo nostro	Sequence
132r–v	O quam mira sunt Deus tua	Sequence
132v–134r	Almiflui a caelorum turba	Sequence
	Palm Sunday	
134v	Occurrunt turbae	Antiphon [20]
	Advent	
135r–136r	Venite omnes exsultemus	Antiphon [3]
	Christmas	
136r–137r	O Maria Iesse virga	Antiphon [4]
	Purification	
137r–v	Ave gratia plena	Antiphon [5]
137v–138r	Adorna thalamum tuum	Antiphon [6]
138r–v	Responsum accepit Symeon	Antiphon [7]
138v	Cum inducerent	Antiphon [8] (incipit)
	Septuagesima Sunday	
138v–139v	Christe pater misericordiarum	Antiphon [19]
	Ash Wednesday	
139v–140r	Immutemus habitum	Antiphon [10]
140r	Exaudi nos . . . quoniam benigna	Antiphon [11]
140r–v	Iuxta vestibulum	Antiphon [12]
	Lent	
140v–141v	Cum sederit filius	Antiphon [13]
141v–142r	Convertimini omnes simul ad deum	Antiphon [14]
	Palm Sunday	
142r	Pueri hebraeorum tollentes	Antiphon [15]
142r–v	Pueri hebraeorum vestimenta	Antiphon [16]
142v–143v	Cum appropinquaret	Antiphon [17]
143v–144r	Cum audisset populus	Antiphon [18]
144r–145v	Gloria laus et honor	Hymn [2]
145v	Ingrediente domino	Responsory [21] (incipit)
145v	Dominus Iesus postquam	Antiphon [22] (incipit)
	Maundy Thursday	
145v–147r	Tellus ac aether iubilent	Hymn [3]
147r	Mandatum novum do vobis	Antiphon [23]
147r	Diligamus nos invicem	Antiphon [24]

Inventory of Rc 1741 cont.

Fol. no.	Text Incipit	Genre [Number] (Remarks)
147r–v	Ubi est caritas (*karitas*)	Antiphon [25]
147v–148r	Postquam surrexit dominus	Antiphon [26]
148r	Domine tu mihi lavas	Antiphon [27]
148r–v	Vos vocatis me magister	Antiphon [28]
148v	Si ego dominus	Antiphon [29]
148v–149r	In diebus illis	Antiphon [30]
149r–v	Maria ergo unxit pedes	Antiphon [31]
149v	Congregavit nos Christus	Antiphon [32]
149v	Ubi fratres in unum	Antiphon [33]
149v–150r	In hoc cognoscent	Antiphon [34]
150r	Maneat in nobis	Antiphon [35] (incipit)
150r	Deus caritas (*karitas*) est	Antiphon [36]
150r	Fratres sit vobis	Antiphon [37]

Good Friday

Fol. no.	Text Incipit	Genre [Number] (Remarks)
150r–151r	Popule meus	Antiphon [38]
151r	Ecce lignum crucis	Antiphon [39]
151r–152r	Vadis propitiatus	Responsory [40]
152r	Adoramus crucem tuam	Antiphon [41]
152r–v	Ego sum alpha et omega	Antiphon [42]
152v	Crucem tuam . . . sanctam resurrectionem	Antiphon [43]
152v–154r	Crux benedicta nitet	Hymn [4]
154r–156r	Crux fidelis	Hymn [5]

Easter

Fol. no.	Text Incipit	Genre [Number] (Remarks)
156r–v	Vidi aquam	Antiphon [44]
156v	In die resurrectionis	Antiphon [45]
156v–157r	Stetit angelus ad sepulchrum	Antiphon [46]
157r–v	Christus resurgens ex mortuis	Antiphon [47]
157v	Dicant nunc iudei	Antiphon [48]
157v–158r	Ex resurrectione tua	Antiphon [49]
158r	Venite omnes adoremus	Antiphon [50]
158r–v	Crucifixum in carne	Antiphon [51]
158v	Propter lignum servi	Antiphon [52]

Ascension

Fol. no.	Text Incipit	Genre [Number] (Remarks)
159r–160v	Rex omnipotens die hodierna	Sequence
160v	Hodie secreta caeli	Antiphon *ante evangelium* [12]

Easter

Fol. no.	Text Incipit	Genre [Number] (Remarks)
161r	Exsurge domine adiuva nos	Antiphon [53]

Easter Monday

Fol. no.	Text Incipit	Genre [Number] (Remarks)
161r–v	Ego sum Deus patarum vestrorum	Antiphon [54]
161v	Populus Sion convertimini	Antiphon [55]
161v–162r	Domine Deus noster qui	Antiphon [56]

Easter Tuesday

Fol. no.	Text Incipit	Genre [Number] (Remarks)
162r	Confinemini domino	Antiphon [57]
162v	Exclamemus omnes ad dominum	Antiphon [58]
162v	Parce domine parce populo	Antiphon [59]

Easter Wednesday

Fol. no.	Text Incipit	Genre [Number] (Remarks)
163r	Cum iocunditate exhibitis	Antiphon [60]
163r–v	Iniquitates nostrae domine	Antiphon [61]

In Time of Tribulation

Fol. no.	Text Incipit	Genre [Number] (Remarks)
163v	Domine non est alius Deus	Antiphon [62]
163v–164r	Exaudi domine deprecationem servorum	Antiphon [63]
164r–v	Miserere domine plebi tuae	Antiphon [64]
164v	Dimitte domine peccata populi	Antiphon [65]
164v–165r	Exaudi Deus deprecationem nostram	Antiphon [66b]
165r–v	Deprecamur te . . . misericordia	Antiphon [67]
165v	Inclina domine . . . et audi	Antiphon [68]
165v–166r	Multa sunt domine peccata	Antiphon [69]
166r	Dimitte domine peccata populi	Antiphon [65] (incipit)
166r–v	Non in iustificationibus	Antiphon [70]
166v	Peccavimus domine et tu	Antiphon [71]
166v–167r	Domine imminuti sumus	Antiphon [72b]
167r–168v	Timor et tremor	Antiphon [73]
168v	Nos peccavimus domine	Antiphon [74]

Inventory of Rc 1741 cont.

Fol. no.	Text Incipit	Genre [Number] (Remarks)
169r	Terribile est Christe	Antiphon [75]
169r–v	De tribulatione clamamus	Antiphon [76]
169v–170r	Rogamus te domine Deus	Responsory [77]
170r–171r	Pro pace regum	Antiphon [78]
171r	Dimitte nobis domine	Antiphon [79]
171r–172r	Oremus dilectissimi nobis	Antiphon [80]
172r–v	Deus qui es benedictus	Antiphon [81]
	In Time of War	
172v	Domine miserere nostri	Antiphon [82]
172v–173r	Exaudi nos domine . . . David	Antiphon [83]
173r	Invocantes dominum exclamemus	Antiphon [84]
173r–v	Convertere . . . et deprecare	Antiphon [85]
173v	Propter peccata nostra	Antiphon [86]
173v–174r	Sicut exaudisti domine	Antiphon [87]
	In Time of Drought	
174r–v	Domine rigans montes	Antiphon [88]
174v	Domine rex Deus Abraham	Antiphon [89]
174v–175r	Respice domine quia aruit	Antiphon [90]
175r–v	Numquid est in idolis	Antiphon [91]
175v	Exaudi domine populum tuum	Antiphon [92]
176r	Si clauso caelo	Antiphon [93]
176r–v	Arridaverunt montes	Antiphon [94]
	In Time of Flood	
176v–177r	Inundaverunt aquae domine	Antiphon [95]
177r	Rupti sunt fontes	Antiphon [96]
177r–v	Non nos demergat domine	Antiphon [97]
177v	Peccavimus domine peccavimus	Antiphon [98]
177v–178r	Qui siccasti mare	Antiphon [99]
	For the Dead	
178r	Libera domine populum tuum	Antiphon [100]
178r–v	Exsurge libera nos Deus	Antiphon [101]
178v–179r	Miserere domine et dic angelo	Antiphon [102]
179r–v	Deus Deus noster respice in nos	Antiphon [103]
179v	Domine Deus rex . . . libera nos	Antiphon [104]
	In Procession with Relics	
179v	Cum iocunditate	Antiphon [60] (incipit)
179v	Ecce populus custodiens	Antiphon [105]
180r	Plateae Jerusalem gaudebunt	Antiphon [106]
180r	De Jerusalem exeunt	Antiphon [107]
180r–v	Ambulantes sancti dei ingredimini	Antiphon [108]
180v	Ambulate sancti dei ad locum	Antiphon [109]
180v	Ambulabunt sancti tui	Antiphon [110]
180v–181r	Sub altare domini	Antiphon [111]
181r	Sanctos portamus sanctorum	Antiphon [112]
181r–v	Ierusalem civitas sancta	Antiphon [113]
181v	In civitate domini	Antiphon [114] (incipit)
181v–182r	Kyrie . . . Emmanuel nobiscum	Litany [1]
182r	Kyrie . . . Sancta Marie te	Litany [2]
182v–183r	Kyrie . . . Domine miserere	Litany [3]
183v–184r	Kyrie . . . Exaudi exaudi	Litany [4]
184v	[blank]	
185r	In civitate domini	Antiphon [114]
185r–v	Benedic domine domus . . . omnes	Antiphon [115]
185v	Gregem tuum domine	Antiphon [116]
185v–186v	Oportet nos mundum	Antiphon [117]
186v	Sint oculi tui aperti	Antiphon [118]
186v	Signum salutis pone	Antiphon [119]
	At the Sprinkling of Holy Water on Sunday	
186v–187v	Agnus Dei . . . Suscipe	Litany [5]
187v	Asperges me	Antiphon [120]
	In Processions on Sunday	
188r–v	Cum venerimus ante conspectum	Antiphon [121]
188v–189v	Omnipotens Deus supplices	Antiphon [122]

Inventory of Rc 1741 *cont.*

Fol. no.	Text Incipit	Genre [Number] (Remarks)
	[*In Litaniis Majoribus et Minoribus*]	
190r	Exaudivit de templo sancto	Introit
190r	Alleluia V Confitemini domino quoniam	Alleluia
190r–191r	Confitebor domino	Offertory
191r	Petite	Communion
	[Sunday within the Octave of Ascension]	
191r	Omnes gentes	Introit
191v	Alleluia V Dominus in Sina	Alleluia
191v	Ascendit Deus	Offertory
191v–192r	Pater cum essem	Communion
	[Chants without rubrics designating feast]	
192r	Conversus Petrus vidit	Responsorium prolixum [126]
192r	Hic est discipulis Iohannes	Responsorium prolixum V [127]
192v	Kyrie eleison (addition)	Kyrie (*sine tropis*)
192v	Kyrie eleison (addition)	Kyrie (*sine tropis*)

Inventory of Rn 1343

Fol. no.	Text Incipit	Genre [Number] (Remarks)
	[Chants without rubrics designating feast]	
1r–v	Te Christe rex supplices	Kyrie prosula [1]
1v	Omnipotens genitor	Kyrie trope [2]
1v–2r	Canamus (*Kanamus*) cunti laudes	Kyrie prosula [3]
2r–v	Lux et origo lucis	Kyrie prosula [4]
2v–3r	Dominator Deus	Kyrie prosula [5]
3r–v	Rex magne domine	Kyrie prosula [6]
3v–4r	Kyrie rex genitor	Kyrie prosula [7]
4r	Kyrie eleison	Kyrie [8] (*sine tropis*)
4r	Kyrie eleison	Kyrie [9] (*sine tropis*)
4r	Kyrie eleison	Kyrie [10] (*sine tropis*)
4r	Kyrie eleison	Kyrie [11] (*sine tropis*)
4r	Kyrie eleison	Kyrie [12] (*sine tropis*)
4r–v	Gloria in excelsis	Gloria in excelsis [1] (*sine tropis*)
4v–5r	Gloria in excelsis	Gloria in excelsis [2] (*sine tropis*)
5r–v	Gloria in excelsis	Gloria in excelsis [3] (*sine tropis*)
5v	Gloria in excelsis	Gloria in excelsis [4] (*sine tropis*)
5v–6r	Gloria in excelsis	Gloria in excelsis [5] (*sine tropis*)
6r–v	Gloria in excelsis	Gloria in excelsis [6] (*sine tropis*)
6v	Gloria in excelsis	Gloria in excelsis [7] (*sine tropis*)
	Christmas	
6v–7v	Pax sempiterna	Troped Gloria in excelsis [8a]
	St. Stephen	
7v	Quem patris ad dextram	Troped Gloria in excelsis [9]
	[St. John Evangelist]	
8r–v	Quem cives caelestes	Troped Gloria in excelsis [10]
	St. Sylvester	
8v	Laus tua Deus	Troped Gloria in excelsis [11]
	Epiphany	
9r–v	Quem novitate	Troped Gloria in excelsis [12]
	Easter	
9v–10r	Cives superni . . . Christus surrexit	Troped Gloria in excelsis [13a]
	Easter Monday	
10v–11r	Alme mundi hodie de morte	Troped Gloria in excelsis [14]
	Ascension	
11r	Alme mundi hodie in caelum	Troped Gloria in excelsis [15]
	[Ss. Senesius and Theopontius]	
11r–v	O laudabilis rex	Troped Gloria in excelsis [16]
	Pentecost	
12r	Laudat in excelsis	Troped Gloria in excelsis [17]
	St. John the Baptist	
12r–13r	Quando regis cunctus	Troped Gloria in excelsis [18]
	[St. Peter]	
13r–v	O gloria sanctorum	Troped Gloria in excelsis [19]

Inventory of Rn 1343 *cont.*

Fol. no.	Text Incipit	Genre [Number] (Remarks)
	[Chants without rubrics designating feast]	
13v	Qui caelicolas	Troped Gloria in excelsis [20]
14r	Deus fortis	Troped Sanctus [1]
14r–v	Pater ingenitus	Troped Sanctus [2]
14v	Pater lumen aeternum	Troped Sanctus [3]
14v	Deus pater ingenite	Troped Sanctus [4]
14v–15r	Mundi fabricator	Troped Sanctus [5]
15r	Admirabilis splendor	Troped Sanctus [6]
15r	Sanctus	Sanctus [8] (*sine tropis*)
15v	Sanctus	Sanctus [9] (*sine tropis*)
15v	Sanctus	Sanctus [10] (*sine tropis*)
15v	Sanctus	Sanctus [11] (*sine tropis*)
16r	Sanctus	Sanctus [12] (*sine tropis*)
15v–16r	Quem cherubim	Troped Sanctus [7]
16r	Qui sedes ad dexteram patris	Troped Agnus Dei [1]
16r–v	Omnipotens aeterna Dei	Troped Agnus Dei [2]
16v	Tu Deus et dominus	Troped Agnus Dei [3]
16v	Suscipe deprecationem . . . Dei patris	Troped Agnus Dei [4]
16v	Ad dextram patris	Troped Agnus Dei [5]
17r	Exaudi domine	Troped Agnus Dei [6]
17r	Suscipe deprecationem . . . Dei	Troped Agnus Dei [7]
17r	Agnus Dei . . . alleluia alleluia	Troped Agnus Dei [8]
17r–v	Salus et vita	Troped Agnus Dei [9]
17v	Agnus Dei	Agnus Dei [10] (*sine tropis*)
	Christmas	
17v	Emitte angelum tuum	Confractorium [1]
	[Holy Saturday]	
17v	Hic est agnus	Confractorium [2]
	[Easter]	
18r	Corpus Christi accepimus	Confractorium [3]
	[St. Sylvester]	
18r	Angeli circumdederunt altare	Confractorium [4]
	First Sunday of Advent	
18r–v	Sanctissimus namque Gregorius	Introit trope [1]
18v	Almipotens verus Deus	Introit trope [2]
18v	Ecce iam Christus	Introit trope [3]
18v	Venturum te cuncti dixerunt	Gradual prosula [1]
18v–19r	Invocavite altissime	Offertory prosula [2]
	Second Sunday of Advent	
19r	Possessor polorum Deus	Offertory prosula [3]
	Third Sunday of Advent	
19r	Qui sedes in alto throno	Gradual prosula [4]
19r	Misericors et clemens famulis	Offertory prosula [5]
	Fourth Sunday of Advent	
19r	A supernis caelorum	Offertory prosula [6]
	Christmas I	
19r–v	Verbo altissimi patris	Introit trope [4]
	Christmas II	
19v	Hora est iam nos	Introit trope [5]
19v	Ecce iam venit hora	Introit trope [6]
19v	Iam surgens aurora	Introit trope [7]
19v–20r	Dierum noctuque	Offertory prosula [7]
	Christmas III	
20r	Verbum caro hodie	Processional antiphon [1]
20r	Hodie salvator mundi per virginem	Introit trope [8]
20r	Hodie exultent iusti natus est	Introit trope [9]
20r–v	Hic enim est de quo prophetae	Introit trope [10]
20v	Audi nos te deprecamur	Alleluia prosula [8]
20v	Alme caeli rex inmortalis	Alleluia prosula [9]
20v–21r	Natus ante saecula Dei filius	Sequence
21r	Tu rex gloriae Christi	Antiphon *ante evangelium* [1]
21v	Hodie natus est Christus	Antiphon *ante evangelium* [2]
21v	Proles virginis matris	Offertory prosula [10]

Inventory of Rn 1343 *cont.*

Fol. no.	Text Incipit	Genre [Number] (Remarks)
	St. Stephen	
21v	Hodie inclitus martyr Stephanus	Introit trope [11]
21v	Grandine lapidum	Introit trope [12]
22r–v	Hanc concordi famulatu	Sequence
22v	Gloria in excelsis Deo	Antiphon *ante evangelium* [3]
22v	Magnus et felix	Communion trope [14]
	St. John Evangelist	
22v	Aeterno genitus genitore	Introit trope [15]
22v	Ille qui dixit	Introit trope [16]
22v–23r	Amor angelorum et gaudium	Introit trope [17]
23r	Iohannes Iesu Christo multum	Sequence
23v	Iste est discipulus	Antiphon *ante evangelium* [4]
23v	Florebit justus ut palma	Offertory trope [19]
	St. Sylvester	
23v	Clementissime Christi confessor	Processional antiphon [2]
23v	Venite populi ad conlaudandum	Introit trope [21]
23v–24r	Hic est Silvester	Introit trope [22]
24r–v	Haec sunt sacra festa	Sequence
24v	Dicit dominus	Antiphon *ante evangelium* [5]
24v	Usque in saeculum saeculi	Offertory trope [23]
25r–v	Laude mirandum digna	Sequence
	Epiphany	
25v	Hodie descendit Christus	Introit trope [24]
25v	Forma speciosissimus	Introit trope [25]
25v–26r	Haec est praeclara dies	Introit trope [26]
26r–v	Festa Christi omnis christianitas	Sequence
26v–27r	Tribus miraculis	Antiphon *ante evangelium* [6]
	Purification	
27r	Adest alma virgo	Introit trope [27]
27r	Psallentes legimus	Introit trope [28]
27r–28v	Concentu parili hic te	Sequence
28r	Omnes patriarchae	Antiphon *ante evangelium* [7]
	Sexagesima Sunday	
28r	Sana Christe rex alme	Tract prosula [11]
	Fourth Sunday of Lent	
28r	Mons magnus est	Tract prosula [12]
	Palm Sunday	
28r–v	Ingresso Iesu	Introit trope [29]
	Easter Sunday	
28v	Hora est surgite/Quem quaeritis	Introit trope [31]
28v	Christus de sepulchro resurrexit	Introit trope [32]
28v	Hodie resurrexit leo fortis	Introit trope [33]
28v–29r	Iam redeunt gaudia	Alleluia prosula [14]
29r	Christe tu vita vera	Alleluia prosula [15]
29r–v	Ecce vicit radix David	Sequence
29v	Laudate dominum de caelis	Antiphon *ante evangelium* [8]
29v–30r	Ab increpatione et ira	Offertory trope [34]
30r	Laus honor virtus	Communion trope [35]
	Easter Monday	
30r–v	Clara gaudia festa paschalia	Sequence
30v–31r	Maria et Maria	Antiphon *ante evangelium* [9]
	Easter Tuesday	
31r	Dic nobis quibus	Sequence
	Octave of Easter	
31v–32r	Eia recolamus laudibus piis digna	Sequence
	Dedication of a Church	
32r–v	Ad templi huius limina	Sequence
	Ss. Senesius and Theopontius	
32v–33r	Cuncti fideles Christi	Introit trope [36]
33r	Sanguine sacrati Christi	Introit trope [37a]
33r–v	Laus tibi Christe patris optimi	Sequence
33v	Isti sunt qui	Antiphon *ante evangelium* [10]

Inventory of Rn 1343 cont.

Fol. no.	Text Incipit	Genre [Number] (Remarks)
	Ascension	
33v	Quem creditis super astra	Introit trope [38]
33v	Hodie redemptor mundi ascendit	Introit trope [39]
34r	Terrigenas summos affatur	Introit trope [40]
34r–v	Summi triumphum regis	Sequence
34v	Hodie secreta caeli	Antiphon *ante evangelium* [12]
	Pentecost	
34v–35r	Hodie spiritus sanctus procedens	Introit trope [42]
35r	Hodie spiritus sanctus processit	Introit trope [43]
35r–36r	Sancti spiritus assit nobis gratia	Sequence
36r	Hodie e caelis	Antiphon *ante evangelium* [13]
	St. John the Baptist	
36r	Hodie exultent iusti . . . Iohannes	Introit trope [45]
36r–v	Deus pater clamat Iohannem	Introit trope [46]
36v	Audite insulae	Introit trope [47]
36v–37r	Alme mundi rex Christe	Sequence
	St. Peter	
37r	Beatissimus Petrus catenis	Introit trope [48]
37r	Hodie sanctissimi patroni nostri	Introit trope [49]
37r–v	Divina beatus Petrus	Introit trope [50]
37v–38r	Pretiosa sollemnitas adest	Sequence
38r	Petre amas me	Antiphon *ante evangelium* [15]
38r–v	Petre summe Christi pastor	Sequence
	Translation of St. Benedict	
38v	A domino impletum	Introit trope [51]
39r–v	Sancti merita Benedicti	Sequence
	St. Lawrence	
39v–40r	Hodie beatus Laurentius levita	Introit trope [53]
40r	Prunas extensa	Introit trope [54]
40r–v	Qui tibi dedit Laurenti	Introit trope [55]
40v–41r	Laurenti David magni martyr	Sequence
41r	Iustum deduxit dominus	Antiphon *ante evangelium* [16]
	Assumption	
41r	Exaudi virgo virginum	Introit trope [56]
41r–v	Ave beata Maria	Introit trope [57]
41v	Nos sinus ecclesiae	Introit trope [58]
41v–42r	Congaudet angelorum chori	Sequence
42r	Beata es quae	Antiphon *ante evangelium* [17]
	Birth of the Blessed Virgin	
42v	O quam clara nitet	Introit trope [59]
42v–43r	Summa stripe genita virgo	Sequence
	Michael Archangel	
43r	Qui patris in caelo	Introit trope [60]
43r–v	Ante Deum semper gloriae	Alleluia prosula [23]
43v	Concussum et percussum	Alleluia prosula [24]
43v	Angele Michael atque Gabriel	Alleluia prosula [25]
43v–44r	Summi regis archangele Michael	Sequence
44v	Tu rex gloriae Christi	Antiphon *ante evangelium* [1] (incipit)
	Ss. Simon and Jude	
44v	Nobile apostolici admirans	Introit trope [61]
44v	Admirans vates proclamat	Introit trope [62]
44v	Consortes tuorum effecti	Introit trope [63]
44v–45r	Clare sanctorum senatus	Sequence
	All Saints	
45r	Sanguinis sacrati Christi	Introit trope [37b] (incipit)
45r–v	Omnes sancti seraphin	Sequence
45v–46r	Gaudent in caelis	Antiphon *ante evangelium* [11]
	St. Martin	
46r	Divini fuerat	Introit trope [64]
46r–47r	Sacerdotem Christi Martinum	Sequence
	Common of the Blessed Virgin Mary	
47r	Psallat turba devota	Alleluia prosula [26]

xxviii

Inventory of Rn 1343 *cont.*

Fol. no.	Text Incipit	Genre [Number] (Remarks)
	St. Andrew	
47r–v	Festus nunc in apostolicis	Introit trope [65]
47v	Hodie beatissimus Andreas	Introit trope [66]
47v	In dulcedine amoris	Alleluia prosula [27]
47v–48r	Deus in tua virtute	Sequence
48r	Salve crux	Antiphon *ante evangelium* [18]
	Trinity Sunday	
48r–v	Alma fulgens crux praeclara	Sequence
48v	Alme domine noli claudere	Alleluia prosula [28]
	Sundays after Pentecost	
48v–49r	Arbiter singulorum facta	Alleluia prosula [29]
49r	Alma voce canamus	Alleluia prosula [30]
49r	Laudes debitas vocibus	Alleluia prosula [31]
49r	Et ab insurgentibus Deus	Alleluia prosula [32]
49r–v	Lingua cor simul clamitet	Alleluia prosula [33]
49v	Laetamente canamus Deo nostro	Sequence
49v–50r	O quam mira sunt Deus tua	Sequence
50r	Stans a longe publicanus	Sequence
50r–v	Almiflui a caelorum turba	Sequence
	Trinity Sunday	
51r	Splendor et imago patris	Introit trope [67]
51r–v	Benedicta semper sancta	Sequence
	Advent	
51v–52v	Venite omnes exsultemus	Antiphon [3]
	Christmas	
52v–53r	O Maria Iesse virga	Antiphon [4]
	Purification	
53r–v	Ave gratia plena	Antiphon [5]
53v	Adorna thalamum tuum	Antiphon [6]
53v	Responsum accepit Symeon	Antiphon [7]
53v	Cum inducerent	Antiphon [8] (incipit)
	Septuagesima	
54r–v	Christe pater misericordiarum	Antiphon [9]
	Ash Wednesday	
54v	Immutemus habitum	Antiphon [10]
54v	Exaudi nos . . . quoniam benigna	Antiphon [11]
54v	Iuxta vestibulum	Antiphon [12]
	Lent	
55r	Cum sederit filius	Antiphon [13]
55r–v	Convertimini omnes simul ad deum	Antiphon [14]
	Palm Sunday	
55v	Pueri hebraeorum tollentes	Antiphon [15]
55v	Pueri hebraeorum vestimenta	Antiphon [16]
55v–56r	Cum appropinquaret	Antiphon [17]
56r–v	Cum audisset populus	Antiphon [18]
56v	Coeperunt omnes trubae	Antiphon [19]
56v–57r	Occurrunt turbae	Antiphon [20]
57r–v	Gloria laus et honor	Hymn [2]
57v	Ingrediente domino	Responsory [21] (incipit)
57v	Dominus Iesus postquam	Antiphon [22]
	Maundy Thursday	
57v–58v	Tellus ac aether iubilent	Hymn [3]
58v	Mandatum novum do vobis	Antiphon [23]
58v	Diligamus nos invicem	Antiphon [24]
58v	Ubi est caritas (*karitas*)	Antiphon [25]
58v–59r	Postquam surrexit dominus	Antiphon [26]
59r	Domine tu mihi lavas	Antiphon [27]
59r	Vos vocatis me magister	Antiphon [28]
59r	Si ego dominus	Antiphon [29]
59r–v	In diebus illis	Antiphon [30]
59v	Maria ergo unxit pedes	Antiphon [31]
59v	Congregavit nos Christus	Antiphon [32]
59v	Ubi fratres in unum	Antiphon [33]

Inventory of Rn 1343 *cont.*

Fol. no.	Text Incipit	Genre [Number] (Remarks)
59v	In hoc cognoscent	Antiphon [34]
59v	Maneat in nobis	Antiphon [35] (incipit)
59v	Deus caritas (*karitas*) est	Antiphon [36]
59v–60r	Fratres sit vobis	Antiphon [37]

Good Friday

Fol. no.	Text Incipit	Genre [Number] (Remarks)
60r	Popule meus	Antiphon [38]
60r–v	Ecce lignum crucis	Antiphon [39]
60v	Vadis propitiatus	Responsory [40]
60v	Adoramus crucem tuam	Antiphon [41]
60v–61r	Ego sum alpha et omega	Antiphon [42]
61r	Crucem tuam . . . sanctam resurrectionem	Antiphon [43]
61r–v	Crux benedicta nitet	Hymn [4]
61v–62v	Crux fidelis	Hymn [5]

Easter

Fol. no.	Text Incipit	Genre [Number] (Remarks)
62v	Vidi aquam	Antiphon [44]
63r	In die resurrectionis	Antiphon [45]
63r	Stetit angelus ad sepulchrum	Antiphon [46]
63r	Christus resurgens ex mortuis	Antiphon [47]
63v	Exsurge domine adiuva nos	Antiphon [53]

Easter Monday

Fol. no.	Text Incipit	Genre [Number] (Remarks)
63v	Ego sum Deus patarum vestrorum	Antiphon [54]
63v	Populus Sion convertimini	Antiphon [55]
63v–64r	Domine Deus noster qui	Antiphon [56]

Easter Tuesday

Fol. no.	Text Incipit	Genre [Number] (Remarks)
64r	Confinemini domino	Antiphon [57]
64r	Exclamemus omnes ad dominum	Antiphon [58]
64r	Parce domine parce populo	Antiphon [59]

Easter Wednesday

Fol. no.	Text Incipit	Genre [Number] (Remarks)
64r–v	Cum iocunditate exhibitis	Antiphon [60]
64r	Iniquitates nostrae domine	Antiphon [61]

In Time of Tribulation

Fol. no.	Text Incipit	Genre [Number] (Remarks)
64v	Domine non est alius Deus	Antiphon [62]
64v–65r	Exaudi domine deprecationem servorum	Antiphon [63]
65r	Miserere domine plebi tuae	Antiphon [64]
65r	Dimitte domine peccata populi	Antiphon [65]
65r	Exaudi Deus deprecationem nostram	Antiphon [66a]
65r–v	Deprecamur te . . . misericordia	Antiphon [67]
65v	Inclina domine . . . et audi	Antiphon [68]
65v	Multa sunt domine peccata	Antiphon [69]
65v	Dimitte domine peccata populi	Antiphon [66] (incipit)
65v	Non in iustificationibus	Antiphon [70]
65v–66r	Peccavimus domine et tu	Antiphon [71]
66r	Domine imminuti sumus	Antiphon [72a]
66r–v	Timor et tremor	Antiphon [73]
66v–67r	Nos peccavimus domine	Antiphon [74]
67r	Terribile est Christe	Antiphon [75]
67r	De tribulatione clamamus	Antiphon [76]
67r–v	Rogamus te domine Deus	Responsory [77]
67v–68r	Pro pace regum	Antiphon [78]
68r	Dimitte nobis domine	Antiphon [79]
68r	Oremus dilectissimi nobis	Antiphon [80]
68r–v	Deus qui es benedictus	Antiphon [81]

In Time of War

Fol. no.	Text Incipit	Genre [Number] (Remarks)
68v	Domine miserere nostri	Antiphon [82]
68v	Exaudi nos domine . . . David	Antiphon [83]
68v–69r	Invocantes dominum exclamemus	Antiphon [84]
69r	Convertere . . . et deprecare	Antiphon [85]
69r	Propter peccata nostra	Antiphon [86]
69r	Sicut exaudisti domine	Antiphon [87]

In Time of Drought

Fol. no.	Text Incipit	Genre [Number] (Remarks)
69r–v	Domine rigans montes	Antiphon [88]
69v	Domine rex Deus Abraham	Antiphon [89]
69v	Respice domine quia aruit	Antiphon [90]

Inventory of Rn 1343 *cont.*

Fol. no.	Text Incipit	Genre [Number] (Remarks)
69v	Numquid est in idolis	Antiphon [91]
69v–70r	Exaudi domine populum tuum	Antiphon [92]
70r	Si clauso caelo	Antiphon [93]
70r	Arridaverunt montes	Antiphon [94]
	In Time of Flood	
70r	Inundaverunt aquae domine	Antiphon [95]
70v	Rupti sunt fontes	Antiphon [96]
70v	Non nos demergat domine	Antiphon [97]
70v	Peccavimus domine peccavimus	Antiphon [98]
70v	Qui siccasti mare	Antiphon [99]
	For the Dead	
71r	Libera domine populum tuum	Antiphon [100]
71r	Exsurge libera nos Deus	Antiphon [101]
71r	Miserere domine et dic angelo	Antiphon [102]
71r–v	Deus Deus noster respice in nos	Antiphon [103]
71v	Domine Deus rex . . . libera nos	Antiphon [104]
	In Procession with Relics	
71r	Cum iocunditate	Antiphon [60] (incipit)
71v	Ecce populus custodiens	Antiphon [105]
71v	Plateae Jerusalem gaudebunt	Antiphon [106]
71v	De Jerusalem exeunt	Antiphon [107]
71v–72r	Ambulantes sancti dei ingredimini	Antiphon [108]
72r	Ambulabunt sancti tui	Antiphon [110]
72r	Sub altare domini	Antiphon [111]
72r	Sanctos portamus sanctorum	Antiphon [11]
72r	Ierusalem civitas sancta	Antiphon [112]
72r–v	Kyrie . . . Emmanuel nobiscum	Litany [1]
72v	Kyrie . . . Sancta Maria te	Litany [2]
72v–73v	Kyrie . . . Domine miserere	Litany [3]
73v	Kyrie . . . Exaudi exaudi	Litany [4]
74r–77r	Humili prece et sincera devotione	Hymn [1]
77r	In civitate domini	Antiphon [114]
77r–v	Benedic domine domus . . . omnes	Antiphon [115]
77v	Gregem tuum domine	Antiphon [116]
77v	Oportet nos mundum	Antiphon [117]
77v	Sint oculi tui aperti	Antiphon [118]
77v–78r	Signum salutis pone	Antiphon [119]
	At the Sprinkling of Holy Water on Sunday	
78r–v	Agnus Dei . . . Suscipe	Litany [5]
78v	Asperges me	Antiphon [120]
	In Processions on Sunday	
78v–79r	Cum venerimus ante conspectum	Antiphon [121]
79r–v	Omnipotens Deus supplices	Antiphon [122]
80v	Ote to stauron (O quando in cruce)	Antiphon [123]
80v–81r	O quando in cruce	Antiphon [124]
81r	O crux gloriosa	Antiphon [125]
81v	O quando in cruce	Antiphon [124] (fragment)

Notes

1. Early northern Italian chants are identified and their relationships to those of other regions discussed in Michel Huglo, "Vestiges d'un ancient répertoire musical de Haute-Italie," in *Bericht über den zweiter Internationaler Kongress für katholische Kirchenmusik* (Vienna, 1955), 142–45; Kenneth Levy, "The Italian Neophytes' Chants," *JAMS* 23 (1970): 181–227; and idem, "Lux de luce: The Origin of an Italian Sequence," *MQ* 59 (1971): 40–61.

2. Regarding the connections between northern and southern Italian chant, see Terence Bailey, "Ambrosian Chant in Southern Italy," *Journal of the Plainsong and Mediaeval Music Society* 6 (1983): 1–7; idem, *The Ambrosian Alleluias* (Egham Surrey, 1983), 51–52; and Thomas Forrest Kelly, "Beneventan and Milanese Chant," *Journal of the Royal Musical Association* 12 (1987): 173–95.

3. Gallican influence in northern Italy is discussed briefly in *New Grove*, s.v. "Ambrosian [Milanese] rite, music of the," by Giacomo Bonifacio Baroffio.

4. See *New Grove*, s.v. "Gallican rite, music of the," by Michel Huglo. Anne Walters Robertson succinctly describes the order of the Gallican Mass in *The Service-Books of the Royal Abbey of Saint-Denis: Images of Ritual and Music in the Middle Ages* (Oxford, 1991), 10–11.

5. For a survey of the repertory at Saint-Denis, see Anne Walters [Robertson], "The Reconstruction of the Abbey Church at St-Denis (1231–81): The Interplay of Music and Ceremony with Architecture and Politics," *Early Music History* 5 (1985): 205–231; and idem, *The Service Books*, 267–71. The practice of singing antiphons before the reading of the gospel was evidently widespread throughout medieval France. The famous thirteenth-century liturgist William Durandus comments on their performance in his *Rationale divinorum officiorum*, ed. Jean Beletho (Naples, 1859), 197. As late as the eighteenth century Edmundo Martène wrote that antiphons *ante evangelium* were sung at Tours, Senlis, Langre, and Bayonne. See his *De antiquis ecclesiae ritibus*, 2d ed., 4 vols. (Antwerp, 1737–38), 4:104.

6. Levy, "The Italian Neophytes' Chants," 187–88, identifies Ravenna, along with Milan and Benevento, as one of three major centers of the pre-Carolingian liturgy in Italy.

7. Gregorio Penco, *Storia del monachesimo in Italia dalle origini alla fine del medio evo*, Collana universale storica, Tempi e Figure, 2d ser., vol. 21 (Rome, 1961), 125.

8. James Borders, "The Northern Italian Antiphons *ante evangelium* and the Gallican Connection," *Journal of Musicological Research* 8 (1988): 1–53.

9. For a discussion of written evidence of the Frankish reform at one northern Italian center, see Borders, "The Cathedral of Verona as a Musical Center in the Middle Ages: Its History, Manuscripts, and Liturgical Traditions," 2 vols. (Ph.D. diss., University of Chicago, 1983).

10. On the use of Gregory's image in the transmission of the Franco-Roman repertory, see Leo Treitler, "Homer and Gregory: The Transmission of Epic Poetry and Plainchant," *MQ* 60 (1974): 334–44. See also Helmut Hucke, "Towards a New Historical View of Gregorian Chant," *JAMS* 33 (1980): 437–67.

11. The librarians of Nonantola did not catalog many service books before the fifteenth century. Judging from the medieval practice at other centers, these codices would normally have been kept in the sacristy, not the library. On the history of the Nonantolan library as it relates to music, see Ave Moderini, *La notazione neumatica di Nonantola*, Instituta et Monumenta pubblicati dalla Biblioteca governativa e civica di Cremona, ser. 2, no. 3, pts. 1–2 (Cremona, 1970), 1:43–50. On the library catalogs and their contents, see Giuseppe Gullotta, *Gli antichi cataloghi e i codici della Abbazia di Nonantola*, Studi e Testi, vol. 182 (Vatican City, 1955); and José Ruysschaert, *Les manuscrits de l'abbaye de Nonantola*, Studi e Testi, vol. 182 *bis* (Vatican City, 1955).

12. This conjecture is an extension of Richard Crocker's research on Latin Kyries summarized in "Troping Hypothesis," *MQ* 52 (1966): 183–203. More recently, David Hiley, *Western Plainchant: A Handbook* (Oxford, 1993), 152, admits the likelihood that many Kyries, for example, contained Latin verses from the moment of their composition.

13. Crocker, "Troping Hypothesis," 187–88.

14. Borders, "The Cathedral of Verona," 1:263–64; 2:467–84.

15. For further discussion of the transmission of the trope repertory in Italy, see Planchart, "Italian Tropes," *Mosaic* 18 (1985): 11–31; and idem, "On the Nature and Transmission and Change in Trope Repertories," *JAMS* 41 (1988): 215–49. See also Planchart's seminal study, *The Repertory of Tropes at Winchester*, 2 vols. (Princeton, 1977), which examines a far wider geographical swath of tropes than the title suggests. A general introduction to this kind of research is found in Planchart, "The Transmission of Medieval Chant," in *Music in Medieval and Modern Europe*, ed. Iain Fenlon (Cambridge, 1981), 347–63. The different historical and geographical influences to which the entire Introit trope repertory was subject are discussed in Hiley, "Some Observations on the Interrelationships between Trope Repertories," in *Research On Tropes*, ed. Gunilla Iversen (Stockholm, 1983), 29–37.

16. Ruysschaert, *Les manuscrits*, 43; Moderini, *La notazione*, 1:44, 50.

17. Borders, "The Northern and Central Italian Trope Repertoire and Its Transmission," in *Atti del XIV Congresso della Società Internazionale di Musicologia: Trasmissione e recezione della forme di cultura musicale*, 3 vols. (Turin, 1989), 3:546.

18. Planchart, "Italian Tropes," 11, describes the local conditions which in part governed the preservation of the Italian trope repertory. He points out that most Italian tropes come down to us in Gradual books, the format of which effectively limited the number of pieces preserved. See also Borders, "Tropes and the New Philology," *Cantus Planus* (Budapest, 1990), 393–94.

19. Hiley, "The Interrelationships," 33, employs the useful metaphor of "diverse waves of influence, each wave leaving a residual deposit on the shore."

20. Borders, "The Northern and Central Italian Trope Repertoire," 546. Hiley points to a similar relationship in "Some Observations," 35, but in *Western Plainchant*, 353, erroneously states that the Nonantolan trope repertory comes mostly from East Frankland.

21. Paul Evans, "Northern French Elements in an Early Aquitanian Troper," in *Speculum musicae artis: Festgabe für Heinrich Husmann zum 60. Geburtstag*, ed. H. Becker and R. Gerlach (Munich, 1970), 103–10.

22. Leach, "The *Gloria in Excelsis Deo* Tropes of the Breme-Novalesa Community and the Repertory in North and Central Italy" (Ph.D. diss., University of North Carolina, 1986).

23. Falconer, "Some Early Tropes to the Gloria" (Ph.D. diss., Princeton University, 1989).

24. For information on the monastery's early elevated status and privileges, see Penco, *Storia del monachesimo*, 113–14. See also A. Gaudenzi, "Il Monastero di Nonantola, Il Ducato di Persiceta e la Chiesa di Bologna," *Bullettino dell'Istituto storico Italiano* 22 (1901): 77–214; and *Vita Anselmi abbatis Nonantulani*, Monumenta Germaniae Historica, Scriptores rerum Langobardicarum et Italicarum saec. VI–XI (Hannover, 1878).

25. Penco, *Storia del monachesimo*, 125.

26. Moderini, *La notazione*, 1:38.

27. Gullotta, *Gli antichi cataloghi*, x.

28. Moderini, *La notazione*, 1:39.

29. Penco, *Storia del monachesimo*, 202–3.

30. This style of musical notation is described in the descriptions of the manuscript sources. The earlier history of the Nonantolan scriptorium is treated in E. A. Lowe, *Codices Latini Antiquiores*, vol. 4 (Oxford, 1947).

31. Moderini, *La notazione*, 1:46.

32. Moderini, *La notazione*, 1:43. This catalog, which is found on fols. 1v–2r of Bologna, Biblioteca Universitaria, MS 2248, lists only two liturgical books, identified as "Antiphonarii de die."

33. According to legend, after the holy oil was consecrated, a flame descended from heaven and set it on fire. Moderini, *La notazione*, 1:40.

34. Hiley, *Western Plainchant*, 353. Other discussions of the traits of Nonantolan notation are found in Dom Grégoire M. Suñol, *Introduction a la paléographie musicale grégorienne* (Paris, 1935), 197–99, and Bruno Stäblein, *Schriftbild der Einstimmigen Musik*, Musikgeschichte in Bildern, vol. 4, no. 3 (Leipzig, 1975), 34–37, who observes important differences among northern Italian notations, which combined traits of French, German, and other Italian styles.

35. Cf. Moderini, *La notazione*, plates 23–40 and 9–22. On developed Nonantolan style notation in Veronese chantbooks, see Borders, "The Cathedral of Verona," 1:281–87.

36. See Michel Huglo et al., *Fonti e paleografia del canto Ambrosiano*, Archivio Ambrosiano, vol. 7 (Milan, 1956), 80; Heinrich Husmann, *Tropen- und Sequenzenhandschriften*, RISM, ser. B.V.1 (Munich-Duisburg, 1964), 170–71; and Moderini, *La notazione*, 1:54.

37. See Huglo et al., *Fonti*, 80–81; Husmann, *Tropen- und Sequenzenhandschriften*, 182; Moderini, *La notazione*, 1:68; and [The Benedictines of Solesmes], *Le graduel romain: édition critique, ii: Les Sources* (Solesmes, 1957), 122.

38. See Huglo et al., *Fonti*, 80; Husmann, *Tropen- und Sequenzenhandschriften*, 185; Moderini, *La notazione*, 1:69; Heinrich Pfaff, "Die Tropen und Sequenzen der Handschrift Rom, Bibl. Naz. Vitt. Emm. 1343 (Sessor. 62) aus Nonantola" (Inaugural-Dissertation, Ludwig-Maximillian University, Munich, 1948), 8–12; and *Les Sources*, 122.

39. Husmann, *Tropen- und Sequenzenhandschriften*, 170–71, 182, and 185.

Introduction to the Ordinary Chants and Tropes

Because numerous surveys of medieval chant address the origins and histories of the individual Ordinary chants and their tropes,[1] the following introduction focuses almost exclusively on the contents of the three Nonantolan sources and their transmission. (For ease of reference, I use the following sigla for each manuscript: Bu 2824 = Bologna, Biblioteca Universitaria, MS 2824; Rc 1741 = Rome, Biblioteca Casanatense, MS 1741; and Rn 1343 = Rome, Biblioteca Nazionale Centrale, MS 1343. Numbers refer to this edition.) The main question addressed is: how did so many chants of different geographical origins find their way to Nonantola?

Kyrie eleison

Rn 1343 and Rc 1741 together preserve twelve Kyries, listed below in table 1 in the order in which they are found in Rn 1343; Bu 2824 has no Kyries in the surviving corpus, but two (nos. 7 and 8) were added near the end of the manuscript in a hand other than that of the main scribe. The notation for these is central Italian rather than Nonantolan. None of these Kyries was provided with a rubric to designate an assignment to a specific feast. Some connection to the liturgical cycle is implied, however, because Rn 1343 and Rc 1741 preserve nearly identical collections of Kyries, and all save one were copied in some order. (The exception is Kyrie no. 5, *Dominator Deus*, which was copied later in the Rc 1741 than in Rn 1343.) The former manuscript lacks two of the five Kyries *sine tropis* found in the latter (nos. 8 and 12), but what if any implications this may have for the local repertory is unclear.

The diverse repertory of Kyrie melodies sung at Nonantola is another clue to their use in the liturgical cycle. Note in the preceding list that chants employing the same melody were not copied sequentially, suggesting that they were considered independent pieces, not alternatives. As such they would likely have been assigned to different feasts.[2] Indeed, only two melodies recur in different guises: Melnicki 39 was sung in connection with *Omnipotens genitor* and *Lux et origo lucis*, and Melnicki 155 was employed with the verse *Dominator Deus* and as the untroped Kyrie 8. Finally, judging from concordances in northern and central Italian manuscripts in which liturgical assignments are provided, it is reasonable to infer that the order of the Kyries in the Nonantolan tropers corresponds to their use during the Church year.

Eight of the ten Kyrie melodies in Nonantolan sources are among the earliest in the recorded repertory. Five of these were known in the Rhineland by the middle of the tenth century, and northern Italy by the beginning of the eleventh. These are Melnicki 39, 47, 55, 68, and 155. Of the remaining three Kyries, Melnicki 151 has concordances in early manuscripts from Saint Gall and Winchester, as well as Apt, Basilique de Ste. Anne, MS 18, which may be Italian; Melnicki 124 and 217 probably originated in Aquitaine, although the latter finds a concordance at Winchester.[3]

TABLE 1
Kyrie Chants in the Nonantolan Tropers

Kyrie eleison	Melnicki no.	Vatican ed.	Rn 1343	Rc 1741	Bu 2824
1. Verse: *Te Christe rex supplices*	55	VI*	1r	5r	—
2. Trope: *Omnipotens genitor*	39	I	1v	6v	—
3. Verse: *Canamus cuncti laudes*	68	XIV	1v	7r	—
4. Verse: *Lux et origo lucis*	39	I	2r	8v	—
5. Verse: *Dominator Deus*	155	XV	2v	12r	—
6. Verse: *Rex magne domine*	124	—	3r	9v	—
7. Verse: *Kyrie rex genitor*	47	VI	3v	10v	103r (addn.)
8. (*sine tropis*)	155	XV	4r	—	104r (addn.)
9. (*sine tropis*)	151	XVIII	4r	12v	—
10. (*sine tropis*)	136	—	4r	12v	—
11. (*sine tropis*)	112?	—	4r	13r	—
12. (*sine tropis*)	217	XVI	4r	—	—

These facts imply that Nonantola was largely dependent on the East Frankish repertory, but a close comparison of the Latin texts reveals a more nuanced story. Of eight Latin Kyries in the earliest East Frankish sources, four have concordances in the Nonantolan tropers. Eliminating from consideration one manuscript grouped with the East Frankish ones—a Rhenish source from Prüm (Paris, Bibliothèque Nationale, fonds latin, MS 9448)—the number of concordances drops to two (*Omnipotens genitor* and *Canamus cuncti*). The Latin Kyrie texts found in Nonantola but not in the East Frankish repertory are probably either imports from the West, like *Te Christe rex* and *Dominator Deus*, or local products, like *Lux et origo lucis*. Thus Nonantola was plainly subject both to Eastern and Western influences, probably at different times. It is not coincidental, then, that the Nonantolan repertory shares traits with that of the Rhineland (as represented by Pn 9448), an area referred to as a zone of transition between East and West. (A direct relationship between Prüm and Nonantola does not seem likely since the readings of Latin Kyries sometimes disagree significantly in their texts and neumations.)

Gloria in excelsis

The Nonantolan tropers yield a total of twenty-one Gloria in excelsis chants, troped and untroped, listed below in table 2 as they appear in Rn 1343. The contents of this source are nearly identical with Rc 1741, except that no. 21, *Hinc laudando patrem*, is found in Nonantolan sources exclusively in Rc 1741. Here it was copied before no. 20, *Qui caelicolas*. From table 2 we may infer three important features of the Nonantolan Gloria in excelsis repertory. First, Bu 2824 preserves the smallest collection: only seven items (nos. 4, 8, 9–13). A close inspection of the manuscript reveals that the number of Glorias was further diminished by the erasure of *Laudat in excelsis* (no. 17) from fols. 8v–9v, on which a later hand has inscribed six responsory verses. Folio 8v also once contained the closing verses of no. 13 (*Cives superni . . . Christus surrexit*).

Second, tropes were added to all but one of the untroped melodies—only Bosse 21 (Gloria in excelsis 6) was not so treated. Of the Gloria in excelsis melodies with tropes, Bosse 51 and 12 were sung the most frequently, four times each in Rn 1343. However, the Rc 1741 scribe employed Bosse 39 instead of 51 and 12 in connection with tropes *Pax sempiterna* (no. 8), *Laus tua Deus* (no. 11), and *Cives superni . . . Christus surrexit* (no. 13).

Third, as indicated on the far right column of the table, the troped Glorias were provided with rubrics clarifying their assignments to various feasts. It is thus not difficult to understand why the Nonantolan tropers correspond in their order. Indeed, Rn 1343

TABLE 2
Gloria Chants in the Nonantolan Tropers

Gloria in excelsis	Bosse no.	Rn 1343	Rc 1741	Bu 282	Assignment
1. (sine tropis)	39	4r–v	13r–14r	—	—
2. (sine tropis)	2 (var.)	4v–5r	14v–15r	—	—
3. (sine tropis)	43	5r–v	15v–16r	—	—
4. (sine tropis)	12	5v	18v–19r	1r–v	—
5. (sine tropis)	11	5v–6r	16v–17r	—	—
6. (sine tropis)	21	6r–v	17v–18r	—	—
7. (sine tropis)	51	6v	14r	—	—
8. Pax sempiterna	51	6v–7r	—	2r	Christmas
	39	—	19v–21r	—	
9. Quem patris ad dexteram	2 (var.)	7v	21r–22r	2r–3r	St. Stephen
10. Quem cives caelestes	43	8r–v	22r–23r	3r–4v	St. John Evangelist
11. Laus tua Deus	12	8v	—	4v–5v	St. Sylvester
	39	—	23r–24r	—	
12. Quem novitate	12	9r–v	24r–25r	5v–7r	Epiphany
13. Cives superni . . . Christus surrexit	51	9v–10r	—	7r–8r	Easter
	39	—	25v–27r	—	
14. Alme mundi hodie de morte	11	10v–11r	27r–v	—	Easter Monday
15. Alme mundi hodie ad caelos	11	11r	27v–28r	—	Ascension
16. O laudabilis rex	51	11r–v	28r–29r	—	Ss. Senesius & Theopontius
17. Laudat in excelsis	51	12r	29r–30r	—	Pentecost
18. Quando regis cunctos	12	12r–13r	30r–32r	—	St. John the Baptist
19. O gloriosa sanctorum	11	13r–v	32r–33v	—	St. Peter
20. Qui caelicolas	12	13v	34v–35v	—	—
21. Hinc laudando patrem	2 (var.)	—	33v–34v	—	Assumption

and Rn 1741 differ only with respect to one piece, no. 20, the only Gloria trope for which an assignment to a feast was not specified.

The Nonantolan repertory of Gloria in excelsis tropes includes the entire pan-Italian repertory identified by Mark Leach: *Quem patris ad dexteram, Quem cives caelestes, Laus tua Deus, Cives superni . . . Christus surrexit,* and *Laudat in excelsis*.[4] To this list should be added two Gloria tropes normally found in northern and central Italian sources: *Pax sempiterna* (no. 8) and *Quem novitate* (no. 12).

Five of these seven pieces (nos. 8–11 and 17) were widely distributed north of the Alps and are found in both West and East Frankish manuscripts before 1200.[5] Of the remaining two, no. 12 (*Quem novitate*) probably originated in Italy; the origin of no. 13 (*Cives superni*) is uncertain, but conceivably could have been written at a northern Italian center.[6] The remaining seven Gloria in excelsis tropes in Nonantolan sources include four with concordances in West Frankish manuscripts (nos. 16, 18, 19, and 21), one with concordances in both East and West Frankland (no. 20), and one with northern Italian counterparts (no. 15, *Alme mundi hodie ad caelos*). *Alme mundi hodie de morte* (no. 14) is a contrafact of this piece which survives exclusively in Nonantolan sources.

Sanctus

The three Nonantolan tropers together yield a total of thirteen Sanctus chants and tropes. Of these, seven are troped (see table 3). The items are listed in the order in which they appear in Rn 1343, except that no. 7 (*Quem cherubim*) in this edition is grouped with the other troped Sanctus melodies. Moreover, Sanctus 13 is found in Nonantola only in Rc 1741. Despite some differences among the three collections—Rc 1741 lacks no. 10; Rn 1343 and Bu 2824 lack no. 13; Bu 2824 contains only eight Sanctus chants, three untroped—the order of the chants is generally the same. The scribe of Rc 1741 copied all troped items in a single group, perhaps disturbing the order in which the chants were performed during the church year (there are no rubrics). Two melodies were employed more than once: Thannabaur 154 (Vatican I) is associated with three different tropes (nos. 1, 2, and 4); no. 9, which is found only in Rn 1343, is a variant of Thannabaur 9, which may have originated at Nonantola. (Thannabaur's reading of melody 9 differs from Nonantolan Sanctus 10 in its greater emphasis on the tone F.)

Of the Nonantolan Sanctus tropes, only one, *Deus Pater ingenite* (no. 4), is found in all early regional repertories.[7] The pattern of early concordances of the remaining items suggests that Nonantola was open to different regional influences, the strongest of which was Aquitanian (nos. 2, 3, and 6). Sanctus 1, *Deus fortis*, with its concordances in early Rhenish, Swiss, central and southeastern French manuscripts, was apparently not known in Aquitania. Finally, two tropes, nos. 5 and 7, may have originated in northern or central Italy since they are found almost exclusively in sources from this area.

Agnus Dei

The Nonantolan tropers have a total of ten Agnus Dei chants, all but one, invariably the last in a series, troped (see table 4). As with the other movements of the Ordinary, the order of Agnus Dei chants in the Nonantolan sources generally corresponds, and Bu 2824 contains fewer items than the other two tropers. Only one melody, Schildbach 209 (var. 2), is employed twice, once with the northern Italian trope *Tu Deus et dominus*, the other in an untroped form (no. 10). Schildbach 236 and 236 (var. 3) are different enough in their particulars to be considered different melodies.

TABLE 3
Sanctus Chants in Nonantolan Sources

Sanctus	Thannabaur no.	Vatican ed.	Rn 1343	Rc 1741	Bu 2824
1. *Deus fortis*	154	I	14r	35v	10r
2. *Pater ingenitus*	154	I	14r	36v	10r
3. *Pater lumen aeternum*	216 (var.)	—	14v	37r	—
4. *Deus pater ingenite*	154	I	14v	37v	—
5. *Mundi fabricator*	223	XV	14v	37v	10v
6. *Admirabilis splendor*	111	—	15r	38r	97r
7. *Quem cherubim*	6	—	15v	39r–v	105r–v
8. (*sine tropis*)	60	—	15r	39v	11v
9. (*sine tropis*)	111 (var.)	—	15v	40r	—
10. (*sine tropis*)	9	—	15v	—	—
11. (*sine tropis*)	9 (var.)	—	15v	40v	11v
12. (*sine tropis*)	32	XVII	16r	40v	12r
13. (*sine tropis*)	57	—	—	41r	102r

TABLE 4
Agnus Dei Chants in the Nonantolan Tropers

Agnus Dei	Schildbach no.	Vatican ed.	Rn 1343	Rc 1741	Bu 2824
1. *Qui sedes ad dexteram*	226	II	16r	41v	12v
2. *Omnipotens aeterna Dei*	78	—	16r	42r	—
3. *Tu Deus et dominus*	209 (var. 2)	—	16v	42r	—
4. *Suscipe deprecationem . . . Dei patris*	236	—	16v	42r	—
5. *Ad dextram patris*	236 (var. 3)	—	16v	43r	13v
6. *Exaudi domine*	87	—	17r	43v	13r
7. *Suscipe deprecationem . . . Dei*	164	XVI	17r	43v	14r
8. *Alleluia alleluia*	19	—	17r	44v	14r
9. *Salus et vita*	81	—	17r	44r	—
10. (*sine tropis*)	209 (var. 2)	—	17v	44v	14r

Of the nine Angus Dei tropes in Nonantolan sources, only two were widely transmitted outside northern Italy. *Qui sedes ad dexteram* (no. 1) is found in nearly all the earliest sources examined by Charles Atkinson.[8] On account of this, its nonpoetic text, and because the piece was often sung in connection with Christmas, it is probably among the earliest Agnus Dei tropes. The other trope, *Omnipotens aeterna Dei* (no. 2), is transmitted in Aquitanian, West Frankish, and Italian sources. Despite its use of relatively sophisticated hexameters rather than prose, it is considered to be among the earliest tropes in the medieval repertory, having been composed toward the end of the tenth century.[9] In addition to these, the element "*Qui sedes ad dexteram patris*" (in no. 7) exists as an independent element in early East and West Frankish sources. The remaining tropes are evidently Italian products. The transmission of one, *Tu Deus et dominus* (no. 3), was limited to the Nonantola-Mantua axis; no. 8 survives exclusively in Nonantolan sources.

Notes

1. The most recent of these is Hiley, *Western Plainchant*, 148–68.
2. For a discussion of this theory, see Bjork, "Early Repertories of the Kyrie Eleison," *Kirchenmusikalisches Jahrbuch* 63–64 (1979–80): 20.
3. A basic survey of the dissemination of early Kyrie melodies is found in Hiley, *Western Plainchant*, 152. Hiley also analyzes Melnicki melodies 55, 68, and 155 (on pp. 153–54).
4. Leach, "The *Gloria in Excelsis Deo* Tropes," 35.
5. Klaus Rönnau, *Die Tropen zum Gloria in excelsis Deo, unter besonderer Berücksichtigung des Repertoires der St. Martial-Handschriften* (Wiesbaden, 1967), 78–81; Leach, "The *Gloria in Excelsis Deo* Tropes," 25–34.
6. Keith Falconer, "The Origin of *Cives superni*," paper read at the 54th Annual Meeting of the American Musicological Society, Baltimore, 6 November 1988. See also idem, "Some Early Tropes to the Gloria," 77–108.
7. Concordances are traced in Gunilla Iversen, *CT VII: Tropes du Sanctus*. Studia Latina Stockholmiensia, vol. 34 (Stockholm, 1990).
8. "The Earliest Settings of the *Agnus Dei* and its Tropes" (Ph.D. diss., University of North Carolina, 1975).
9. Atkinson, "The Earliest Settings," 198.

Critical Apparatus

List of Manuscript Sigla

APT 17	Apt, Basilique de Ste. Anne, MS 17
APT 18	Apt, Basilique de Ste. Anne, MS 18
Bu 7	Bologna, Biblioteca Universitaria, MS Q 7
Bu 2824	Bologna, Biblioteca Universitaria, MS 2824
BAs 5	Bamberg, Staatliche Bibliothek, MS Lit. 5
BAs 6	Bamberg, Staatliche Bibliothek, MS Lit. 6
BV 34	Benevento, Biblioteca Capitolare, MS 34
BV 35	Benevento, Biblioteca Capitolare, MS 35
BV 39	Benevento, Biblioteca Capitolare, MS 39
Ccc 473	Cambridge, Corpus Christi College, MS 473
CA 60	Cambrai, Bibliothèque Municipale, MS 60
CA 75	Cambrai, Bibliothèque Municipale, MS 75
IV 60	Ivrea, Biblioteca Capitolare, MS 91 (Bollati LX)
Kl 15	Kassel, Murhardsche Bibliothek, MS 4° MS theol. 25
Lbm 14	London, British Library, Cotton MS Caligula A. xiv
Lbm 19768	London, British Library, Additional MS 19768
Mah 288	Madrid, Biblioteca Nacional, MS 288
Mah 289	Madrid, Biblioteca Nacional, MS 289
Mbs 14083	Munich, Bayerische Staatsbibliothek, MS clm. 14083
Mbs 14322	Munich, Bayerische Staatsbibliothek, MS clm. 14322
Mza 75	Monza, Biblioteca Capitolare, MS C 12/75
Mza 76	Monza, Biblioteca Capitolare, MS C 13/76
MOd 7	Modena, Biblioteca Capitolare (Duomo), MS O.I.7
MZ 452	Metz, Bibliothèque Municipale, MS 452
Ob 27	Oxford, Bodleian Library, MS Selden supra 27
Ob 222	Oxford, Bodleian Library, MS Douce 222
Ob 775	Oxford, Bodleian Library, MS Bodley 77
Pa 1169	Paris, Bibliothèque de l'Arsenal, MS 1169
Pn 778	Paris, Bibliothèque Nationale, fonds latin, MS 778
Pn 903	Paris, Bibliothèque Nationale, fonds latin, MS 903
Pn 909	Paris, Bibliothèque Nationale, fonds latin, MS 909
Pn 1084	Paris, Bibliothèque Nationale, fonds latin, MS 1084
Pn 1118	Paris, Bibliothèque Nationale, fonds latin, MS 1118
Pn 1119	Paris, Bibliothèque Nationale, fonds latin, MS 1119
Pn 1235	Paris, Bibliothèque Nationale, fonds latin, MS 1235
Pn 1240	Paris, Bibliothèque Nationale, fonds latin, MS 1240
Pn 9448	Paris, Bibliothèque Nationale, fonds latin, MS 9448
Pn 9449	Paris, Bibliothèque Nationale, fonds latin, MS 9449
Pn 10508	Paris, Bibliothèque Nationale, fonds latin, MS 10508
Pn 10510	Paris, Bibliothèque Nationale, fonds latin, MS 10510
Pn 13252	Paris, Bibliothèque Nationale, fonds latin, MS 13252
PAc 20	Padua, Biblioteca Capitolare, MS A 20
PAc 47	Padua, Biblioteca Capitolare, MS A 47
PAs 697	Padua, Biblioteca del Seminario Vescovile, MS 697
PCsa 65	Piacenza, Biblioteca e Archivio di San Antonio, MS 65
PS 119	Pistoia, Biblioteca Capitolare (Cattedrale), MS C 119
PS 120	Pistoia, Biblioteca Capitolare (Cattedrale), MS C 120

PS 121	Pistoia, Biblioteca Capitolare (Cattedrale), MS C 121
Ra 123	Rome, Biblioteca Angelica, MS 123
Rc 1741	Rome, Biblioteca Casanatense, MS 1741
Rn 1343	Rome, Biblioteca Nationale Centrale Vittorio Emanuele III, MS 1343 (olim Sessoriano 62)
Rv 52	Rome, Biblioteca Valliceliana, MS C 52
Rvat 602	Rome, Biblioteca Apostolica Vaticana, Urb. lat. 602
SGs 381	Saint Gall, Stiftsbibliothek, MS 381
SGs 484	Saint Gall, Stiftsbibliothek, MS 484
Tn 18	Turin, Biblioteca Nazionale Universitaria, MS F.IV.18
Tn 20	Turin, Biblioteca Nazionale Universitaria, MS G.V.20
VCd 146	Vercelli, Biblioteca Capitolare (Duomo), MS 146
VCd 161	Vercelli, Biblioteca Capitolare (Duomo), MS 161
VCd 162	Vercelli, Biblioteca Capitolare (Duomo), MS 162
VEcap 90	Verona, Biblioteca Capitolare, MS XC
VEcap 107	Verona, Biblioteca Capitolare, MS CVII
VO 39	Volterra, Biblioteca Guarnacci, MS L.3.39
Wn 1609	Vienna, Österreichische Nationalbibliothek, MS 1609

List of Works Cited

Atkinson, "The Earliest Agnus Dei Melody" = Atkinson, Charles M. "The Earliest Agnus Dei Melody and Its Tropes." *JAMS* 30 (1977): 1–19.

Atkinson, "The Earliest Settings" = Atkinson, Charles M. "The Earliest Settings of the *Agnus Dei* and Its Tropes." Ph.D. diss., University of North Carolina, 1975.

Bjork, "The Early Frankish Kyrie Text" = Bjork, David. "The Early Frankish Kyrie Text: A Reappraisal." *Viator* 12 (1981): 9–35.

Bjork, "Early Repertories" = Bjork, David. "Early Repertories of the *Kyrie eleison*." *Kirchenmusikalisches Jahrbuch* 63–64 (1979–80): 9–43.

Bjork, "The Kyrie Trope" = Bjork, David. "The Kyrie Trope." *JAMS* 33 (1980): 1–41.

CT 4 = Iversen, Gunilla. *Corpus Troporum IV: Tropes de l'Agnus Dei*. Studia Latina Stockholmiensia, vol. 26. Stockholm, 1980.

CT 7 = Iverson, Gunilla. *Corpus Troporum VII: Tropes du Sanctus*. Studia Latina Stockholmiensia, vol. 34. Stockholm, 1990.

David, "Le trope 'Sanctus pater' " = David, R. L. "Le trope 'Sanctus pater'." *RdCG* 36 (1932): 129–40.

Gautier, *Les Tropes* = Gautier, Léon. *Histoire de la poésie liturgique au moyen âge: Les Tropes*. 1886. Reprint. Ridgewood, N.J., 1966.

Grosspellier, "Le Kyrie paschal" = Grosspellier, A. "Le Kyrie paschal 'Lux et origo lucis' avec tropes." *RdCG* 14 (1905–6): 135–36.

Husmann, "Sinn und Wesen" = Husmann, Heinrich. "Sinn und Wesen der Tropen: Veranschaulicht an den Introitustropen des Weihnachtsfestes." *Archiv für Musikwissenschaft* 16 (1959): 135–47.

Kelly, "Introducing the *Gloria*" = Kelly, Thomas Forrest "Introducing the *Gloria in excelsis*." *JAMS* 38 (1984): 479–505.

Leach, "The *Gloria in Excelsis Deo* Tropes" = Leach, Mark Alan. "The *Gloria in Excelsis Deo* Tropes of the Breme-Novalesa Community and the Repertory in North and Central Italy." Ph.D. diss., University of North Carolina, 1986.

Lewis and Short, *A Latin Dictionary* = Lewis, Charlton T., and Charles Short. *A Latin Dictionary*. Rev. ed. Oxford, 1879.

Norberg, *Versification médiévale* = Norberg, Dag. *Introduction à l'étude de la versification latine médiévale*. Studia Latina Stockholmiensia 5. Stockholm, 1958.

Pfaff, *Die Tropen* = Pfaff, Heinrich. "Die Tropen und Sequenzen der Handschrift Rom, Bibl. Naz. Vitt. Emm. 1343 (Sessor. 62) aus Nonantola." Inaugural-Dissertation, Ludwig-Maximillian University, Munich, 1948.

Planchart, *Repertory* = Planchart, Alejandro Enrique. *The Repertory of Tropes at Winchester*. 2 vols. Princeton, 1977.

Roederer, *Festive Troped Masses* = Roederer, Charlotte. *Festive Troped Masses from the Eleventh Century: Christmas and Easter in the Aquitaine*. Collegium Musicum: Yale University, 2d ser., vol. 11. Madison, 1989.

Rönnau, "Regnum tuum solidum" = Rönnau, Klaus. "Regnum tuum solidum." In *Festschrift Bruno Stäblein*. Edited by Martin Ruhnke, 195–205. Kassel, 1967.

Rönnau, *Die Tropen zum Gloria* = Rönnau, Klaus. *Die Tropen zum Gloria: Unter besonderer Berücksichtigung des Repertoires des St. Martial-Handschriften*. Wiesbaden, 1967.

Schlager, *Alleluia-Melodien* = Schlager, Karlheinz, ed. *Alleluia-Melodien II ab 1100*. Monumenta Monodica Medii Aevi, vol. 8. Kassel, 1987.

Stäblein, *Hymnen* = Stäblein, Bruno, ed. *Hymnen I: Die mittelalterlichen Hymnenmelodien des Abendlandes*. Monumenta Monodica Medii Aevi, vol. 1. Kassel, 1956.

Strunk, "Tropus and Troparion" = Strunk, Oliver. "Tropus and Troparion." In *Speculum Musicae Artis. Festgabe für Heinrich Husmann*. Edited by Heinz Becker and Reinhard Gerlach, 305–11. Munich, 1940. Reprinted in *Essays on Music in the Byzantine World*. New York, 1977. Pp. 268–76.

Van Deusen, *Music at Nevers* = Van Deusen, Nancy. *Music at Nevers Cathedral: Principal Sources of Medieval Chant*. 2 vols. Musicological Studies, vol. 30, nos. 1–2. Henryville, Ottawa, and Binningen, 1980.

Vecchi, *Troparium* = Vecchi, Giuseppe, ed. *Troparium Sequentiarium Nonantulanum: Cod. Casanat. 1741*. Monumenta Lyrica Medii Aevi Italica, I: Latina. Modena, 1955.

Editorial Methods

Arrangement and Identification of Ordinary Chants and Tropes

Ordinary chants in this volume are grouped into four categories: Kyrie eleison, Gloria in excelsis, Sanctus, and Agnus Dei. Within each category, chants are normally presented and numbered sequentially according to the order of Rn 1343, the older of the two most comprehensive Nonantolan tropers (the other being Rc 1741). The melodies are identified by the numbers assigned to them in the standard catalogs of the Ordinary repertory by Melnicki, Bosse, Thannabaur, and Schildbach, and in modern Vatican and Milanese editions of plainchant.

Text incipits of tropes or verses are also included in the headings to individual pieces in the commentary and in the music where applicable. Because these incipits also serve as uniform titles in the edition, their spelling has been standardized for ease of access and recognition according to normal classical spellings reported in Lewis and Short, *A Latin Dictionary*. Thus *Canamus cunti laudes* is the uniform title for Kyrie eleison no. 3, despite the fact that Nonantolan scribes spelled the first word "*Kanamus*." Proper names, including *Deus* but not *dominus*, are also capitalized in the uniform titles but nowhere else unless indicated in the typical readings. Finally, the manuscript source of the chant selected as the typical reading, along with inclusive folio numbers, is signaled by boldface type in the commentaries; the source is also provided at the beginning of the first line of the music.

Selection and Presentation of Versions and Variants

In most cases, the versions of chants in this edition come from Rn 1343. The decision to treat this manuscript as the typical source rests on two observations concerning the three Nonantolan tropers and their relationship. First, Rn 1343 is earlier and thus closer to the presumed original source than Rc 1741, which is otherwise comparable to Rn 1343 in its scope and contents. Second, the text and melodic readings in Bu 2824, which is perhaps the earliest Nonantolan source but the one containing the fewest items, generally agree with those in Rn 1343 but not as frequently with Rc 1741. One should note, however, that the versions of chants in Rn 1343 and Bu 2824 are not necessarily more correct textually or musically than Rc 1741. As a practical matter, the editor also notes that a facsimile edition of Rc 1741 (Vecchi, *Troparium*) is widely available for comparison with this edition.

In certain cases, however, a version of a chant other than that in Rn 1343 has been selected for inclusion in the edition. This applies if the Rn 1343 text or music reading is marred by extensive lacunae or obvious mistakes. Regardless of which source has been judged typical, all the available Nonantolan readings may be reassembled from the variants listed in the commentary. Of course, pieces not found in Rn 1343 but in one or both of the other tropers are identified as such.

Typical Texts and Translations

Ordinary chant texts are centered in the commentary; trope elements and verses are printed flush to the left margin. These tropes and verses are provided with arabic numerals enclosed in square brackets based on their sequence in the piece.

Typical texts in the edition are rendered diplomatically. In exceptional cases, however, editorial emendations have been made to clarify meaning. These are always given in square brackets. The Nonantolan tropers exclude nearly all punctuation, but the scribes did use capital letters to mark the beginnings of new periods and, for this reason, the capitalization of the typical readings has been scrupulously retained. The resultant long lines are divided into sense units in the text edition to clarify the structure of the chants and to render syntax understandable without added punctuation. The musical settings of these texts, however, are printed as through-composed.

Spellings have also been retained from the manuscript sources in both the commentary and the music. Hence the letters *i* and *j* are treated as the same letter (i), following the practice of the Nonantolan scribes. Only text variants that have a bearing on meaning, syntax, or pronunciation are reported in the commentary. Thus, variants of orthography, such as differences in the use of *c* and *t* in words like *gratias*, are not indicated. Moreover, although the *ae* ligature (in Rn 1343 and Bu 2824) or *e-caudata* (in Rc 1741) are presented in the typical readings as in the manuscript source, the differing practices of the scribes with respect to their use are not reported, nor are variants noted. Errors in a single word or letter of the typical text have been corrected in translation and cued in the commentary. Oversights and errors in initial letters, to which the rubricating scribe of Rn 1343 was unfortunately prone, have been corrected based on concordant readings.

Standard contractions and suspension found in the texts—such as for ℘ for *per*, ℘ for *pro*, ℘ for *qui*, ℔; for *-bus*, and the *nomina sacra* including *Xpistus* for *Christus*—have been resolved in the texts of the edition and commentary without comment. Truncated or heavily abbreviated phrases of the base chant texts, however, have been reproduced as they are found in the typical source, with abbreviations expanded within angle brackets. Angle brackets also indicate the continuation of chant texts where the scribe used the Latin word *usque* along with the first and last few words of the phrase. Thus, *Benedictus qui venit* usque *excelsis* appears as *Benedictus qui venit <in nomine domini. Hosanna in> excelsis*. Note that the word *usque* (meaning "all the way to") does not appear in the text edition. All other editorial revisions and additions are placed within square brackets.

English translations are provided for all the Latin texts. These translations employ modern liturgical English in the style of the New American Catholic Edition of the Bible (New York, 1961) and *The Saint Andrew Daily Missal* (Bruges, 1962). Literary sources for the tropes in Holy Scripture, the writings of the Fathers, and in the liturgy are traced in the appropriate *Corpus Troporum* volumes. In the present edition, no consistent attempt has been made to duplicate these references, although they are sometimes discussed in the commentaries. Similarly, certain irregularities in the standard Latin meters are alluded to but not discussed.

The Notation of Music in the Edition

Following modern scholarly custom, chants in this edition are notated in stemless black noteheads on five-line staves with either bass clef or treble clef transposed down an octave. In addition to stemless noteheads, two special signs are also employed. The first is an italic *n* for the oriscus, which signals a prolongation of the preceding note or a note repetition. The second is the liquescent, which is transcribed as two slurred notes, the second being smaller and in parentheses as in Roederer, *Festive Troped Masses*; the slurs are placed under the notes with a verticule. Nonantolan scribes used liquescent neumes in connection with most diphthongs and liquid consonants. In addition, the singing of B-flat is occasionally indicated in Rc 1741 by an additional green line (besides the yellow and red ones). Where B-flat is clearly called for in a chant melody, a flat sign has been placed on the staff. In all other cases nothing has been added.

All notes sung to a single syllable are printed under a slur. Slurs within slurs indicate ligated notes; gapped slurs show sub-groupings of notes within aggregate neumes. The manuscript readings generally correspond in the subgroupings of neumes; the few variants that do occur are not reported in the critical apparatus because they have not been judged to affect performance significantly. Although bar lines were obviously not notated by the Nonantolan scribes, single bars are employed in the edition to distinguish the trope elements from the phrases of the Ordinary texts and to close certain other sections of music. Double bars are found at the ends of pieces.

All music not found in the typical source is given in square brackets, particularly the portions of standard chants which the scribes left unnotated. Repeats in Kyries without tropes not indicated in the manuscripts but assumed in liturgical performance are added. Single hyphens have been inserted between syllables in the text indicating divisions according to the rules of syllabification in Latin classical verse. Thus *Chris-te* is preferred over *Chri-ste*, and *Be-ne-dic-tus* over *Be-ne-di-ctus*.

Pitch is designated in the commentary according to the medieval gamut, beginning on the lowest line of the bass clef:

Γ A B C D E F G a b-flat b c d e f g

Commentaries

Each commentary includes:

- SOURCE of text and music gives the location of each chant in the Nonantolan manuscripts. The main source of the text and music in the edition is indicated in **boldface.**
- REFERENCES to books, editions, periodical articles, and dissertations in which information about the chant may be found. (See the lists of abbreviations and works cited.)
- A TEXT COMMENTARY which describes the structure of the text (those in standard meters are designated as such) and briefly surveys other aspects, such as its meaning and liturgical or historical background. The discussions of Kyries concentrate exclusively on the structure of the texts.
- The TEXT AND TRANSLATION of the main source.
- An overview of the DISTINCTIVE VARIANTS that differentiate the Nonantolan readings from those found in other sources. Here, special attention has been devoted to concordances in northern and central Italian manuscripts—to treat more fully the range of European concordances for all the chants discussed would have represented a project well beyond the scope of this edition. (The sigla for manuscripts cited in the commentaries are generally those employed in RISM.) As is the case with MELODIC VARIANTS, the manuscript source of the variant is indicated in boldface type. When multiple

tropes or verses are involved, the portion of the text in which the variant appears is identified by its verse number in square brackets. Thereafter follow the variant words or phrases and the readings from the typical text. Individual variants are separated by a semicolon; variants in the different manuscript sources are separated by a period.

- A listing of MELODIC VARIANTS in the Nonantolan tropers based on the approaches of Stäblein, *Hymnen*, and Schlager, *Alleluia-Melodien*. The manuscript source of the melodic variants is indicated in **boldface** type. Thereafter follow individual words in italics with the unaffected syllables in parentheses; in some melismatic chants, particularly in the Kyrie eleison, the affected syllable may stand alone with a dash or dashes. When tropes or verses are involved, the portion of the text in which the variant appears is identified by its verse number in square brackets. The letters of the medieval gamut represent the pitches of the scale (see above). Liquescent notes are indicated in parentheses. The oriscus is represented by a tilde (~) placed next to the letter name designating its pitch. Letters are grouped in two ways, either with a space between groups of letters to indicate groupings of neumes over the same syllable or with an apostrophe to indicate a syllable break. Individual variants are separated by a semicolon; variants in the different manuscript sources are separated by a period.

Kyrie eleison 1

MELNICKI 55; VATICAN *ad lib.* VI

VERSE: *Te Christe rex supplices*

SOURCES
Rn 1343 fol. 1r–v
Rc 1741 fols. 5r–6v

REFERENCES
AH 47, no. 2; Bjork, "The Early Frankish Kyrie Text," 16–18; Bjork, "Early Repertories," 21, 31; Gautier, *Les Tropes*, 235; Pfaff, *Die Tropen*, 90; Planchart, *Repertory*, 2:259–63.

TEXT COMMENTARY
The symmetry evident in the first two groups of three lines contrasts with the variety of the last five, which differ from one another both in length and structure. The openings of vv. [1–3] are metrically identical (4pp), as are the three eleven-syllable lines that follow (11pp), though these have different endings (6p, 5p, and 5pp, respectively). Vv. [4–6] are similarly organized into three phrases, the first and second having the same metrical structure (6pp + 6pp), the third with two different endings (5p and 6p).

TEXT AND TRANSLATION
[1] Te christe rex
supplices exoramus cunctipotens
ut nobis digneris eleyson
        Kyrrieleyson
[2] Te decet laus
cum tripudio iugiter unde te
poscimus semper eleyson
        Kyrrieleyson
[3] O bone rex
qui super astra sedes et dominans
cuncta gubernans eleyson
        Kyrrieleyson
[4] O theos agie
salva[n]s vivifice
redemptor mundi eleyson
        Christeleyson
[5] Canentum ante te
precibus annue
tuque nobis semper eleyson
        Christeleyson
[6] Temet devota plebs
implorat iugiter
ut illi digneris eleyson
        Christeleyson
[7] Clamat incessanter nunc quoque concio et dicit eleyson
        Kyrrieleyson
[8] Miserere fili dei vivi nobis tu eleyson
        Kyrrieleyson
[9] In excelsis deo magna sit gloria æterno regi
        Kyrrieleyson
[10] Qui nos redemit proprio sanguine
ut vivificaret a morte
[11] Dicamus incessanter omnes una voce eleyson

*

[1] You, O Christ, almighty King,
we suppliants ask
that You deign to have mercy.
        Lord, have mercy.
[2] Yours be praise forever
with exultation, whence
we beseech You: have mercy.
        Lord, have mercy.
[3] O good King,
who sits (enthroned) above the stars, reigning and governing all things, have mercy.
        Lord, have mercy.
[4] O holy, saving God,
vivify,
Redeemer of the world, have mercy.
        Christ, have mercy.
[5] Accede to the prayers of those
who sing before You
and always have mercy.
        Christ, have mercy.

[6] The faithful people
beseech You continually
so that You may deign to have mercy.
    Christ, have mercy.
[7] The assembled now also cry out incessantly and say: have mercy.
    Lord, have mercy.
[8] Have Thou mercy on us, Son of the living God, have mercy.
    Lord, have mercy.
[9] To God in the highest, great be the glory to the eternal King!
    Lord, have mercy.
[10] He who redeemed us with His own blood to restore life from death.
[11] Let us all sing incessantly in one voice: have mercy.

DISTINCTIVE VARIANTS

Rc 1741 [4] *salvans* for *salvas*. Unlike the Nonantolan tropers and VEcap 107, most northern Italian MSS transmit the Aquitanian text reading of v. [2]: "Tibi laus decet cum tripudio qua tibi petimus decantes eleyson." Italian sources preserve different arrangements of vv. [4–9]; Tn 18 and PS 121, for example, reverse the order of vv. [4–6]. In v. [8], Italian readings are distinct as a group from the Aquitanian, "Miserere nostri fili David tu nobis eleyson."

MELODIC VARIANTS

Rc 1741 [1] *rex* abc; *-ley-* cbb~G aGF FED . . . ; [2] *-ley-* cbb~a; [4] *ley-* acb GFa Gcc~baGFE F(G); [6] *-ley-* . . . cc~baG EF(G); [7] *Kyr-* Gbcdd~; [8] *Kyr-* dddc; [9] *de(o)* dcb; *re(gi)* a; *Kyr-* Gbcdd~; [10] *(incessan)ter* cc~.

Kyrie eleison 2

MELNICKI 39; VATICAN I

TROPE: *Omnipotens genitor*

SOURCES
Rn 1343 fol. 1v
Rc 1741 fols. 6v–7r

REFERENCES
AH 47, no. 3; Bjork, "Early Repertories," 21; Bjork, "The Kyrie Trope," 10–11, 15, 26–31; Gautier, *Les Tropes*, 229–36; Pfaff, *Die Tropen*, 89–90.

TEXT COMMENTARY

Hexameters. *Omnipotens genitor* comprises three groups of three lines devoted, in turn, to each of the three persons of the Trinity. Vv. [1] and [2] clearly refer to God the Father and to his act of creation. Only as the trope's Trinitarian program unfolds does it become clear that the Father is also the subject of v. [3]—it could only have been He who, by sending Jesus to earth (vv. [4–6]), had mercy on the sins of mankind. The third section of text begins with v. [7], in which the Holy Spirit is named and his relationship to the Father and Son specified. (Cf. Bjork, "The Kyrie Trope," 30, who calls the text Christocentric.)

TEXT AND TRANSLATION

[1] Omnipotens genitor lumenque et lucis origo
    Kyrrieleyson
[2] De nichilo iussu verbi qui cuncta creasti
    Kyr<rieleyson>
[3] Humano generi peccati pondere presso
    Kyr<rieleyson>
[4] Ad cęnum terrę missus genitoris ab arce
    Christeleyson
[5] Qui indueras carnem casta de virgine natus
    Christe<leyson>
[6] Et mundi culpam mundasti sanguine fuso
    Christe<leyson>
[7] Aequalis patri seu nato spiritus alme
    Kyrrieleyson
[8] Omnia conformans illi simul atque gubernans
    Kyr<rieleyson>
[9] Trinus personis deus maiestate sed unus
    Kyrrieleyson
            *
[1] Almighty Father, both light and source of light.
    Lord, have mercy.
[2] From nothingness by commanding word You have created all things.
    Lord, have mercy.
[3] On the human race kept down by the weight of sin.
    Lord, have mercy.
[4] Sent to the filth of earth from the Father's citadel.
    Christ, have mercy.
[5] You who assumed flesh, born of the chaste virgin.
    Christ, have mercy.
[6] And You cleansed the guilt of the world with the blood You shed.
    Christ, have mercy.
[7] Nourishing Spirit, equal to the Father or the Son.
    Lord, have mercy.
[8] Conforming all things to Him and at the same time also governing.
    Lord, have mercy.
[9] Three in persons but one God in majesty.
    Lord, have mercy.

DISTINCTIVE VARIANTS

Rn 1343 [4] *coenum* for *cęnum*; [6] *Ut mundi culpa* for *Et mundi culpam*; [8] *illis atque* for *illi simul atque*. The arrangement of trope elements before the Ordinary invocations in Nonantolan MSS and VEcap 107 may have led to the addition of v. [8], which is found in only these three manuscripts. (In all other readings of the trope save one, Pn 9448, the tropes follow the Ordinary invocations.) Unlike the Nonantolan MSS and VEcap 107, most other sources, including East Frankish ones, have a different opening for v. [5] (*Indueras*). In v. [9], the variant "deus in maiestate" is found solely in Nonantolan MSS and VEcap 107, instead of the more widely transmitted "deus in deitate."

MELODIC VARIANTS

Rn 1343 [1] *Omnipotens* a'G'F'G; *(Kyrri)e* abc; [2] *De* b; *ver(bi)* bb(a); [5] *car(nem)* aa(g); [6] *mundas(ti)* b(a)'aa~g; [7] *(Kyrri)e* dedcb . . . ; [8] *confor(mans)* de'dd(c); *simul* om.; [9] *(Kyrri)e* . . . edd~cb dbaG.

Kyrie eleison 3

MELNICKI 68; VATICAN XIV

VERSE: *Canamus cuncti laudes*

SOURCES
Rn 1343 fols. 1v–2r
Rc 1741 fols. 7r–8v

REFERENCES
AH 47, no. 29; Bjork, "Early Repertories," 21, 31; Pfaff, *Die Tropen*, 82, 90–91.

TEXT COMMENTARY

The symmetry of vv. [1–3] and [4–6] contrasts with the three longer, more loosely organized closing verses. Vv. [1–3] are the same length, with similar accentuation patterns; 11p + 7p is the apparent model. Vv. [4–6] resemble one another in their organization of 7p + 6p + 7p or 8p, although the meter varies. V. [9] is a paraphrase of the Latin hymn *Quem terra pontus aethera*, the first stanza of which reads:

> *Quem terra, pontus, aethera*
> *collunt, adorant, praedicant*
> *trinam regentem machinam*
> *claustrum Mariae baiulat.*

TEXT AND TRANSLATION

[1] Kanamus cuncti laudes hymnificas soli deo placitas
    Kyrrieleyson
[2] Qui pius salvet semper et protegat se sequentes in evo
    Kyr<rieleyson>
[3] Quem nunc adoramus glorificantes et laudantes devote
    Kyr<rieleyson>
[4] Christo melos et odas clamantes psallimus sic lętantes devote
    Christeleyson
[5] Obediunt omnia illi quę facta sunt cęli terreque et aquę
    Christe<leyson>
[6] Quem supera cęlorum atque angelica venerantur agmina
    Christe<leyson>
[7] Fac nos tuis insistere laudibus amenis quas pręcinerunt summa pręsagia
    Kyrrieleyson
[8] Doxa patri ac pariter filio edito spiritui sancto canamus omnes voce sonanti
    Kyr<rieleyson>
[9] Quem terra pontus ethera
    colunt atque adorant
    predicant regentem trinam iuste machinam
    te precamur ut nunc et semper
    eleyson ymas
        Kyrrieleyson ymas

*

[1] Let us together sing pleasing, hymnic praises to the one true God.
    Lord, have mercy.
[2] Let the benevolent One ever preserve and protect those who follow Him in eternity.
    Lord, have mercy.
[3] Whom we now adore, glorifying and praising devotedly.
    Lord, have mercy.
[4] We sing songs and odes to Christ, proclaiming (and) thus rejoicing devotedly:
    Christ, have mercy.
[5] All things created obey Him, the heavens and also the lands and the water.
    Christ, have mercy.
[6] Whom the higher and also the angelic hosts of heaven adore.
    Christ, have mercy.
[7] Make us devote ourselves to Your delightful praises, which have foretold the most important presagings.
    Lord, have mercy.
[8] Glory be to the Father and likewise to the Son issued (from Him, and) to the Holy Spirit; let us all sing in a resounding voice:
    Lord, have mercy.
[9] Whom the earth, the sea, the serene sky worship, adore, and proclaim;
    O Triple Scheme of the Just One,
    we beseech that You now and forever have mercy on us.
        Lord, have mercy.

DISTINCTIVE VARIANTS

Rn 1343 [1] *placita* for *placitas*; [6] *superat* for *supera*; [7] *precenerunt* for *precinerunt*; [9] *trinum* for *trinam*. Northern Italian manuscripts transmit three somewhat different versions of the text for v. [4]. All are apparently related to the East Frankish version,

"Christe melos et odas clamantes psallimus sic laetantes in eo." The Nonantolan tropers and VEcap 107 alone have a different ending: "laetantes devote." The widely transmitted line, "Almipotens qui regis alta caelorum simul et cuncta moderaris terrena," is lacking in Nonantolan MSS and VEcap 107. Differences in the order of lines and minor text variants in vv. [5] (*facta sunt* for *factura*) and [7] distinguish the northern Italian readings from those of other regions.

Melodic Variants

Rn 1343 [1] *(pla)ci(tas)* G; *(Kyrri)e* . . . DEFGG~F; [2] *(pi)us* GaG; [4] *(lae)tan(tes)* a; *(Chris)te* accacc~ . . . ; [5] *(om)ni(a)* G; [7] *(a)me(nis)* b; *(prece)ne(runt)* b; *sum(ma)* b(a); [8] *(edi)to* e; *sanc(to)* bb(a); *(so)nan(ti)* bb(a); [9] *(pre)ca(mur)* d; *(e)ley(son)* b(a); *y(mas)* ab; *(Kyrri)e* bdeed edb cbG bdcba bG.

Kyrie eleison 4

Melnicki 39; Vatican I

Verse: *Lux et origo lucis*

Sources

Rn 1343 fols. 2r–v
Rc 1741 fols. 8v–9v

References

AH 47, no. 12; Bjork, "Early Repertories," 31; Grosspellier, "Le Kyrie pascal," 135–38; Pfaff, *Die Tropen*, 91; Planchart, *Repertory*, 2:252–54.

Text Commentary

The text is organized into three sets of three lines of different length: eleven, fifteen, and thirteen syllables respectively, all with accents on the penult. (The *leyson* refrain and the vocative *Christe* in vv. [4–6] do not figure into the syllable counts.) The text is not Trinitarian—the Holy Spirit is never mentioned—but the first and second sets of verses are devoted to epithets and characterizations of the Father and Son, respectively. In the last set, v. [8] refers to the Father, but the subject of vv. [7] and [9] is unclear.

Text and Translation

[1] Lux et origo lucis
    summe deus eleyson
        Kyrrieleyson
[2] Qui solus potens
    miserere nobis eleyson
        Kyrr\<ieleyson\>
[3] In cuius nutu
    constat cuncta nobis eleyson
        Kyr\<rieleyson\>
[4] Per crucem redemptis
    a morte perhenni spes nostra
    christe eleyson
        Christeleyson

[5] O mundi redemptor
    salus et humana rex pie
    christe eleyson
        Christe\<leyson\>
[6] Qui es verbum patris
    verbum caro factum lux vera
    christe eleyson
        Christe\<leyson\>
[7] Adonay domine deus
    iudex iuste eleyson
        Kyrrieleyson
[8] Qui machinam gubernat rerum
    alme pater eleyson
        Kyrr\<ieleyson\>
[9] Quem solum laus et honor decet
    nunc et semper eleyson
        Kyrrieleyson

*

[1] Light and source of light,
    supreme God, have mercy.
        Lord, have mercy.
[2] Who alone is powerful,
    have mercy on us, have mercy.
        Lord, have mercy.
[3] Upon whose command all things
    are constituted for us.
        Lord, have mercy.
[4] By the cross redeemed
    from eternal death, our hope,
    Christ, have mercy.
        Christ, have mercy.
[5] O Redeemer of the world
    and salvation of mankind,
    gracious King, Christ, have mercy.
        Christ, have mercy.
[6] You who are the Word of the Father,
    the Word made flesh,
    the True Light, Christ, have mercy.
        Christ, have mercy.
[7] Ruler, Lord God,
    righteous Judge, have mercy.
        Lord, have mercy.
[8] Who governs the scheme of things,
    sustaining Father, have mercy.
        Lord, have mercy.
[9] (To) whom alone praise and honor is due,
    now and forever, have mercy.
        Lord, have mercy.

Distinctive Variants

Rc 1741 [3] *constant* for *constat*. Northern Italian sources preserve a number of different arrangements of lines, though always in the same groupings of three. Ra 123, MOd 7, Rv 52, and PAc 47 transmit a variant of v. [1] (see Planchart, *Repertory*) which is set to the same music as in the Nonantolan MSS. This is not the case with v. [4] as it is found in Rv 52, "Ad cuius vocem omnes sancti clamant eleyson." This line is considerably shorter than vv. [5] and [6], necessitating a distinct setting apparently derived from the melody of vv. [1–3]. Bjork, "Early Repertories," 31, suggests that the text may be of northern Italian origin.

Melodic Variants

Rc 1741 [1] *sum(me)* cc~; [2] *(mise)re(re)* cc~; [3] *cunc(ta)* cc~; [6] *(fac)tum* a; *ve(ra)* c; [7] *de(us)* ed; [8] *(guber)nat* d; [9] *so(lum)* aa~.

Kyrie eleison 5

Melnicki 155; Vatican XV

Verse: *Dominator Deus*

Sources
Rn 1343 fols. 2v–3r
Rc 1741 fol. 12r–v

References
AH 47, no. 35; Bjork, "Early Repertories," 23, 26, 31; Pfaff, *Die Tropen*, 91.

Text Commentary
Symmetrical organization of three sets of three lines. Note the prominent *-e* assonance, which results in end rhyme throughout. The opening six lines of the prosula are relatively short: 10pp and 4p + 8pp. Compared with these, vv. [7–9] are longer and display more variety in their organization: [7] 4p + 6p + 6pp; [8] 5pp + 6p + 6pp; [9] 4p + 6p + 4pp.

Text and Translation
[1] Dominator deus piisime
           Kyrrieleyson
[2] Fons et origo lucis perpetuę
           Kyr<rieleyson>
[3] Verbi tui pater ingenite
           Kyr<rieleyson>
[4] Incarnate tu quoque pie domine
           Christeleyson
[5] Lux de luce deus de deo genite
           Christe<leyson>
[6] Salus vita via veritas idemque
           Christe<leyson>
[7] Consolator pie flamen quoque alme vivifice
           Kyrrieleyson
[8] Patris natique qui es summus amor deus luciflue
           Kyr<rieleyson>
[9] Sine fine regnans nos guberna mitissime
           Kyrrieleyson
                *
[1] Ruler, most benevolent God.
           Lord, have mercy.

[2] Fount, source of everlasting light.
           Lord, have mercy.
[3] Of Your word, unbegotten Father.
           Lord, have mercy.
[4] You, incarnate and benevolent Lord.
           Christ, have mercy.
[5] Light from light, God begotten from God.
           Christ, have mercy.
[6] Salvation, life, the way, the truth, and the Selfsame.
           Christ, have mercy.
[7] Kindly comforter, generous priest, bring us life.
           Lord, have mercy.
[8] To the Father and the Son, You who are supreme love, O luminous God. (Read *natoque*)
           Lord, have mercy.
[9] Reigning without end, rule over us most gently.
           Lord, have mercy.

Distinctive Variants
Rn 1343 [2] *Consorigo lucis* for *Fons origo*; [7] *flamme* for *flamen*; [8] *Patri* for *Patris*. Northern Italian manuscripts yield few regional differences in text. V. [6] is probably a variant of "Salus vita qui es plebis deicole," found in Pn 778, Pn 903, and Pn 9448.

Melodic Variants
Rn 1343 [1] *(Do)mina(tor)* D'E; [2] *Consorigo* D'D'E'D; [3] *(Ver)bi tu(i)* D'E; [4] (transposed) *Incarnate* d'c'd'b (etc.); [5] (transposed) *Lux de luce* d'c'd'b (etc.); [6] (transposed) *Salus vita* d'c'd'b (etc.); [7] (transposed) *Consolator* d'de'e'c (etc.); *(pi)e flamme quo(que)* b'c'a'b; [8–9] notation lacking.

Kyrie eleison 6

Melnicki 124

Verse: *Rex magne domine*

Sources
Rn 1343 fol. 3r–v
Rc 1741 fols. 9v–10v

References
AH 47, no. 11a; Bjork, "Early Repertories," 24; Pfaff, *Die Tropen*, 91.

Text Commentary
Rough symmetry of groups of prose lines set to the same music (3 + 3 + 4 + 1). Corresponding lines differ in the number of syllables.

Text and Translation
[1] Rex magne domine quem sancti adhorant eleyson
           Kyrrieleyson

[2] Voces nostras tu nobis digneris hodie exaudire
    Kyrr<ieleyson>
[3] Vivificandus est deus homo simul et cuncta eleyson
    Kyrr<ieleyson>
[4] O agie infiniteque iudex noster nostras preces suscipe eleyson
    Christeleyson
[5] Fons et origo lucis perpetue vita salus pax æterna domine
    Christe<leyson>
[6] Qui de supernis descendere voluisti propter hominem quem fecisti eleyson
    Christe<leyson>
[7] Consolator qui es alme quoque vivifice eleyson
    Kyrrieleyson
[8] Lux de luce deus de deo genite redemptor noster eleyson
    Kyrr<ieleyson>
[9] Auctor cælorum deus æternę vere qui polum formasti necne solum
    Kyrr<ieleyson>
[10] Ab omni malo tu nos defende alme christe de cælis miserere
[11] Servos tuos audi piissime eleyson [e]leyson

*

[1] Great King, Lord whom the saints adore, have mercy.
    Lord, have mercy.
[2] Deign to hear our voices today.
    Lord, have mercy.
[3] Let the God-Man, together with all things, be restored to life, have mercy.
    Lord, have mercy.
[4] O holy and infinite One, our Judge, accept our prayers, have mercy.
    Christ, have mercy.
[5] Fount and origin of everlasting light, life, salvation, peace, eternal Lord.
    Christ, have mercy.
[6] You who willed to descend from heaven because of man, whom You created, have mercy.
    Christ, have mercy.
[7] You who are the kindly Comforter, vivify us, have mercy.
    Lord, have mercy.
[8] Light from Light, God begotten from God, our Redeemer, have mercy.
    Lord, have mercy.
[9] Creator of the heavens, God immortal true, You who fashioned the heavens and the sun. (Read *necnon*)
    Lord, have mercy.
[10] From every evil protect us, propitious Christ, from heaven have mercy.
[11] Hear, O most benevolent One, Your servants, have mercy, have mercy.

DISTINCTIVE VARIANTS

Unlike the Aquitanian sources for v. [1], readings in the Nonantolan tropers and other Italian MSS lack the word *semper* (*adorant semper eleyson*) and, in v. [2], *rex caeli* (*hodie rex caeli exaudire*). All Italian versions preserve the same text readings for vv. [3–6] with the exception of Ob 222, which has in v. [3]: "Mirificandus es deus et homo simul tu nostri eleyson." (These lines and their Aquitanian counterparts may be compared in *AH* 47:66–68.) The order of vv. [7–8] is reversed in Rv 52. There is considerable variation among northern and central Italian sources in the order and content of the last three lines.

MELODIC VARIANTS

Rc 1741 [1] *san(cti)* FF(E); *(e)ley(son)* DD(E); *Kyrri)e* EDC DFF~D; [8] *de(o)* cc~; *(e)ley(son)* F(G); [9] *Auctor ce(lorum)* G'G'ac; [10] *(de)fen(de)* c(b); *al(me)* a(G).

Kyrie eleison 7

MELNICKI 47; VATICAN VI

VERSE: *Kyrie rex genitor*

SOURCES
Rn 1343 fols. 3v–4r
Rc 1741 fols. 10v–11v

REFERENCES
AH 47, no. 15; Planchart, *Repertory*, 2:250–51; Pfaff, *Die Tropen*, 91.

TEXT COMMENTARY

Prose lines whose organization follows largely from the musical form of the Kyrie, though lines set to the same music do not necessarily correspond in length (compare vv. [7] and [9]).

TEXT AND TRANSLATION

[1] Kyrrie rex genitor ingenite vera essentia eleyson
    Kyrrieleyson
[2] Kyrrie luminis fons et rerum conditor eleyson
    Kyrrieleyson
[3] Kyrrie qui nos tuę imaginis signasti specie eleyson
    Kyr<rieleyson>
[4] Christe qui perfecta es sapientia eleyson
    Christeleyson
[5] Christe lux oriens per quem sunt omnia eleyson
    Christe<leyson>
[6] Christe deiforma humanę particeps eleyson
    Christe<leyson>

[7] Kyrrie spiritus vivifice vitę vis eleyson
    Kyrrieleyson
[8] Kyrrie utriusque donum in quo cuncta eleyson
    Kyrrieleyson
[9] Kyrrie expurgator scelerum et largitor gratię
    Kyrrie<leyson>
[10] Quesumus propter nostras offensas noli nos relinquere
[11] O consolator dolentis animę eleyson leyson

*

[1] Lord, King, Creator unbegotten, true Essence, have mercy.
    Lord, have mercy.
[2] Lord, Source of light and Creator of all things, have mercy.
    Lord, have mercy.
[3] Lord, who marked us with the character of Your image, have mercy.
    Lord, have mercy.
[4] Christ, You who are perfect wisdom, have mercy.
    Christ, have mercy.
[5] Christ, morning Light, through whom all things exist, have mercy.
    Christ, have mercy.
[6] Christ, Image of God, sharing in human (life), have mercy.
    Christ, have mercy.
[7] Lord, vivifying spirit, power of life, have mercy.
    Lord, have mercy.
[8] Lord, Gift of each, in whom all things, have mercy.
    Lord, have mercy.
[9] Lord, Cleanser of crimes and Giver of grace.
    Lord, have mercy.
[10] We implore You not to abandon us on account of our offenses.
[11] O Consoler of the sorrowful soul, have mercy.

DISTINCTIVE VARIANTS
    Rn 1343 [6] *deiformam* for *deiforma;* [9] *expurgatos* for *expurgator.* For v. [6], Ob 222 alone preserves "Christi dei forma continens omnia eleyson." In v. [8], northern Italian sources transmit *utriusque donum* for the French *utriusque vapor.*

MELODIC VARIANTS
    Rn 1343 [1] *(Kyrri)e(leyson)* bbc~; [10] *(relique)re* . . . fgfd dcdfe fgfd fedc efd; *(conso)la(tor)* a; *(eley)son* ad~. . . .

Kyrie eleison 8

MELNICKI 155; VATICAN XV
SOURCE
Rn 1343 fol. 4r

TEXT AND TRANSLATION
    Kyrrieleyson [Kyrrieleyson Kyrrieleyson]
    Christeleyson [Christeleyson Christeleyson]
    Kyrrieleyson [Kyrrieleyson] Kyrrieleyson

*

    Lord, have mercy.
    Christ, have mercy.
    Lord, have mercy.

Kyrie eleison 9

MELNICKI 151; VATICAN XVIII
SOURCES
Rn 1343 fol. 4r
Rc 1741 fol. 12v

MELODIC VARIANTS
    Rc 1741 *Kyr-* ccc~b; *Kyr-* ccc~b.

TEXT AND TRANSLATION
See Kyrie eleison 8.

Kyrie eleison 10

MELNICKI 136
SOURCES
Rn 1343 fol. 4r
Rc 1741 fol. 12v

TEXT AND TRANSLATION
See Kyrie eleison 8.

MELODIC VARIANTS
    Rc 1741 *Kyrrie* cc~'a'aG; *(Kyrri)e* dc; *Kyr(rie)-* cc~.

Kyrie eleison 11

MELNICKI 112 (?)
SOURCES
Rn 1342 fol. 4r
Rc 1741 fol. 13r

TEXT AND TRANSLATION
See Kyrie eleison 8.

MELODIC VARIANTS
    Rc 1741 *(Chris)te ley(son)* ee~'de(d); *Kyrrieleyson* edd~'c' cefe'de(d)'dcb.

Kyrie eleison 12

MELNICKI 217; VATICAN XVI
SOURCE
Rn 1343 fol. 4r

TEXT AND TRANSLATION
See Kyrie eleison 8.

Gloria in excelsis 1

BOSSE 39; GLORIA A

SOURCES
Rn 1343 fol. 4r–v
Rc 1741 fols. 13r–14r

TEXT AND TRANSLATION

Gloria in excelsis deo
Et in terra pax hominibus bone voluntatis
Laudamus te
Benedicimus te
Adoramus te
Glorificamus te
Gracias agimus tibi propter magnam gloriam tuam
Domine deus rex cælestis
Deus pater omnipotens
Domine fili unigenite
Hiesu christe
Domine deus
Agnus dei
Filius patris
Qui tollis peccata mundi
Miserere nobis
Qui tollis peccata mundi
Suscipe deprecationem nostram
Qui sedes ad dexteram patris
miserere nobis
Quoniam Tu solus sanctus
Tu solus dominus
Tu solus altissimus
Hiesu christe
Cum sancto spiritu in gloria dei patris
Amen

*

Glory to God in the highest:
And on earth peace to men of good will.
We praise You.
We bless You.
We worship You.
We glorify You.
We give You thanks for Your great glory.
O Lord God, heavenly King,
God the Father almighty,
O Lord, the only-begotten Son,
Jesus Christ.
O Lord God,
Lamb of God,
Son of the Father,
You who take away the sins of the world
have mercy on us.
You who take away the sins of the world
receive our prayer.
You who sit at the right hand of the Father
have mercy on us.
For You alone are the holy one,
You alone are the Lord,
You alone are the most high,
Jesus Christ,
with the Holy Spirit
in the glory of God the Father.
Amen.

MELODIC VARIANTS
Rc 1741 *(ex)cel(sis)* abaa(G); *ter(ra)* aa~; *(volun)ta(tis)* GabaG; *Lau(damus)* Ga(G); *glor(iam)* bcbGaba; *tuam* bcdcaG aba'aG Gabb~a; *pa(ter)* b; *u(nigenite)* cc~ba; *(unigeni)te* GaG GaGEE~D; *(Mi)se(rere)1* cc~bG; *(no)bis* aG Gabb~a; *(dexte)ram* a(G); *(Mi)se(rere)2* cc~bG; *al(tissimus)* c(a); *pa(tris)* cc~bG aba; *Amen* [see below]

♪ A - men

Gloria in excelsis 2

BOSSE 2 (VAR.); MILAN IV

SOURCES
Rn 1343 fol. 4v–5r
Rc 1741 fols. 14v–15r

TEXT AND TRANSLATION
See Gloria in excelsis 1.

MELODIC VARIANTS
Rc 1741 *glo(riam)* DC; *(Do)mi(ne)1* FE; *celes(tis)* EF'E; *om(nipotens)* D(C); *(Do)mi(ne)2* FE; *(Do)mi(ne)3* FE; *(Ag)nus* EF; *(mi)se(rere)1* EE~DC; *(solus do)mi(nus)* DC; *dei pa(tris)* D'EF'DECC~A.

Gloria in excelsis 3

BOSSE 43; VATICAN XV

SOURCES
Rn 1343 fol. 5r–v
Rc 1741 fols. 15v–16r

TEXT AND TRANSLATION
See Gloria in excelsis 1.

MELODIC VARIANTS
Rc 1741 *(excel)sis* G; *(bo)ne* GG~; *(volun)ta(tis)* FF~; *(Benedici)mus* E; *(A)do(ramus)* FG; *propter* D'F; *glo(riam)* GG~; *ce(lestis)* G; *(uni)ge(nite)* a; *Domin(e)* D'F; *(Mi)se(rere)1* GG~; *no(bis)1* F; *suscipe* D'F'G; *nos(tram)* F; *(mi)se(rere)2* GG~; *no(bis)2* F; *(so)lus1* G; *al(tissimus)* a: *Chris(te)* Ga; *spi(ritu)* G; *A(men)* DEFF~EDC(D).

Gloria in excelsis 4

BOSSE 12; VATICAN I

SOURCES
Rn 1343 fol. 5v
Rc 1741 fols. 18v–19r
Bu 2824 fol. 1r–v

TEXT AND TRANSLATION
See Gloria in excelsis 1.

MELODIC VARIANTS
Rc 1741 *(ex)cel(sis)* EE(C); *(Et) in* EF; *(vo)lunta(tis)* DE(D)'DD~; *Glo(rificamus)* EE~; *a(gimus)* EE~; *(glori)am* GaG; *om(nipotens)* GG~F; *u(nigenite)* FF~E; *Qui se(des)* aG'ab; *(Misere)re no(bis)2* DC'D; *pa(tris)* D; *Amen* GG~FGaa~GFE' . . . DD~C CDEDD~C. **Bu 2824** *(ex)cel(sis)* E(C); *in* EF; *(vo)lunta(tis)* DE(D)'DD~; *Glo(rificamus)* EE~; *(glori)am* GaG; *ut se(des)* aG'ab; *(so)lus (dominus)* GaG; *(A)men* EFGGFDD~C GFEDC DEDD~C.

Gloria in excelsis 5

BOSSE 11; VATICAN XIV

SOURCES
Rn 1343 fols. 5v–6r
Rc 1741 fols. 16v–17r

TEXT AND TRANSLATION

Gloria in excelsis deo
Et in terra pax hominibus bone voluntatis
Laudamus te
Benedicimus te
Adoramus te
Glorificamus te
Gracias agimus tibi propter magnam tuam gloriam
Domine rex cælestis
Deus pater omnipotens
Domine fili unigenite hiesu christe et sancte spiritus
Domine deus
Agnus dei
Filius patris
Qui tollis peccata mundi miserere nobis
Qui tollis peccata mundi
Suscipe deprecationem nostram
Qui sedes ad dexteram patris miserere nobis
Quia tu solus sanctus
Tu solus dominus
Tu solus altissimus hiesu christe
Cum sancto spiritu in gloria dei patris
Amen

*

Glory to God in the highest:
And on earth peace to men of good will:
We praise You.
We bless You.
We worship You.
We glorify You.
We give You thanks for Your great glory.
O Lord, heavenly King,
God the Father almighty,
O Lord, the only-begotten Son,
Jesus Christ, and the Holy Spirit.
O Lord God,
Lamb of God,
Son of the Father,
You who take away the sins of the world
have mercy on us.
You who take away the sins of the world
Receive our prayer.
You who sit at the right hand of the Father
have mercy on us.
For You alone are the holy one,
You alone are the Lord,
You alone are the most high,
Jesus Christ,
with the Holy Spirit
in the glory of God the Father.
Amen.

MELODIC VARIANTS
Rc 1741 *(ex)cel(sis)* F; *de(o)* DD~; *(bo)ne voluntatis* DC'D'DE(D)'DD~; *(Laudamus) te* CD; *(Benedi)cimus* D'DE'; *(omni)po(tens)* DD~; *Chri(ste)1* CC~; *sanc(te)* DD(C); *Qui (tollis)2* ED; *(Suscri)pe* D; *(nos)tram* EE~; *pa(tris)* DD~; *no(bis)2* ABA; *solus altissimus* EG'E'D'E'DC'EE~; *Chri(ste)2* CC~; *(spiri)tu* DD~; *pa(tris)* CC~; *(A)men* BA.

Gloria in excelsis 6

BOSSE 21

SOURCES
Rn 1343 fol. 6r–v
Rc 1741 fols. 17v–18r

TEXT AND TRANSLATION
See Gloria in excelsis 1.

MELODIC VARIANTS
Rc 1741 *(ex)cel(sis)* cc(b); *ho(minibus)* Ga(c); *(vo)lun(tatis)* F(G); *(Prop)ter* a(c); *(u)nigeni(te)* ba'bc'a; *(Susci)pe* G; *(solus san)ctus* Ga.

Gloria in excelsis 7

BOSSE 51; VATICAN XI
SOURCES
Rn 1343 fol. 6v
Rc 1741 fol. 14r

TEXT AND TRANSLATION

    Gloria in excelsis deo
Et in terra pax hominibus bone voluntatis
        Laudamus te
       [B]enedicimus te

*

   Glory to God in the highest:
And on earth peace to men of good will.
        We praise You.
        We bless You.

MELODIC VARIANTS

Rc 1741 in FE; de(o) EE~; (homi)ni(bus) FE; bo(ne) FE; (vo)lun(tatis) F.

Gloria in excelsis 8a

BOSSE 51; VATICAN XI

TROPE: *Pax sempiterna*

SOURCES

Rn 1343 fols. 6v–7v LAUS IN. N<ativitate>. D<omi>NI.

Bu 2824 fol. 2r (no rubric)

REFERENCES

AH 47, nos. 168 and 242; *BTC* II/2, 22, 28–31; Leach, "The Gloria in Excelsis Deo Tropes," 97–115; Norberg, *Versification médiévale*, 94–101; Rönnau, "Regnum tuum solidum"; Pfaff, *Die Tropen,* 99, 103, 183; Planchart, *Repertory,* 2:292–97; Rönnau, *Die Tropen zum Gloria,* 159–60, 213–16.

TEXT COMMENTARY

Accentual verse of three to five units, comprising five or six syllables ending in a paroxytone. This pattern,

    ´   ´   ´   ´
~ ~ ~ ~ ~ + ~ ~ ~ ~ ~
   ´   ´   ´   ´
~ ~ ~ ~ ~ + ~ ~ ~ ~ ~

which Norberg calls rhythmic Adonics, was typically employed in Agnus Dei tropes of Italian provenance.

TEXT AND TRANSLATION

      Gloria in excelsis deo
 <Et in terra pax hominibus> bone voluntatis

[1] Pax sempiterna
    christus illuxit
    gloria tibi
    pater excelse
           Laudamus te

[2] Ymnum canentes
    hodie quem terris
    angeli fuderunt
    christo nascente
          Bene[dicimus te]

[3] Natus est nobis
    hodie salvator
    in trinitate
    semper colendus
          Adoramus [te]

[4] Quem vagientem
    inter angusti
    antra presepi
    angelorum cetus
    laudat exultans
         Glorificam<us te>

[5] Cuius a sede
    lux benedicta
    caliginoso
    orbis refulsit
      Gra<tia>s agimus <tibi propter magnam
          gloriam tuam
      Domine deus rex caelestis
      Deus pater omnipotens
       Domine fili unigenite
          Hiesu christe
          Domine deus
           Agnus dei
          Filius patris
    Qui tollis> peccata mundi

[6] Ultro mortali
    hodie indutus
    carne precamur
        Mis<erere> nob<is>
     <Qui tollis peccata mundi
    Suscipe deprecationem nostram
    Qui sedes ad dexteram patris>
        mis<erere> nob<is>

[7] O ineffabilis rex et ammirabilis
    ex virgine matre hodie prodisti
    mundo quem subvenisti
       Q<uonia>m tu solus s<an>c<tu>s
        <Tu solus dominus
        Tu solus> altissim<us>

[8] Regnum tuum solidum
    permanebit indivisum
    inconcussum
    sine fine perhenne
    Te adorant et conlaudant
    simul omnes
    virtutes angelice
    et nos supplices
    conlaudamus tuum nomen
    Qui permanebit in æternum.
          Hiesu christe
   <Cum sancto spiritu in gloria dei patris>
           Am<en>

*

Glory to God in the highest:
And on earth peace to men of good will.

[1] Christ, the perpetual Peace, is manifest!
Glory to You, O exalted Father!
We praise You.

[2] Today the angels, singing (this) hymn,
spread the news of the begotten Christ to all lands.
We bless You.

[3] Today the Savior, to be worshipped in the Trinity,
is born to us.
We worship You.

[4] Whom, crying amid the narrow confines of the small manger, the company of
angels extols, exulting:
We glorify You.

[5] From whose throne a blessed light shown bright onto a dark world.
We give You thanks for Your great glory.
O Lord God, heavenly King
God the Father almighty
O Lord, the only-begotten Son,
Jesus Christ.
O Lord God,
Lamb of God,
Son of the Father,
You who take away the sins of the world

[6] (Who) today willingly assumed human flesh, we pray:
Have mercy on us.
You who take away the sins of the world
receive our prayer.
You who sit at the right hand of the Father
have mercy on us.

[7] O ineffable and admirable King,
today You came forth from a virgin mother into the world,
which You came to redeem.
For You alone are the holy one,
You alone are the Lord,
You alone are the most high.

[8] Your reign shall endure,
sound, undivided, constant,
without end, forever.
All the angelic powers at once
worship and extol You.
And we supplicants praise Your name,
which shall endure forever,
Jesus Christ,
with the Holy Spirit
in the glory of God the Father.
Amen

DISTINCTIVE VARIANTS

The East Frankish Christmas trope *Pax sempiterna*, one of the oldest Gloria in excelsis tropes in the repertory, circulated in northern Italy in three somewhat different versions. Of these, the one found in the Nonantolan tropers was the most widely disseminated. (It is also found in VEcap 107, MOd 7, Mza 76, PAc 47, PS 121, Ra 123, Vo 39, and the Vercelli MSS.) The Nonantolan version, however, is distinguished from all the others in v. [8] by the employment of the *Regnum* prosula, *Permanebit in aeternum*.

Gloria in excelsis 8b

BOSSE 39; GLORIA A

TROPE: *Pax semipterna*

SOURCE
Rc 1741 fols. 19v–21r (no rubric)

TEXT AND TRANSLATION

Gloria in excelsis d<e>o
<Et in terra pax hominibus> bone voluntatis

[1] Pax sempiterna
christus illuxit
gloria tibi
pater excelse
Laud<amus te>

[2] Hymnum canentes
hodie quem terris
angeli fuderunt
christo nascente
Bened<icimus te>

[3] Natus est nobis
hodie salvator
in trinitate
semper colendus
Ador<amus te>

[4] Quem vagientem
inter angusti
antra presępis
angelorum coetus
laudat exultans
Glorif<icamus te>

[5] Cuius a sede
lux benedicta
caliginoso
orbi refulsit
Gra<tia>s ag<imus> <tibi propter magnam
gloriam tuam
Domine deus rex caelestis
Deus pater omnipotens
Domine fili unigenite
Hiesu christe
Domine deus
Agnus dei
Filius patris
Qui tollis> pecc<ata> mundi

[6] Ultro mortali
hodie indutum
carne precamur

lii

Mis\<erere\> nob\<is\>
\<Qui tollis peccata mundi
Suscipe deprecationem nostram
Qui sedes ad dexteram patris\>
mis\<erere\> nob\<is\>

[7] O ineffabilis rex et admirabilis
ex virgine matre hodie prodisti
mundo quem subvenisti
Q\<uonia\>m tu \<solus sanctus
Tu solus dominus
Tu solus\> altissim\<us\>

[8] Regnum tuum solidum
permanebit indivisum
inconcussum
sine fine perhenne
Te adorant et collaudant
simul omnes
virtutes angelicę
Et nos supplices
collaudamus tuum nomen
Quod permanebit in eternum
Hiesu christe
\<Cum sancto spiritu in gloria dei patris\>
Amen

*

Glory to God in the highest:
And on earth peace to men of good will.

[1] Christ, the perpetual Peace, is manifest!
Glory to You, O exalted Father!
We praise You.

[2] Today the angels, singing (this) hymn,
spread the news of the begotten Christ to all lands.
We bless You.

[3] Today the Savior, to be worshipped in the Trinity,
is born to us.
We worship You.

[4] Whom, crying amid the narrow confines of the small manger, the company of
angels extols, exulting:
We glorify You.

[5] From whose throne a blessed light shown bright onto a dark world.
We give You thanks for Your great glory.
O Lord God, heavenly King,
God the Father almighty,
O Lord, the only-begotten Son,
Jesus Christ.
O Lord God,
Lamb of God,
Son of the Father,
You who take away the sins of the world,

[6] (Who) today willingly assumed human flesh, we pray:
Have mercy on us.

You who take away the sins of the world
receive our prayer.
You who sit at the right hand of the Father
have mercy on us.

[7] O ineffable and admirable King,
today You came forth from a virgin mother into the world,
which You came to redeem.
For You alone are the holy one,
You alone are the Lord,
You alone are the most high,

[8] Your reign shall endure,
sound, undivided, constant,
without end, forever.
All the angelic powers at once
worship and extol You.
And we suppliants praise Your name,
which shall endure forever,
Jesus Christ,
with the Holy Spirit
in the glory of God the Father.
Amen

Gloria in excelsis 9

BOSSE 2 (VAR.); MILAN IV

TROPE: *Quem patris ad dextram*

SOURCES
Rn 1343 fol. 7r Laus in [natale] s\<an\>c\<t\>i stephani
Rc 1741 fols. 21r–22r LAUS IN.N\<atale\>. S\<ancti\>. Step\<hani\>
Bu 2824 fols. 2r–3r i\<n\> [natale] s\<ancti\> step\<ha\>ni

REFERENCES
AH 47, no. 171; *BTC* II/2, 22, 29–41; Leach, "The *Gloria in Excelsis Deo* Tropes," 272–90; Pfaff, *Die Tropen*, 99; Planchart, *Repertory*, 2:306–9; Rönnau, *Die Tropen zum Gloria*, 48, 155–56, 174.

TEXT COMMENTARY
Hexameters. Given that the earliest source of the trope, Pn 1240, and many later witnesses are Aquitanian, and on stylistic grounds, Rönnau argues that it originated there before 936 A.D.

TEXT AND TRANSLATION

Gloria in excelsis d\<e\>o
\<Et in terra pax hominibus bone\> voluntatis

[1] Quem patris ad dextram collaudant omnia verbum
Laud\<amus te\>

[2] Omnia quem sanctum benedicunt condita regem
Ben\<edicimus te\>

liii

[3] Tellus atque polus mare quem veneranter adorant
  Adora<mus te>
[4] Glorificant agnum cives quem digniter almi
  Glorif<icamus te>
[5] Gracia sanctorum splendor decus et diadema
  Gra<tia>s ag<imus> <tibi propter magnam> gl<ori>am tua<m>
[6] Culpas gestorum solvens sine crimine solus
  D<omi>ne d<eu>s rex <caelestis
  Deus pater omnipotens
  Domine fili unigenite
  Hiesu Christe
  Domine deus
  Agnus dei
  Filius patris
  Qui tollis peccata mundi miserere nobis
  Qui tollis peccata mundi
  Suscipe deprecationem nostram
  Qui sedes ad dexteram patris miserere nobis
  Quoniam> tu sol<us> s<an>c<tu>s
[7] Insons omnipotens nostris tu parce ruinis
  Tu sol<us> d<ominus>
[8] Cuncta tenens et cuncta fovens et cuncta perornans
  Tu sol<us> al<tissimus> hiesu christe
[9] Nos nostrasque preces cęlo describe redemptor
  Cum s<an>c<t>o sp<irit>u
  <in gloria dei patris>
  Amen

*

Glory to God in the highest:
And on earth peace to men of good will.
[1] Whom, at the right hand of the Father, all things praise, the Word:
  We praise You.
[2] Holy King, whom all created things bless:
  We bless You.
[3] Whom the earth, the heavens, and the sea reverently adore:
  We worship You.
[4] Lamb, whom genial citizens worthily glorify:
  We glorify You.
[5] Favor of the Saints, Splendor, Glory, Crown:
  We give You thanks for Your great glory.
[6] Absolving the failures of (our) actions, alone without sin
  O Lord God, heavenly King,
  God the Father almighty,
  O Lord, the only-begotten Son,
  Jesus Christ,
  O Lord God,
  Lamb of God,
  Son of the Father,
  You who take away the sins of the world have mercy on us.
  You who take away the sins of the world receive our prayer.
  You who sit at the right hand of the Father have mercy on us.
  You alone are the holy one,
[7] Guiltless, all powerful One, spare our failings!
  You alone are the Lord.
[8] Possessing all and sustaining all and adorning all,
  You alone are most high, Jesus Christ.
[9] Convey us and our prayers to heaven, Redeemer!
  With the Holy Spirit
  in the glory of God the Father.
  Amen.

DISTINCTIVE VARIANTS

Rn 1343 [1] *collaudat* for *collaudant*; [2] *quæ* for *quem*; [5] *Gracias* for *Gracia*; [9] *nostras quæ* for *nostrasque*. **Bu 2824** [6] *solve* for *solvens*. Although *Quem patris ad dextram* probably originated in Aquitania, the opening of v. [1] of the Nonantolan and other Italian versions agrees more closely with northern French readings, suggesting that it may have been transmitted from there to Italy (see Leach, "The *Gloria in Excelsis Deo* Tropes," 289). The order of vv. [1–5] remains the same in Italian sources despite some differences in the cues to the Ordinary chant. The order of vv. [6–8], on the other hand, is variable.

MELODIC VARIANTS

Rn 1343 [2] *(bene)dicunt con(dita)* G'G'F; [5] *(splen)-dor* EFG; [6] *ges(torum)* FF~E; [8] *cunc(ta)* 2 F(E); *(per)-or(nans)* EE(D).

Gloria in excelsis 10

BOSSE 43; VATICAN XV

TROPE: *Quem cives caelestes*

SOURCES

Rn 1343 fol. 8r–v (no rubric)
Rc 1741 fols. 22r–23r Laus in N<atale>. S<ancti>. ioh<ann>is ev<an>g<elistae>.
Bu 2824 fols. 3r–4v in [natale] s<an>c<t>i ioh<anni>s eva<n>g<e>l<istae>

REFERENCES

BTC II/2, 22, 32–36; Leach, "The *Gloria in Excelsis Deo* Tropes," 305–23; Pfaff, *Die Tropen*, 99; Planchart, *Repertory*, 2:300–304; Rönnau, *Die Tropen zum Gloria*, 148–52, 175, 193, 213.

TEXT COMMENTARY

Trope texts are in prose. Note the connection between the trope elements and preceding lines of the Ordinary chant in vv. [3–6].

TEXT AND TRANSLATION

Gloria in excelsis deo
[1] Quem cives cælestes sanctum clamantes laude frequentant
   Et in t\<er\>ra pax hominibus bone voluntatis
[2] Quam ministri domini verbo incarnato terrenis promiserant
   Laudam\<us te\>
[3] Laudibus cuius astra matutina insistunt
   Benedic\<imus te\>
[4] Per quem omne sacrum et benedictio conceditur atque angetur
   Adoram\<us\> te
[5] Omnipotens adorande colende tremende venerande
   Glorificam\<us\> te
[6] Et creatura creantem plasma plasmantem figulum figmentum
   Gra\<tia\>s agimus tibi \<propter magnam\> gl\<ori\>am tuam
[7] Hymnum maiestati gracias autem pietati ferentes
   D\<omi\>ne d\<eu\>s rex cæl\<estis\>
   \<Deus pater omnipotens
   Domine\> fili unigenite
   Hiesu christe
[8] Hiesu christe altissime quem quisquis adorat in spiritu et veritate oportet orare
   D\<omi\>ne d\<eu\>s agnus \<dei filius patris
   Qui tollis peccata mundi miserere nobis
   Qui tollis peccata mundi suscipe deprecationem nostram
   Qui sedes ad dexteram patris miserere nobis
   Quoniam to solus santus
   Tu solus dominus\>
   tu sol\<us\> altissimus
[9] Qui venisti hiesu christe et precioso sanguine tuo nos redemisti
   Cum sancto spiritu in gloria d\<e\>i patris am\<en\>

*

Glory to God in the highest:
[1] Whom the citizens of heaven celebrate with praise proclaiming holy.
   And on earth peace to men of good will,
[2] Which the servants of the Lord promised to the world by the Word incarnate.
   We praise You
[3] To whose praises the morning stars lend themselves.
   We bless You
[4] Through whom everything holy and blessed is given and increased.
   We worship You,
[5] Almighty One, to be adored, revered, feared, and venerated.
   We glorify You
[6] And creating as creature, forming as figure, making as made.
   We give You thanks for Your great glory.
[7] A hymn to the Sovereign, giving thanks for piety,
   O Lord God, heavenly King,
   God the Father almighty,
   O Lord, the only-begotten Son,
   Jesus Christ.
[8] Most high, Jesus Christ, whom all adore in spirit and in truth, it is fitting to pray:
   O Lord God,
   Lamb of God,
   Son of the Father,
   You who take away the sins of the world have mercy on us.
   You who take away the sins of the world receive our prayer.
   You who sit at the right hand of the Father have mercy on us.
   For You alone are the holy one,
   You alone are the Lord,
   You alone are the most high,
[9] You who came, Jesus Christ, and with Your precious blood redeemed us
   with the Holy Spirit
   in the glory of God the Father. Amen.

DISTINCTIVE VARIANTS

Rc 1741 [6] *Ut* for *Et.* **Bu 2824** [1] *cælestem . . . laudes* for *cælestes . . . laude;* [6] *Ut* for *Et;* [7] *maiestatis* for *maiestati. Quem cives caelestes* is among the oldest Gloria in excelsis tropes in the repertory; it is found in nearly all early regional repertories. Vv. [1–8], as they were known in Nonantola, resemble most other northern and central Italian versions of the trope. For v. [9], however, the Nonantolan MSS and VEcap 107 have the variant line, "Qui venisti hiesu christe et precioso sanguine tuo redemisti," distinctive for its incorporation of a portion of the Ordinary text, "Jesu Christe."

The three Nonantolan sources differ as to the cue to v. [8]:

Rn 1343 . . . *usque* fili unigenite Hiesu christe;
Rc 1741 Domine deus rex;
Bu 2824 Domine deus rex *usque* fili unigenite.

Since v. [8] incorporates the Ordinary text, "Jesu Christe," but with a different melodic setting than that found in Bosse 43, it is possible that Christ's name was invoked successively—at the end of the Gloria phrase and the beginning of v. [8]—as in RoN 1343.

MELODIC VARIANTS
   Rc 1741 *(in) ex(celsis)* dd~; [1] *ce(lestes)* dd~; [2] *(in)car(nato)* cd(c); [4] *et* dd~; [6] *(crea)tu(ra)* aa~; [8] *(veri)ta(te)* aa~; *(o)por(tet)* aa~; [9] *san(guine)* d; *nos* dd~. **Bu 2824** *(in) ex(celsis)* d; [1] *(ho)mi(nibus)* de; *(volun)ta(tis)* c; [9] *san(guine)* d.

Gloria in excelsis 11a

BOSSE 12; VATICAN I

TROPE: *Laus tua Deus*

SOURCES
Rn 1343 fol. 8v LAUS.IN.N<atale>.S<ancti>.SILV<est>RI.
Bu 2824 fols. 4v–5v Laus in [natale] s<an>c<t>i Silvestri

REFERENCES
AH 47, pp. 282–83; *BTC* II/2, 22, 25–28; Gautier, *Les Tropes*, 269; Leach, "The *Gloria in Excelsis Deo* Tropes," 216–39; Pfaff, *Die Tropen*, 100–101; Planchart, *Repertory*, 2:276–82; Rönnau, *Die Tropen zum Gloria*, 140–47, 173, 211–12, 249–51; Rönnau, "*Regnum tuum solidum.*"

TEXT COMMENTARY
   Trope texts are in prose. Like *Quem cives caelestes*, *Laus tua Deus* is one of the oldest tropes of the Gloria in excelsis; it is included in early sources from the East and West Frankish traditions, as well as northern Italy. Because the trope is generally concerned with the kingship of Christ, the wandering vv. [5, 7, 8] and *Regnum tuum solidum permanebit in aeternum* were probably associated with *Laus tua Deus* originally (see Planchart, *Repertory*, 2:297).

TEXT AND TRANSLATION

        Gloria in excelsis deo
    <Et in terra pax hominibus> bone voluntatis
[1] Laus tua deus resonet coram te rex
        Laudam<us te>
[2] Qui venisti propter nos rex angelorum deus
        Bene<dicimus te>
[3] In sede maiestatis tuæ
        Adoramus te
[4] Veneranda trinitas
        Glorificamus te
[5] Gloriosus es rex israhel in throno patris tui
    Gra<tia>s agimus tibi <propter magnam
        gloriam tuam
        Domine deus rex caelestis
        Deus pater omnipotens
        Domine fili unigenite>
        Hiesu christe
[6] Domine deus redemptor israhel
        D<omi>ne deus agnus d<e>i
        <Filius patris
        Qui tollis peccata mundi
        Miserere nobis
        Qui tollis peccata mundi
        Suscipe deprecationem nostram
        Qui sedes ad dexteram patris
        Miserere nobis
        Quoniam> tu solus s<an>c<tu>s
[7] Deus fortis et inmortalis
        Tu solus d<omi>n<u>s
[8] Cælestium terrestrium et infernorum rex
        Tu solus altissimus
[9] Regnum tuum <solidum
    permanebit indivisum
    inconcussum
    sine fine perhenne
    Te adorant et conlaudant
    simul omnes
    virtutes angelice
    et nos supplices
    conlaudamus tuum nomen
    Qui permanebit in aeternum>
        Hiesu christe
        [Cum sancto spiritu
        in gloria dei patris
        Amen]
        *

    Glory to God in the highest:
    And on earth peace to men of good will.
[1] Let praise of You, O God, resound before You, O King!
        We praise You.
[2] You who came for our sake, King of the angels, God:
        We bless You.
[3] On the throne of Your majesty:
        We worship You.
[4] Trinity to be venerated:
        We glorify You.
[5] You are glorious, King of Israel, on Your Father's throne!
    We give You thanks for Your great glory.
        O Lord God, heavenly King,
        God the Father almighty,
        O Lord, the only-begotten Son,
        Jesus Christ.
[6] O Lord God, Redeemer of Israel:
        O Lord God,
        Lamb of God,
        Son of the Father,
    You who take away the sins of the world
        have mercy on us.
    You who take away the sins of the world
        receive our prayer.

You who sit at the right hand of the Father
have mercy on us.
For You alone are the holy one.
[7] Mighty and immortal God:
You alone are the Lord.
[8] King of all things in heaven, on the earth, and below the earth,
You alone are the most high.
[9] Your reign shall endure,
sound, undivided, constant,
without end, forever.
All the angelic powers at once
worship and extol You.
And we suppliants praise Your name,
which shall endure forever,
Jesus Christ,
with the Holy Spirit
in the glory of God the Father.
Amen.

Distinctive Variants

The Nonantolan readings correspond for the most part to the version found in the earliest northern Italian sources of the trope, VEcap 90, Mza 75, and Mza 76. Like these readings, the Nonantolan version closes with the line *Regnum tuum*, but with the prosula *Permanebit indivisum*; Aquitanian and St. Gall sources have different prosulae. Bu 2824 differs from all the other transmissions of the trope complex in that it includes the following tenth verse, which unfortunately lacks musical notation:

Hiesu christe
[10] Christe cælorum rex alme voces nostras inclite vocibus angelorum adiuge
Cum sancto spiritu [in gloria dei patris Amen]

*

Jesus Christ,
[10] Supportive, glorious Christ, King of the angels, add our voices to the
voices of the angels,
With the Holy Spirit in the glory of God the Father.
Amen.

Melodic Variants
Bu 2824 [3] *(tu)ae* . . . dedd~ca dd~cb; [5] *(tu)i* . . . dedd~ca dd~cb; [7] *De(us)* cbc caGacc~b; *et* bcdd~.

Gloria in excelsis 11b

Bosse 39; Gloria A
Trope: *Laus tua Deus*
Source
Rc 1741 fols. 23r–24r Laus in Nat<ale> S<an>c-<t>i Silv<est>ri.

Text and Translation

Gloria in excelsis d<e>o
<Et in terra pax hominibus bone> vol<untatis>
[1] Laus tua deus resonet coram te rex
Laud<amus te>
[2] Qui venisti propter nos rex angelorum deus
Ben<edicimus te>
[3] In sede maiestatis tuę
Ador<amus te>
[4] Veneranda trinitas
Glor<ificamus te>
[5] Gloriosus es rex israhel in throno patris tui
Gra<tia>s <agimus tibi propter magnam
gloriam tuam
Domine deus rex caelestis
Deus pater omnipotens
Domine fili unigenite>
hiesu christe
[6] Domine deus redemptor israhel
D<omi>ne d<eu>s agn<us> <dei
Filius patris
Qui tollis peccata mundi
Miserere nobis
Qui tollis peccata mundi
Suscipe deprecationem nostram
Qui sedes ad dexteram patris
Miserere nobis
Quoniam> tu sol<us> s<an>c<tu>s
[7] Deus fortis et immortalis
Tu sol<us> d<ominu>s
[8] Cęlestium terrestrium et infernorum rex
Tu solus altissimus
[9] Regnum tuu<m> <solidum
permanebit indivisum
inconcussum
sine fine perhenne
Te adorant et conlaudant
simul omnes
virtutes angelice
et nos supplices
conlaudamus tuum nomen
Qui permanebit in eternum
Hiesu christe
Cum sancto spiritu
in gloria dei patris
Amen>

*

Glory to God in the highest:
And on earth peace to men of good will.
[1] Let praise of You, O God, resound before You, O King!
We praise You.
[2] You who came for our sake, King of the angels, God:
We bless You.

lvii

[3] On the throne of Your majesty:
   We worship You.
[4] Trinity to be venerated:
   We glorify You.
[5] You are glorious, King of Israel, on Your Father's throne!
   We give You thanks for Your great glory.
   O Lord God, heavenly King,
   God the Father almighty,
   O Lord, the only-begotten Son,
   Jesus Christ.
[6] O Lord God, Redeemer of Israel:
   O Lord God,
   Lamb of God,
   Son of the Father,
   You who take away the sins of the world
   have mercy on us.
   You who take away the sins of the world
   receive our prayer.
   You who sit at the right hand of the Father
   have mercy on us.
   For You alone are the holy one.
[7] Mighty and immortal God:
   You alone are the Lord.
[8] King of all things in heaven, on the earth, and below the earth,
   You alone are the most high.
[9] Your reign shall endure,
   sound, undivided, constant,
   without end, forever.
   All the angelic powers at once
   worship and extol You.
   And we suppliants praise Your name,
   which shall endure forever,
   Jesus Christ,
   with the Holy Spirit
   in the glory of God the Father.
   Amen.

Gloria in excelsis 12

BOSSE 12; VATICAN I

TROPE: *Quem novitate*

SOURCES
Rn 1343 fol. 9r–v LAUS IN EPIPHANIA
   D<omi>NI
Rc 1741 fols. 24r–25r Laus in epiphania
Bu 2824 fols. 4v–7r Laus in epy<p>h<ania> d<omi>ni

REFERENCES
   AH 47, nos. 209 and 220; *CT* 4, 249; Leach, "The *Gloria in Excelsis Deo* Tropes," 80–82, 116–26; Pfaff, *Die Tropen*, 100, 103; Rönnau, *Die Tropen zum Gloria*, 80.

TEXT COMMENTARY
   In accentual meter; vv. [1–7] comprise three or four units of five syllables ending in a paroxytone, a meter favored in Italian tropes for the Agnus Dei and Gloria in excelsis. (See above, Gloria in excelsis 8a.) Given its frequent appearance in Italian sources, *Quem novitate* may be of Italian origin.

TEXT AND TRANSLATION
   Gloria in excelsis deo
   [Et in terra pax hominibus
      bone voluntatis]
[1] Quem novitate
   sideris actus
   laudat eous
      Laudamus [te]
[2] Qui benedicis
   flumina fontis
   tinctus in undis
      Benedic<imus te>
[3] Qui magus offert
   poplite flexo
   mistica dona
      Adoramus te
[4] Gloria cuius
   prima colorem
   atque saporem
   mutat aquarum
      Glorificamus te
[5] Te fore verum
   aurea clamant
   munera regem
      Gra<tia>s agimus tibi <propter magnam>
         gl<ori>am tuam
[6] Te deitatis
   nomine signant
   thura colendum
      D<omi>ne d<eu>s rex cæl<estis>
         <Deus pater omnipotens
         Domine fili> unigenite
[7] Carnis amictum
   teque subisse
   mirra fatetur
      Hiesu christe
         <Domine deus
         Agnus dei
         Filius patris
   Qui tollis peccata mundi miserere nobis
      Qui tollis peccata mundi
      Suscipe deprecationem nostram
      Qui sedes ad dexteram patris
         Miserere nobis
      Quoniam tu solus sanctus
         Tu solus dominus>
         tu solus altissimus

[8] Conditor generis humani redemptor idemque
[9] Regnum tuum solidum
 ineffabile sine fine sine principio
 Sapientia dei patris æterni
 Salvare venisti nos
 Nasci dignatus de virgine
 Et nunc deus et homo regnas o domine dominator
 Permanebis in æternum
  Hiesu christe
  [Cum sancto spiritu
  in gloria dei patris
  Amen]

*

Glory to God in the highest:
And on earth peace to men of good will.
[1] Whom the magus from the East,
 led by the newness of the star,
 praises:
  We praise You.
[2] You who bless
 the waters of the fountain,
 bathed in the waves:
  We bless You.
[3] To whom the magus,
 on bended knee,
 offers mystical gifts:
  We worship You.
[4] Whose pristine glory
 changes the color
 and the taste of the waters:
  We glorify You.
[5] The tributes of gold
 proclaim that You are about to be
 the true King:
  We give You thanks for Your great glory.
[6] The frankincenses signify that
 You (are) to be revered
 with the name of deity.
  O Lord God, heavenly King,
  God the Father almighty,
  O Lord, the only-begotten Son,
[7] And the myrrh shows
 that You have assumed
 the cloak of the flesh,
  Jesus Christ
  O Lord God,
  Lamb of God,
  Son of the Father,
 You who take away the sins of the world
  have mercy on us.
 You who take away the sins of the world
  receive our prayer.
 You who sit at the right hand of the Father
  have mercy on us.
 For You alone are the holy one,
 You alone are the Lord,
 You alone are most the most high.
[8] Creator of the human race and self-same Redeemer,
[9] Your ineffable dominion will remain complete,
 without beginning, without end;
 By the wisdom of God, the eternal Father,
 You came to save us;
 deigned to be born of the virgin,
 and now, God and Man, You reign, O Lord, Ruler.
 (Your reign) will last forever,
  Jesus Christ,
  with the Holy Spirit
  in the glory of God the Father.
  Amen

DISTINCTIVE VARIANTS
Rc 1741 [3] *Cui* for *Qui*; [7] cue *altissimus* changed to *dominus*; [8] cue *Tu solus altissimus* added after the trope verse. **Bu 2824** [1] *notitati* for *novitate*; [2] *benedicit* for *benedicis*; [3] *Cui* for *Qui*. The version of *Quem novitate* known in Nonantola was similar to all other Italian readings except Ob 222 (see Leach; it is found in still another version in two sources closely linked to the Italian tradition, APT 17 and 18). The Nonantolan tropers differ from other readings by the inclusion of v. [8], which does not observe the meter of the core verses, and by the use of the *Regnum* prosula, *Ineffabilis sine fine*.

MELODIC VARIANTS
Rc 1741 [1] *lau(dat)* CCDD CFGa; [7] *Car(nis)* CD; *(sub)is(se)* DD~; [8] *(re)demp(tor)* D(C); [9] *so(lidum)* FEF FDC; *sine (fine)* E'F; *(ae)ter(ni)* FF(E); *(ho)mo* D; *(eter)num* AΓ. **Bu 2824** [2] *undis* EFD C(E)'E; *sine (fine)* E'F; *(ho)mo* D; *(Perma)ne(bit)* FF~E.

Gloria in excelsis 13a

BOSSE 51; VATICAN XI

TROPE: *Cives superni . . . Christus surrexit*

SOURCES
Rn 1343 fols. 9v–10r LAUS IN PASCHA
Bu 2824 fols. 7r–8r Laus i<n> pasca d<omini>

REFERENCES
AH 47, nos. 167 and 169a; *BTC* II/2, 22, 12–15; Gautier, *Les Tropes*, 260; Husmann, "Sinn und Wesen," 136–37; Kelly, "Introducing the Gloria"; Leach, "The *Gloria in Excelsis Deo* Tropes," 127–82; Norberg, *Versification médiévale*, 94–101; Pfaff, *Die Tropen*, 100–101; Planchart, *Repertory*, 2:292–97; Rönnau, *Die Tropen zum Gloria*, 104–7, 194–96, 217; Oliver Strunk, "Tropus and Troparion," 272–76; Van Deusen, *Music at Nevers*, 91–92.

TEXT COMMENTARY

Accentual meter is a pattern known as rhythmic Adonics (see Gloria in excelsis 8 and 12).

TEXT AND TRANSLATION

    Gloria in excelsis deo
    [Et in terra pax hominibus bone voluntatis]

[1] Cives superni hodie suam
simul et nostram nunciant mundo
festivitatem gloriam deo
resonemus omnes christo surgente
    Laudamus [te]

[2] Christus surrexit dulcibus hymnis
omnipotenti modulemur eia
    Benedic<imus te>

[3] Figens illa cruci
    Adoramus te

[4] Optime rector generis humani
qui voluisti vulnera curare
filii cruore
    Glorificamus [te]

[5] Iam liberati mortis a vinculo
et libertati redditi vere
    Gra<tia>s agimus [tibi]

[6] Qui deminutos angelorum chorus
hodie restaurans multos inferno
abstrahens funesto
    Propter magna<m> gl<ori>am tuam

[7] Protege verum pascha celebrantes
    Domine deus rex cælestis
    <Deus> pat<er> om<ni>p<oten>s

[8] Presta ne nobis veteris fermenti quid misceatur
    D<omi>ne fili <unigenite> hiesu christe

[9] Azima sincera ques[u]mus largire
    D<omi>ne d<eu>s agnus d<e>i
    <Filius patris
    Qui tollis peccata mundi
    Miserere nobis
    Qui tollis peccata mundi
    Suscipe>
    dep<re>cationem nostram

[10] Misericors et clemens
    Qui sedes ad dexte[ram] <patris
    Miserere nobis
    Quoniam tu solus sanctus>
    tu sol<us> d<omi>n<u>s

[11] Pius ac benignus serenus et severus
    Tu solus altissimus

[12] Atque potentissimus
    Hiesu christe
    <Cum sancto spiritu
    in gloria dei patris>
    am<en>

    *

    Glory to God in the highest:
    And on earth peace to men of good will.

[1] Today the citizens of heaven
announce to the world their and our joy together:
    Let us sound forth on (the occasion of) Christ's rising: Glory to God!
    We praise You.

[2] Christ is risen. Let us sing delightful hymns to the omnipotent One, ah!
    We bless You.

[3] Fastening Him to the cross:
    We worship You.

[4] Most blessed Ruler of the human race,
You who willed to heal our wounds
with the blood of Your Son:
    We glorify You.

[5] Now, released from the bondage of death
and truly made free:
    We give You thanks,

[6] You who restored the diminished choirs of angels
by drawing many away from eternal damnation
for Your great glory.

[7] Protect those who celebrate the true Pasch,
    O Lord God, heavenly King,
    God the Father almighty.

[8] Grant that nothing of the old leaven is mixed in us,
    O Lord, the only-begotten Son,
    Jesus Christ.

[9] Grant, we ask, sincere leaven,
    O Lord God,
    Lamb of God,
    Son of the Father,
    You who take away the sins of the world
    have mercy on us.
    You who take away the sins of the world
    receive our prayer.

[10] Merciful and kind,
You who sit at the right hand of the Father
have mercy on us.
For You alone are the holy one,
You alone are the Lord,

[11] Loyal and benign, serene and stern,
    You alone are most high

[12] And also most powerful,
    Jesus Christ.
    With the Holy Spirit
    in the glory of God the Father.
    Amen.

DISTINCTIVE VARIANTS

Bu 2824 [6] *Qua* for *Qui*; *restaurat* for *restaurans*. The transmission scheme of *Cives superni . . . Christus surrexit* is perhaps the most complex in the repertory of Gloria tropes. The text comes down to us in three main groups: Aquitanian, northern French, and Italian. (Its origins have been ascribed variously to Italy by Blume, Rönnau, and Falconer, and to France by Leach.) Even within the Italian tradition there were two distinct versions. The Nonantolan readings, along with those in PS 121 and Vo 39, are distinguished by their placement of v. [3], "Figens illa (illum) cruci," between "Benedicimus te" and "Adoramus te," a position which makes little sense grammatically—hence the correction of *illa* to *illum* in RoC 1741 (see Gloria in excelsis 13b). Leach argues that this ordering indicates that Nonantolan and related readings were adapted from an earlier Italian or French version of the trope, in which this element follows "Qui tollis peccata mundi." In this case, the neuter plural accusative pronoun, *illa*, would refer to *peccata* and would be translated: "Nailing those (sins) to the Cross."

Melodic Variants

Bu 2824 [2] *(dulci)bus hym(nis)* d'c; [4] *(Op)ti(me)* a(G); *(hu)ma(ni)* babcb; *(volu)isti* e'b; [5] *li(berati)* cb; [7–12] the music and text were scraped off to provide space for another chant (*Quis regis Israel*).

Gloria in excelsis 13b

Bosse 39; Gloria A

Trope: *Cives superni . . . Christus surrexit*

Source

Rc 1741 fols. 25v–27r LAUS IN DOM<inica> PASCHE

Text and Translation

  Gloria in excelsis deo
  <Et in terra pax hominibus bone> voluntatis
[1] Cives superni hodie suam
 simul et nostram nunciant mundo
 festivitatem gloriam deo
 resonemus omnes christo surgente
  Laud<amus te>
[2] Christus surrexit dulcibus hymnis
 omnipotenti modulemur eia
  Ben<edicimus te>
[3] Figens illum cruci
  Ador<amus te>
[4] Optime rector generis humani
 qui voluisti vulnera curare
 filii cruore
  Glorif<icamus te>
[5] Iam liberati mortis a vinculo
 et libertati redditi vere
  Gra<tia>s ag<imus> t<ib>i
[6] Qui deminutos angelorum choros
 hodie restauras multos inferno
 abstrahens funesto
  P<ro>pt<er> mag<nam> [gloriam tuam]
[7] Protege verum pascha celebrantes
  D<omi>ne d<eus> rex [caelestis
  Deus pater] om<ni>p<oten>s

[8] Presta ne nobis veteris fermenti quid misceatur
  D<omi>ne fili unig<enite> [Hiesu christe]
[9] Azima sincera quęsumus largire
  D<omi>ne d<eus> ag<nus> <dei
  Filius patris
  Qui tollis peccata mundi
  Miserere nobis
  Qui tollis peccata mundi
  Suscipe> dep<re>c<ationem> n<ost>ram
[10] Misericors et clemens
  Qui sedes <ad dexteram patris
  Miserere nobis
  Quoniam tu solus sanctus>
  tu sol<us> d<ominus>
[11] Pius ac benignus serenus et severus
  Tu sol<us> alt<issimus>
[12] Atque potentissimus
  Hiesu [christe
  Cum sancto spiritu
  in gloria dei patris
  Amen]

    *

  Glory to God in the highest:
  And on earth peace to men of good will.
[1] Today the citizens of heaven
 announce to the world their and our joy together:
 Let us sound forth on (the occasion of) Christ's rising: Glory to God!
  We praise You.
[2] Christ is risen. Let us sing delightful hymns to the omnipotent One, ah!
  We bless You.
[3] Fastening Him to the cross:
  We worship You.
[4] Most blessed Ruler of the human race,
 You who willed to heal our wounds
 with the blood of Your Son:
  We glorify You.
[5] Now, released from the bondage of death
 and truly made free:
  We give You thanks,
[6] You who restored the diminished choirs of angels
 by drawing many away from eternal damnation,
  for Your great glory.
[7] Protect those who celebrate the true Pasch,
  O Lord God, heavenly King,
  God the Father almighty.
[8] Grant that nothing of the old leaven is mixed in us,
  O Lord, the only-begotten Son,
  Jesus Christ.
[9] Grant, we ask, sincere leaven,
  O Lord God,
  Lamb of God,

Son of the Father,
You who take away the sins of the world
have mercy on us.
You who take away the sins of the world
receive our prayer.
[10] Merciful and kind,
You who sit at the right hand of the Father
have mercy on us.
For You alone are the holy one,
You alone are the Lord,
[11] Loyal and benign, serene and stern,
You alone are most high
[12] And also most powerful,
Jesus Christ.
With the Holy Spirit
in the glory of God the Father.
Amen.

Gloria in excelsis 14

BOSSE 11; VATICAN XIV

TROPE: *Alme mundi hodie de morte*

SOURCES
Rn 1343 fols. 10v–11r LAUS IN F<e>R<ia> .II. De albis
Rc 1741 fol. 27r–v Fer<ia> .ii. de albis

REFERENCES
Leach, "The *Gloria in Excelsis Deo* Tropes," 325–27; Pfaff, *Die Tropen*, 100; Rönnau, *Die Tropen zum Gloria*, 80.

TEXT COMMENTARY
Trope texts are in prose; note the parallelisms in vv. [1–6], which are similar in length (between 14 and 16 syllables). Moreover, vv. [1, 2, 4, 5] end with *cursus planus*, which is a common prose rhythm at ends of lines. V. [1] of Gloria in excelsis 15, "Alme mundi . . . in caelum," however, does not follow this pattern.

TEXT AND TRANSLATION

Gloria in excelsis deo
[Et in terra pax hominibus bone voluntatis]
[1] Alme mundi hodie de morte victor redisti
Lauda[mus te]
[2] Qui nos redemisti proprio sanguine o rex angelorum
Ben<edicimus te>
[3] Rex angelorum atque archangelorum deus
Ador<amus te>
[4] Quem laudant sol atque luna et universa creata tua
Glorific<amus te>
[5] Qui genus humanum revocasti ad pristinam vitam
Gra<tia>s agim<us> <tibi propter magnam gloriam tuam
Domine rex caelestis
Deus pater omnipotens
Domine fili unigenite hiesu christe et sancte spiritus
Domine deus
Agnus dei
Filius patris
Qui tollis peccata mundi miserere nobis
Qui tollis peccata mundi
Suscipe deprecationem nostram
Qui sedes ad dexteram patris miserere nobis
Quia> tu solus s<an>c<tu>s
[6] Hoc nomen est tibi in fine et ante omnia secula
Tu sol<us> d<ominus>
[7] Et non est alius in æternum
Tu solus altissimus
[8] Cui regnum est sine fine
In secula seculorum
Hiesu christe
<Cum sancto spiritu in gloria dei patris> amen

*

Glory to God in the highest:
And on earth peace to men of good will.
[1] Generous Conqueror of the world, today You have come back from death!
We praise You.
[2] You who have redeemed us with Your own blood, O King of the angels:
We bless You.
[3] King of the angels and God of the archangels:
We worship You.
[4] Whom the sun and the moon and all creation praise:
We glorify You.
[5] You who restored the human race to (its) original life:
We give You thanks for Your great glory.
O Lord God, heavenly King,
God the Father almighty,
O Lord, the only-begotten Son,
Jesus Christ.
O Lord God,
Lamb of God,
Son of the Father,
You who take away the sins of the world
have mercy on us.
You who take away the sins of the world
receive our prayer.
You who sit at the right hand of the Father
have mercy on us.
For You alone are the holy one.
[6] This name is Yours in the end and before eternity:
You alone are the Lord.

[7] And there is no other into eternity.
You alone are most high,
[8] To whom is the kingdom without end, forever and ever,
Jesus Christ with the Holy Spirit
in the glory of God the Father.
Amen.

DISTINCTIVE VARIANTS
See Gloria in excelsis 15.

MELODIC VARIANTS
Rc 1741 *(ex)cel(sis)* F(E); [1] *Al(me)* EDD~; *mun(di)* DE(D); [3] *Rex* E; [6] *an(te)* EFE; [7] *alius* FE'DE'DD~C; [8] *secula* FE'DE'DD~C.

Gloria in excelsis 15

BOSSE 11; VATICAN XIV
TROPE: *Alme mundi hodie in caelum*
SOURCES
Rn 1343 fol. 11r LAUS IN ASCENSA D<omi>NI
Rc 1741 fols. 27v–28r Laus in ascens<a> d<omini>

TEXT AND TRANSLATION
Gloria in excelsis deo
<Et in terra pax hominibus> bone voluntatis
[1] Alme mundi hodie in cælum victor ascendisti

*

Glory to God in the highest:
And on earth peace to men of good will.
[1] Generous Conqueror of the world, today You have ascended into heaven!
[2–8] (Same as vv. [2–8] of Gloria in excelsis 14.)

DISTINCTIVE VARIANTS
Rc 1741 [1] *ad cęlos* for *in cælum*. In addition to the RoN 1343 and RoC 1741, the Gloria trope *Alme mundi hodie in caelum* is found in two other northern Italian MSS, VEcap 107 and PS 121. In these sources the trope comprises ten lines. The Nonantolan tropers lack the wandering line, "Domine deus rex israhel" (PS 121: *redemptor*), found in the other readings between vv. [5] and [6]. This element is employed in Gloria in excelsis 17. The version of VEcap 107 and PS 121 also includes the *Regnum* prosula, *Permanebit in aeternum*, which was sung in Nonantola in connection with Gloria in excelsis 8a/b and 11a/b.

MELODIC VARIANTS
Rc 1741 [1] *Al(me)* EDD~; *mun(di)* DE(D); *ascen-(disti)* D'E.

Gloria in excelsis 16

BOSSE 51; VATICAN XI
TROPE: *O laudabilis rex*
SOURCES
Rn 1343 fol. 11r–v (No rubric)
Rc 1741 fols. 28r–29r Laus in Natalis. S<an>c<t>orum Senesii. <et> Theopontii.

REFERENCES
AH 47, nos. 177 and 221; Leach, "The *Gloria in Excelsis Deo* Tropes," 188–97; Pfaff, *Die Tropen*, 100, 103; Planchart, *Repertory*, 2:286–88; Rönnau, *Die Tropen zum Gloria*, 113–16, 171–72, 209–210, 234–35.

TEXT COMMENTARY
Trope texts are in prose; vv. [1–2] and [3–4] have a rough symmetry. The first pair comprises epithets in the vocative with *-e* assonance, ending in "deus." Vv. [3–4] are both divided by the conjunction "et" and again end in "deus." The structure of v. [5] (4 + 7p) is similar to v. [4] (5 + 7p).

TEXT AND TRANSLATION
Gloria in excelsis deo
<Et in terra pax hominibus> bon<e> vol<untatis>
[1] O laudabilis rex domine deus
Laudamus [te]
[2] Adonay benedicte deus
Ben<edicimus te>
[3] O adoranda et beata trinitas deus
Ador<amus te>
[4] Glorificande et metuende deus
Glorifi[camus te]
[5] Rex seculorum domine hiesu christe
Gra<tia>s agim<us> <tibi propter magnam gloriam tuam
Domine deus rex caelestis
Deus pater omnipotens
Domine> fili unig<enite>
[6] Misertus esto nostri qui redemisti mundum tuo sacro sanguine
Hiesu christe
<Domine deus
Agnus dei
Filius patris
Qui tollis peccata mundi miserere nobis
Qui tollis> pecc<ata> mundi
[7] Pax salus et vita hominum tibi gloria
Suscipe dep<re>c<ationem nostram>
[8] Nobis in terris miserere deus alme
Qui sedes <ad dexteram patris> mis<erere> nobis

[9] Æterni sapientia patris
   Q<uonia>m tu solus s<an>c<tu>s
[10] Tu lux via et spes nostra
   Tu solus d<omi>n<u>s
[11] O virtus honor dei patris et gloria omnium vita
   mori voluisti pro cunctis o bone rex
   Tu solus altissimus
[12] Sceptrum regni nobilem
   lumen æterni
   qui splendore
   sed de tuo lumine
   Sacræ æcclesiæ
   sociasti
   ammirabili dote
   Dignare proles
   absolvere dilecte
   Sponsæ tuæ
   divo piamine
   Permanebis in æternum
      Hiesu christe
   <cum sancto spiritu in gloria dei patris>
      am<en>
         *
   Glory to God in the highest:
   And on earth peace to men of good will.
[1] O praiseworthy King, Lord God:
      We praise You.
[2] Lord, blessed God:
      We bless You.
[3] O honored and blessed Trinity, God:
      We worship You.
[4] To be glorified and revered, God:
      We glorify You.
[5] King of the ages, Lord Jesus Christ:
      We give You thanks for Your great glory.
      O Lord God, heavenly King,
         God the Father almighty,
      O Lord, the only-begotten Son,
[6] Be merciful to us, You who redeemed the world
   with Your sacred blood,
         Jesus Christ.
      O Lord God,
         Lamb of God,
         Son of the Father,
      You who take away the sins of the world
         have mercy on us.
      You who take away the sins of the world:
[7] Peace, welfare, and life of mankind,
      Glory to You!
         Receive our prayer.
[8] Have mercy on us on earth, sustaining God,
   You who sit at the right hand of the Father
         have mercy on us.
[9] Wisdom of the eternal Father:
      You alone are the holy one.
[10] You, our light, way, and hope:
      You alone are the Lord.

[11] O virtue, honor of God, the Father of all things.
   You chose life over death for all, O good King:
      You alone are most high.
[12] Noble scepter of the kingdom,
   Eternal light,
   which in a wonderful way
   suffuses the Holy Church
   with its rays:
   Deign to absolve
   Your childrens' sins
   by the expiation of Your spouse.
   You will remain forever,
      Jesus Christ,
      with the Holy Spirit
   in the glory of God the Father
      Amen.

DISTINCTIVE VARIANTS
Rc 1741 [12] *nobile* for *nobilem*; *splendorem* for *splendore*. Of the versions of *O laudabilis rex* that circulated in Italy, those found in the Nonantolan tropers and VEcap 107 are the longest, resembling more closely than the others the readings in northern French and Norman-Sicilian sources. Nonantolan MSS and VEcap 107 are further distinguished from other Italian versions by the use of the *Regnum* variant, *Sceptrum regni nobilem*, with the prosula, *Lumen aeterne*. Like the trope, this prosula finds concordances in northern French and Norman-Sicilian sources.

MELODIC VARIANTS
Rc 1741 [1] *rex* aa~; [3] *(ado)ran(da)* bb~; *et* b(a); [6] *es(to)* acc~b; *(rede)mis(ti)* Gab; [8] *(mise)rere* c′b; *al(me)* bcbb~abc; [10] *et* baa(G); [11] *(vi)ta* c; [12] *(do)te* EGabb; *(dilec)te* dbe . . .; *(piami)ne* dedca abcdd; *(Perma)ne(bis)* cb.

Gloria in excelsis 17

BOSSE 51: VATICAN XI

TROPE: *Laudat in excelsis*

SOURCES
Rn 1343 fol. 12r Laus in pen<te>costen.
Rc 1741 fols. 29v–30r Laus

REFERENCES
AH 47, no. 170a; *BTC* II/2, 22, 19–21; Leach, "The *Gloria in Excelsis Deo* Tropes," 195–215; Pfaff, *Die Tropen*, 77, 100; Planchart, *Repertory*, 2:270–73; Rönnau, *Die Tropen zum Gloria*, 151–54, 210–11, 231–32, 249.

TEXT COMMENTARY
Vv. [1–4] and [6], the core of the trope, are in elegiac couplets or distichs. The opening hexameters are generally reserved for the acclamations of heaven, elegiac pentameter for earthly creations. Leach makes

a useful connection between the language of *Laudat in excelsis* and Theodulphus's hymn, *Gloria laus et honor*.

TEXT AND TRANSLATION

    Gloria in excelsis deo
  [Et in terra pax hominibus bone voluntatis]
[1] Laudat in excelsis cælum terramque regentem
  angelicus cetus laudat et omnis homo
     Laud<amus te>
[2] Te benedicit ovans angelorum celsa potestas
  et mortalis homo te benedicit ovans
     Ben<edicimus te>
[3] Te veneranter adorat cunta caterva polorum
  te tellus pelagus laudat adorat amat
     Ador<amus te>
[4] Glorificant dominum rutilancia sydera cæli
  glorificant te rex cuncta creata tua
     Glorif<icamus> <te
  Gratias agimus tibi propter magnam gloriam tuam
    Domine deus rex caelestis
    Deus pater omnipotens
   Domine fili unigenite> hiesu christe
[5] Domine deus redemptor hisrahel
    D<omi>ne d<eu>s agnus d<e>i
    <Filius patris
  Qui tollis peccata mundi miserere nobis
   Qui tollis peccata mundi
  Suscipe> dep<re>c<ationem> n<ost>ram
[6] Qui super astra sedes ad dextram patris in alto
  rex cælo famulis tu miserere tuis
  Qui sedes <ad dexteram patris miserere nobis
    Quoniam tu solus sanctus
    Tu solus dominus>
    tu [solus] altis[simus]
[7] Regnum tuum [solidum
  permanebit indivisum
  inconcussum
  sine fine perhenne
  Te adorant et collaudant
  simul omnes
  virtutes angelicae
  et nos supplices
  collaudamus tuum nomen
  Qui permanebit in aeternum]
    Hiesu [christe
    Cum sancto spiritu
    in gloria dei patris
     Amen]

      *

  Glory to God in the highest:
  And on earth peace to men of good will.
[1] The angelic host extols (Him) who rules heaven and earth,
  and all mankind gives praise.
    We praise You.
[2] The great power of the angels triumphantly blesses You,
  and mortal man joyfully blesses You!
    We bless You.
[3] All the planets of the heavens reverently adore You;
  the earth, the sea praise, adore, and love You.
    We worship You.
[4] The glowing constellations of heaven glorify the Lord,
  the whole of Your creation glorifies You.
    We glorify You.
  We give You thanks for Your great glory.
    O Lord God, heavenly King,
    God the Father almighty,
    O Lord, the only-begotten Son,
    Jesus Christ.
[5] Lord God, Redeemer of the people of Israel,
    O Lord God,
    Lamb of God,
    Son of the Father,
  You who take away the sins of the world
    have mercy on us
  You who take away the sins of the world
    receive our prayer.
[6] You who sit above the stars on high at the right hand
  of God the Father, heavenly King, have mercy on Your servants,
  You who sit at the right hand of the Father
    have mercy on us.
    For You alone are the holy one,
    You alone are the Lord,
    You alone are most high.
[7] Your reign shall endure,
  sound, undivided,
  constant,
  without end, forever.
  All the angelic powers
  at once worship and extol You.
  And we suppliants
  praise Your name,
  which shall endure forever,
    Jesus Christ,
    with the Holy Spirit
    in the glory of God the Father.
     Amen.

DISTINCTIVE VARIANTS

Rc 1741 [1] *coetus* for *cetus*; [6] *dexteram* for *dextram*. The Nonantolan version is distinct from other Italian readings of *Laudat in excelsis* by the use of the wandering prose line, "Domine deus redemptor israhel" (v. [5]) and the *Regnum* prosula, *Permanebit indivisum*. The wandering line "Regnum tuum solidum" is found in the Vercelli MSS and Vo 39, but without the prosula. *Laudat in excelsis* was erased from Bo 2824.

MELODIC VARIANTS
   Rc 1741 [1] *(ter)ram(que)* aa~; [3] *(polo)rum* cb: *(pe)la(gus)* aa~; [4] *(cre)a(ta)* aa~g; [5] *(Do)mi(ne)* cb; [6] *dexteram* e'd'd; *(al)to* cb; [7] *Reg(num)* Ga(G).

Gloria in excelsis 18

BOSSE 12; VATICAN I

TROPE: *Quando regis cunctos*

SOURCES
Rn 1343 fols. 12r–13r Laus in s<an>c<t>i io-h<ann>is bapt<istae>
Rc 1741 fols. 30v–32r (no rubric)

REFERENCES
AH 47, nos. 179 and 219; Leach, "The *Gloria in Excelsis Deo* Tropes," 336–38; Pfaff, *Die Tropen,* 100, 103; Rönnau, *Die Tropen zum Gloria,* 138, 220–21.

TEXT COMMENTARY
   Hexameters; vv. [3–4, 6–8, 10–11] are Leonine. The *Regnum* prosula, *Per te Christe,* displays some metrical patterns and rhyme. Note for example the trochaic rhythm of the first, third, and last lines; and the rhyme with proparoxytone endings of the second, fourth, and sixth lines (*omnipotentissime / vivifice / clementissime*).

TEXT AND TRANSLATION
   Gloria in excelsis d<e>o
   <Et in terra pax hominibus bone>
   vol<untatis>
[1] Quando regis cunctos semper gratanter homones
   Laud<amus te>
[2] Complacuit tibimet mortem rex iure subire
   Ben<edicimus te>
[3] Ablato loeto vitam perfundis honestam
   Ador<amus te>
[4] Glorificant temet mites in tempore voces
   Glorif<icamus te>
[5] Tu nobis aperis cęlestia regna polorum
   Gr<atia>s ag<imus> <tibi propter magnam>
   gl<ori>am tua<m>
[6] Cęlorum sistis factor telluris et auctor
   D<omi>ne d<eus> rex cęl<estis>
[7] Tu rector mitis per secula cuncta manebis
   D<eu>s pat<er> om<ni>p<oten>s
[8] Esto principium cunctarum congrue rerum
   D<omi>ne fili unig<enite> hiesu christe
[9] Quem cecinit iohannes in clauso viscere matris
   D<omi>ne d< eus> <agnus dei filius> patris
[10] Poscimus ecce pater pellas delicta potenter
   Qui tol<lis> <peccata mundi miserere nobis
   Qui tollis peccata mundi
   Suscipe> dep<re>c<ationem> n<ost>ram

[11] Protege servorum clementer corda tuorum
   Qui sed<es> <ad dexteram patris
   Miserere nobis
   Quoniam tu solus sanctus
   tu sol<us> d<omi>n<u>s
[12] Cuncta regis et cuncta tenens et cuncta gubernas
   Tu sol<us> alt<issimus>
[13] Regnum tuum solidum
   per te christe sistit
   omnipotentissime
   Qui in cruce signum
   nobis dedisti vivifice
   Te laudamus
   rex clementissime
   Tibi laus et honor
   permanebit in ęternum
      Hiesu christe
      [Cum sancto spiritu
      in gloria dei patris
      Amen]

*

   Glory to God in the highest:
   And on earth peace to men of good will.
[1] Who ruleth graciously all men:
   We praise You.
[2] It pleased You to submit to death as rightful King.
   We bless You.
[3] With death withdrawn, You inspire a noble life.
   We worship You.
[4] Gentle voices glorify You on earth (i.e., in earthly time).
   We glorify You.
[5] You open the celestial regions of the heavens to us.
   We give You thanks for Your great glory.
[6] You are the Creator of the heavens and Maker of the earth,
   Lord God, heavenly King.
[7] You, gentle Ruler, shall abide for all ages,
   God the Father almighty.
[8] Be Thou the fit origin of all things,
   O Lord, only-begotten Son, Jesus Christ.
[9] Of whom John sang from within his mother's womb:
   O Lord God,
   Lamb of God,
   Son of the Father.
[10] Lo! We beg You, Father, with Your powers cast out our transgressions,
   You who take away the sins of the world have mercy on us.
   You who take away the sins of the world receive our prayer.

[11] Indulgently protect the souls of Your servants,
You who sit at the right hand of the Father
have mercy on us.
For You alone are the holy one,
You alone are the Lord.
[12] All reigning and all comprehending and all governing
You alone are most high.
[13] Your reign stands firm
for You, Christ almighty,
You who on the cross
gave to us the sign, vivify!
We praise You,
most merciful King.
Your glory and honor
shall last forever,
Jesus Christ,
with the Holy Spirit
in the glory of God the Father.
Amen.

Distinctive Variants

Rn 1343 [3] *leto* for *loeto*; [4] *tement* for *temet*; [12] *tenens* for *tenes*. The only northern Italian sources for *Quando regis* are the Nonantolan MSS and VEcap 107; in France outside Aquitaine, it is also found in Pa 1169 and Pn 10508, whose readings differ in the order of vv. from the Aquitanian sources. Moreover, the northern Italian version of the trope begins with the line "Quando regis . . . ," which is a variant of the presumed Aquitanian original, "Qui regis actus semper gratanter humanos." All the non-Aquitanian versions close with the *Regnum* prosula, *Per te Christe*.

Melodic Variants

Rn 1343 [1] *(Quan)do* cc~b; *cunc(tos)* aa(G); [3] *(per)fun(dis)* abaa(G); [4] *(te)ment* c; [5] *no(bis)* cc~b; [6] *Cæ(lorum)* ED; [8] *Es(to)* ED; [9] *in* Ga; [10] (transposed) *Poscimus* c′df′f (etc.); *(po)ten(ter)* edcdd(e); [11] (transposed) *Protege* e′d′c (etc.); [12] (transposed) *Cuncta regis* ce(f)′f′f′dedc (etc.); *cunc(ta tenens)* gf(e); *gu(bernas)* e; [13] *(clementissi)me* dbee~dc . . .; *(æ)ternum* F(G)′FE.

Gloria in excelsis 19

Bosse 11; Vatican XIV

Trope: *O gloria sanctorum*

Sources
Rn 1343 fol. 13r-v (no rubric)
Rc 1741 fols. 32r-33v Laus in N<atale>.S<ancti>. Petri

References
AH 47, no. 172; Leach, "The *Gloria in Excelsis Deo* Tropes," 328-31; Pfaff, *Die Tropen*, 100; Planchart, *Repertory*, 2:282-85; Rönnau, *Die Tropen zum Gloria*, 109-113, 209, 228-30.

Text Commentary
Vv. [1-4] are in prose with dactylic rhythm which is disrupted by the substitution in these lines of *Petrus* for the original *Iohannes*. (The Nonantolan/Mantuan version is an adaptation of an earlier Aquitanian trope for St. John the Evangelist [*AH* 47, no. 172; Rönnau, *Die Tropen zum Gloria*, 113].) Vv. [5-8] in dactylic hexameters or elegiac couplets.

Text and Translation

Gloria in excelsis deo
[Et in terra pax hominibus bone voluntatis]
[1] O gloria sanctorum lausque angelorum
quam secutus est sanctus petrus
Lauda[mus te]
[2] O decus et virtus lausque beata sanctorum
quam laudat sanctus petrus
Benedi[cimus te]
[3] Angelicus tibi a[d]stat clarissimus ordo
cum quo te semper glorificat sanctus petrus
Ador<amus te>
[4] Cantemus tibi laudes de pectore toto
teque cum sancto benedicamus petro
Glo<ri>fic<amus te>
[5] Glorificant dominum rutilancia sydera cæli
glorificant te rex cuncta creata tua
Gra<tia>s ag<imus> <tibi propter magnam>
tuam gl<ori>am
[6] Vita salus bonitas karitas sapientia christe
Domine rex <caelestis
Deus pater omnipotens
Domine fili unigenite
Hiesu christe> et s<an>c<t>æ sp<iritu>s
[7] Bonum omne pariter cuncta per secula christe
D<omi>ne d<eu>s agnus <dei
Filius patris
Qui tollis peccata mundi miserere nobis
Qui tollis peccata mundi
Suscipe> dep<re>c<ationem> n<ost>ram
[8] Angelicis sorte coniunctus iste catervis
assistit iugiter vultibus ecce tuis
Qui sedes ad d<exteram> <patris
miserere nobis
Quia tu solus sanctus
Tu solus dominus
Tu solus> altis[simus]
[9] Tibi laus imperium salus victoria et gracia potestas gloria decus et honor
permanebit in æternum
Hiesu christe

[Cum sancto spiritu
in gloria dei patris
Amen]

*

Glory to God in the highest:
And on earth peace to men of good will.
[1] O Glory of the saints and Praise of the angels,
whom St. Peter followed:
We praise You.
[2] O Splendor and Virtue and blessed Praise of the saints,
whom St. Peter adores:
We bless You.
[3] The most brilliant angelic rank waits upon You,
together with whom St. Peter forever glorifies:
We worship You.
[4] From the soul we sing Your praises,
and with St. Peter we bless You:
We glorify You.
[5] The glowing constellations of heaven glorify the Lord;
all Your creatures glorify You.
We give You thanks for Your great glory.
[6] Life, deliverance, goodness, charity, wisdom, O Christ:
O Lord God, heavenly King,
God the Father almighty,
O Lord, only-begotten son,
Jesus Christ and the Holy Spirit.
[7] Every good equally for all time, O Christ:
O Lord God,
Lamb of God,
Son of the Father,
You who take away the sins of the world
have mercy on us.
You who take away the sins of the world
receive our prayer.
[8] Happily conjoined with the angelic ranks,
behold he forever places himself in Your sight:
You who sit at the right hand of the Father
have mercy on us.
For You alone are the holy one,
You alone are the Lord,
You alone are the most high.
[9] Praise, dominion, salvation, victory, and grace;
Your power, glory, splendor, and honor will endure forever,
Jesus Christ,
with the Holy Spirit
in the glory of God the Father.
Amen.

DISTINCTIVE VARIANTS
Rc 1741 [3] *adstat* for *astat*; [6] *cue hiesu christe* for *cue et s<an>c<t>ae sp<iritu>s*. The order of core vv. [3–4] is reversed in the Nonantolan tropers compared with all other sources. Vv. [5–8] appear to have been written in imitation of the four preceding lines. V. [5] is an adaptation of v. [4] of Gloria in excelsis 9.

MELODIC VARIANTS
Rc 1741 *(ex)cel(sis)* c; [1] *san(ctus)* b(a); [2] *(bea)ta* G; [3] *or(do)* cc(b); *te* d; [5] *si(dera)* de; *(cre)a(ta)* aa~G; [6] *(bo)ni(tas)* Gb; [7] *(om)ne* aa~; [8] *(con)iunc(tus)* b(a); *tu(is)* ab; [9] *(po)tes(tas)* ed; *per(manebit)* cc~baGacb cc~baGacb acb bcdedcb. . . .

Gloria in excelsis 20

BOSSE 12; VATICAN I

TROPE: *Qui caelicolas*

SOURCES
Rn 1343 fol. 13v (no rubric)
Rc 1741 fols. 34v–35v (no rubric)

REFERENCES
AH 47, no. 189; Leach, "The *Gloria in Excelsis Deo* Tropes," 332–35; Pfaff, *Die Tropen,* 100; Rönnau, *Die Tropen zum Gloria,* 162–63, 176, 220.

TEXT COMMENTARY
Trope texts are in prose, but with rhymes between pairs of lines throughout. Vv. [1–2] and [4–5] are similar; vv. [3] and [6] do not follow their plan, being respectively shorter and longer. Blume remarks that this type of organization is unusual for such an early East Frankish trope.

TEXT AND TRANSLATION
Gloria in excelsis deo
<Et in terra pax hominibus> bon<e>
vol<untatis>
[1] Qui cælicolas et terrigenas federe sancto socias et exornas
Laud<amus te>
[Benedicimus te
Adoramus te]
[2] Quem laudat chorus et benedicit superus adorant te cuncta sydera turme
Glorif<icamus te>
[Gratias agimus tibi
propter magnam gloriam tuam]
[3] Quia tu nos redimeras cum finem seculi imposueras ut ante tempora decreveras
D<omi>ne d<eu>s rex [caelestis
Deus pater omnipotens]
[4] Non minus clementiæ quam potentiæ diviciis locuples perhenniter manens
D<omi>ne fili unig<enite> <hiesu christe
Domine deus
Agnus dei
Filius patris
Qui tollis peccata mundi miserere nobis

Qui tollis peccata mundi
Suscipe> dep<re>c<ationem> n<ost>ram
[5] Christe de patre lumen de luce summe de summo nostra faveto
Qui sed<es> <ad dexteram patris
Miserere nobis
Quoniam tu solus sanctus>
tu sol<us> d<ominus>
[6] Qui mundo victo hostemque subiecto patris virtute cooperante redemptor et tutor splendens gloriosæ
Tu solus alt<issimus> <Hiesu christe
Cum sancto spiritu in gloria dei patris>
am<en>

*

Glory to God in the highest:
And on earth peace to men of good will.
[1] You who unite and reconcile the inhabitants of heaven and earth in holy league:
We praise You.
We bless You.
We worship You.
[2] Whom the heavenly chorus lauds and praises; all the heavenly throngs worship You.
We glorify You.
We give You thanks for Your great glory.
[3] For You had redeemed us when You brought an age to a close, as before time You had decreed,
O Lord God, heavenly King,
God the Father almighty.
[4] Not less by forbearance than power; remaining ever rich and abundant.
O Lord, the only-begotten Son,
Jesus Christ.
O Lord God,
Lamb of God,
Son of the Father,
You who take away the sins of the world have mercy on us.
You who take away the sins of the world receive our prayer.
[5] Christ (begotten) from the Father; light from light, most high from most high,
favor us:
You who sit at the right hand of the Father have mercy on us.
For You alone are the holy one,
You alone are the Lord.
[6] Who, the word having been conquered and the enemy subdued by the Father's powers, the Redeemer and Guardian working with Him, and shining forth in glory:
You alone are most high,
Jesus Christ,
with the Holy Spirit
in the glory of God the Father.
Amen.

DISTINCTIVE VARIANTS

Rc 1741 [1] *foedere* for *federe*. The collation of minor text variants provided in *AH* suggests that *Qui caelicolas* reached northern Italy via northern France or the Rhineland. The order of vv. [4–5] are reversed in Rv 52; there are also minor text variants in that source that place it further on the periphery than Nonantola.

MELODIC VARIANTS

Rc 1741 *(ex)cel(sis)* EE(C); [4] *(perhenni)ter* GaG; [6] *(hostem)que* FF~E; *(virtu)te* E.

Gloria in excelsis 21

BOSSE 2 (VAR.); MILAN IV

TROPE: *Hinc laudando patrem*

SOURCE

Rc 1741 fols. 33v–34v Laus in assu<m>p<tione> s<an>c<t>e marie

REFERENCES

AH 47, no. 180; Leach, "The *Gloria in Excelsis Deo* Tropes," 297–99; Rönnau, *Die Tropen zum Gloria*, 125.

TEXT COMMENTARY

Hexameters. *Hinc laudando patrem* is related textually and musically to *Quem patris ad dexteram* (Gloria in excelsis 9).

TEXT AND TRANSLATION

Gloria in excelsis deo
<Et in terra pax hominibus bone>
volunt<atis>
[1] Hinc laudando patrem hiesu cum neumate divo
Laud<amus te>
[2] Cuncta creans verbo salvansque et quod benedicunt
Ben<edicimus te>
[3] Quem mare terra polus sub lege fatentur et orant
Ador<amus te>
[4] Celsa hominem ima deum pium amando tremendoque iustum
Glor<ificamus te>
[5] Gracia lex nobis virtus sapientia patris
Gra<tia>s ag<imus> <tibi propter magnam gloriam tuam
Domine deus rex caelestis
Deus pater omnipotens
Domine fili unigenite
Hiesu christe
Domine deus
Agnus dei
Filius patris
Qui tollis peccata mundi miserere nobis
Qui tollis peccata mundi
Suscipe> dep<recationem> n<ost>ram

[6] Esto benigne pius miseris sine crimine solus
Qui sed<es> <ad dexteram patris
miserere nobis
Quoniam tu solus sanctus
Tu solus dominius
Tu solus altissimus> hiesu christe
[7] Sit tua pax terris tibi doxa resultet in altis
Cum s<an>c<t>o [spiritu
in gloria dei patris
Amen]

*

Glory to God in the highest:
And on earth peace to men of good will.
[1] Hence, praising the Father, Jesus, with the Holy Spirit:
We praise You.
[2] Creating and preserving all things by the word and which they bless:
We bless You.
[3] Whom, under the law, the sea, the land, and the heavens acknowledge and beseech:
We worship You.
[4] The heavens (glorify) the Man, and the depths (glorify) in love and fear the benevolent just One:
We glorify You.
[5] Grace, a law unto us; virtue, wisdom of the Father:
We give You thanks for Your great glory.
O Lord God, heavenly King,
God the Father almighty,
O Lord, the only-begotten Son,
Jesus Christ,
O Lord God,
Lamb of God,
Son of the Father,
You who take away the sins of the world
have mercy on us.
You who take away the sins of the world
receive our prayer.
[6] You, kind One, who alone are without sin, be generous to the wretched:
You who sit at the right hand of the Father
have mercy on us.
For You alone are the holy one,
You alone are the Lord,
You alone are most high,
Jesus Christ
[7] Let your peace be on earth, let glory on high resound to You:
With the Holy Spirit
in the glory of God the Father.
Amen.

DISTINCTIVE VARIANTS

Although *Hinc laudando patrem* is found in some of the earliest Aquitanian sources (Pn 1118 and 1084) and two northern Italian tropers predating the Nonantolan MSS (VEcap 107 and Ob 222), the trope is found in only one of the three Nonantolan tropers. Its text is nearly identical to the version in VEcap 107.

Sanctus 1

THANNABAUR 154; VATICAN I

TROPE: *Deus fortis*

SOURCES
Rn 1343 fol. 14r
Rc 1741 fols. 35v–36v
Bu 2824 fol. 10r (fragment)

REFERENCES
CT 7 (no. 34), 95–97; Gautier, *Les Tropes,* 162; Pfaff, *Die Tropen,* 92.

TEXT COMMENTARY

Prose lines lack symmetry; vv. [1–3] are constructed according to a Trinitarian principle. V. [4] alludes to the text of the Gloria in excelsis. Vv. [5–6] resemble in expression the northern Italian antiphon *ante evangelium* for Christmas, *Tu rex gloriae*. Even though this trope is the first in the series its text does not refer specifically to Christmas and thus may also have been performed on other feasts.

TEXT AND TRANSLATION

Sanctus
[1] Deus fortis
Sanctus
[2] Filius excelsi
Sanctus dominus
[3] Spiritus sanctus qui regnas in trinitate
Deus sabaoth
[4] Te laudat te adorat te glorificat omnis creatura tua
Pleni sunt cęli et terra gloria tua
[5] Tu ergo salva nos domine
salva nos qui redemisti nos
Osanna in excelsis
[6] Tibi omnes angeli et archangeli
tibi omnis tua sancta proclamat ęcclesia
Benedictus qui venit in nomine domini
[7] Tuum est domine regnum tua potestas
tibi honor et imperium
per cuncta secula
Osanna in excelsis

*

Holy,
[1] Mighty God,
Holy,
[2] Son of the most High,
Holy Lord,

[3] Holy Spirit, You who reign in the Trinity,
      God of Hosts.
[4] All Your creation praises You, worships You,
      glorifies You.
      Heaven and earth are filled
      with Your glory.
[5] Save us now, O Lord, save us, You who redeemed us.
      Hosanna in the highest.
[6] All the angels and archangels,
   all Your Holy Church cry out to You:
      Blessed is He who comes
      in the name of the Lord.
[7] Yours, O Lord, is the power (and) sovereignty!
   Honor and dominion to You
   for all eternity!
      Hosanna in the highest.

Distinctive Variants

Rn 1343 [2] *excelsi* for *excelsi*; [3] *regnans* for *regnas*. *Sanctus Deus fortis* is found in a three-line version in a number of early sources outside Italy (including Pn 9448, SGs 484, and SGs 381) and two early Italian MSS, Ra 123 and Tn 20. Vv. [4–6] were added to this early form of the trope in Italy. They are found in the Nonantolan MSS, VEcap 107, Rv 52, MOd 7, Tn 18, PAc 47, and Rvat 602. These elements are fairly stable in their transmission, but with the following three exceptions: (a) in VEcap 107 v. [5] reads "salva nos domine salvator qui redemisti," which is preferable to the Nonantolan reading, in which the words *salva nos* are repeated. (The scribe of Rvat 602 simply omitted the repetition, "salva nos domine qui redemisti"); (b) in PAc 47 and MOd 7, v. [6] begins with the opening text and music of v. [7], "Tuum est domine regnum tua potestas tibi omnis tua sancta," and v. [7] has the text and music for v. [6], "Tibi omnes angeli et archangeli tibi honor"; (c) the scribe of Rvat 602 combined vv. [7] and [6]. Finally, *Sanctus Deus fortis* concludes with the Osanna prosula, *Omniumque rex regum* (see example 1), in Ra 123, VCd 162, MOd 7, Tn 18, and PAc 47; this prosula is associated with *Sanctus Pater ingenitus* in Tc 18 (Planchart, *Repertory*, 2:324).

Melodic Variants

Rn 1343 [2] *(Fili)us* DC; [5] *sal(va)* Ga; *do(mine)* GF; *(Osan)na* GF; [6] *om(nes)* G; *(arch)an(geli)* Ga; *(sanc)ta* EFGFDD~C; *qui* G; [7] *tu(a)* GF; *(impe)ri(um)* FED; *per* EFGFDD~C; *(Osan)na* DC EFGaa~G aaGFE.

Sanctus 2

Thannabaur 154; Vatican I

Trope: *Pater ingenitus*

Sources
Rn 1343 fol. 14r–v
Rc 1741 fols. 36v–37r
Bu 2824 fol. 10r–v

References

CT 7 (no. 97), 149–50; Pfaff, *Die Tropen*, 92; Planchart, *Repertory*, 1:277–79, 341; 2:323–34.

Text Commentary

Prose trope without symmetry; vv. [1–3] are organized according to a Trinitarian principle. V. [4] would seem to refer to the childrens' welcome of Christ on Palm Sunday (see processional antiphons *Pueri hebraeorum tollentes* and *Pueri hebraeorum vestimenta*), but the trope was copied second in the series, too soon to have been sung on that feast. The reference could conceivably relate to the gospel for the feast of St. Stephen, which foretells Christ's triumphal entry into Jerusalem. Remarkably, this feast's gospel closes with the words "Benedictus qui venit in nomine domini," that is, the same portion of the Sanctus with which v. [4] is associated here: "Jerusalem, Jerusalem! . . . How often would I have gathered thy children together, as a hen gathers her young under her wings, but thou wouldst not! Behold, your house is left to you desolate. For I say to you, you shall not see me henceforth until you shall say, 'Blessed is he who comes in the name of the Lord!'" (Matt. 23:37–39).

Text and Translation

               Sanctus
[1] pater ingenitus
               Sanctus
[2] Orbis redemptor filius
               Sanctus dominus
[3] Vivificans spiritus pollens in trinitate
               Deus sabaoth
               Pleni sunt cæli et terra gloria tua
               Osanna in excelsis
[4] Cuius in laude voces dabant pueri
   regem christum conlaudantes in altissimis
               Benedictus qui venit in nomine domini
               Osanna in excelsis

*

               Holy
[1] Father unbegotten,
               Holy
[2] Son, Redeemer of the world,
               Holy Lord,
[3] Life-giving, powerful Spirit in the Trinity,
      God of Hosts.
      Heaven and earth are filled with Your glory.
      Hosanna in the highest.

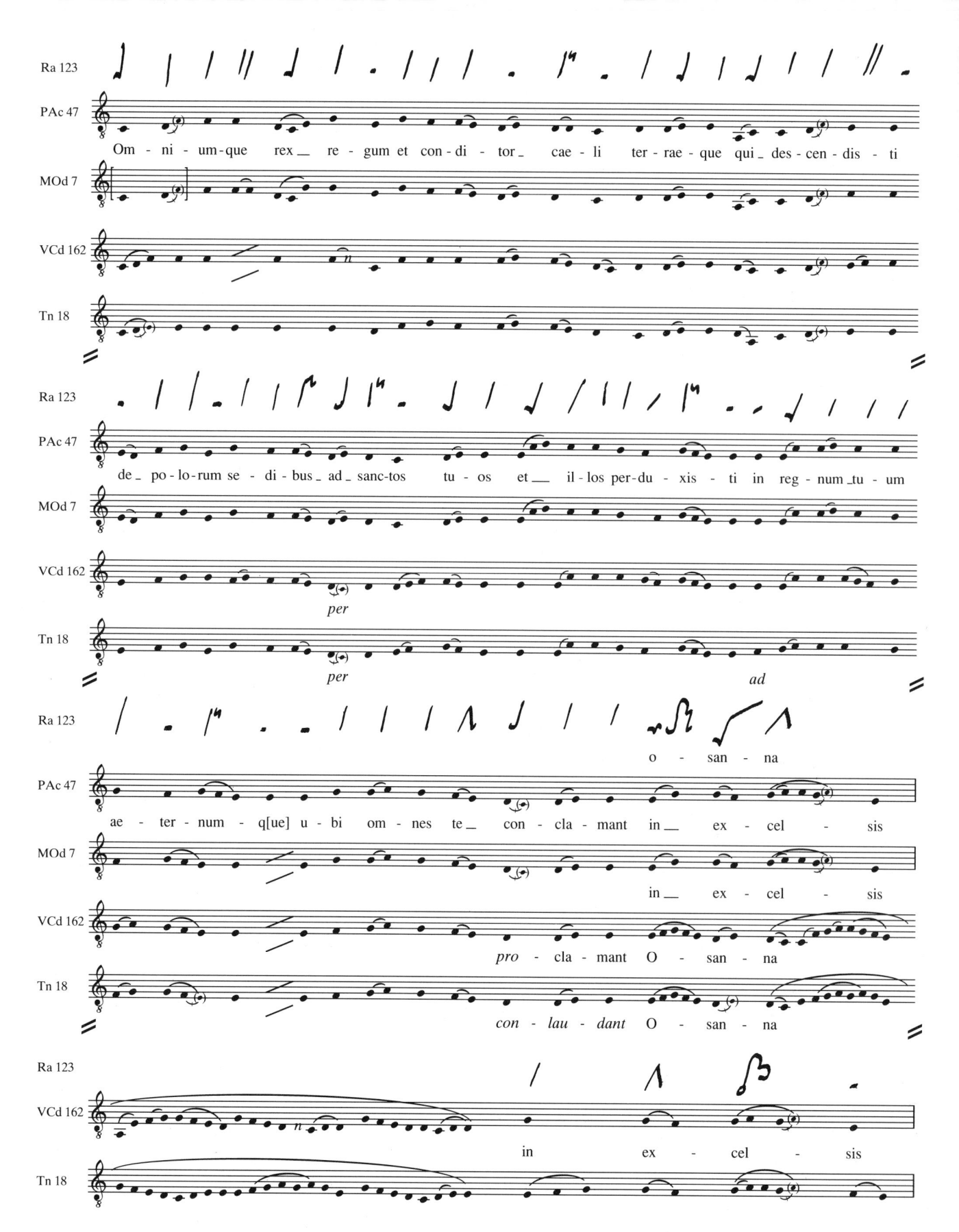

Example 1. Osanna Prosula *Omniumque rex regum* in Five Northern Italian Manuscripts

[4] In whose praise the children gave (their) voices,
extolling Christ the King in the highest.
Blessed is He who comes
in the name of the Lord.
Hosanna in the highest.

DISTINCTIVE VARIANTS

The version of *Sanctus pater ingenitus* that comes down to us in the Nonantolan MSS is also found in Italy in VEcap 107 and IV 60, the latter without musical notation. Two other Italian readings of this Aquitanian trope are abbreviated (Rv 52 and MOd 7); the version found in Tn 18 is extended by the Osanna prosula *Omniumque rex regum* (see Sanctus 1).

MELODIC VARIANTS

Rc 1741 [1] *Pa(ter)* GG~F; [3] *spi(ritus)* ED; *pol(lens)* EF(G); *ce(li)* GF; *(tu)a* DC; *(Osan)na* GG~F; [4] *(re)gem* FG(F); *chri(stum)* FE; *(conlau)dan(tes)* DD~; *qui* a; *in nomine . . . excelsis* omitted. **Bu 2824** [1] *Pa(ter)* GG~F; [3] *pol(lens)* EF(G); *qui* a.

Sanctus 3

THANNABAUR 216 (VAR.)

TROPE: *Pater lumen aeternum*

SOURCES
Rn 1343 fol. 14v
Rc 1741 fol. 37r

REFERENCES
CT 7 (no. 98), 150–51; David, "Le trope 'Sanctus pater' "; Pfaff, *Die Tropen*, 92; Planchart, *Repertory*, 1:277–80, 340–41; 2:325–26.

TEXT COMMENTARY
Prose trope; vv. [1–3] follow the same Trinitarian principle observed above.

TEXT AND TRANSLATION

Sanctus
[1] Pater lumen æternum
Sanctus
[2] Genitus ex deo deus
Sanctus dominus
[3] Spiritus maiestate consimilis
Deus sabaoth
Pleni sunt cæli et terra gloria tua
Osanna in excelsis
Benedictus qui venit in nomine domini
Osanna in excelsis

*

Holy
[1] Father, Eternal Light,
Holy
[2] God begotten from God,
Holy Lord,
[3] Spirit, like in majesty.
God of Hosts.
Heaven and earth are filled with Your glory.
Hosanna in the highest.
Blessed is He who comes
in the name of the Lord.
Hosanna in the highest.

DISTINCTIVE VARIANTS

The versions of *Pater lumen aeternum* found in the Nonantolan MSS and most other Italian sources are essentially identical to the texts that circulated in Aquitaine. Italian MSS PS 121 and Vo 39 include three additional lines (see example 2).

MELODIC VARIANTS

Rc 1741 [1] *San(ctus)* DEFG; [2] *Ge(nitus)* EGabb~a; [3] *(con)si(milis)* FE; *(Bene)dic(tus)* FE.

[4] Tri - nus per - so - na - li - ter et u - nus es - sen - ti - a - li - ter *Pleni sunt caeli . . .*

[5] Qui cae - lum ter - ram - que re - gis et cunc - ta tu - e - ris *Osanna . . .*

[6] Mun - di sal - va - tor om - ni - um pi - us at - que re - demp - tor *Benedictus . . .*

Example 2. Sanctus *Pater lumen aeternum* vv. [5–6] from PS 121

Sanctus 4

THANNABAUR 154; VATICAN I
TROPE: *Deus pater ingenite*
SOURCES
Rn 1343 fol. 14v
Rc 1741 fols. 36v–37r

REFERENCES
CT 7 (no. 40), 101–3; Pfaff, *Die Tropen*, 92; Planchart, *Repertory*, 1:277–79, 281; 2:320–23.

TEXT COMMENTARY
Prose trope; vv. [1–3] follow the same Trinitarian principle observed in Sanctus 1–3.

TEXT AND TRANSLATION

     Sanctus
[1] Deus pater ingenite
     Sanctus
[2] Filius eius unigenitus
     Sanctus dominus
[3] Spiritus sanctus paraclitus ab utroque procedens
    Deus sabaoth
  <Pleni sunt caeli et terra gloria tua
    Osanna in excelsis
  Benedictus qui venit in nomine domini
    Osanna in excelsis>

     *

     Holy
[1] God, Father unbegotten,
     Holy,
[2] His only-begotten Son
     Holy Lord,
[3] Holy Spirit, the Paraclite, proceeding from both.
    God of Hosts.
  Heaven and earth are filled with Your glory.
    Hosanna in the highest.
    Blessed is He who comes
    in the name of the Lord.
    Hosanna in the highest.

DISTINCTIVE VARIANTS
Rc 1741 [2] *deus unigenite* for *eius unigenitus*. All northern and central Italian sources of *Deus pater ingenite*—the Nonantolan tropers, VEcap 107, Rv 52, Tn 18 and 20—furnish the same three-line version of the trope found in MSS of French and German provenance.

MELODIC VARIANTS
Rc 1741 [2] *(Fili)us de(us)* aG'ab.

Sanctus 5

THANNABAUR 223; VATICAN XV
TROPE: *Mundi fabricator*
SOURCES
Rn 1343 fols. 14v–15r
Rc 1741 fols. 37v–38r
Bu 2824 fols. 10v–11v

REFERENCES
CT 7 (no. 76), 134–35; Pfaff, *Die Tropen*, 93.

TEXT COMMENTARY
Prose trope with assonance and rhyme in vv. [1] (*fabricator/rector*), [3] (*flammis/detergis*), and [4] (*famulis/tuis*). The word order in v. [2], which is divided in half by the conjunction *et*, makes for a palendromic effect: "ipsius patris et aequalis dominus." V. [4] alludes to the events recounted in the gospel for Palm Sunday.

Unlike the preceding Sanctus tropes, *Mundi fabricator* is Christocentric.

TEXT AND TRANSLATION

     Sanctus
[1] Mundi fabricator et rector
     Sanctus
[2] Unice ipsius patris et equalis dominus
    Sanctus dominus deus sabaoth
[3] Mundi qui culpas almis flammis mire detergis
    Pleni sunt cæli et terra gloria tua
    Osanna in excelsis
[4] Nobis nunc famulis miserere tuis
  cuius in laude puerorum turba devota prompsit
    Benedictus qui venit in nomine domini
    Osanna in excelsis

     *

     Holy
[1] Maker and Master of the world,
     Holy,
[2] Solely of the Father Himself and equal Lord.
    Holy Lord, God of Hosts.
[3] You who cleanse the sins of the world with bountiful flames.
  Heaven and earth are filled with Your glory.
    Hosanna in the highest.
[4] Have pity on us, Your servants,
  in whose praise the multitude of children shouted devotedly:
    Blessed is He who comes
    in the name of the Lord.
    Hosanna in the highest.

Distinctive Variants

Rn 1343 [2] *patri* for *patris*; [3] *almi* for *almis*; [4] *devote promsit* for *devota prompsit*. **Rc 1741** [4] *devote* for *devota*. Besides the Nonantolan MSS, *Mundi fabricator* is found in only a few other sources, mostly Italian. The text is essentially the same in all cases. In Mah 289 the melodic setting of the trope differs considerably from that found in the other MSS (example 3).

Melodic Variants

Rn 1343 [2] *(Sanctus domi)nus* E; [3] *(ter)ra* C; [4] *prom(sit)* C(D); *(qui) ve(nit)* FF~ED; *(O)san(na)* G; *(ex)cel(sis)* EF(E). **Rc 1741** [1] *rec(tor)* DED; [2] *(ip)si(us)* FGF; *(Sanctus domi)nus* E; [3] *(de)ter(gis)* CDEF; *et* F(E); *(ex)cel(sis)* EF(E); [4] *fa(mulis)* FE; *(tur)ba* DEFEDC; *(promp)sit* DED; *(qui) ve(nit)* FF~ED; *(O)san(na)* G; *(ex)cel(sis)* EF(E).

Example 3. Sanctus *Mundi fabricator* from Mah 289

lxxv

Sanctus 6

THANNABAUR 74

TROPE: *Admirabilis splendor*

SOURCES
Rn 1343 fol. 15r
Rc 1741 fols. 38r–39r
Bu 2824 fol. 97r–v

REFERENCES
CT 7 (no. 1), 67–68; Pfaff, *Die Tropen,* 93; Planchart, *Repertory,* 1:277–79, 2:316–17.

TEXT COMMENTARY
Prose trope; vv. [1–3] are constructed according to a Trinitarian principle.

TEXT AND TRANSLATION

Sanctus
[1] Ammirabilis splendor inmarcessibilisque lux pater deus
S<an>c<tu>s
[2] Verbum quod erat in principio apud deum
S<an>c<tu>s
[3] Paraclitus sanctusque spiritus
Dominus deus sabaoth
Pleni sunt cæli et terra gloria tua
Osanna in excelsis
[4] Cui omne flectitur genu et omnis lingua proclamat dicens
Benedictus qui venit in nomine domini
Osanna in excelsis

*

Holy
[1] Wonderful Brilliance and unapproachable Light, God the Father
Holy
[2] Word, which was in the beginning with God,
Holy
[3] Paraclite and Holy Spirit,
Lord, God of Hosts.
Heaven and earth are filled with Your Glory.
Hosanna in the highest.
[4] To whom every knee is bent
and every tongue cries out, saying:
Blessed is He who comes
in the name of the Lord.
Hosanna in the highest.

DISTINCTIVE VARIANTS
Rc 1741 [1] *inaccessibilisque* for *inmarcessibilisque*. Sanctus 6 is copied in a different hand than the main corpus in Bu 2824.

V. [1] exists in two slightly different versions in Italian sources: *splendor inmarcessibilisque* (Rn 1343, Bu 2824, Rv 52, MOd 7, PS 121, PAc 47, Bu 7) and *splendor inaccessibilisque* (Rc 1741), which is the version in APT 17, as well as the Aquitanian and Winchester tropers. The variant, *splendor inestimabilisque,* preserved in Pn 9449, Mah 289 and 288, was not transmitted to Italy. Northern and central Italian sources preserve three different arrangements of cues to v. [3], a line which is lacking in PAc 47 (see Planchart, *Repertory,* 2:316–17). The version of v. [3] found in Rv 52 is closest to that which circulated in Aquitaine.

MELODIC VARIANTS
Rc 1741 [1] *in(accessibi)lis(que)* GD' . . . dcb; [3] *(san)ctus(que)* ED ED D(C); *cae(li)* baG; *(Osan)na* aG cbaa~g; [4] *(O)san(na)* cb(a). **Bu 2824** *(inmar)cessibilis* abc'c'bc'dcb; [3] *cae(li)* baG; *(O)san(na)* cb; [4] *(O)san(na)* cb(a).

Sanctus 7

THANNABAUR 63

TROPE: *Quem cherubim*

SOURCES
Rn 1343 fols. 15v–16r
Rc 1741 fol. 39r–v
Bu 2824 fol. 105r–v

REFERENCES
CT 7 (no. 118), 165–66; Pfaff, *Die Tropen,* 93.

TEXT COMMENTARY
Prose trope with rhyme (vv. [1–2] and [4–5]). The first three lines lack the Trinitarian program observed in other Sanctus tropes, but v. [3] contains a doxology. V. [1] is apparently drawn from the Te Deum: "Tibi Cherubim et Seraphim incessabili voce proclamant." Vv. [4–5] are reminiscent of the Palm Sunday processional antiphons *Pueri hebraeorum tollentes* and *Cum audisset populus.*

TEXT AND TRANSLATION

Sanctus
[1] Quem cherubim atque seraphim incessanter proclamant
Sanctus
[2] Qui senas alas habent quotidie decantant
Sanctus Dominus deus sabaoth
[3] Patri prolique flamminique almo
qui est ante secula nunc et in evum
Pleni sunt cæli et terra gloria tua
Osanna in excelsis
[4] Cui pueri hebreorum obviantes clamabant
Benedictus qui venit in nomine domini

lxxvi

[5] Et ple[b]s hebrea vociferantes vaticinantes dicebant
Osanna in excelsis

*

Holy,
[1] Whom the cherubim and seraphim unceasingly proclaim
Holy,
[2] They who have six wings each sing daily:
Holy Lord, God of Hosts.
[3] In the Father and the Son and the Holy Spirit, who (was) before time, is now and into eternity.
Heaven and earth
are filled with Your Glory.
Hosanna in the highest.
[4] To whom the children of the Hebrews, coming to meet (Him), cried out:
Blessed is He who comes
in the name of the Lord.
[5] And the shouting, prophesying Hebrew multitude affirmed:
Hosanna in the highest.

DISTINCTIVE VARIANTS

Italian sources yield three slightly different readings for the beginning of v. [3]: *Patri prolique flamminique* (Nonantolan MSS, Rvat 602); *Pater prolique flamineo* (Rv 52, MOd 7, Bu 7, BV 34); and *Pater proles cum flamineo* (PS 121). It is lacking in Tn 18. In MOd 7, the same verse is divided between successive phrases of the Sanctus: "Pater prolique flamineo almo PLENI SUNT CAELI ET TERRA GLORIA TUA Qui es ante secula nunc et in evum OSANNA IN EXCELSIS."

The remaining text variants in the Italian versions of the trope either involve word transposition (Tn 18, v. [2] reads *habentalas*; Rv 52, v. [5] reads *vaticinantes vociferantes*) or other minor variants (Tn 18, v. [5] reads *vociferantes obviantes dicebant*).

MELODIC VARIANTS

Rc 1741 [2] *(quotidi)e* cb; [3] *(glo)ri(a)* a; [4] *(nomi)ne* cb. **Bu 2824** [2] *(cotidi)e* cb; *(de)can(tant)* abaG; *(sa)ba(oth)* aG; [3] *(glo)ri(a)* a; [4] *(nomi)ne* cb.

Sanctus 8

THANNABAUR 60

SOURCES
Rn 1343 fol. 15r
Rc 1741 fols. 39v–40r
Bu 2824 fol. 11v

TEXT AND TRANSLATION

Sanctus S<an>c<tu>s S<an>c<tu>s Dominus deus sabaoth
Pleni sunt cæli et terra gloria tua
Osanna in excelsis
Benedictus qui venit in nomine domini
Osanna in excelsis

*

Holy, Holy, Holy Lord, God of Hosts.
Heaven and earth are filled with your glory.
Hosanna in the highest.
Blessed is He who comes in the name of the Lord.
Hosanna in the highest.

MELODIC VARIANTS
Rc 1741 *(de)us* a; *(tu)a* GFGabaG; *(O)san(na)1* cc. **Bu 2824** *(tu)a* GFGabaG; *(O)san(na)* cc; *in (nomine)* b.

Sanctus 9

THANNABAUR 111 (VAR.)
SOURCES
Rn 1343 fol. 15v
Rc 1741 fol. 40r–v

TEXT AND TRANSLATION

Sanctus Sanctus Sanctus dominus deus sabaoth
Pleni sunt cęli et terra gloria tua
Osanna in excelsis
Benedictus qui venit in nomine domini
Osanna in excelsis

*

Holy, Holy, Holy Lord, God of Hosts.
Heaven and earth are filled with your glory.
Hosanna in the highest.
Blessed is He who comes in the name of the Lord.
Hosanna in the highest.

DISTINCTIVE VARIANTS
The opening of the Rn 1343 reading through "*gloria tua*" is notated a tone higher than Rc 1741 and most other sources of this melody.

MELODIC VARIANTS
Rn 1343 (N.B. pitch level corrected) *sunt* aba; *Benedic(tus)* C'DE'Ga; *qui ve(nit)* Ga'GF; *do(mini)* aba.

Sanctus 10

THANNABAUR 9
SOURCE
Rn 1343 fol. 15v

TEXT AND TRANSLATION
See Sanctus 8.

Sanctus 11

THANNABAUR 10

SOURCES
Rn 1343 fol. 15v
Rc 1741 fol. 40v
Bu 2824 fols. 11v–12r

TEXT AND TRANSLATION
See Sanctus 8.

MELODIC VARIANTS
Rc 1741 *(Sanc)tus* DEFE'FEDCC~ . . . ; *Pleni* CE'E.

Sanctus 12

THANNABAUR 32; VATICAN XVII

SOURCES
Rn 1343 fol. 16r
Rc 1741 fols. 40v–41r
Bu 2824 fol. 12r–v

TEXT AND TRANSLATION
See Sanctus 8.

MELODIC VARIANTS
Rc 1741 *de(us)* Ga; *et* CD; *tu(a)* Gaa~G; *(Osan)na1* EFGFD; *(do)mi(ni)* G; *(Osan)na2* EFGFD; *excelsis* DE'D'C. **Bu 2824** *et* CED; *tu(a)* Gaa~G; *(Osan)na1* EFGFED.

Sanctus 13a

THANNABAUR 57
SOURCE
Rc 1741 fol. 41r–v

TEXT AND TRANSLATION
See Sanctus 8.

Sanctus 13b

THANNABAUR 57
SOURCE
Bu 2824 fol. 102r

TEXT AND TRANSLATION
See Sanctus 8.

Agnus Dei 1

SCHILDBACH 226; VATICAN II
TROPE: *Qui sedes ad dexteram patris*
SOURCES
Rn 1343 fol. 16r
Rc 1741 fol. 41v
Bu 2824 fols. 12v–13r

REFERENCES
Atkinson, "The Earliest Agnus Dei Melody," 12–19; Atkinson, "The Earliest Settings," 83–104; *CT* 4 (no. 63), 220, 222, 229–40; Gautier, *Les Tropes*, 164; Pfaff, *Die Tropen*, 94; Planchart, *Repertory*, 1:283–85, 287, 291, 2:326–35.

TEXT COMMENTARY
In prose; the three elements (which have no inherent relationship to one another) comprise a series of appositives reminiscent of the Gloria in excelsis. Some expressions are direct borrowings (*Qui sedes ad deteram patris*), others merely allude to the Ordinary text (*rex, lux, pax*).

TEXT AND TRANSLATION

Agnus dei
qui tollis peccata mundi
Miserere nobis
[1] Qui sedes ad dexteram patris solus invisibilis rex
Mise[rere nobis]
[2] Rex regum gaudium angelorum deus
Misere[re nobis]
[3] Lux indeficiens pax perpetua hominumque redemptio eia
Dona [nobis pacem]
*
Lamb of God,
You who take away the sins of the world,
have mercy on us.
[1] You who sit at the right hand of the Father, sole unseen King,
have mercy on us.
[2] King of kings, delight of the angels, God,
have mercy on us.
[3] Unfailing Light, universal Peace and Redemption of men, ah,
grant us peace.

DISTINCTIVE VARIANTS
Bu 2824 [3] *redemptio christe eia Misere<re nobis>* for *redemptio eia Dona [nobis pacem]*. The order of lines given here is by far the most common arrangement. In v. [3], VEcap 107 and other northern Italian manuscripts preserve the variant, *omniumque redemptio*.

MELODIC VARIANTS
Rc 1741 [1] *(se)des* EFGF FDF; *dexteram* F'FE'DE(D); [2] *an(gelorum)* G. **Bu 2824** [3] *(redemptio) christe* without neumes.

Agnus Dei 2

SCHILDBACH 78
TROPE: *Omnipotens aeterna Dei*

SOURCES
Rn 1343 fol. 16r–v
Rc 1741 fol. 42r

REFERENCES
AH 47, no. 385; Atkinson, "The Earliest Settings," 196–201; *CT* 4 (no. 41), 220, 222; Pfaff, *Die Tropen*, 94; Planchart, *Repertory*, 1:283–87, 290, 2:336–38.

TEXT COMMENTARY
Hexameters. Appositives referring to Christ. V. [2] was drawn from the Credo text, "lumen de lumine."

TEXT AND TRANSLATION
Agnus dei
qui tollis peccata mundi
Miserere nobis
[1] Omnipotens æterna dei sapientia christe
[M]isere[re nobis]
[2] Verum subsistens vero de lumine lumen
Mise[rere nobis]
[3] [O]ptima perpetue concedens gaudia vitæ
Dona [nobis pacem]

*

Lamb of God,
You who take away the sins of the world,
have mercy on us.
[1] All powerful, eternal wisdom of God, Christ,
have mercy on us.
[2] Remaining true, Light from true light,
have mercy on us.
[3] Granting the greatest joys of perpetual life,
grant us peace.

DISTINCTIVE VARIANTS
Rc 1741 [3] *perpetuę* for *perpetue*. Nonantolan MSS and the other Italian and French sources of *Omnipotens aeterna Dei* lack the Aquitanian variant in v. [1] *aeterne* for *aeterna*. The reading of v. [3] in VEcap 107 differs slightly from most other Italian ones in that it preserves the variant *perpetua*, also found in Aquitanian readings.

MELODIC VARIANTS
Rc 1741 *(pec)ca(ta)* ed edc cba; [1] *(eterna) de(i)* dc.

Agnus Dei 3

SCHILDBACH 209 (VAR. 2)
TROPE: *Tu Deus et dominus*
SOURCES
Rn 1343 fol. 16v
Rc 1741 fol. 42r–v

REFERENCES
AH 47, no. 411; *CT* 4 (no. 74), 220, 260, 262, 264; Pfaff, *Die Tropen*, 95.

TEXT COMMENTARY
Hexameters. V. [1] derives from the second element of the widely disseminated Proper trope, *Terrigenas*, for the Ascension Introit, *Viri Galilaei*. In the Nonantolan tropers, the Introit trope element takes the form: "Sic deus et homo caelorum compos et orbis" (see *CT* 3, 204). Like other Italian Agnus Dei tropes, this one addresses Christ in the second person (*tu*) and employs the vocative, *Christe*.

TEXT AND TRANSLATION
Agnus dei
qui tollis peccata mundi
Miserere nobis
[1] Tu deus et dominus cælorum compos et orbis
christe
Mise[rere nobis]
[2] In sede etherea qui regnas cum patre deus
Dona [nobis pacem]

*

Lamb of God,
You who take away the sins of the world,
have mercy on us.
[1] You, God and Lord, possessing the heavens and
the earth, O Christ,
have mercy on us.
[2] You who reign on the celestial throne with God
the Father,
grant us peace.

DISTINCTIVE VARIANTS
Tu Deus et dominus comes down to us only in two Nonantolan tropers and VEcap 107. The only difference between the texts is found in v. [1], for which VEcap 107 reads: *compos et orbis eia*. The final word here and in Nonantolan MSS, *Christe*, disrupts the meter (see *CT* 4:88).

MELODIC VARIANTS
Rc 1741 [1] *(cę̧lo)rum* E; *chris(te)* FEC EFD; [2] *cum* ED(C).

Agnus Dei 4

SCHILDBACH 236
TROPE: *Suscipe deprecationem . . . Dei patris*
SOURCES
Rn 1343 fol. 16v
Rc 1741 fol. 42v

REFERENCES
CT 4 (no. 72), 220, 253–59, 260; Planchart, *Repertory*, 1:290–91, 2:340–42.

TEXT COMMENTARY
Trope texts are in prose. *Suscipe deprecationem . . . Dei patris* is apparently an adaptation of Agnus Dei

no. 7, whose text and melody stem from the litany and/or the Gloria in excelsis.

TEXT AND TRANSLATION

Agnus dei
qui tollis peccata mundi
Miserere nobis
[1]   Suscipe deprecationem nostram filius dei patris
Mise[rere nobis]
[2]   Qui sedes ad dexteram patris
Dona [nobis pacem]

*

Lamb of God,
You who take away the sins of the world,
have mercy on us.
[1]   Receive our prayer, Son of God the Father,
have mercy on us.
[2]   You who sit at the right hand of the Father,
grant us peace.

DISTINCTIVE VARIANTS

This form of the trope survives only in the three Nonantolan tropers and VEcap 107. The Nonantolan text of v. [1] differs slightly from that found in VEcap 107: "nostram in filius dei patris." Moreover, v. [2] is cued in VEcap 107 to *Miserere nobis*, rather than to *Dona nobis pacem*.

Suscipe deprecationem . . . Dei patris is probably a local adaptation of the more widely transmitted Agnus Dei 7, *Suscipe deprecationem . . . Dei patris*, which is associated with Schildbach 164 rather than 236. The former trope melody is considerably more elaborate than the tonus-like setting of *Suscipe deprecationem . . . Dei patris*.

MELODIC VARIANTS

Rc 1741 *tol(lis)* Ga(G); *no(bis)* GF; [1] *de(i)* GG~F; [2] *(dex)te(ram)* FE.

Agnus Dei 5

SCHILDBACH 236 (VAR. 3)

TROPE: *Ad dextram patris*

SOURCES
Rn 1343 fol. 16v
Rc 1741 fol. 43r
Bu 2824 fol. 13v

REFERENCES
AH 47, no. 430; CT 4 (no. 1), 220, 222, 260–61, 263–4; Pfaff, *Die Tropen*, 94.

TEXT COMMENTARY

Trope texts are in prose, with rough symmetry among the three elements and *-e* assonance. Like other Italian Agnus Dei tropes, this one refers to Christ in the second person and often employs the vocative (*alme, pastor, bone, sancte, benigne*). Iversen remarks that the prayer-like tone of v. [3] is typically Italian.

TEXT AND TRANSLATION

Agnus dei
Qui tollis peccata mundi
Miserere nobis
[1]   Ad dextram patris resides qui semper salva et parce tuis alme
Qui tol<lis> [peccata mundi
miserere nobis]
[2]   Quos tuo sancto redemisti cruore absque labe custodi pastor bone
Qui tol<lis> [peccata mundi
miserere nobis]
[3]   Ut te ducente possimus venire ad te sancte cuncti benigne
Qui tollis [peccata mundi
dona nobis pacem]

*

Lamb of God,
You who take away the sins of the world,
have mercy on us.
[1]   You who forever sit at the right hand of the Father, generously save and spare
your people,
You who take away the sins of the world,
have mercy on us.
[2]   Those whom you have redeemed with your holy blood, keep without blemish,
O good shepherd,
You who take away the sins of the world,
have mercy on us.
[3]   That with you leading we may come to You, O holy, all-benevolent one,
You who take away the sins of the world,
grant us peace.

DISTINCTIVE VARIANTS

Bu 2824 [1] *residens* for *resides*; v. [3] lacking. The many sources of this Italian trope yield a variety of lines and organizations, along with many minor text variants. The most significant differences between Nonantolan readings and related versions occur in v. [3], for which Ra 123, Tn 17, PS 697, and PAc 20 all read *venire ad te pater*; VEcap 107: *patrem*. The reference to God the Father (*Pater*) seems out of place among lines referring exclusively to Christ. Following this logic, it is probably a substitute for the vocative "sancte," leading one to suspect that the Nonantolan version is closer to the presumed original than the tropes with "pater."

MELODIC VARIANTS

Rn 1344 *(Mise)re(re)* EFEDD~; *no(bis)* DEDD~C; [1] *resides qui semper* D'EF'D'ED'C'C; *par(ce)* FED~; [2] *tu(o)* E; [3] *san(cte)* EFEDD(C). **Bu 2824** *(mise)re(re)* EFEDD~; *no(bis)* DEDD~C; [2] *tu(o)* E.

Agnus Dei 6

SCHILDBACH 87

TROPE: *Exaudi domine*

SOURCES
Rn 1343 fol. 17r
Rc 1741 fol. 43v
Bu 2824 fol. 13r–v

REFERENCES
AH 47, no. 432; CT 4 (no. 23), 220, 222, 260, 262; Pfaff, *Die Tropen*, 94.

TEXT COMMENTARY

In prose; with rough symmetry among the three elements, but without assonance.

TEXT AND TRANSLATION

    Agnus dei
    qui tollis peccata mundi
    Miserere nobis
[1] Exaudi domine rex cælorum populorum genitus
    Qui tollis [peccata mundi
    Miserere nobis]
[2] Tuam domine deprecamur supplices clemenciam
    Qui tol[lis peccata mundi
    Miserere nobis]
[3] Largitor pacis pacem perpetuam tribue nobis
    Qui tollis [peccata mundi
    Dona nobis pacem]
    *
    Lamb of God,
    You who take away the sins of the world,
    have mercy on us.
[1] Hear, O Lord, King of the heavens, the lamentations of your people,
    You who take away the sins of the world,
    have mercy on us.
[2] We suppliants plead, O Lord, for your clemency,
    You who take away the sins of the world,
    have mercy on us.
[3] Imparter of peace, grant us perpetual peace,
    You who take away the sins of the world,
    grant us peace.

DISTINCTIVE VARIANTS

Besides the Nonantolan tropers, *Exaudi domine* survives in only three other Italian MSS: MOd 7, PAc 47, and VCd 162. Only the version found in the first of these observes the order and number of lines in the Nonantolan trope. This does not necessarily mean, however, that there was a direct relationship between MOd 7 and the Nonantolan MSS, since only the latter have the cue "Qui tollis." The trope elements in MOd 7 and PAc 47 precede the invocation "Agnus dei"; in VCd 162, the cue is "Miserere nobis." The melodic variants in MOd 7, particularly for v. [3], give the impression that it was closer to the readings in PAc 47 and VCd 162 than to those in the Nonantolan tropers (see example 4).

MELODIC VARIANTS

Rc 1741 *tol(lis)* cdedcd; [2] *(suppli)ces* cb; *(tribu)e* cb; *(no)bis* abcdcb abcG.

Agnus Dei 7

SCHILDBACH 164; VATICAN XVI

TROPE: *Suscipe deprecationem . . . Dei*

SOURCES
Rn 1343 fol. 17r
Rc 1741 fols. 43v–44r
Bu 2824 fol. 14r

REFERENCES
CT 4 (no. 62), 223, 253–59, 260; Planchart, *Repertory*, 1:290–91, 2:340–42.

TEXT COMMENTARY

Trope texts are in prose. The use of a simple recitation tone in the musical setting led Planchart to conclude that the trope derives from the litany rather than the Gloria in excelsis.

TEXT AND TRANSLATION

    Agnus dei
    qui tollis peccata mundi
    Miserere nobis
[1] Suscipe deprecationem nostram filius dei
    Agnus dei
    [qui tollis peccata mundi
    Miserere nobis]
[2] Qui sedes ad dexteram patris miserere nobis
    [Agnus dei
    qui tollis peccata mundi
    Dona nobis pacem]
    *
    Lamb of God,
    You who take away the sins of the world,
    have mercy on us.
[1] Receive our prayer, Son of God,
    Lamb of God, You who take away the sins of the world,
    have mercy on us.

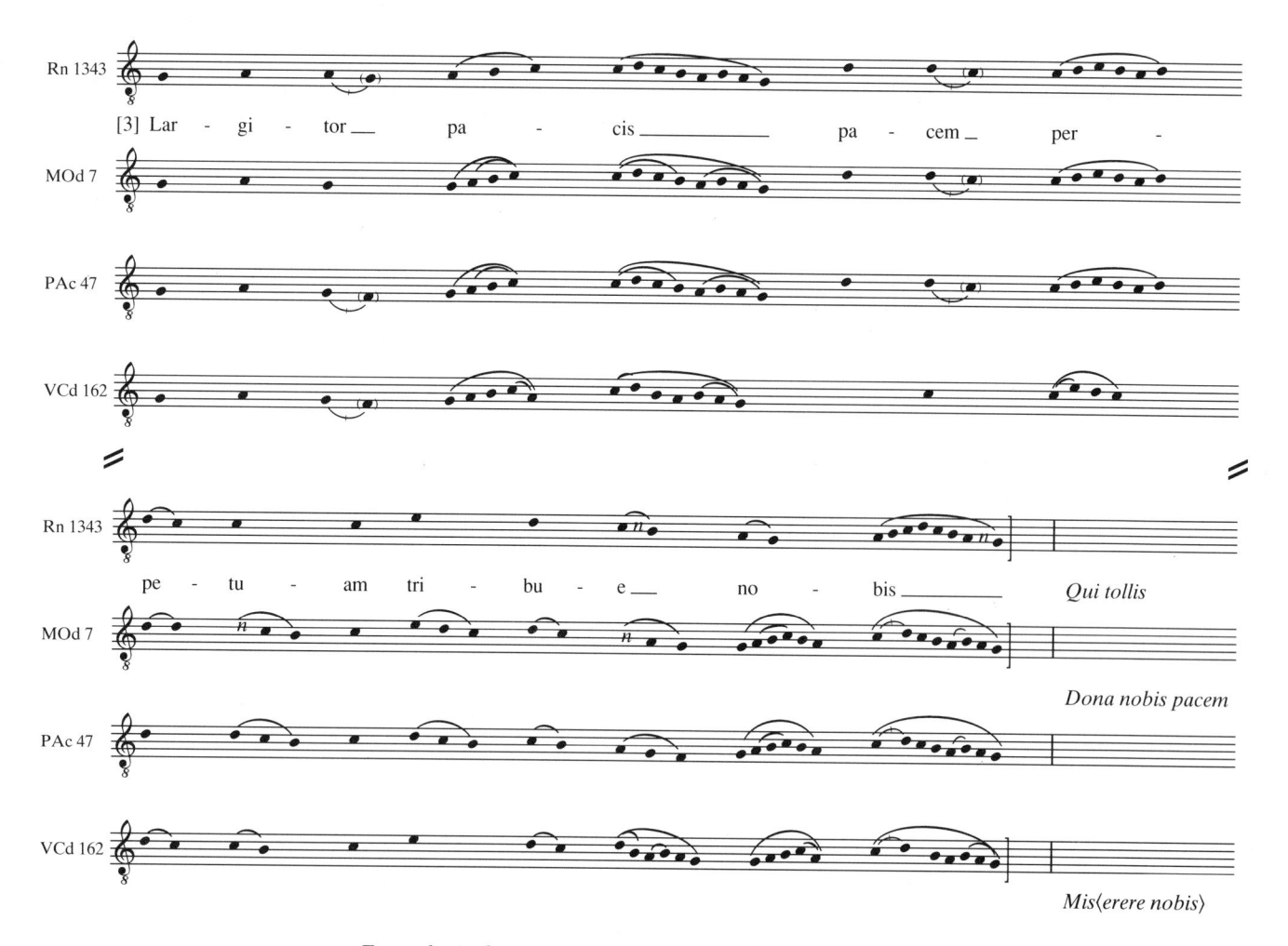

Example 4. Comparison of Sanctus *Exaudi domine* v. [3]

[2] You who sit at the right hand of the Father, pray for us,
    Lamb of God, You who take away the sins of the world,
        grant us peace.

Distinctive Variants

The three Nonantolan tropers preserve a unique form of this trope. Because the elements are cued to the beginning of the Ordinary text, as opposed to "Miserere nobis," Iversen proposed a separate category of structure for this and a few other Italian Agnus Dei tropes. Perhaps this form evolved from the single line introduction, "Qui sedes ad dexteram patris," which is found in numerous sources inside and outside Italy, including East Frankish ones copied before 1050.

The version of v. [1] known in Nonantola was shorter than those sung at other centers. *CT 4* lists only a single text variant of no relevance to transmission.

Melodic Variant
Rc 1741 *mun(di)* GG~.

Agnus Dei 8

Schildbach 19
Agnus Dei . . . miserere nobis alleluia alleluia

Sources
Rn 1343 fol. 17r
Rc 1741 fol. 44v
Bu 2824 fol. 14r

Reference
CT 4 (no. 7), 260.

Text and Translation

Agnus dei
qui tollis peccata mundi
Miserere nobis
alleluia alleluia

*

Lamb of God,
You who take away the sins of the world,
have mercy on us,
alleluia, alleluia.

DISTINCTIVE VARIANTS
Rn 1343 *mundi Agnus miserere* for *mundi Miserere nobis*.

MELODIC VARIANTS
Rn 1343 (*mundi*) *Agnus* (*miserere*) bd'c. **Rc 1741** (*pecca*)*ta* cdcc~b; *al*(*leluia*)*2* e(d).

Agnus Dei 9

SCHILDBACH 81
TROPE: *Salus et vita*
SOURCES
Rn 1343 fol. 17r–v
Rc 1741 fol. 44r–v
Bu 2824 fol. 100r–v

REFERENCES
AH 47, no. 431; CT 4 (no. 66), 220, 222, 260, 265; Gautier, *Les Tropes*, 164; Pfaff, *Die Tropen*, 94.

TEXT COMMENTARY
Accentual meter whose model is apparently the rhythmic Adonic (5p + 5p). V. [1] is a series of appositives, while in v. [2] the suppliants beg Christ to hear their prayers.

TEXT AND TRANSLATION

>   Agnus dei
>   qui tollis peccata mundi
>   miserere nobis

[1] Salus et vita
pax perpetua
lux indeficiens
amator bonus
>   Agnus [dei
>   qui tollis peccata mundi
>   Miserere nobis]

[2] Supplicum preces
benigne exaudi
atque tuis miserere
famulis
>   Dona [nobis pacem]

*

>   Lamb of God,
>   You who take away the sins of the world,
>   have mercy on us.

[1] Salvation and Life, universal Peace, unfailing Light, good Friend,
>   Lamb of God,
>   You who take away the sins of the world,
>   have mercy on us.

[2] Hear, O generous One, the prayers of your suppliants, and have mercy on your servants,
>   Grant us peace.

DISTINCTIVE VARIANTS
Rc 1741 [1] cued to *Mise*[*rere nobis*]; **Rn 1343** [2] cue *Dona* [*nobis pacem*] lacking. The two-element form of the Italian trope *Salus et vita* survives in five Italian manuscripts: the three Nonantolan tropers, MOd 7, and BV 34 (in which it was copied twice). The other versions of the trope comprise three elements. Only Rc 1741 and Bu 2824 cue v. [2] to *Dona* <*nobis pacem*>; the others indicate *Agnus* <*dei*>. The second cue is lacking in Rn 1343.

MELODIC VARIANTS
Rn 1343 *mun*(*di*) abaGFab(a); [1] *per*(*petua*) cdd~cb; [2] (*be*)*nig*(*ne*) cdd~cb.

Agnus Dei 10

SCHILDBACH 209 (VAR. 2)
SOURCES
Rn 1343 fol. 17v
Rc 1741 fol. 44v
Bu 2824 fol. 14r

TEXT AND TRANSLATION

>   Agnus dei
>   qui tollis peccata mundi
>   miserere nobis
>   [Agnus dei
>   qui tollis peccata mundi
>   miserere nobis
>   Agnus dei
>   qui tollis peccata mundi
>   dona nobis pacem]

*

>   Lamb of God,
>   You who take away the sins of the world,
>   have mercy on us.
>   Lamb of God,
>   You who take away the sins of the world,
>   have mercy on us.
>   Lamb of God,
>   You who take away the sins of the world,
>   grant us peace.

MELODIC VARIANTS
None.

Plate 1. Bologna, Biblioteca Universitaria, MS 2824, fols. 12v–13r, including Sanctus no. 12 and Agnus Dei 1 and 6.

Plate 2. Rome, Biblioteca Nazionale, MS 1343 (*olim* Sessoriano 62), fols. 15v–16r, including Sanctus nos. 9, 10, 11, 12, 7 (fol. 16r) and Agnus Dei 1.

Kyrie eleison 1
Melnicki 55; Vatican *ad lib.* VI
Te Christe rex supplices

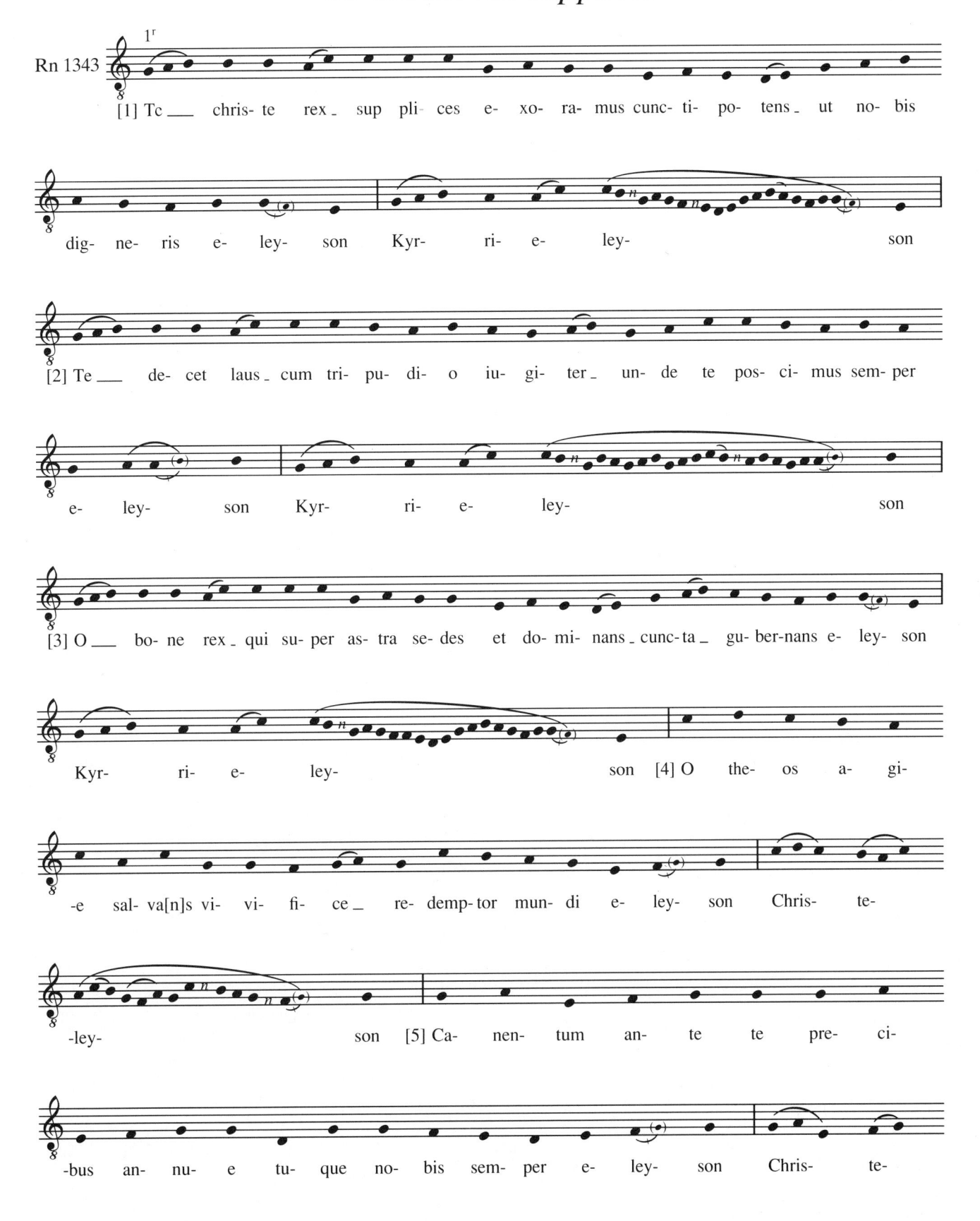

Rn 1343

[1] Te christe rex supplices exoramus cunctipotens ut nobis digneris eleyson Kyrrie eleyson

[2] Te decet laus cum tripudio iugiter unde te poscimus semper eleyson Kyrrie eleyson

[3] O bone rex qui super astra sedes et dominans cuncta gubernans eleyson Kyrrie eleyson

[4] O theos agie salva[n]s vivifice redemptor mundi eleyson Christeleyson

[5] Canentum ante te precibus annue tuque nobis semper eleyson Christe-

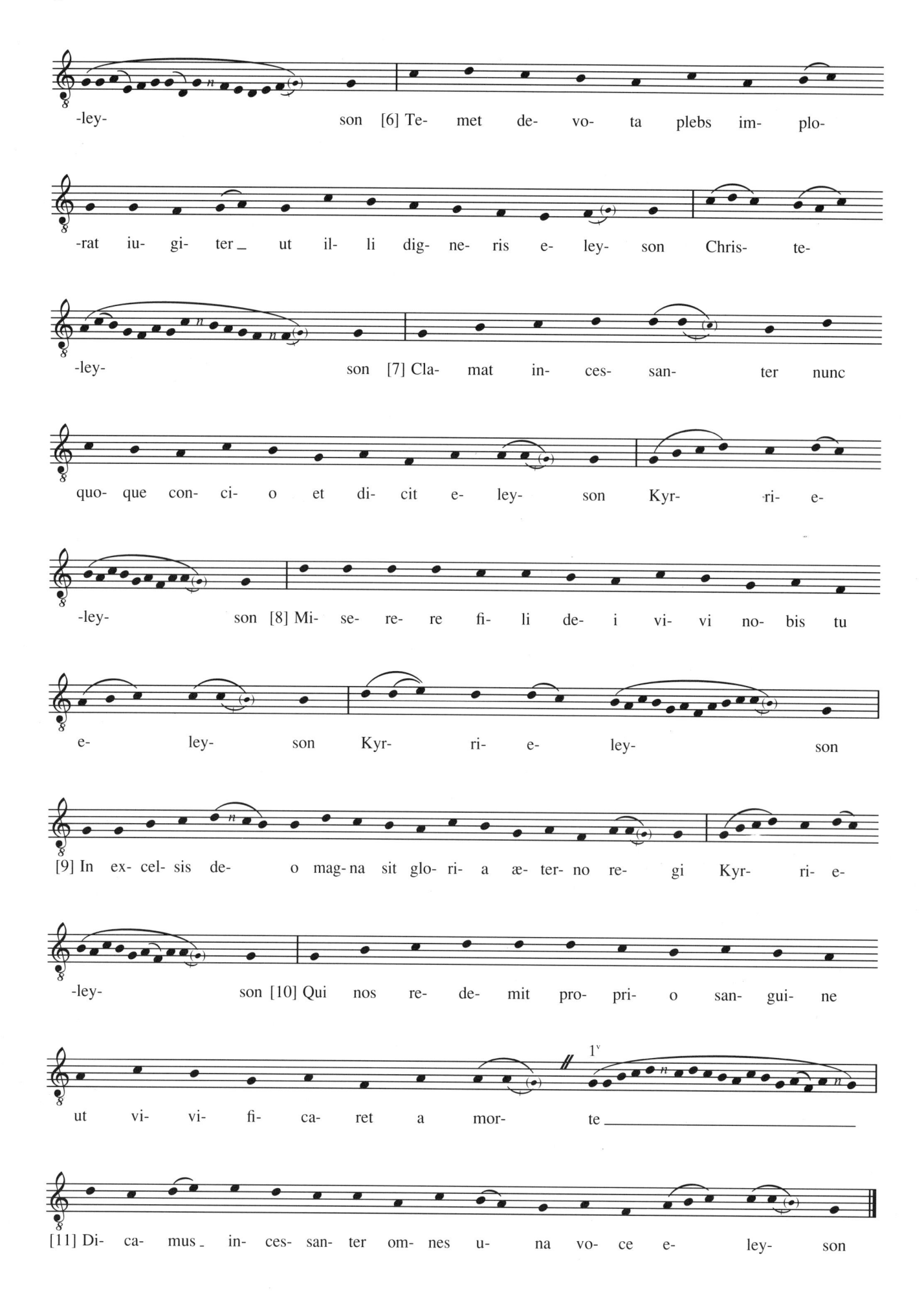

-ley- son [6] Te- met de- vo- ta plebs im- plo- -rat iu- gi- ter ut il- li dig- ne- ris e- ley- son Chris- te- -ley- son [7] Cla- mat in- ces- san- ter nunc quo- que con- ci- o et di- cit e- ley- son Kyr- ri- e- -ley- son [8] Mi- se- re- re fi- li de- i vi- vi no- bis tu e- ley- son Kyr- ri- e- ley- son [9] In ex- cel- sis de- o mag- na sit glo- ri- a æ- ter- no re- gi Kyr- ri- e- -ley- son [10] Qui nos re- de- mit pro- pri- o san- gui- ne ut vi- vi- fi- ca- ret a mor- te [11] Di- ca- mus in- ces- san- ter om- nes u- na vo- ce e- ley- son

Kyrie eleison 2
Melnicki 39; Vatican I
Omnipotens genitor

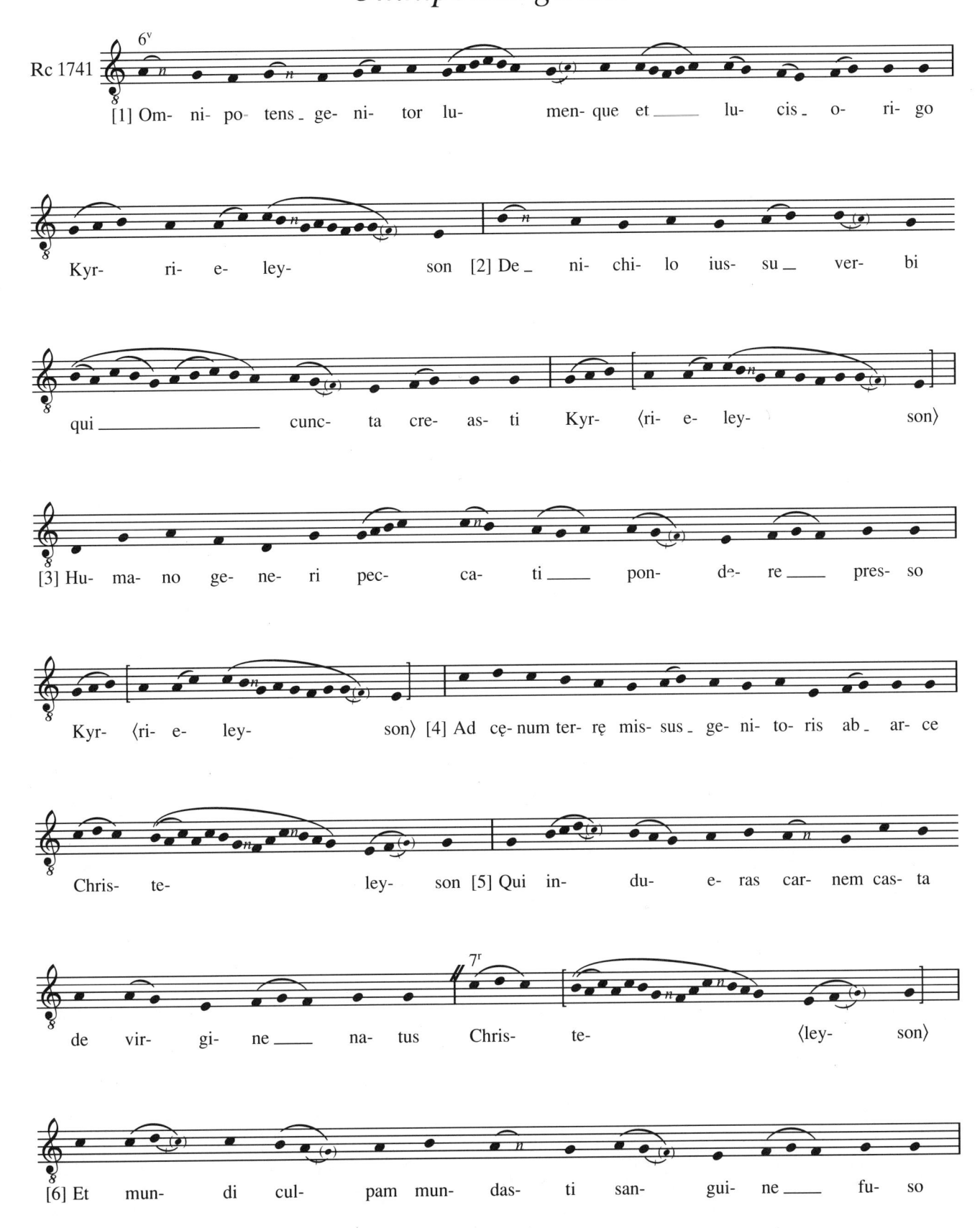

[1] Omnipotens genitor lumenque et lucis origo Kyrrieleyson [2] De nichilo iussu verbi qui cuncta creasti Kyr⟨rieleyson⟩ [3] Humano generi peccati pondere presso Kyr⟨rieleyson⟩ [4] Ad cęnum terrę missus genitoris ab arce Christeleyson [5] Qui indueras carnem casta de virgine natus Christe⟨leyson⟩ [6] Et mundi culpam mundasti sanguine fuso

Chris- te- ⟨ley- son⟩ [7] Ae- qua- lis pa- tri se- u na- to spi- ri- tus al- me Kyr- ri- -e- ley- son [8] Om- ni- a con- for- mans il- li si- mul at- que gu- ber- nans Kyr- ⟨ri- e- ley- son⟩ [9] Tri- nus per- so- nis de- us ma- ies- ta- te sed u- nus Kyr- ri- e- ley- son

Kyrie eleison 3
Melnicki 68; Vatican XIV
Canamus cuncti laudes

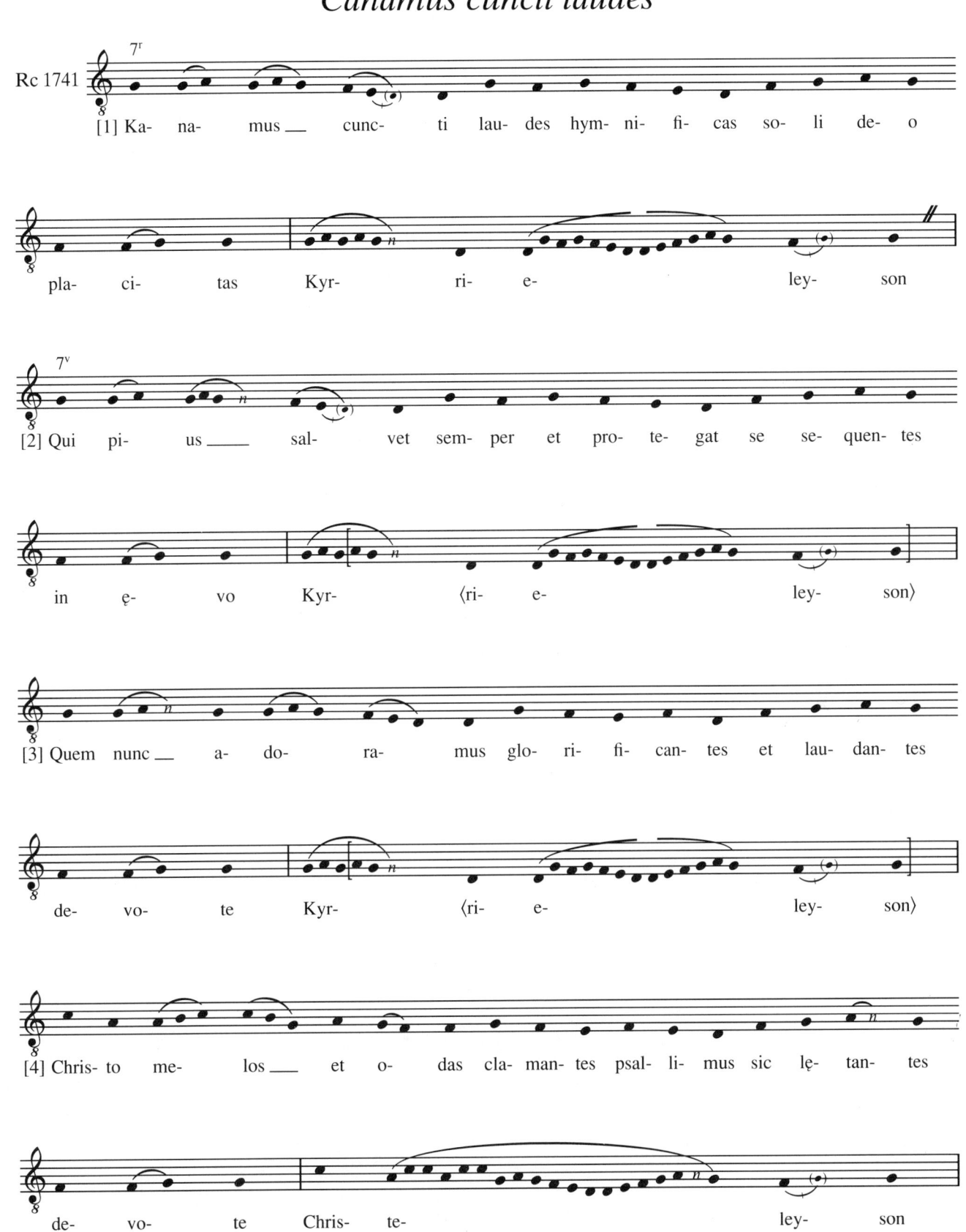

Rc 1741

[1] Ka- na- mus cunc- ti lau- des hym- ni- fi- cas so- li de- o pla- ci- tas Kyr- ri- e- ley- son

[2] Qui pi- us sal- vet sem- per et pro- te- gat se se- quen- tes in ę- vo Kyr- ⟨ri- e- ley- son⟩

[3] Quem nunc a- do- ra- mus glo- ri- fi- can- tes et lau- dan- tes de- vo- te Kyr- ⟨ri- e- ley- son⟩

[4] Chris- to me- los et o- das cla- man- tes psal- li- mus sic lę- tan- tes de- vo- te Chris- te- ley- son

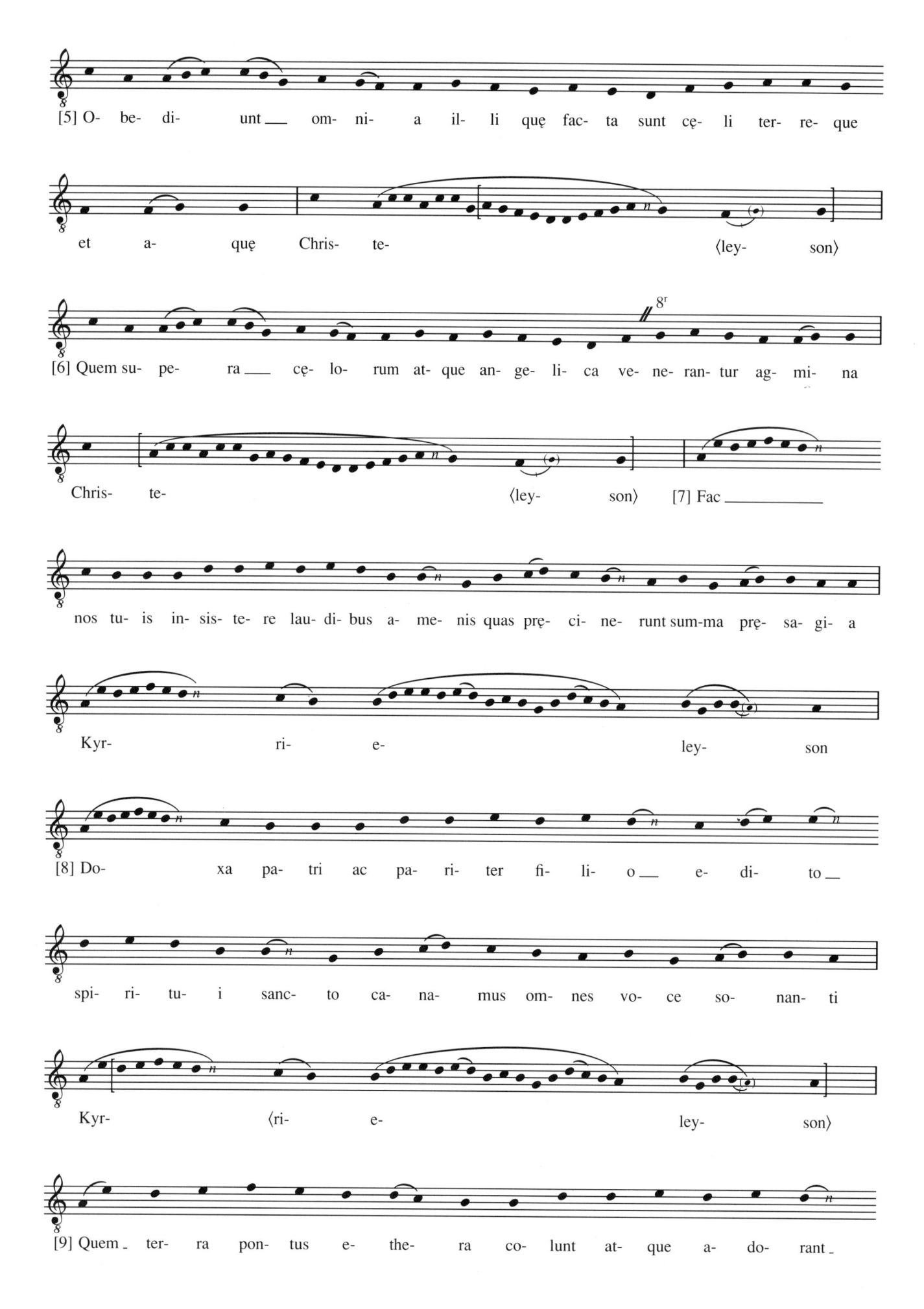

[5] O- be- di- unt omni- a il- li quę fac- ta sunt cę- li ter- re- que et a- quę Chris- te- ⟨ley- son⟩

[6] Quem su- pe- ra cę- lo- rum at- que an- ge- li- ca ve- ne- ran- tur ag- mi- na Chris- te- ⟨ley- son⟩ [7] Fac nos tu- is in- sis- te- re lau- di- bus a- me- nis quas prę- ci- ne- runt sum- ma prę- sa- gi- a Kyr- ri- e- ley- son

[8] Do- xa pa- tri ac pa- ri- ter fi- li- o e- di- to spi- ri- tu- i sanc- to ca- na- mus om- nes vo- ce so- nan- ti Kyr- ⟨ri- e- ley- son⟩

[9] Quem terra pon- tus e- the- ra co- lunt at- que a- do- rant

prę- di- cant re- gen- tem tri- nam iu- ste ma- chi- nam te pre- ca- mur

ut nunc et sem- per e- ley- son y- mas

Kyr- ri- e-

-ley- son y- mas

Kyrie eleison 4
Melnicki 39; Vatican I
Lux et origo lucis

Rn 1343

[1] Lux et o- ri- go lu- cis sum- me de- us e- ley- son Kyr- ri- e-

-ley- son [2] Qui so- lus po- tens mi- se- re- re no- bis e- ley- son

Kyr- r⟨i- e- ley- son⟩ [3] In cui- us nu- tu

con- stat cunc- ta no- bis e- ley- son Kyr- ⟨ri- e- ley- son⟩

[4] Per cru- cem re- demp- tis a mor- te per- hen- ni spes nos- tra chris- te e- ley- son

Chris- te- ley- son [5] O mun-di re-demp-tor

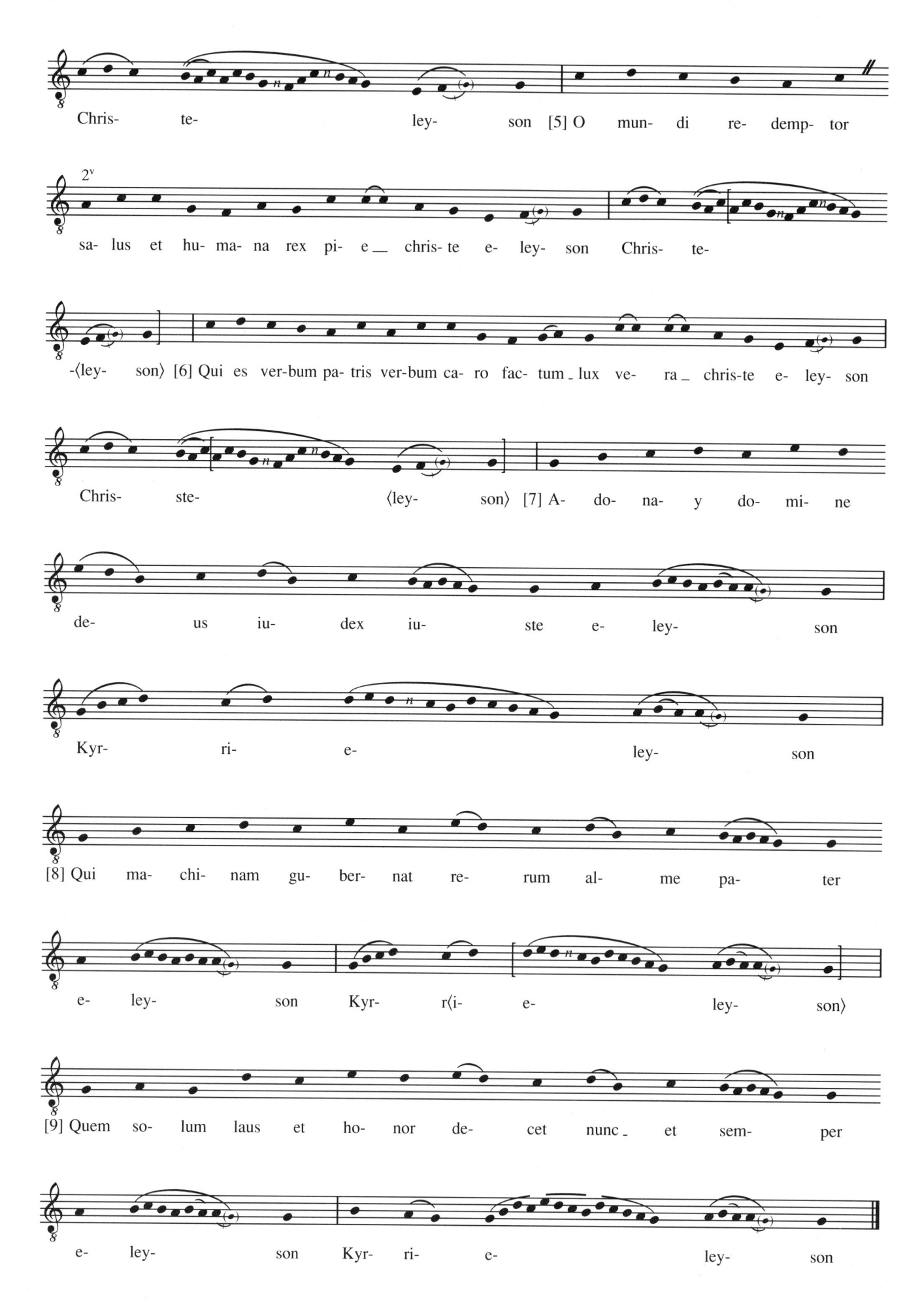

sa- lus et hu- ma- na rex pi- e chris-te e- ley- son Chris- te-

-⟨ley- son⟩ [6] Qui es ver-bum pa- tris ver-bum ca- ro fac- tum lux ve- ra chris-te e- ley- son

Chris- ste- ⟨ley- son⟩ [7] A- do- na- y do- mi- ne

de- us iu- dex iu- ste e- ley- son

Kyr- ri- e- ley- son

[8] Qui ma- chi- nam gu- ber- nat re- rum al- me pa- ter

e- ley- son Kyr- r⟨i- e- ley- son⟩

[9] Quem so- lum laus et ho- nor de- cet nunc et sem- per

e- ley- son Kyr- ri- e- ley- son

Kyrie eleison 5
Melnicki 155; Vatican XV
Dominator Deus

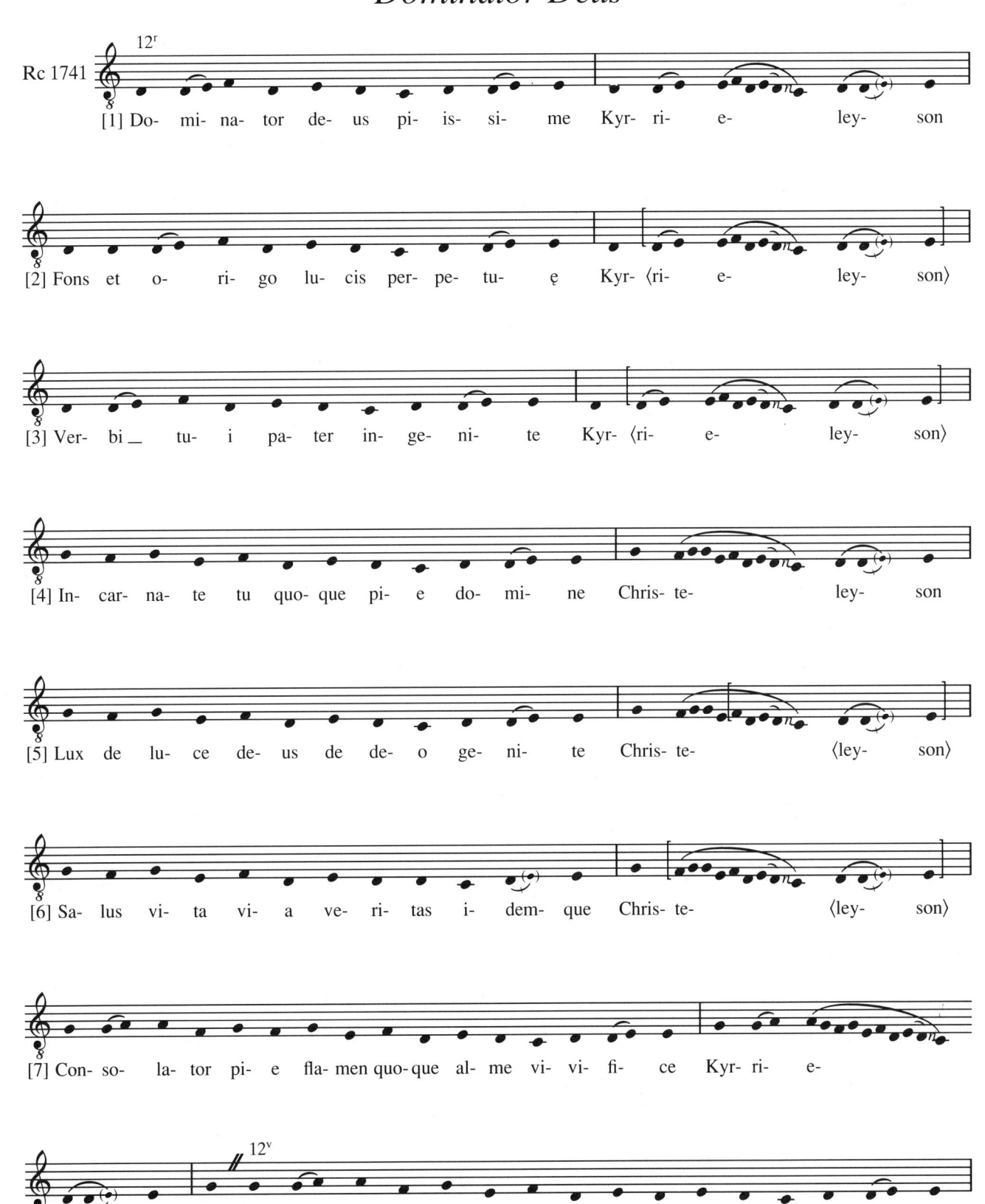

Rc 1741

[1] Do- mi- na- tor de- us pi- is- si- me Kyr- ri- e- ley- son

[2] Fons et o- ri- go lu- cis per- pe- tu- ę Kyr- ⟨ri- e- ley- son⟩

[3] Ver- bi tu- i pa- ter in- ge- ni- te Kyr- ⟨ri- e- ley- son⟩

[4] In- car- na- te tu quo- que pi- e do- mi- ne Chris- te- ley- son

[5] Lux de lu- ce de- us de de- o ge- ni- te Chris- te- ⟨ley- son⟩

[6] Sa- lus vi- ta vi- a ve- ri- tas i- dem- que Chris- te- ⟨ley- son⟩

[7] Con- so- la- tor pi- e fla- men quo- que al- me vi- vi- fi- ce Kyr- ri- e-

-ley- son [8] Pa- tris na- ti- que qui es sum- mus a- mor de- us lu- ci- flu- e

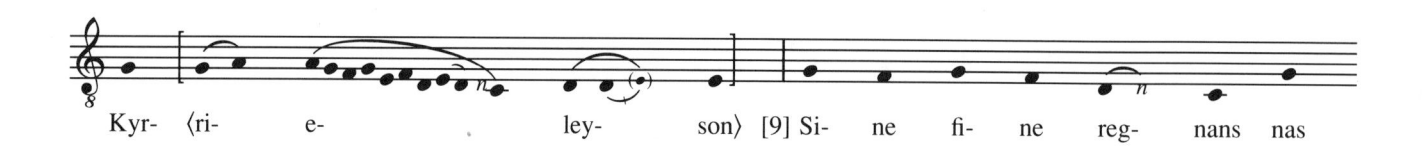

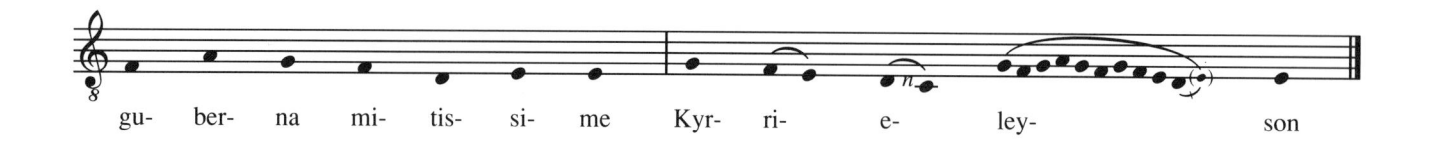

10

Kyr- ⟨ri- e- ley- son⟩ [9] Si- ne fi- ne reg- nans nas-

-gu- ber- na- mi- tis- si- me Kyr- ri- e- ley- son

Kyrie eleison 6
Melnicki 124
Rex magne domine

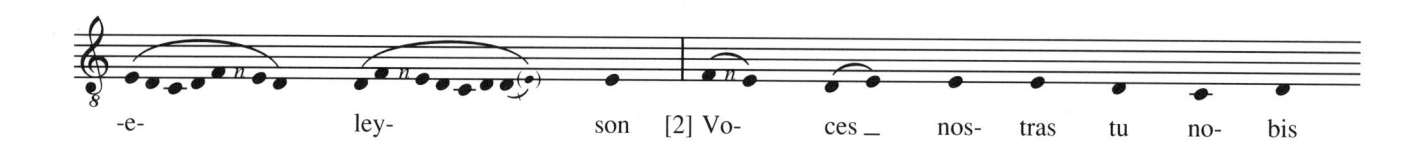

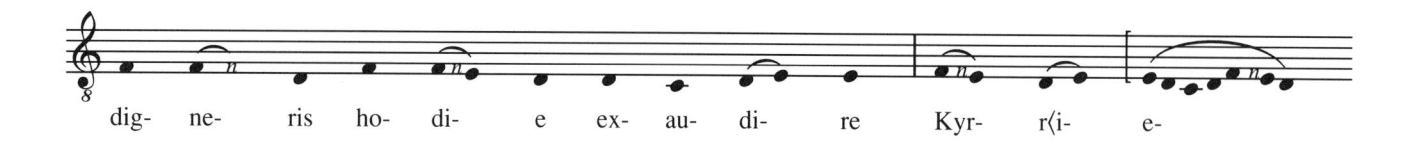

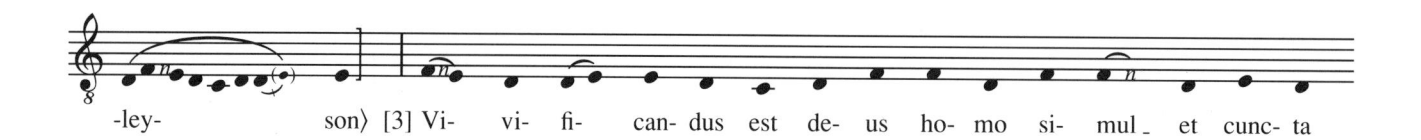

Rn 1343

[1] Rex mag- ne do- mi- ne quem sanc- ti a- dho- rant e- ley- son Kyr- ri-

-e- ley- son [2] Vo- ces nos- tras tu no- bis

dig- ne- ris ho- di- e ex- au- di- re Kyr- r⟨i- e-

-ley- son⟩ [3] Vi- vi- fi- can- dus est de- us ho- mo si- mul et cunc- ta

e- ley- son Kyr- r⟨i- e- ley- son⟩

[4] O a- gi- e in- fi- ni- te que iu- dex nos- ter nos- tras pre- ces sus- ci- pe e- ley- son

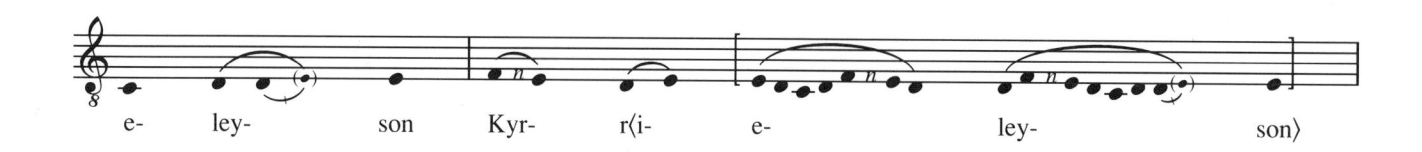

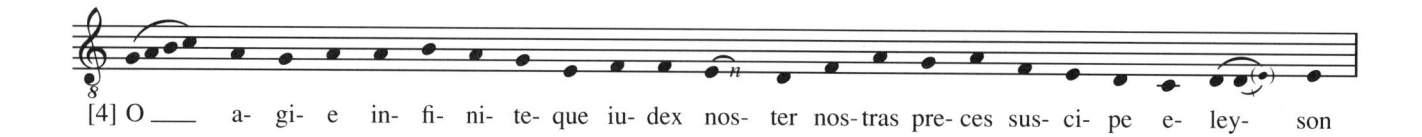

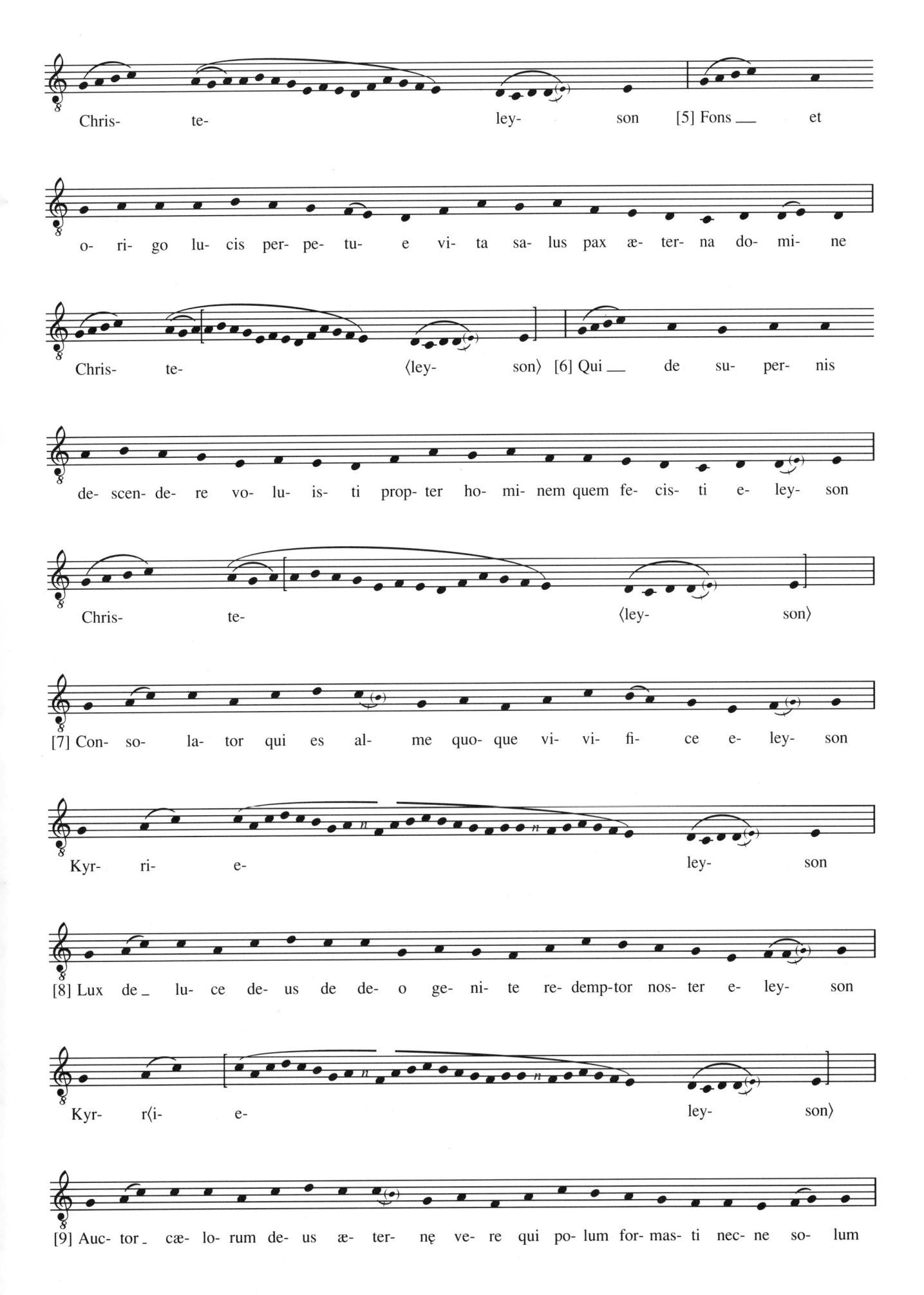

Chris- te- ley- son [5] Fons ___ et o- ri- go lu- cis per- pe- tu- e vi- ta sa- lus pax æ- ter- na do- mi- ne Chris- te- ⟨ley- son⟩ [6] Qui ___ de su- per- nis de- scen- de- re vo- lu- is- ti prop- ter ho- mi- nem quem fe- cis- ti e- ley- son Chris- te- ⟨ley- son⟩

[7] Con- so- la- tor qui es al- me quo- que vi- vi- fi- ce e- ley- son Kyr- ri- e- ley- son

[8] Lux de ___ lu- ce de- us de de- o ge- ni- te re- demp- tor nos- ter e- ley- son Kyr- r⟨i- e- ley- son⟩

[9] Auc- tor ___ cæ- lo- rum de- us æ- ter- nę ve- re qui po- lum for- mas- ti nec- ne so- lum

Kyr- r⟨i- e- ley- son⟩

[10] Ab om- ni ma- lo tu nos de- fen- de al- me chris- te de cæ- lis

mi- se- re- re [11] Ser- vos tu- os

au- di pi- is- si- me e- ley- son [e]- ley- son

Kyrie eleison 7
Melnicki 47; Vatican VI
Kyrie rex genitor

Rc 1741

[1] Kyr- ri- e rex ge- ni- tor in- ge- ni- te ve- ra es- sen- ti- a e- ley- son

Kyr- ri- e- ley- son [2] Kyr- ri- e lu- mi- nis

fons et re- rum con- di- tor e- ley- son Kyr- ri- e-

-ley- son [3] Kyr- ri- e qui nos tu- ę i- ma- gi- nis sig- nas- ti

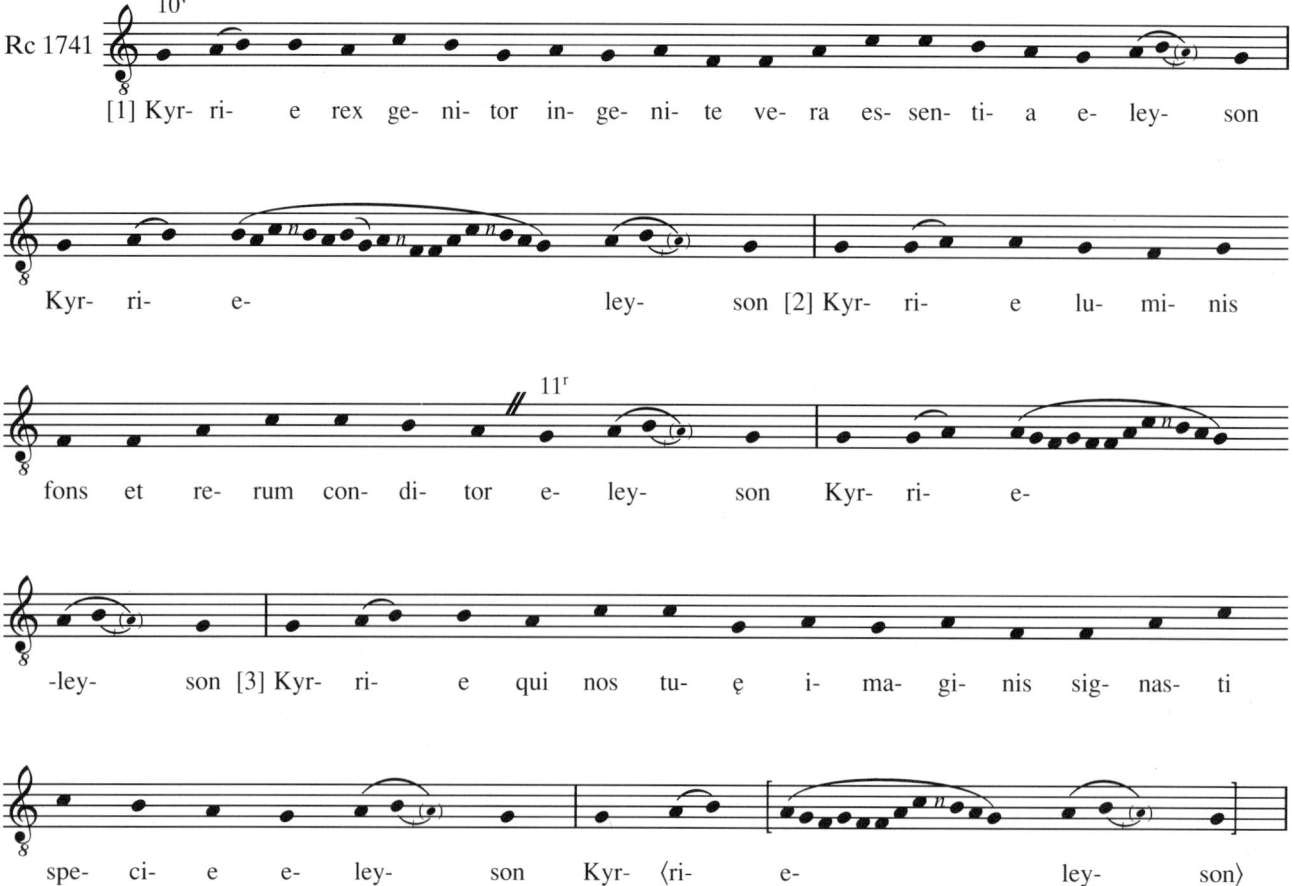

spe- ci- e e- ley- son Kyr- ⟨ri- e- ley- son⟩

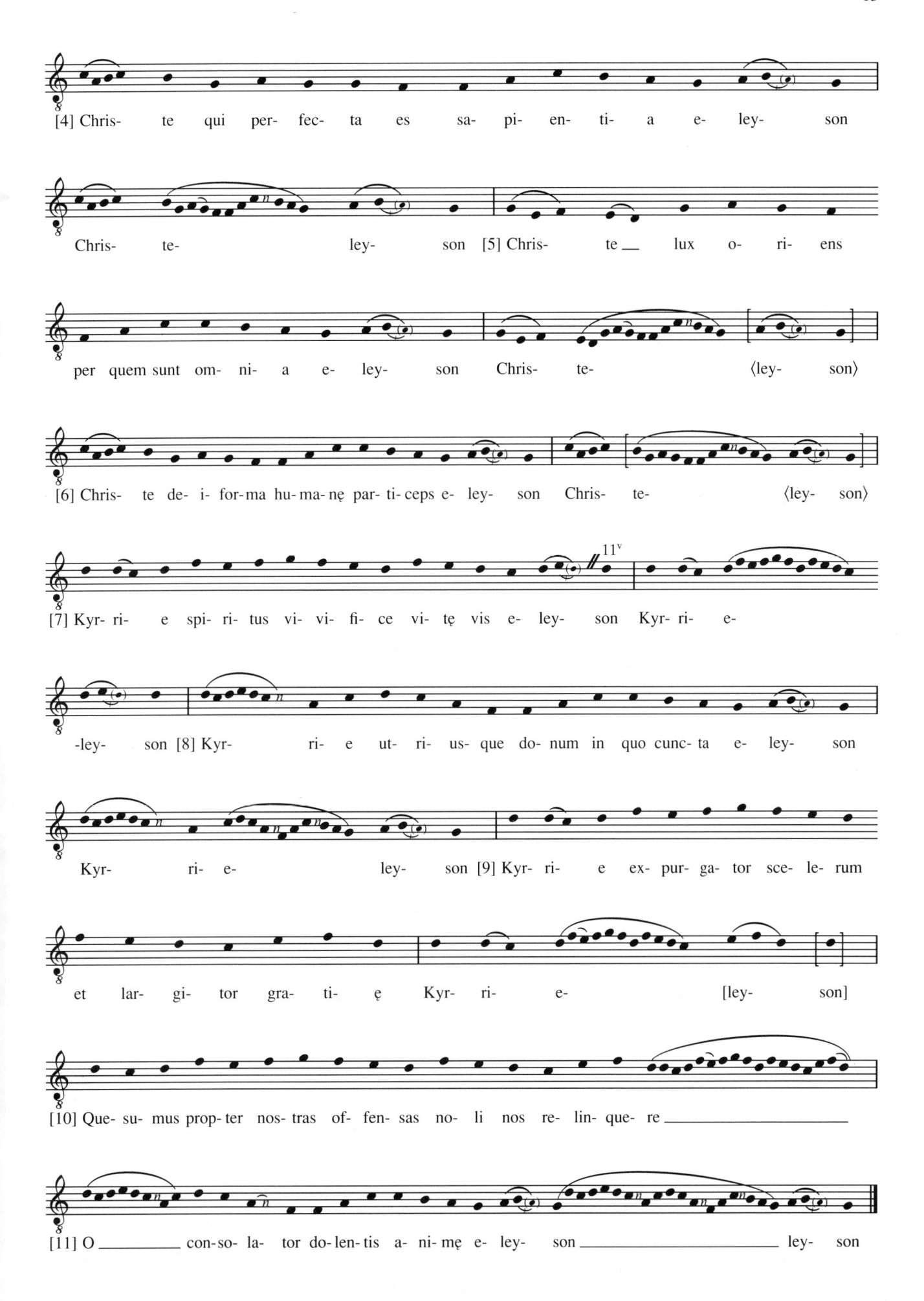

[4] Christe qui perfecta es sapientiae eleyson Christe eleyson [5] Christe lux oriens per quem sunt omnia eleyson Christe ⟨leyson⟩ [6] Christe dei forma humanę particeps eleyson Christe ⟨leyson⟩ [7] Kyrrie spiritus vivifice vitę vis eleyson Kyrrie eleyson [8] Kyrrie utriusque donum in quo cuncta eleyson Kyrrie eleyson [9] Kyrrie expurgator scelerum et largitor gratię Kyrrie [leyson] [10] Quesumus propter nostras offensas noli nos relinquere [11] O consolator dolentis animę eleyson leyson

Kyrie eleison 8
Melnicki 155; Vatican XV

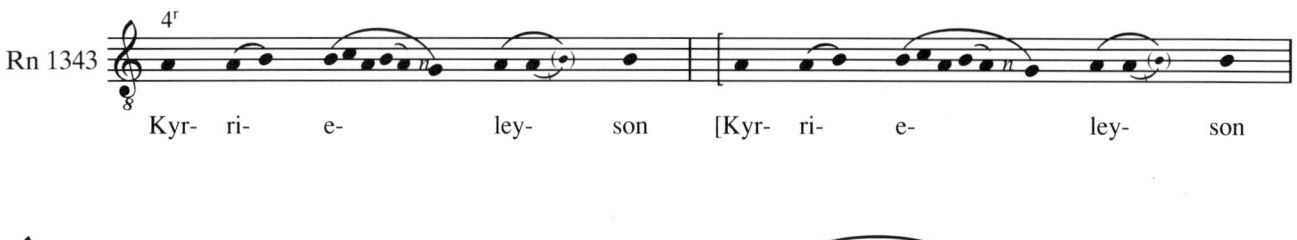

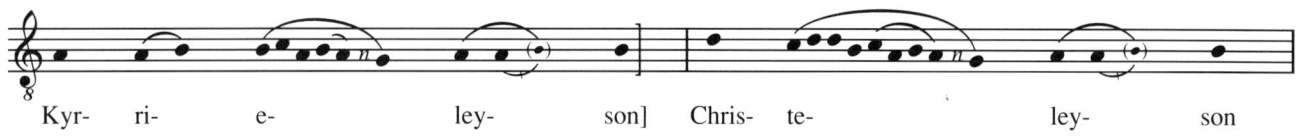

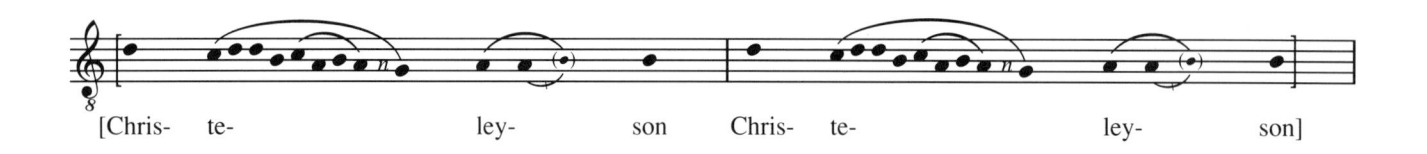

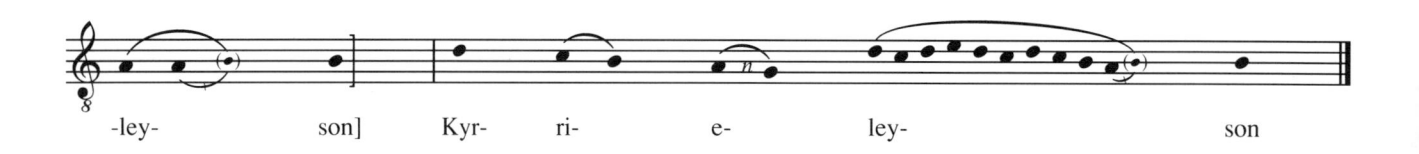

Kyrie eleison 9
Melnicki 151; Vatican XVIII

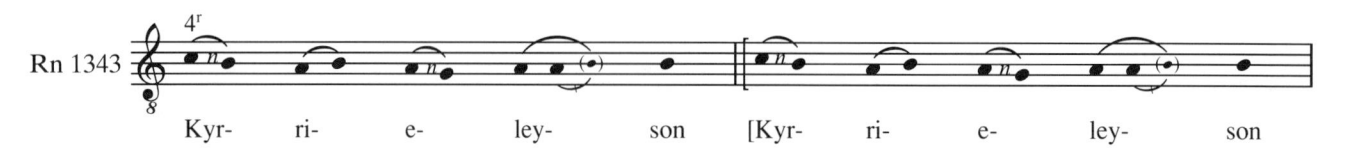

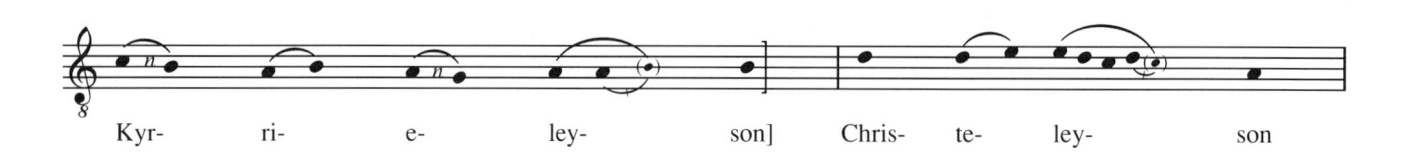

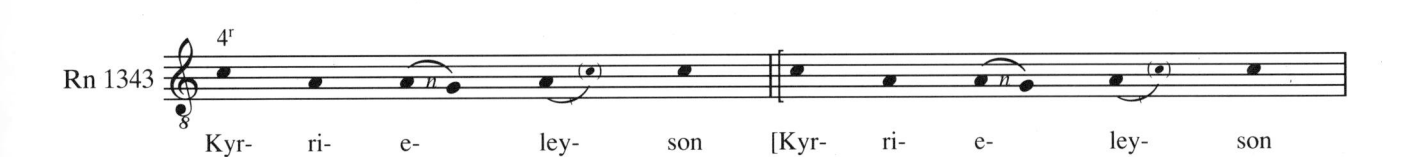

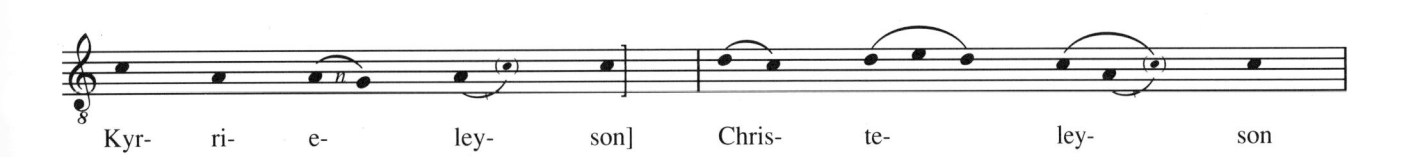

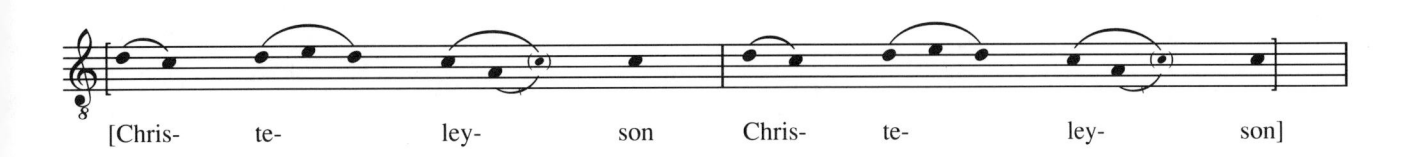

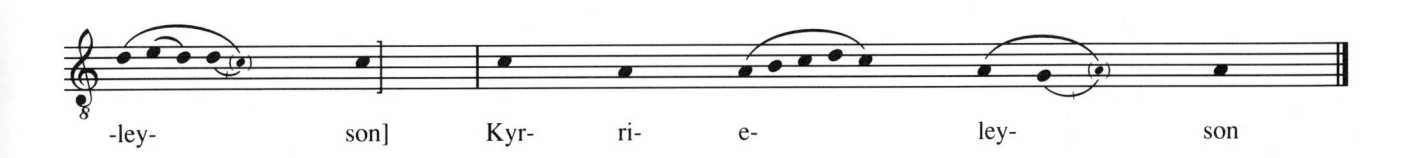

Kyrie eleison 10
Melnicki 136

Kyrie eleison 11
Melnicki 112 (?)

Gloria in excelsis 1
Bosse 39; Gloria A

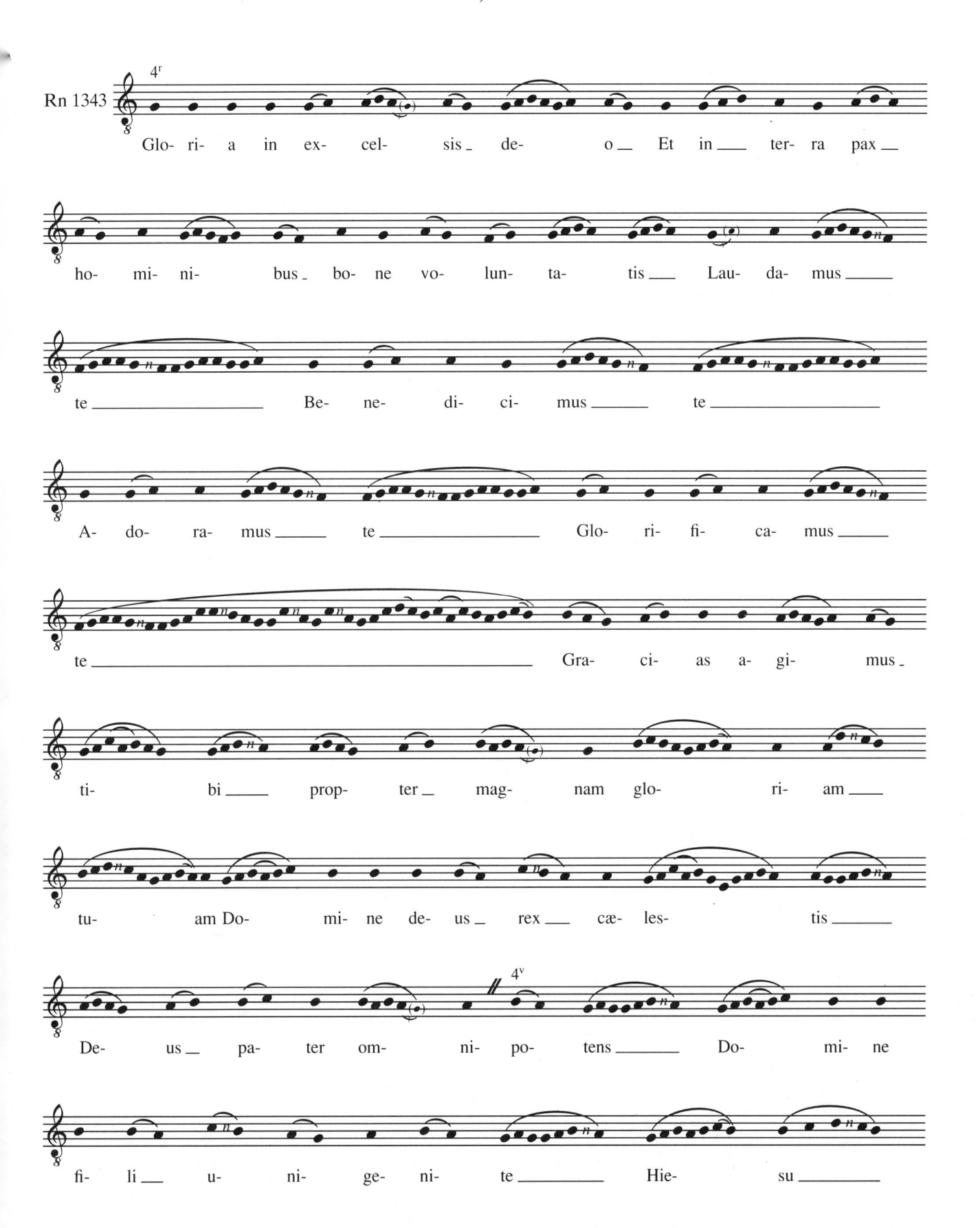

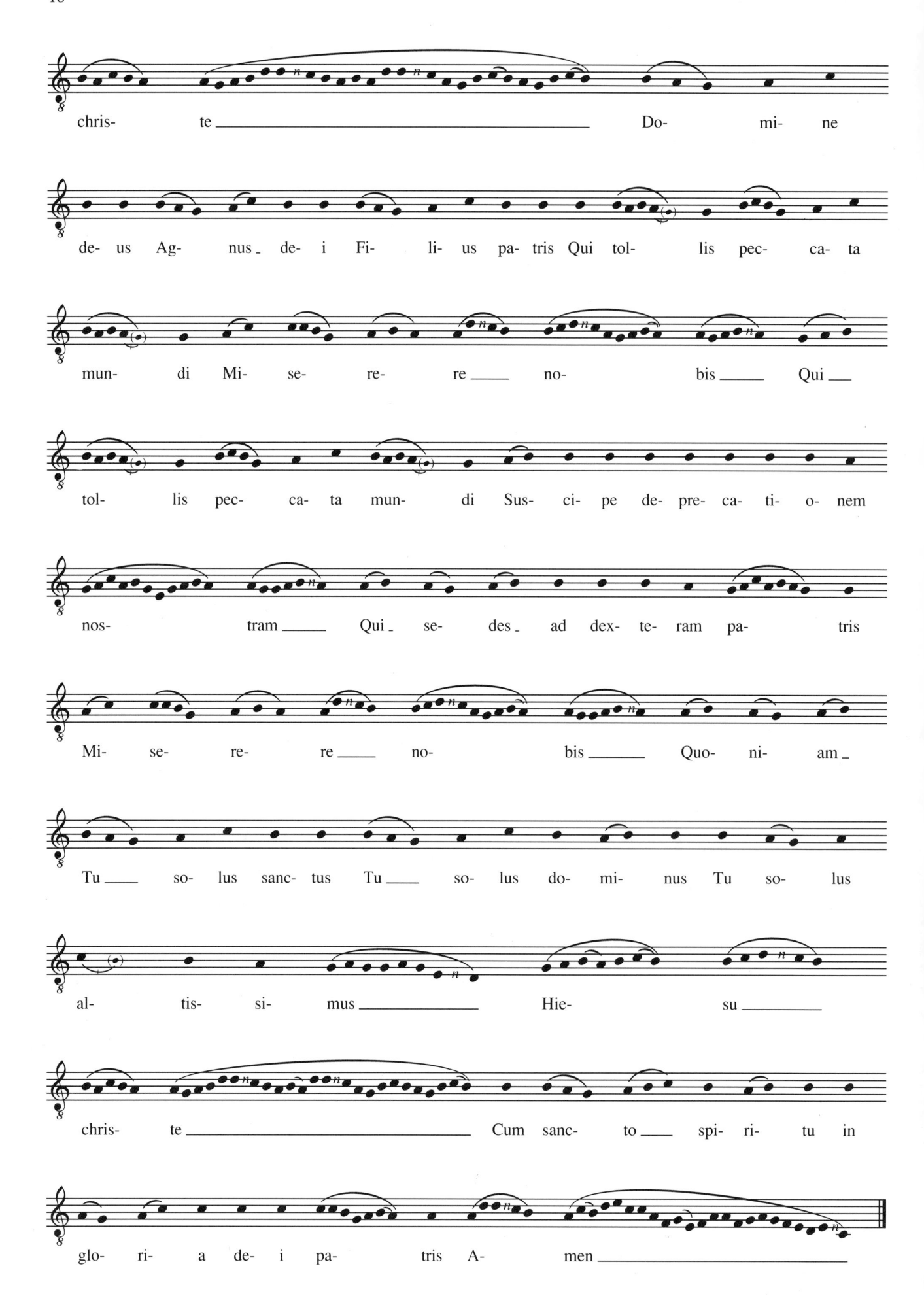

chris- te _____ Do- mi- ne
de- us Ag- nus de- i Fi- li- us pa- tris Qui tol- lis pec- ca- ta
mun- di Mi- se- re- re _____ no- bis _____ Qui _____
tol- lis pec- ca- ta mun- di Sus- ci- pe de- pre- ca- ti- o- nem
nos- tram _____ Qui se- des ad dex- te- ram pa- tris
Mi- se- re- re _____ no- bis _____ Quo- ni- am _____
Tu _____ so- lus sanc- tus Tu _____ so- lus do- mi- nus Tu so- lus
al- tis- si- mus _____ Hie- su _____
chris- te _____ Cum sanc- to _____ spi- ri- tu in
glo- ri- a de- i pa- tris A- men _____

Gloria in excelsis 2
Bosse 2 (var.); Milan IV

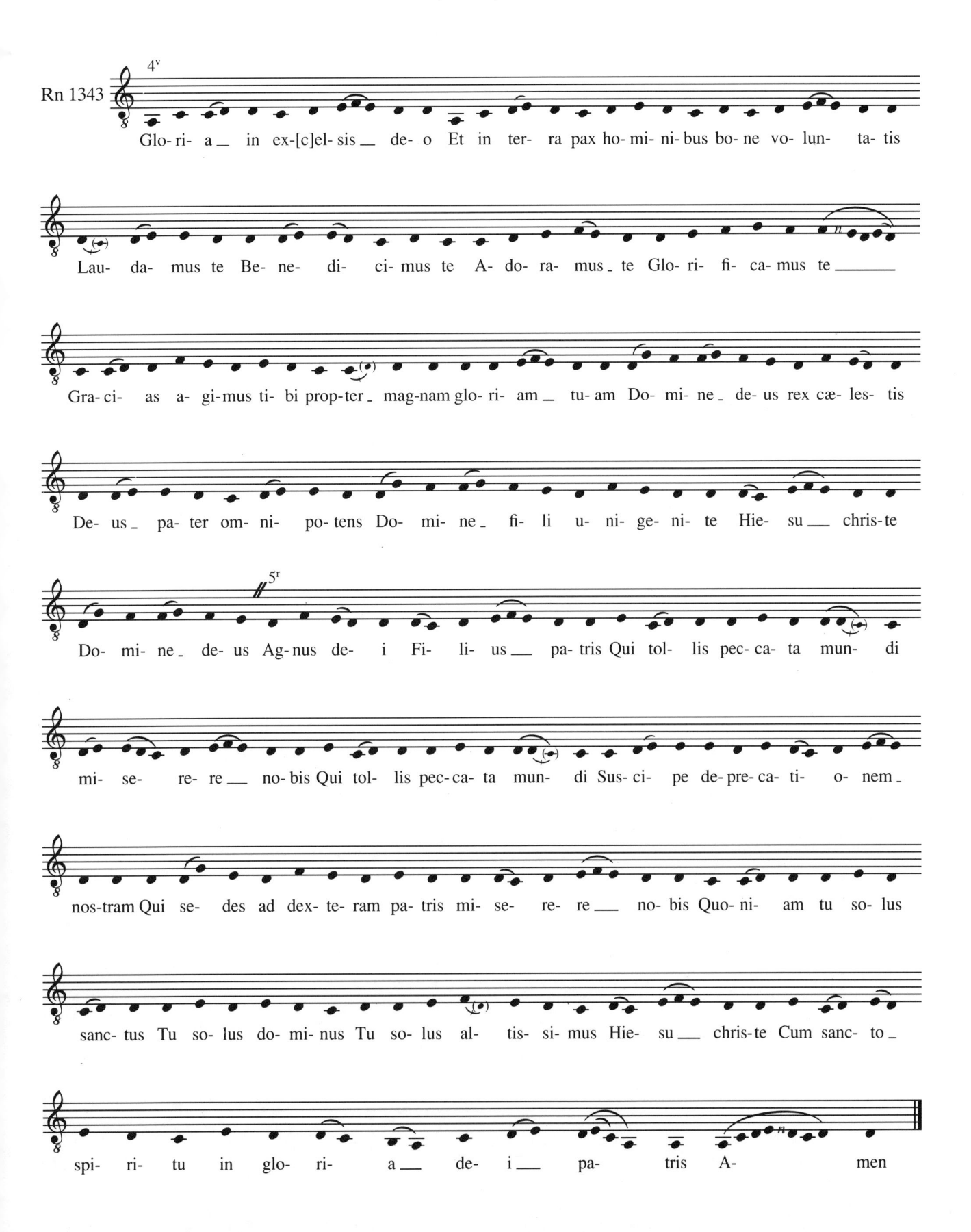

Rn 1343

Glo- ri- a in ex-[c]el- sis de- o Et in ter- ra pax ho- mi- ni- bus bo- ne vo- lun- ta- tis

Lau- da- mus te Be- ne- di- ci- mus te A- do- ra- mus te Glo- ri- fi- ca- mus te

Gra- ci- as a- gi- mus ti- bi prop- ter mag- nam glo- ri- am tu- am Do- mi- ne de- us rex cæ- les- tis

De- us pa- ter om- ni- po- tens Do- mi- ne fi- li u- ni- ge- ni- te Hie- su chris- te

Do- mi- ne de- us Ag- nus de- i Fi- li- us pa- tris Qui tol- lis pec- ca- ta mun- di

mi- se- re- re no- bis Qui tol- lis pec- ca- ta mun- di Sus- ci- pe de- pre- ca- ti- o- nem

nos- tram Qui se- des ad dex- te- ram pa- tris mi- se- re- re no- bis Quo- ni- am tu so- lus

sanc- tus Tu so- lus do- mi- nus Tu so- lus al- tis- si- mus Hie- su chris- te Cum sanc- to

spi- ri- tu in glo- ri- a de- i pa- tris A- men

Gloria in excelsis 3
Bosse 43; Vatican XV

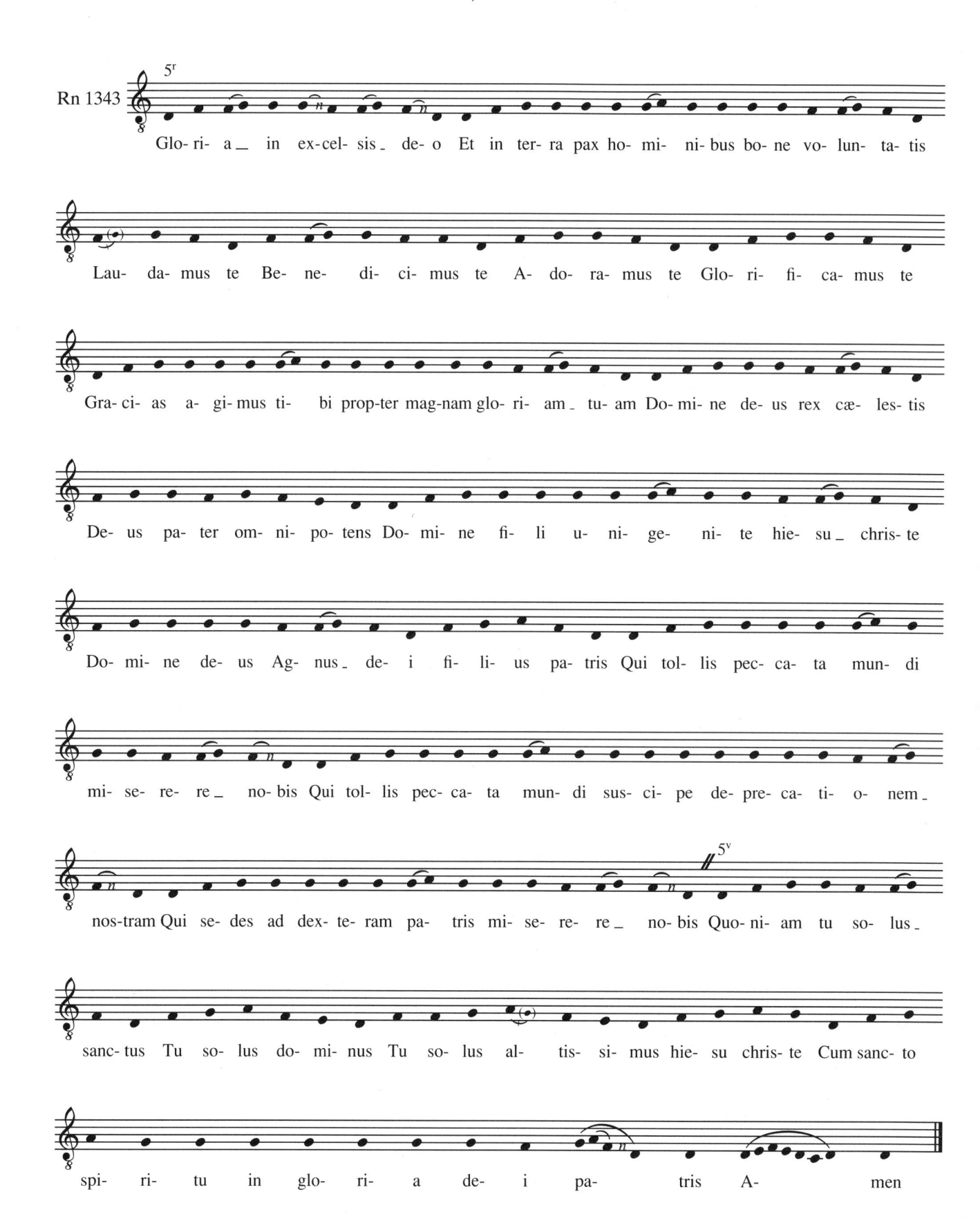

Rn 1343

Glo- ri- a in ex-cel- sis de- o Et in ter- ra pax ho- mi- ni- bus bo- ne vo- lun- ta- tis

Lau- da- mus te Be- ne- di- ci- mus te A- do- ra- mus te Glo- ri- fi- ca- mus te

Gra- ci- as a- gi- mus ti- bi prop-ter mag-nam glo- ri- am tu- am Do- mi- ne de- us rex cæ- les- tis

De- us pa- ter om- ni- po- tens Do- mi- ne fi- li u- ni- ge- ni- te hie- su chris- te

Do- mi- ne de- us Ag- nus de- i fi- li- us pa- tris Qui tol- lis pec- ca- ta mun- di

mi- se- re- re no- bis Qui tol- lis pec- ca- ta mun- di sus- ci- pe de- pre- ca- ti- o- nem

nos-tram Qui se- des ad dex- te- ram pa- tris mi- se- re- re no- bis Quo- ni- am tu so- lus

sanc- tus Tu so- lus do- mi- nus Tu so- lus al- tis- si- mus hie- su chris- te Cum sanc- to

spi- ri- tu in glo- ri- a de- i pa- tris A- men

Gloria in excelsis 4
Bosse 12; Vatican I

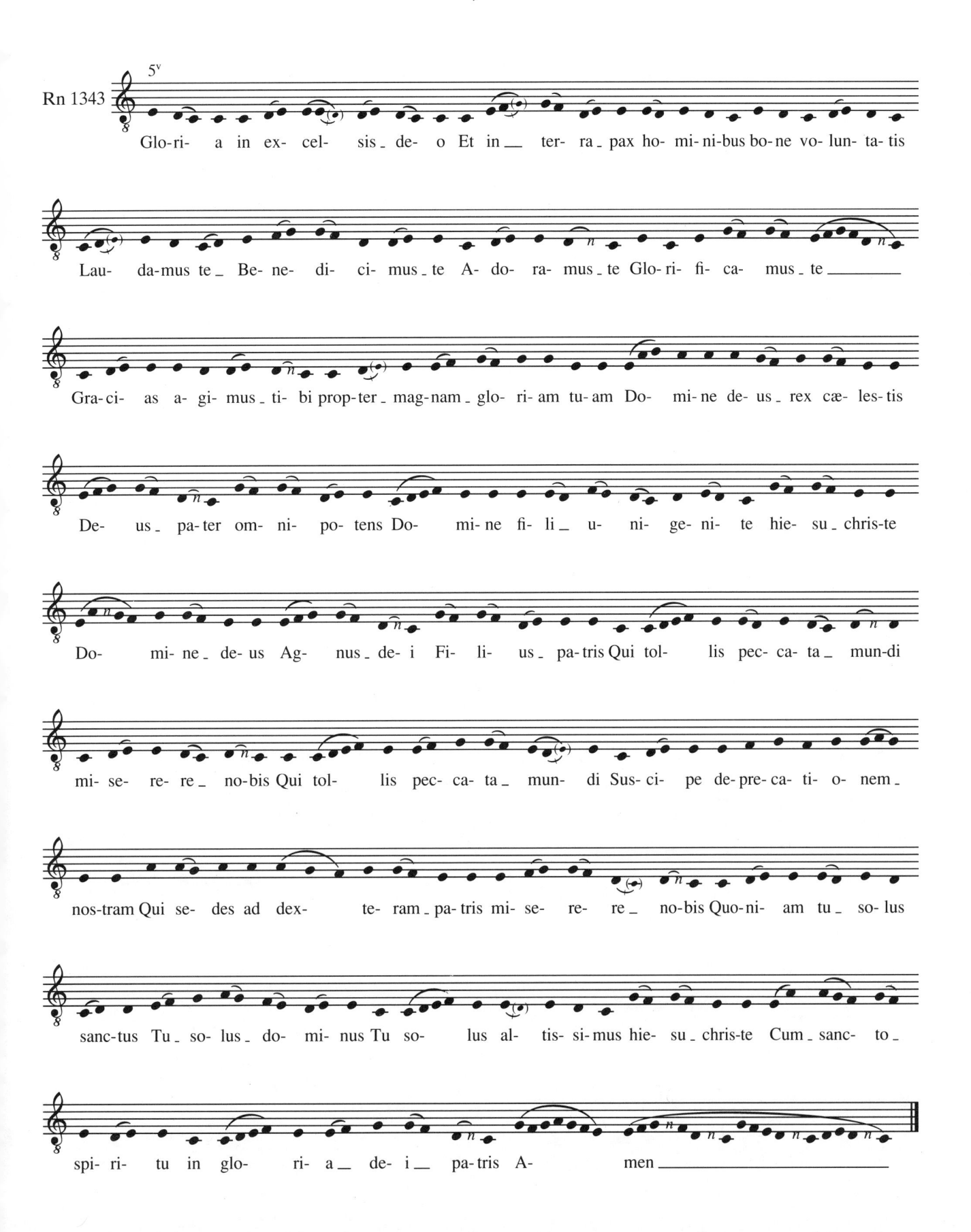

Gloria in excelsis 5
Bosse 11; Vatican XIV

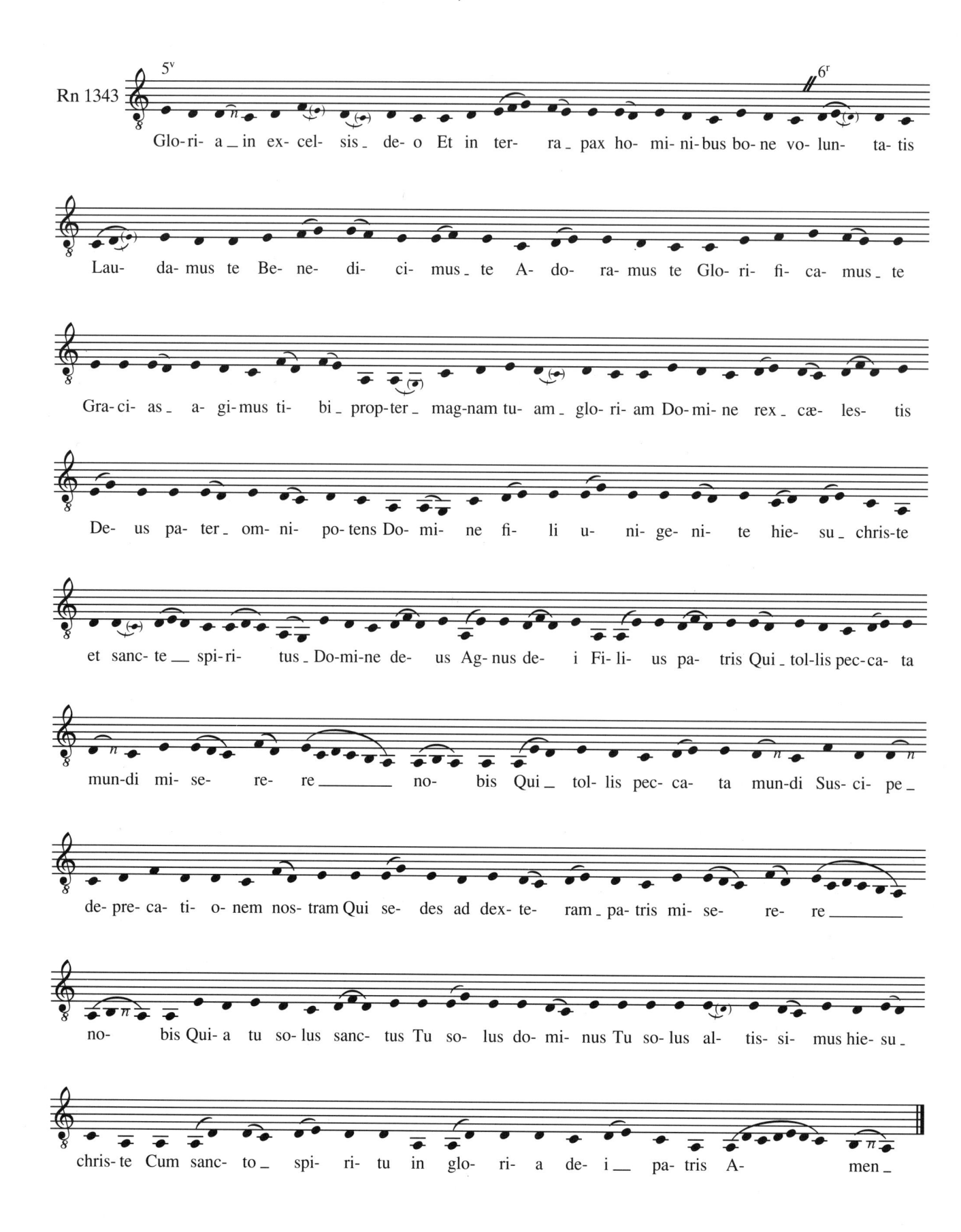

Rn 1343

Glo- ri- a in ex- cel- sis de- o Et in ter- ra pax ho- mi- ni- bus bo- ne vo- lun- ta- tis

Lau- da- mus te Be- ne- di- ci- mus te A- do- ra- mus te Glo- ri- fi- ca- mus te

Gra- ci- as a- gi- mus ti- bi prop- ter mag- nam tu- am glo- ri- am Do- mi- ne rex cæ- les- tis

De- us pa- ter om- ni- po- tens Do- mi- ne fi- li u- ni- ge- ni- te hie- su chris- te

et sanc- te spi- ri- tus Do- mi- ne de- us Ag- nus de- i Fi- li- us pa- tris Qui tol- lis pec- ca- ta

mun- di mi- se- re- re no- bis Qui tol- lis pec- ca- ta mun- di Sus- ci- pe

de- pre- ca- ti- o- nem nos- tram Qui se- des ad dex- te- ram pa- tris mi- se- re- re

no- bis Qui- a tu so- lus sanc- tus Tu so- lus do- mi- nus Tu so- lus al- tis- si- mus hie- su

chris- te Cum sanc- to spi- ri- tu in glo- ri- a de- i pa- tris A- men

Gloria in excelsis 6
Bosse 21

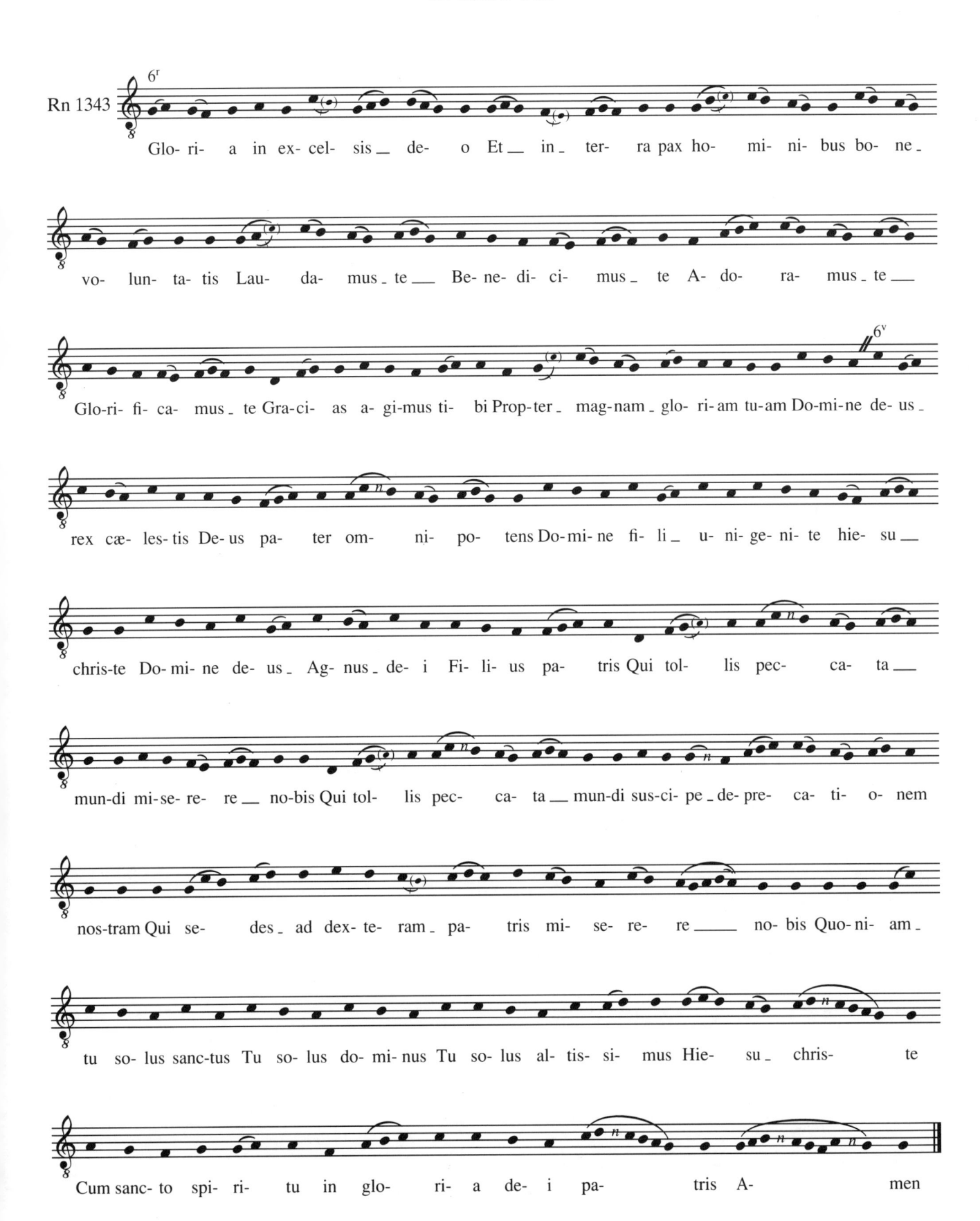

Gloria in excelsis 7
Bosse 51; Vatican XI

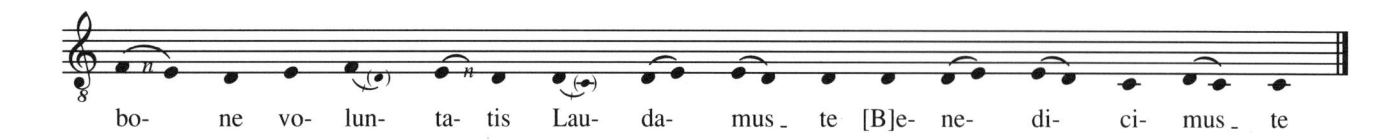

Rn 1343

Glo- ri- a in ex- cel- sis de- o Et in ter- ra pax ho- mi- ni- bus bo- ne vo- lun- ta- tis Lau- da- mus te [B]e- ne- di- ci- mus te

Gloria in excelsis 8a
Bosse 51; Vatican XI
Pax sempiterna

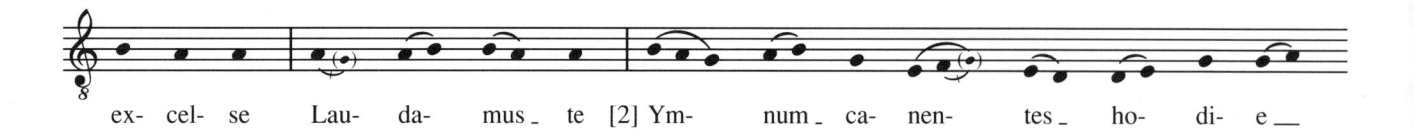

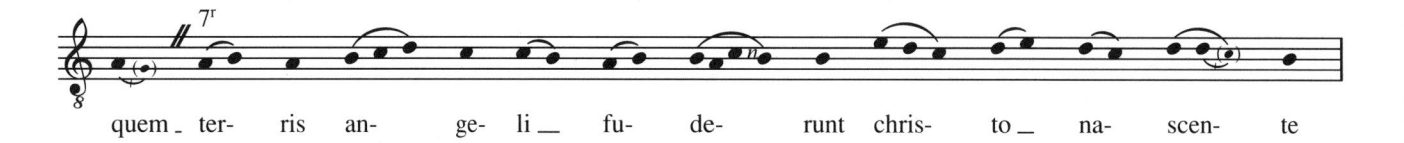

Rn 1343

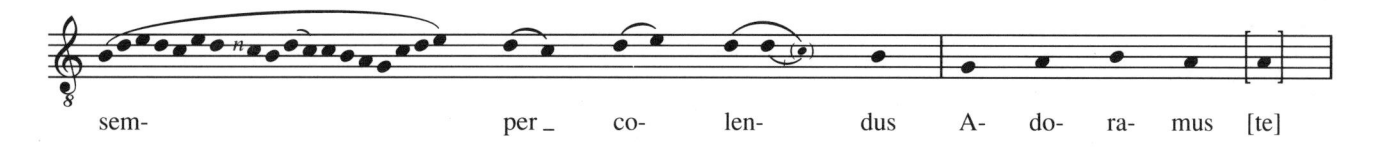

Glo- ri- a in ex- cel- sis de- o ⟨Et in ter- ra pax ho- mi- ni- bus⟩ bo- ne vo- lun- ta- tis [1] Pax sem- pi- ter- na chris- tus il- lu- xit glo- ri- a ti- bi pa- ter ex- cel- se Lau- da- mus te [2] Ym- num ca- nen- tes ho- di- e quem ter- ris an- ge- li fu- de- runt chris- to na- scen- te Be- ne- [di- ci- mus te] [3] Na- tus est no- bis ho- di- e sal- va- tor in tri- ni- ta- te sem- per co- len- dus A- do- ra- mus [te]

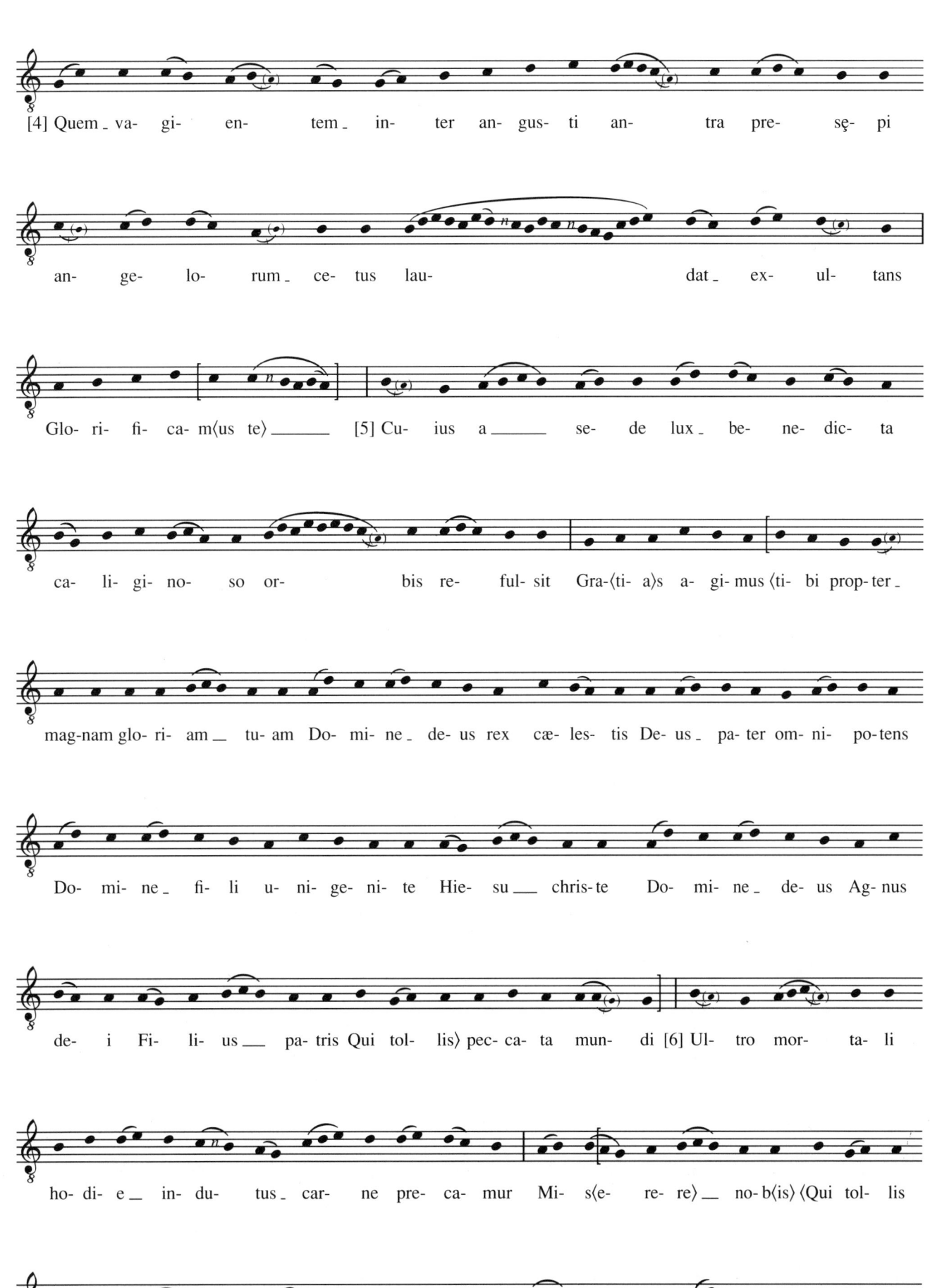

[4] Quem va- gi- en- tem in- ter an- gus- ti an- tra pre- sę- pi an- ge- lo- rum ce- tus lau- dat ex- ul- tans Glo- ri- fi- ca- m⟨us te⟩ [5] Cu- ius a se- de lux be- ne- dic- ta ca- li- gi- no- so or- bis re- ful- sit Gra-⟨ti- a⟩s a- gi- mus ⟨ti- bi prop- ter magnam glo- ri- am tu- am Do- mi- ne de- us rex cæ- les- tis Deus pa- ter om- ni- po- tens Do- mi- ne fi- li u- ni- ge- ni- te Hie- su chris- te Do- mi- ne de- us Ag- nus de- i Fi- li- us pa- tris Qui tol- lis⟩ pec- ca- ta mun- di [6] Ul- tro mor- ta- li ho- di- e in- du- tus car- ne pre- ca- mur Mi- s⟨e- re- re⟩ no- b⟨is⟩ ⟨Qui tol- lis pec- ca- ta mun- di Sus- ci- pe de- pre- ca- ti- o- nem nos- tram Qui se- des ad dex- te- ram pa-

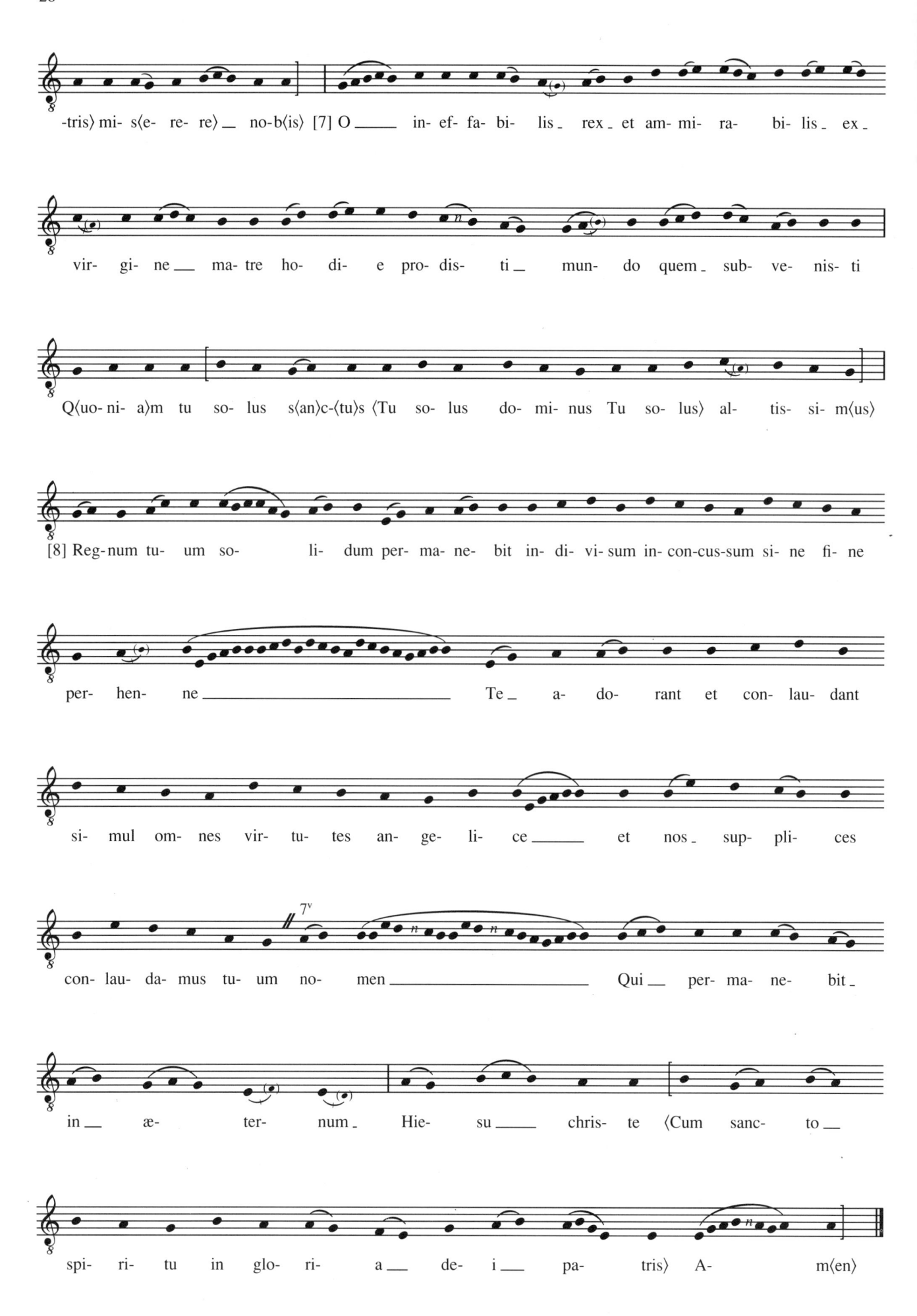

-tris⟩ mi- s⟨e- re- re⟩ no-b⟨is⟩ [7] O in- ef- fa- bi- lis rex et am-mi- ra- bi- lis ex

vir- gi- ne ma- tre ho- di- e pro- dis- ti mun- do quem sub- ve- nis- ti

Q⟨uo- ni- a⟩m tu so- lus s⟨an⟩c-⟨tu⟩s ⟨Tu so- lus do- mi- nus Tu so- lus⟩ al- tis- si- m⟨us⟩

[8] Reg- num tu- um so- li- dum per- ma- ne- bit in- di- vi- sum in- con-cus-sum si- ne fi- ne

per- hen- ne Te a- do- rant et con- lau- dant

si- mul om- nes vir- tu- tes an- ge- li- ce et nos sup- pli- ces

con- lau- da- mus tu- um no- men Qui per- ma- ne- bit

in æ- ter- num Hie- su chri- ste ⟨Cum sanc- to

spi- ri- tu in glo- ri- a de- i pa- tris⟩ A- m⟨en⟩

Gloria in excelsis 8b
Bosse 39; Gloria A
Pax sempiterna

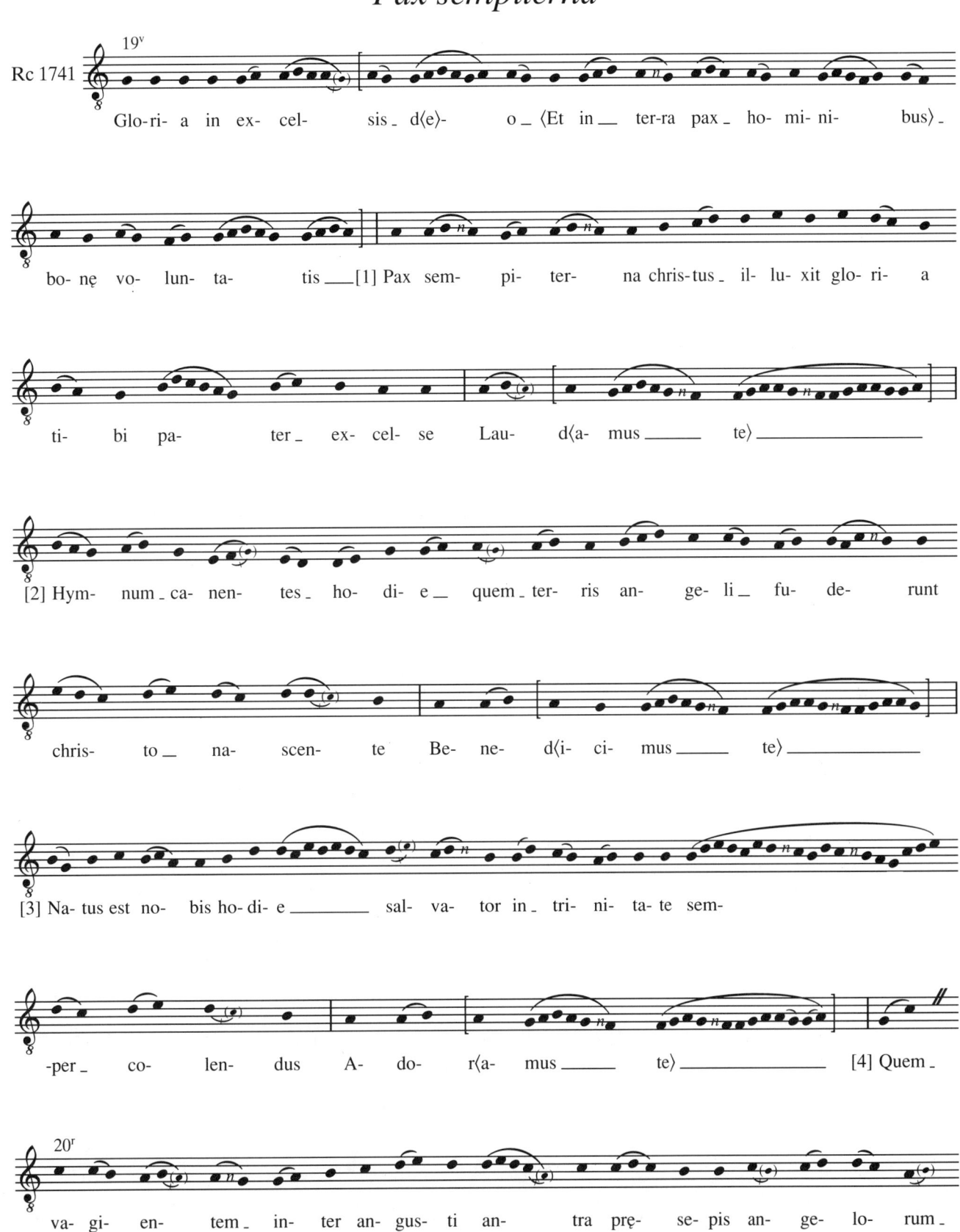

Glo-ri- a in ex- cel- sis d⟨e⟩- o ⟨Et in ter-ra pax ho- mi- ni- bus⟩ bo- nę vo- lun- ta- tis [1] Pax sem- pi- ter- na chris-tus il- lu- xit glo- ri- a ti- bi pa- ter ex- cel- se Lau- d⟨a- mus te⟩

[2] Hym- num ca- nen- tes ho- di- e quem ter- ris an- ge- li fu- de- runt chris- to na- scen- te Be- ne- d⟨i- ci- mus te⟩

[3] Na- tus est no- bis ho- di- e sal- va- tor in tri- ni- ta- te sem- -per co- len- dus A- do- r⟨a- mus te⟩ [4] Quem va- gi- en- tem in- ter an- gus- ti an- tra pre- se- pis an- ge- lo- rum

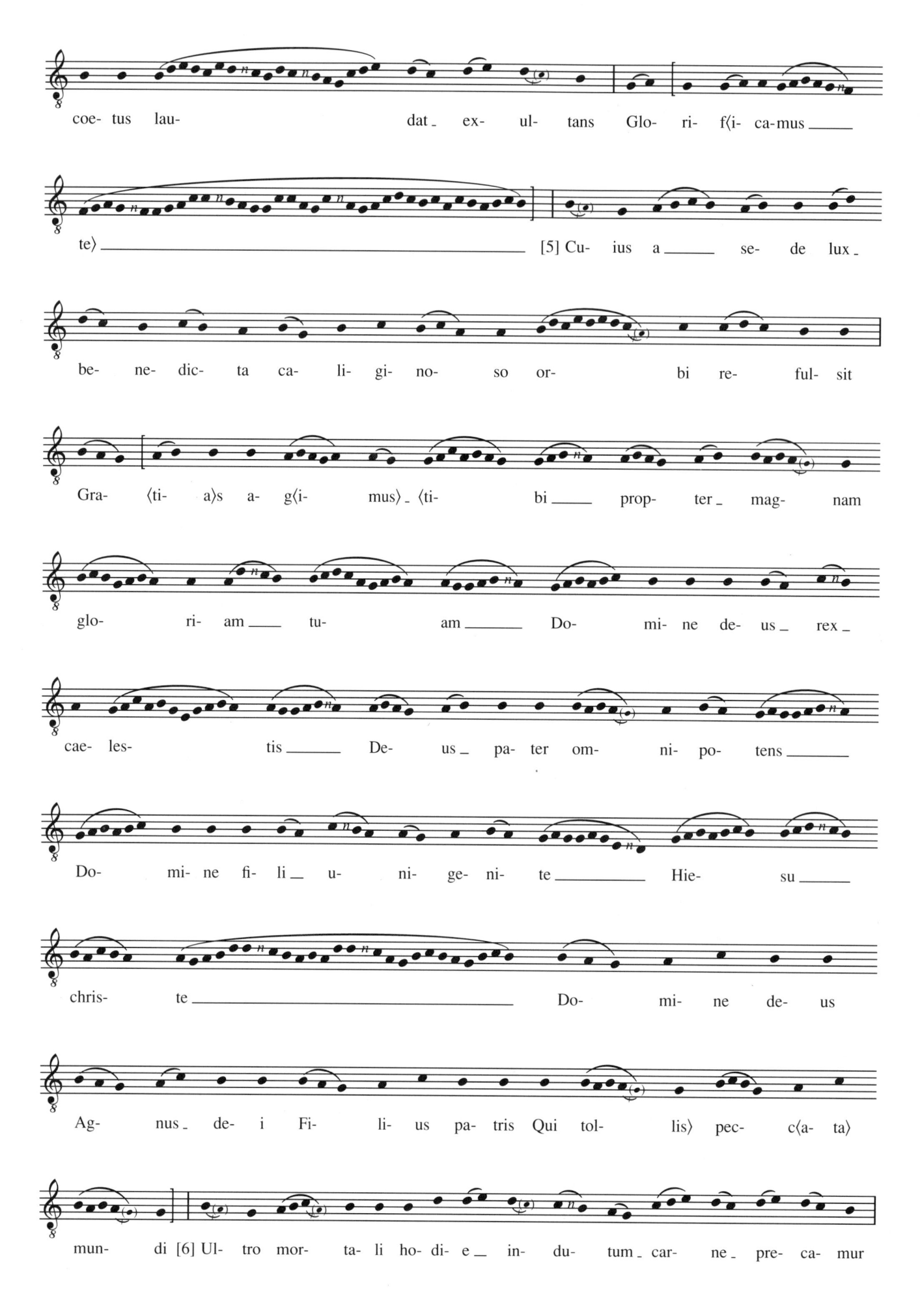

coe- tus lau- dat ex- ul- tans Glo- ri- f⟨i- ca- mus te⟩ [5] Cu- ius a se- de lux be- ne- dic- ta ca- li- gi- no- so or- bi re- ful- sit Gra- ⟨ti- a⟩s a- g⟨i- mus⟩ ⟨ti- bi propter magnam glo- ri- am tu- am Do- mi- ne de- us rex cae- les- tis De- us pa- ter om- ni- po- tens Do- mi- ne fi- li u- ni- ge- ni- te Hie- su chris- te Do- mi- ne de- us Ag- nus de- i Fi- li- us pa- tris Qui tol- lis⟩ pec- c⟨a- ta⟩ mun- di [6] Ul- tro mor- ta- li ho- di- e in- du- tum car- ne pre- ca- mur

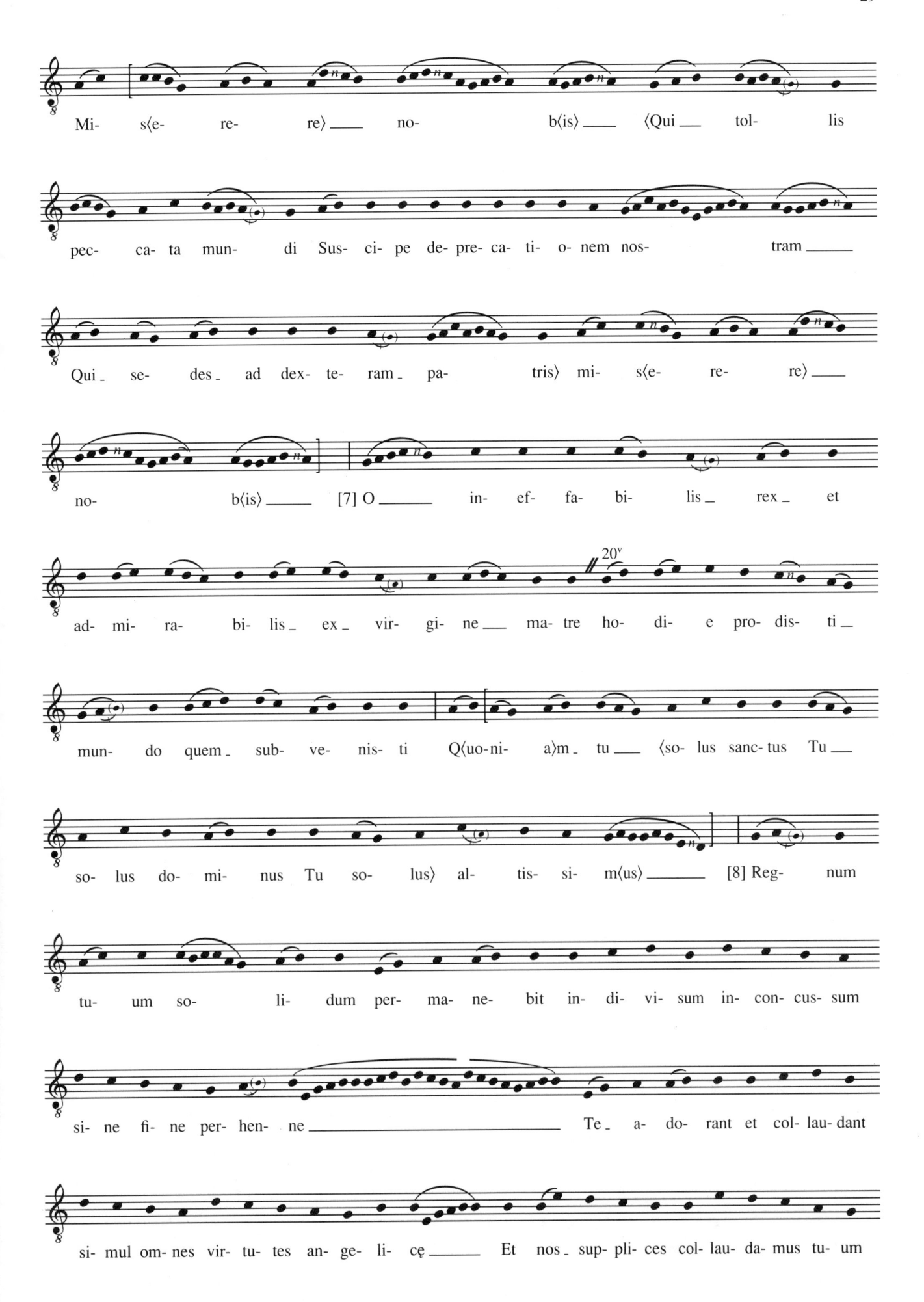

Mi- s⟨e- re- re⟩ no- b⟨is⟩ ⟨Qui tol- lis pec- ca- ta mun- di Sus- ci- pe de- pre- ca- ti- o- nem nos- tram Qui se- des ad dex- te- ram pa- tris⟩ mi- s⟨e- re- re⟩ no- b⟨is⟩ [7] O in- ef- fa- bi- lis rex et ad- mi- ra- bi- lis ex vir- gi- ne ma- tre ho- di- e pro- dis- ti mun- do quem sub- ve- nis- ti Q⟨uo- ni- a⟩m tu ⟨so- lus sanc- tus Tu so- lus do- mi- nus Tu so- lus⟩ al- tis- si- m⟨us⟩ [8] Reg- num tu- um so- li- dum per- ma- ne- bit in- di- vi- sum in- con- cus- sum si- ne fi- ne per- hen- ne Te a- do- rant et col- lau- dant si- mul om- nes vir- tu- tes an- ge- li- cę Et nos sup- pli- ces col- lau- da- mus tu- um no- men ____ Quod _ per- ma- ne- bit _ in _ e- ter- num _

Hie- su ____ chris- te ____

⟨Cum sanc- to ____ spi- ri- tu in glo- ri- a de- i pa- tris⟩

A- men ____

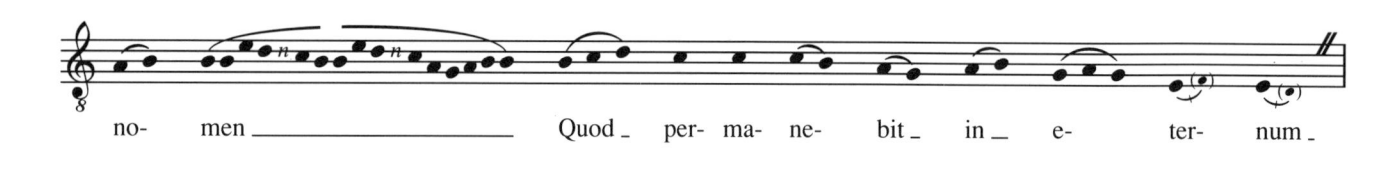

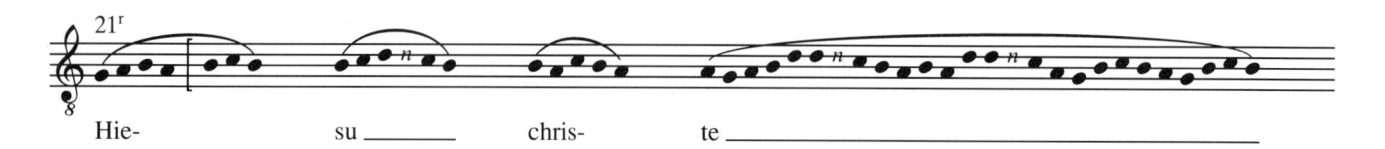

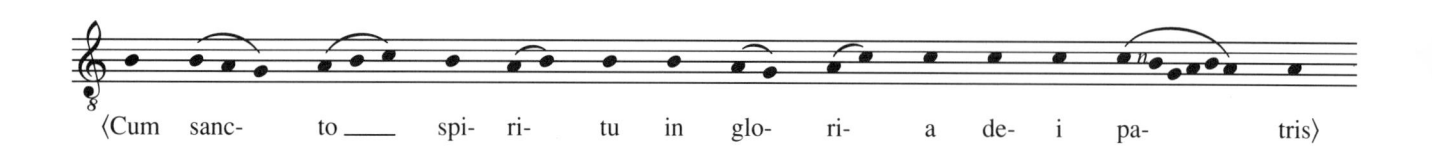

Gloria in excelsis 9
Bosse 2 (var.); Milan IV
Quem patris ad dextram

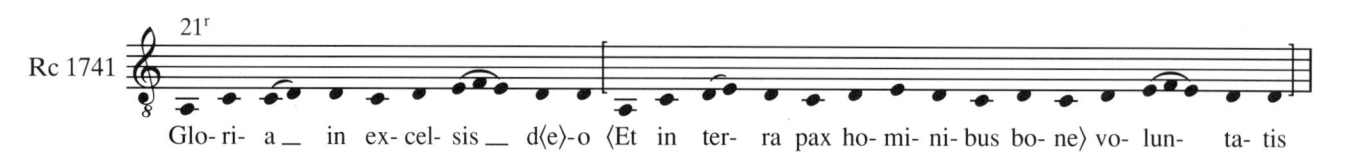

Rc 1741

Glo- ri- a _ in ex- cel- sis _ d⟨e⟩-o ⟨Et in ter- ra pax ho- mi- ni- bus bo- ne⟩ vo- lun- ta- tis

[1] Quem _ pa- tris _ ad _ dex- tram col- lau- dant om- ni- a ____ ver- bum

Lau- d⟨a- mus te⟩ [2] Om- ni- a quem _ sanc- tum _ be- ne- di- cunt _ con- di- ta re- gem

Be- n⟨e- di- ci- mus te⟩ [3] Tel- lus at- que _ po- lus ma- re quem ve- ne- ran- ter a- do- rant A- do-ra-⟨mus te⟩ [4] Glo- ri- fi- cant ag- num

ci- ves quem dig- ni- ter al- mi Glo- ri- f⟨i- ca- mus te⟩

[5] Gra- ci- a sanc- to- rum splen- dor de- cus et di- a- de- ma

Gra- ⟨ti- a⟩s a- g⟨i- mus⟩ ⟨ti- bi prop- ter mag- nam⟩ gl⟨o- ri⟩- am tu- a⟨m⟩

[6] Cul- pas ges- to- rum sol- vens si- ne cri- mi- ne so- lus

D⟨o- mi⟩- ne d⟨e- u⟩s rex ⟨cae- les- tis De- us pa- ter om- ni- po- tens Do- mi- ne

fi- li u- ni- ge- ni- te Hie- su chris- te Do- mi- ne de- us Ag- nus de- i

Fi- li- us pa- tris Qui tol- lis pec- ca- ta mun- di mi- se- re- re no- bis

Qui tol- lis pec- ca- ta mun- di Sus- ci- pe de- pre- ca- ti- o- nem nos- tram

Qui se- des ad dex- te- ram pa- tris mi- se- re- re no- bis Quo- ni- am⟩ tu so- l⟨us⟩

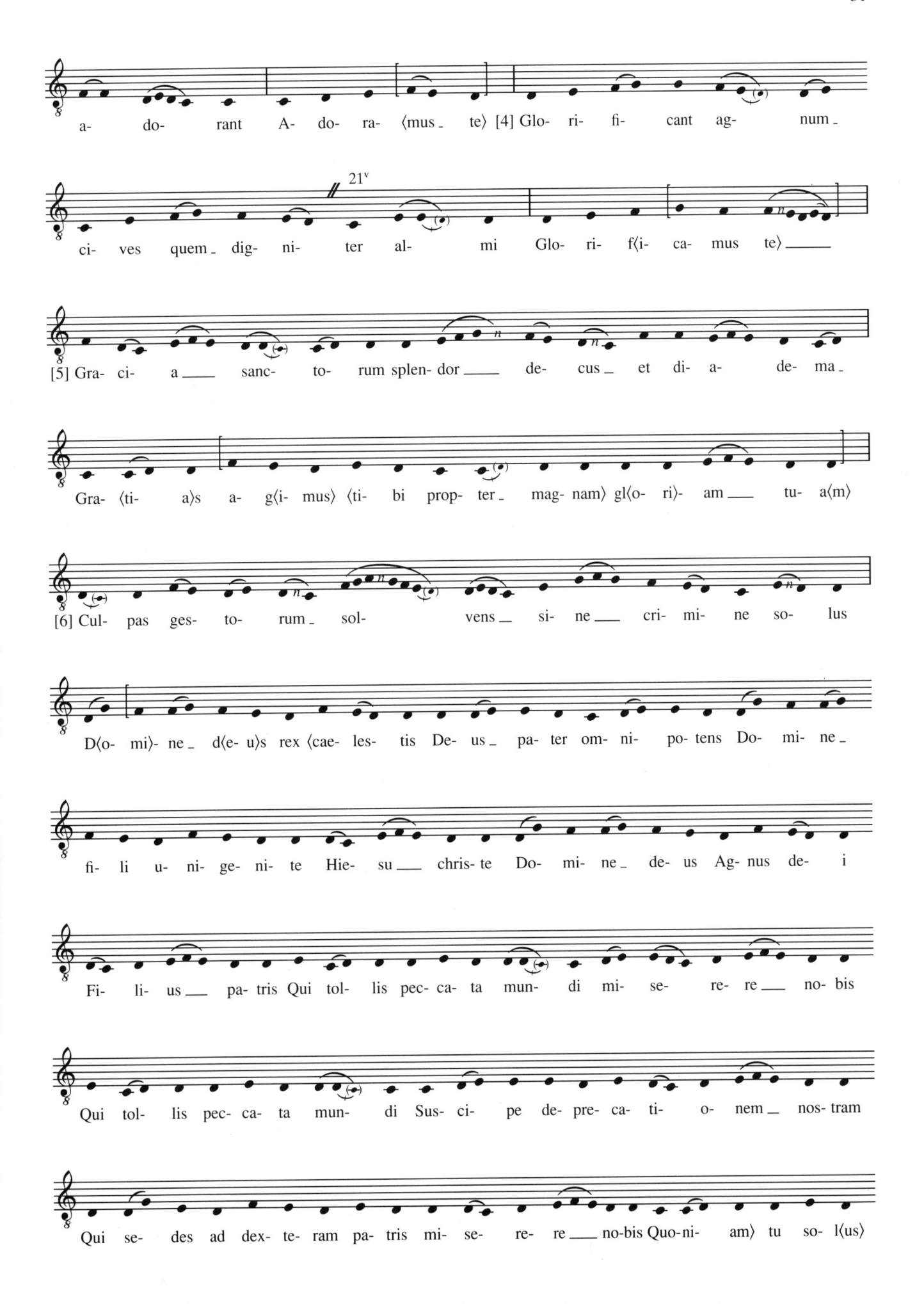

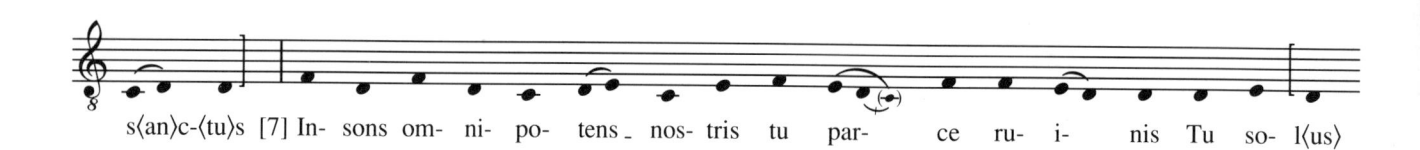

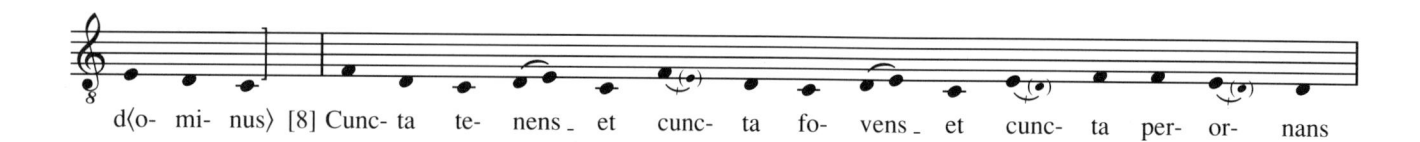

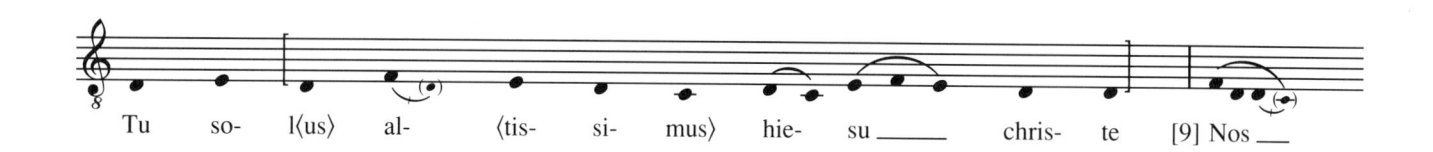

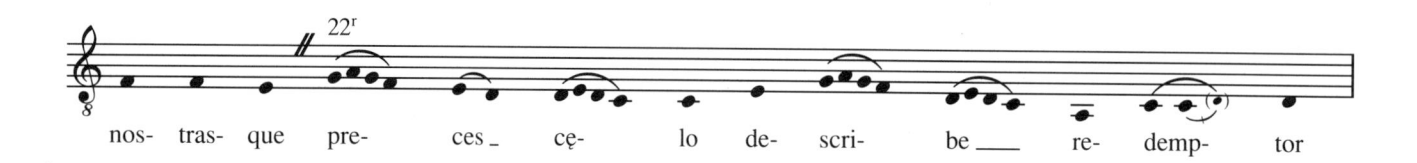

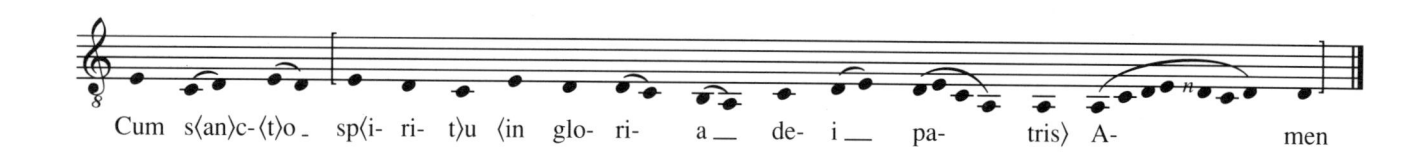

s⟨an⟩c-⟨tu⟩s [7] In- sons om- ni- po- tens nos- tris tu par- ce ru- i- nis Tu so- l⟨us⟩ d⟨o- mi- nus⟩ [8] Cunc- ta te- nens et cunc- ta fo- vens et cunc- ta per- or- nans Tu so- l⟨us⟩ al- ⟨tis- si- mus⟩ hie- su christe [9] Nos nos- tras- que pre- ces cę- lo de- scri- be re- demp- tor Cum s⟨an⟩c-⟨t⟩o sp⟨i- ri- t⟩u ⟨in glo- ri- a dei pa- tris⟩ A- men

Gloria in excelsis 10
Bosse 43; Vatican XV
Quem cives caelestes

Rn 1343

Glo- ri- a in ex- cel- sis de- o [1] Quem ci- ves cæ- les- tes sanc-tum cla- man-tes lau- de fre- quen- tant Et in t⟨er⟩- ra pax ho- mi- ni- bus bo- ne vo- lun- ta- tis [2] Quam mi- nis- tri do- mi- ni ver- bo in- car- na- to ter- re- nis pro- mi- se- rant Lau- da- m⟨us te⟩ [3] Lau- di- bus cu- ius as- tra ma- tu- ti- na in- sis- tunt

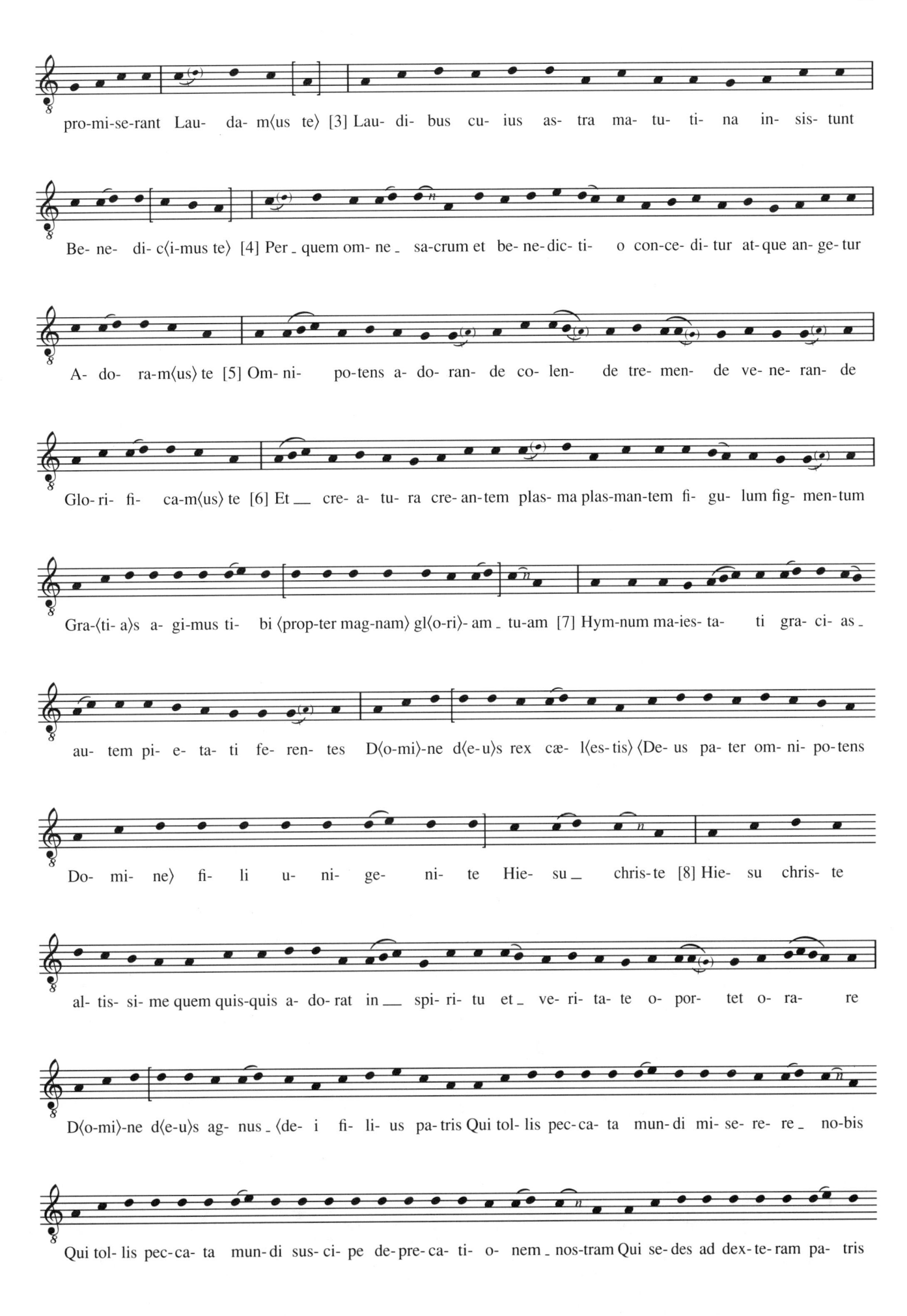

Be- ne- di- c⟨i-mus te⟩ [4] Per quem om- ne sa-crum et be- ne- dic- ti- o con- ce- di- tur at-que an- ge- tur

A- do- ra- m⟨us⟩ te [5] Om- ni- po-tens a- do- ran- de co- len- de tre- men- de ve- ne- ran- de

Glo- ri- fi- ca-m⟨us⟩ te [6] Et cre- a- tu- ra cre- an-tem plas- ma plas-man-tem fi- gu- lum fig- men-tum

Gra-⟨ti- a⟩s a- gi-mus ti- bi ⟨prop-ter mag-nam⟩ gl⟨o-ri⟩- am tu-am [7] Hym-num ma-ies- ta- ti gra- ci- as

au- tem pi- e- ta- ti fe- ren- tes D⟨o-mi⟩-ne d⟨e-u⟩s rex cæ- l⟨es-tis⟩ ⟨De- us pa- ter om- ni- po-tens

Do- mi- ne⟩ fi- li u- ni- ge- ni- te Hie- su chris-te [8] Hie- su chris- te

al- tis- si- me quem quis-quis a- do- rat in spi- ri- tu et ve- ri- ta- te o- por- tet o- ra- re

D⟨o-mi⟩-ne d⟨e-u⟩s ag- nus ⟨de- i fi- li- us pa-tris Qui tol- lis pec-ca- ta mun-di mi- se- re- no-bis

Qui tol- lis pec-ca- ta mun-di sus- ci- pe de- pre- ca- ti- o- nem nos-tram Qui se-des ad dex-te-ram pa- tris mi- se- re- re nobis Quo-ni- am tu so- lus sanc-tus Tu so- lus do- mi-nus⟩ tu so- l⟨us⟩ al- tis- si- mus

[9] Qui ve- nis- ti hie- su chris- te et pre- ci- o- so san- gui- ne tu- o nos re- de- mis- ti

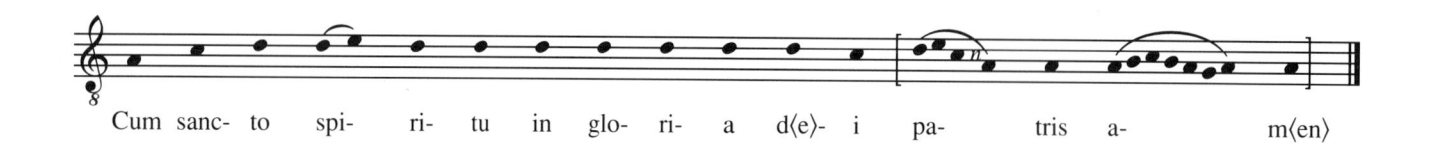

Cum sanc- to spi- ri- tu in glo- ri- a d⟨e⟩- i pa- tris a- m⟨en⟩

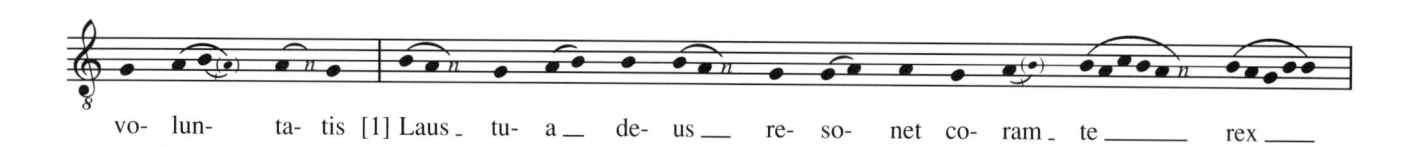

Gloria in excelsis 11a
Bosse 12; Vatican I
Laus tua Deus

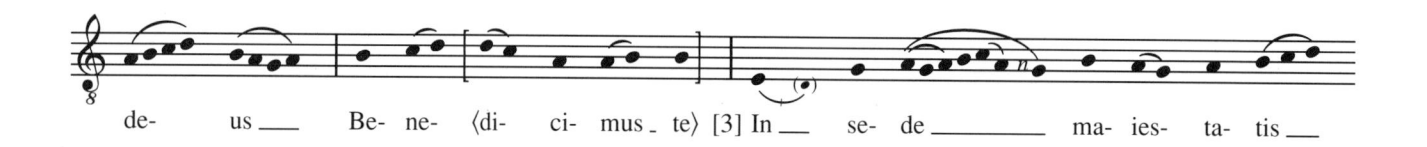

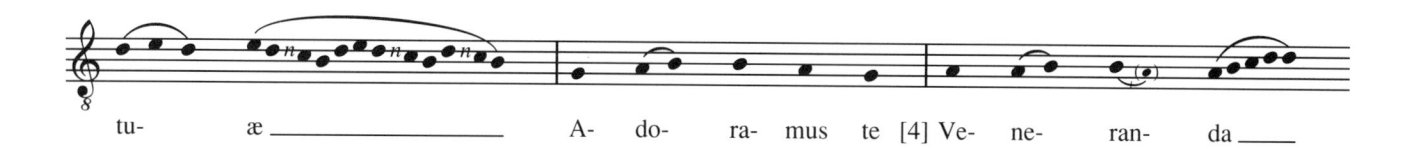

Rn 1343

Glo- ri- a in ex- cel- sis de- o ⟨Et in ter- ra pax ho- mi- ni- bus⟩ bo- ne

vo- lun- ta- tis [1] Laus tu- a de- us re- so- net co- ram te rex

Lau- da- m⟨us te⟩ [2] Qui ve- nis- ti prop- ter nos rex an- ge- lo- rum

de- us Be- ne- ⟨di- ci- mus te⟩ [3] In se- de ma- ies- ta- tis

tu- æ A- do- ra- mus te [4] Ve- ne- ran- da

tri- ni- tas ___ Glo- ri- fi- ca- mus_ te _____ [5] Glo- ri- o- sus_ es_ rex

is- ra- hel in_ thro- no ___ pa- tris ___ tu- i _____ Gra- ⟨ti- a⟩s

a- gi- mus_ ti- bi ⟨prop- ter_ mag- nam_ glo- ri- am tu- am Do- mi- ne de- us_

rex cae- les- tis De- us_ pa- ter om- ni- po- tens Do- mi- ne fi- li_ u- ni- ge- ni- te⟩

Hie- su_ chris- te [6] Do- mi- ne_ de- us re- demp- tor is- ra- hel _____

D⟨o- mi⟩- ne_ de- us ag- nus_ d⟨e⟩- i ⟨Fi- li- us_ pa- tris

Qui tol- lis pec- ca- ta_ mun- di Mi- se- re- re_ no- bis Qui tol- lis

pec- ca- ta_ mun- di Sus- ci- pe de- pre- ca- ti- o- nem_ nos- tram Qui se- des ad _

dex- te- ram_ pa- tris Mi- se- re- re_ no- bis Quo- ni- am⟩ tu_ so- lus

s⟨an⟩c-⟨tu⟩s [7] De- us for- tis et in- mor- ta- lis
Tu so- lus d⟨o- mi⟩- n⟨u⟩s [8] Cæ- les- ti- um ter- res- tri- um
et in- fer- no- rum rex Tu so- lus al- tis- si- mus [9] Reg- num
tu- um ⟨so- li- dum per- ma- ne- bit in- di- vi- sum in- con- cus- sum si- ne fi- ne
per- hen- ne Te a- do- rant et con- lau- dant si- mul om- nes
vir- tu- tes an- ge- li- ce et nos sup- pli- ces con- lau- da- mus tu- um
no- men Qui per- ma- ne- bit in
ae- ter- num⟩ Hie- su chris- te [Cum sanc- to spi- ri- tu in
glo- ri- a de- i pa- tris A- men]

Gloria in excelsis 11b
Bosse 39; Gloria A
Laus tua Deus

te⟩

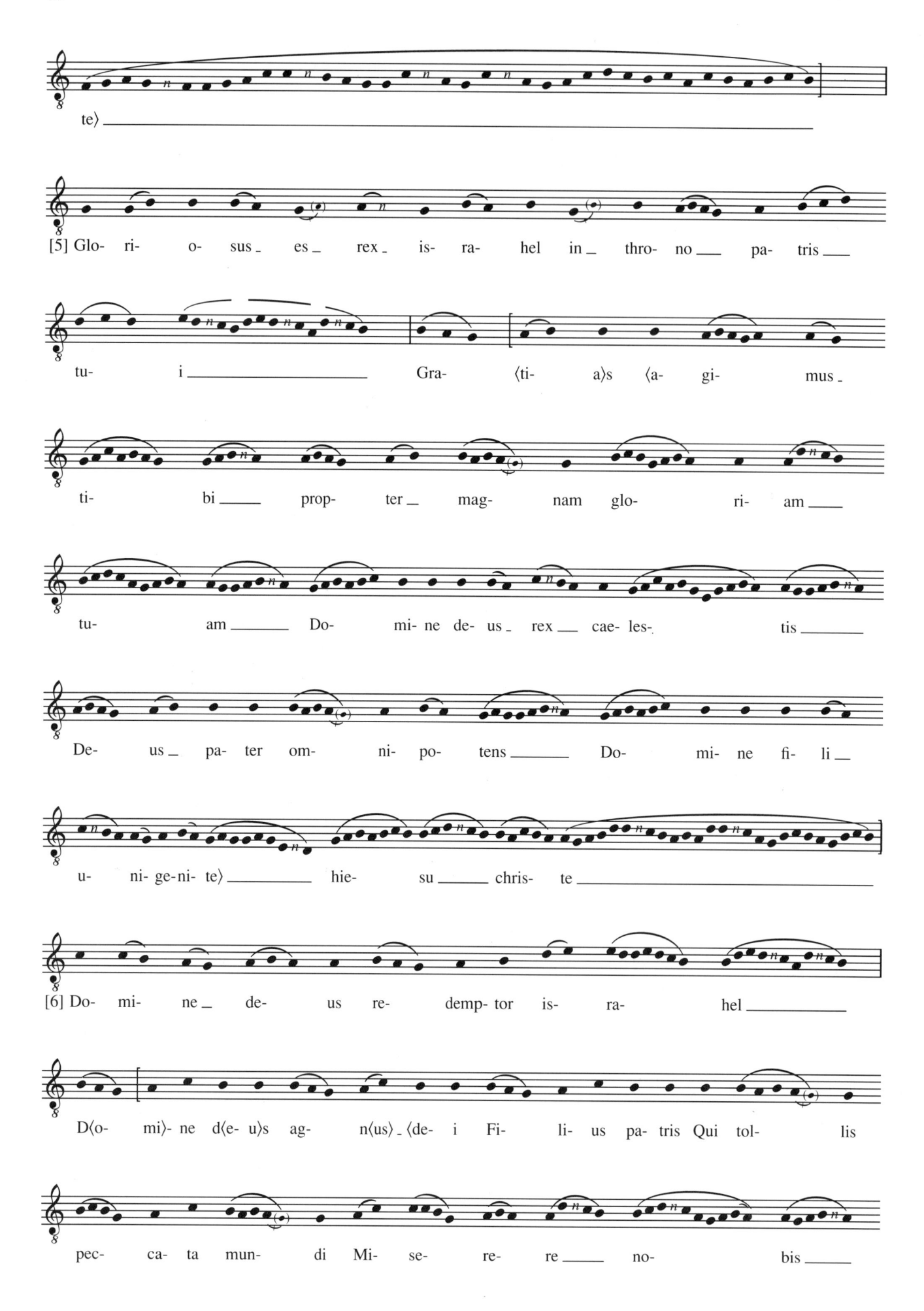

[5] Glo- ri- o- sus es_ rex_ is- ra- hel in_ thro- no_ pa- tris_

tu- i _____ Gra- ⟨ti- a⟩s ⟨a- gi- mus_

ti- bi ____ prop- ter_ mag- nam glo- ri- am ____

tu- am ____ Do- mi- ne de- us_ rex_ cae- les- tis ____

De- us_ pa- ter om- ni- po- tens ____ Do- mi- ne fi- li _

u- ni- ge- ni- te⟩ ____ hie- su_ chris- te ____

[6] Do- mi- ne_ de- us re- demp- tor is- ra- hel ____

D⟨o- mi⟩- ne d⟨e- u⟩s ag- n⟨us⟩_ ⟨de- i Fi- li- us pa- tris Qui tol- lis

pec- ca- ta mun- di Mi- se- re- re ____ no- bis ____

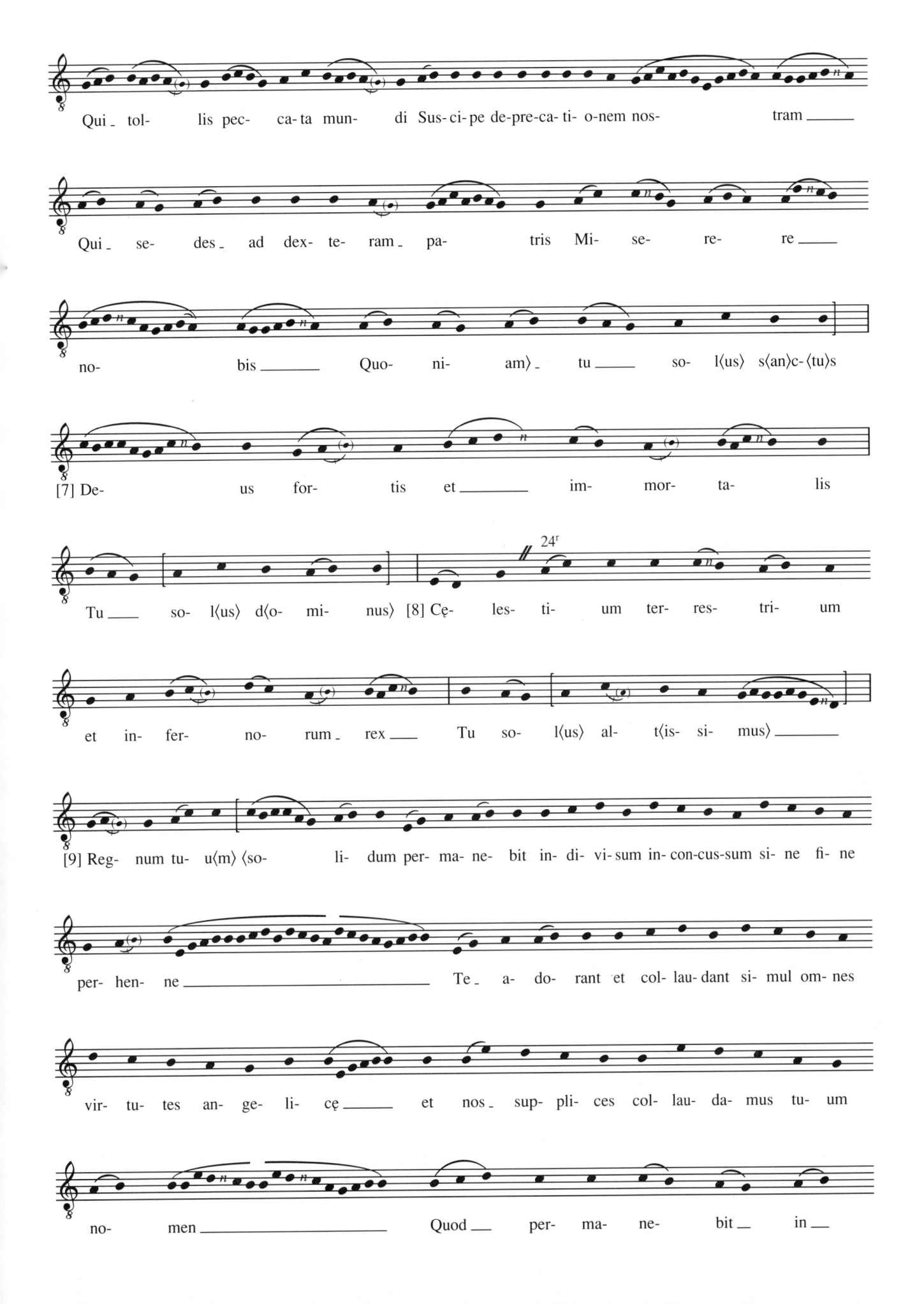

Qui tol- lis pec- ca-ta mun- di Sus-ci-pe de-pre-ca-ti- o-nem nos- tram

Qui se- des ad dex-te- ram pa- tris Mi- se- re- re

no- bis Quo- ni- am tu so- l⟨us⟩ s⟨an⟩c-⟨tu⟩s

[7] De- us for- tis et im- mor- ta- lis

Tu so- l⟨us⟩ d⟨o- mi- nus⟩ [8] Cę- les- ti- um ter- res- tri- um

et in- fer- no- rum rex Tu so- l⟨us⟩ al- t⟨is- si- mus⟩

[9] Reg- num tu- u⟨m⟩ ⟨so- li- dum per- ma- ne- bit in- di- vi-sum in-con-cus-sum si- ne fi- ne

per- hen- ne Te a- do- rant et col- lau- dant si- mul om- nes

vir- tu- tes an- ge- li- cę et nos sup- pli- ces col- lau- da- mus tu- um

no- men Quod per- ma- ne- bit in

e- ter- num Hie- su chris- te

Cum sanc- to spi- ri- tu in glo- ri- a de- i

pa- tris A- men⟩

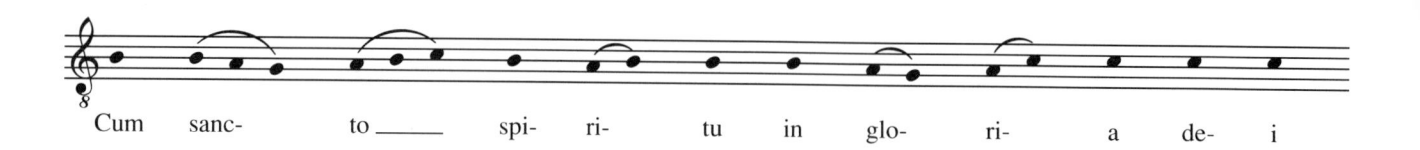

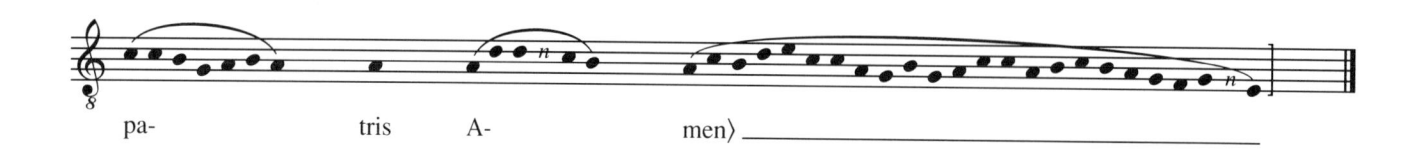

Gloria in excelsis 12
Bosse 12; Vatican I
Quem novitate

Rn 1343

Glo- ri- a in ex- cel- sis de- o [Et in ter- ra pax ho- mi- ni- bus bo- ne

vo- lun- ta- tis] [1] Quem no- vi- ta- te si- de- ris ac- tus lau- dat e- o- us

Lau- da- mus [te] [2] Qui be- ne- di- cis flu- mi- na fon- tis tinc- tus in un- dis

Be- ne- di- c⟨i- mus te⟩ [3] Qui ma- gus of- fert po- pli- te fle- xo mis- ti- ca do- na

A- do- ra- mus te [4] Glo- ri- a cu- ius pri- ma co- lo- rem at- que sa- po- rem mu- tat a- qua- rum

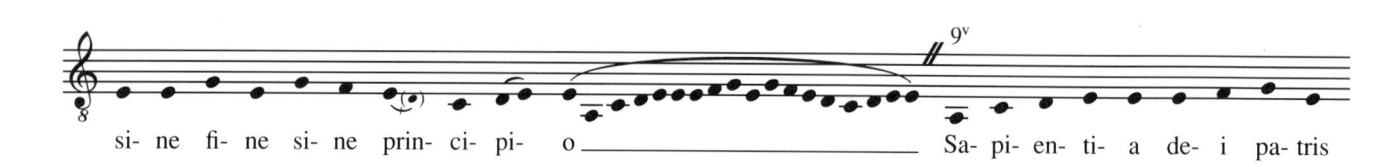

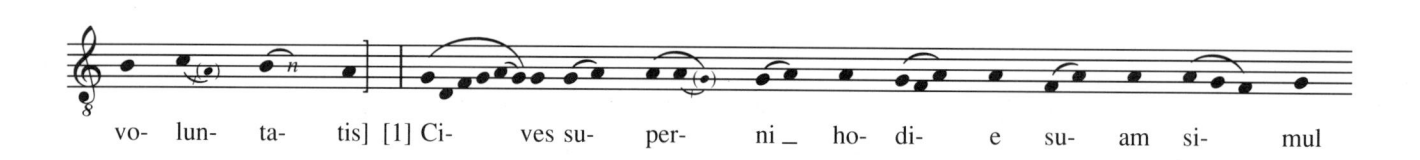

Gloria in excelsis 13a
Bosse 51; Vatican XI
Cives superni . . . Christus surrexit

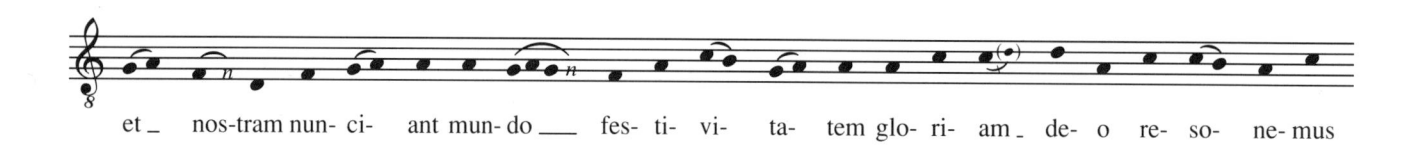

sur- re- xit dul- ci- bus hym- nis omni- po- ten- ti

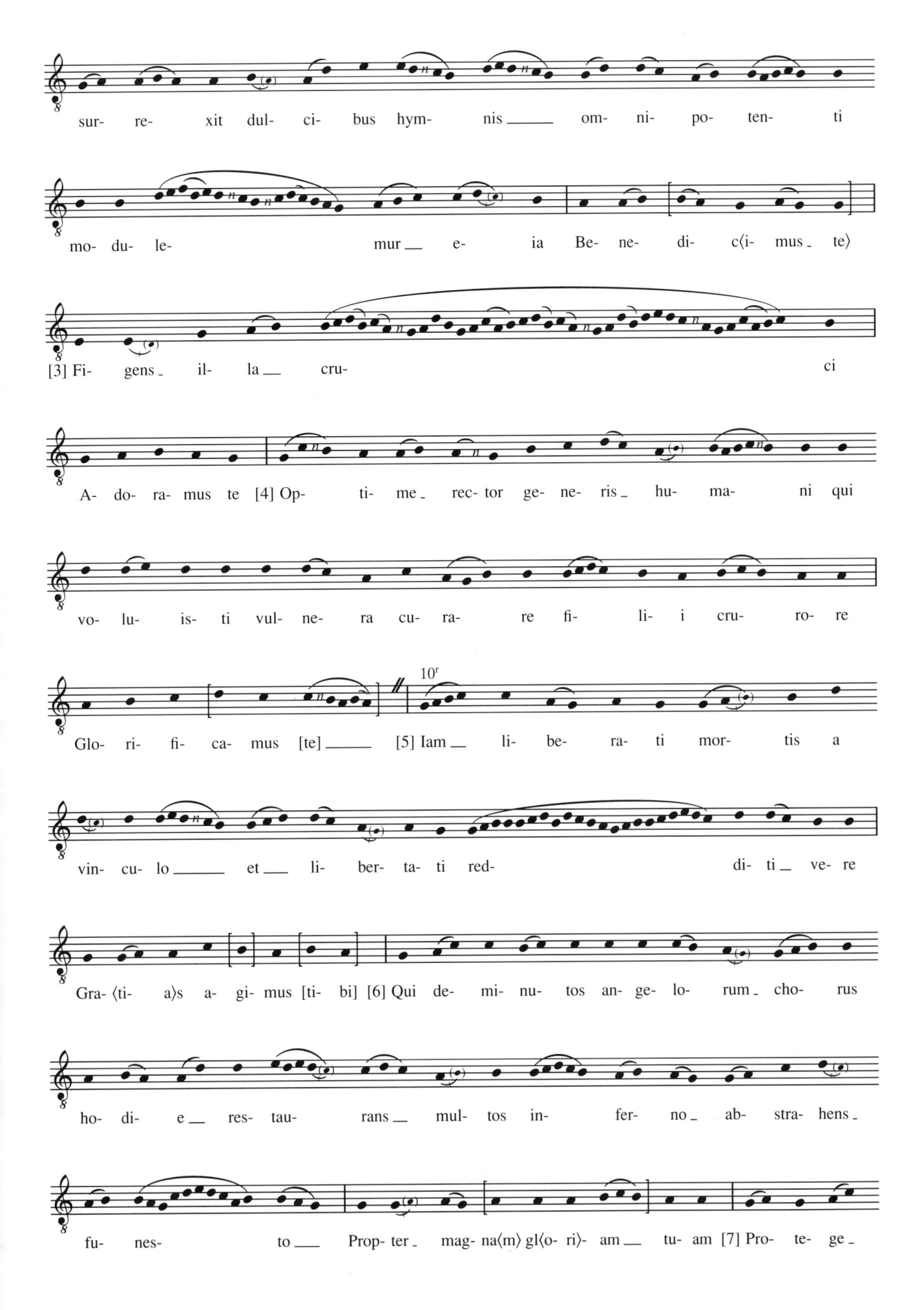

mo- du- le- mur e- ia Be- ne- di- c⟨i- mus te⟩

[3] Fi- gens il- la cru- ci

A- do- ra- mus te [4] Op- ti- me rec- tor ge- ne- ris hu- ma- ni qui

vo- lu- is- ti vul- ne- ra cu- ra- re fi- li- i cru- o- re

Glo- ri- fi- ca- mus [te] [5] Iam li- be- ra- ti mor- tis a

vin- cu- lo et li- ber- ta- ti red- di- ti ve- re

Gra- ⟨ti- a⟩s a- gi- mus [ti- bi] [6] Qui de- mi- nu- tos an- ge- lo- rum chor- us

ho- di- e res- tau- rans mul- tos in- fer- no ab- stra- hens

fu- nes- to Prop- ter mag- na⟨m⟩ gl⟨o- ri⟩- am tu- am [7] Pro- te- ge

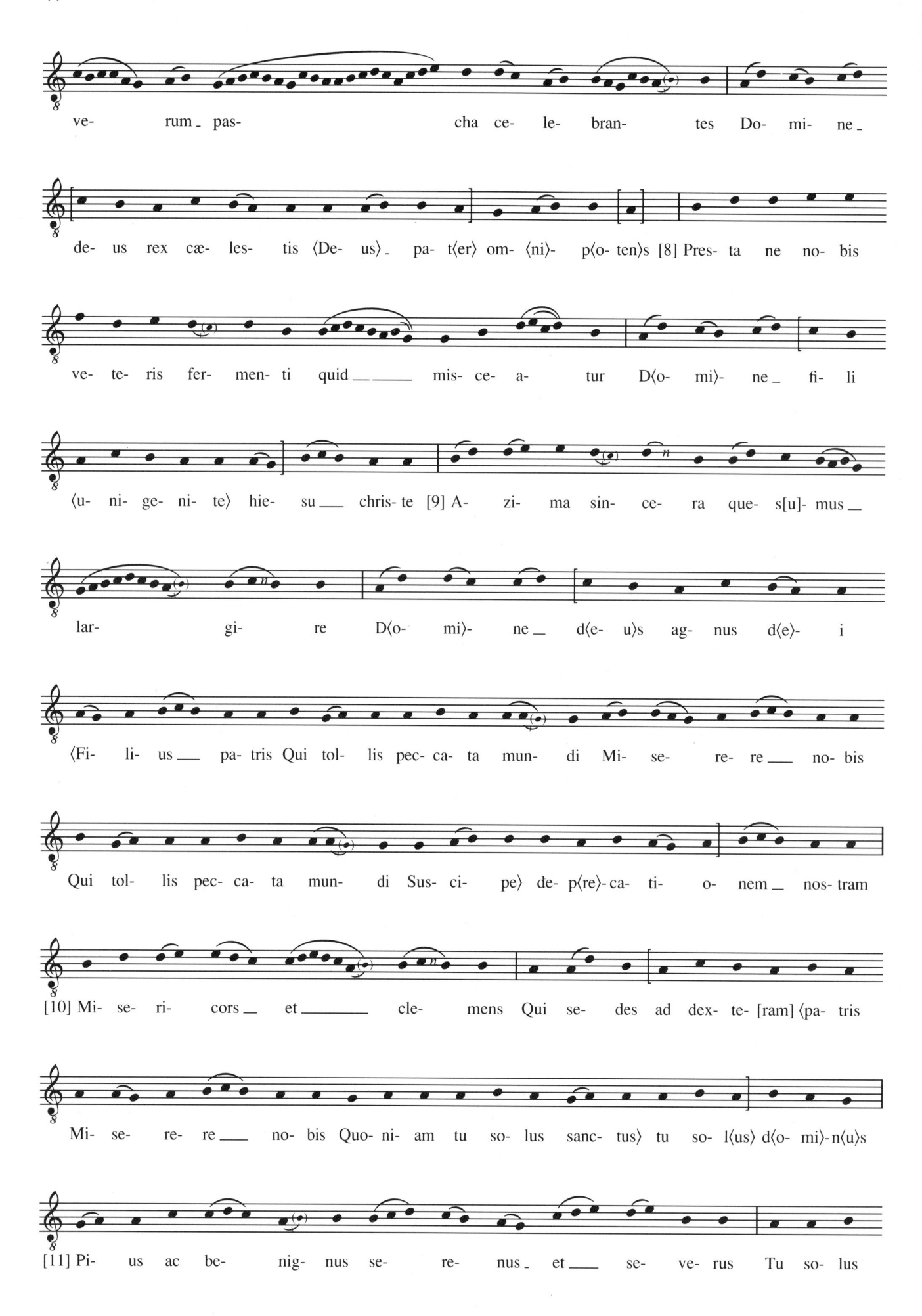

verum pas- cha ce- le- bran- tes Do- mi- ne
de- us rex cæ- les- tis ⟨De- us⟩ pa⟨t⟨er⟩ om- ⟨ni⟩- p⟨o- ten⟩s [8] Pres- ta ne no- bis
ve- te- ris fer- men- ti quid mis- ce- a- tur D⟨o- mi⟩- ne fi- li
⟨u- ni- ge- ni- te⟩ hie- su chris- te [9] A- zi- ma sin- ce- ra ques[u]- mus
lar- gi- re D⟨o- mi⟩- ne d⟨e- u⟩s ag- nus d⟨e⟩- i
⟨Fi- li- us pa- tris Qui tol- lis pec- ca- ta mun- di Mi- se- re- re no- bis
Qui tol- lis pec- ca- ta mun- di Sus- ci- pe⟩ de- p⟨re⟩- ca- ti- o- nem nos- tram
[10] Mi- se- ri- cors et cle- mens Qui se- des ad dex- te- [ram] ⟨pa- tris
Mi- se- re- re no- bis Quo- ni- am tu so- lus sanc- tus⟩ tu sol⟨us⟩ d⟨o- mi⟩-n⟨u⟩s
[11] Pi- us ac be- nig- nus se- re- nus et se- ve- rus Tu so- lus

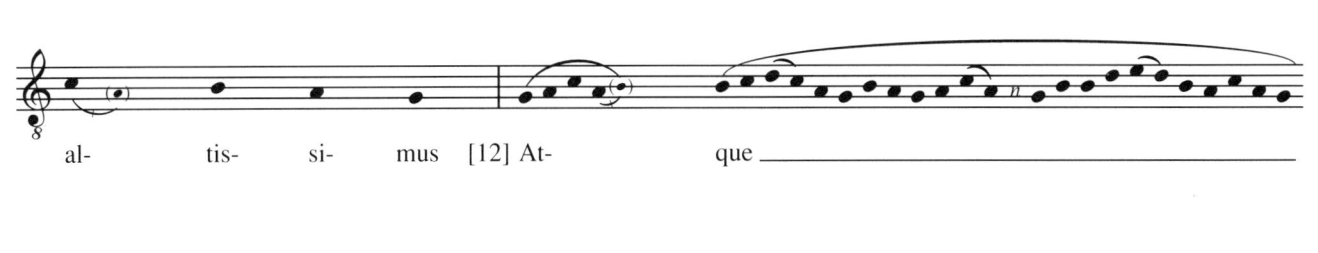

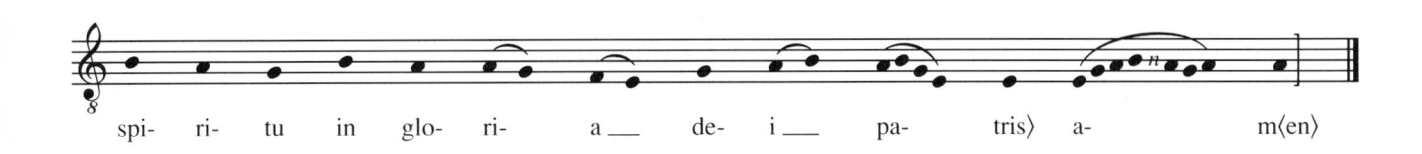

al- tis- si- mus [12] At- que

po- ten- tis- si- mus Hie- su chris- te ⟨Cum sanc- to

spi- ri- tu in glo- ri- a de- i pa- tris⟩ a- m⟨en⟩

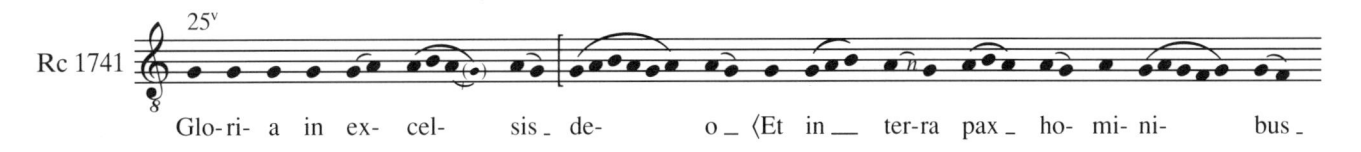

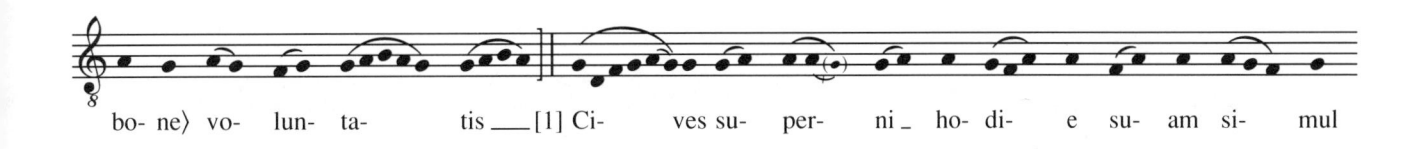

Gloria in excelsis 13b
Bosse 39; Gloria A
Cives superni . . . Christus surrexit

Rc 1741

Glo- ri- a in ex- cel- sis de- o ⟨Et in ter-ra pax ho- mi- ni- bus

bo- ne⟩ vo- lun- ta- tis [1] Ci- ves su- per- ni ho- di- e su- am si- mul

et nos-tram nun- ci- ant mun- do fes- ti- vi- ta- tem glo- ri- am de- o re- so- ne- mus

om- nes chris- to sur- gen- te Lau- d⟨a- mus te⟩

[2] Chris- tus sur- re- xit dul- ci- bus hym- nis om- ni- po- ten- ti mo- du- le- mur e- ia Ben(e- di- ci- mus te)

[3] Fi- gens il- lum cru- ci A- do- r(a- mus te) [4] Op- ti- me rec- tor ge- ne- ris hu- ma- ni qui vo- lu- is- ti vul- ne- ra cu- ra- re fi- li- i cru- o- re Glo- ri- f(i- ca- mus te) [5] Iam li- be- ra- ti mor- tis a vin- cu- lo et li- ber- ta- ti red- di- ti ve- re Gra- (ti- a)s a- g(i- mus) t(i- b)i

[6] Qui de- mi- nu- tos an- ge- lo- rum cho- ros ho- di- e re- stau- ras mul- tos in- fer- no ab- stra- hens fu- nes- to

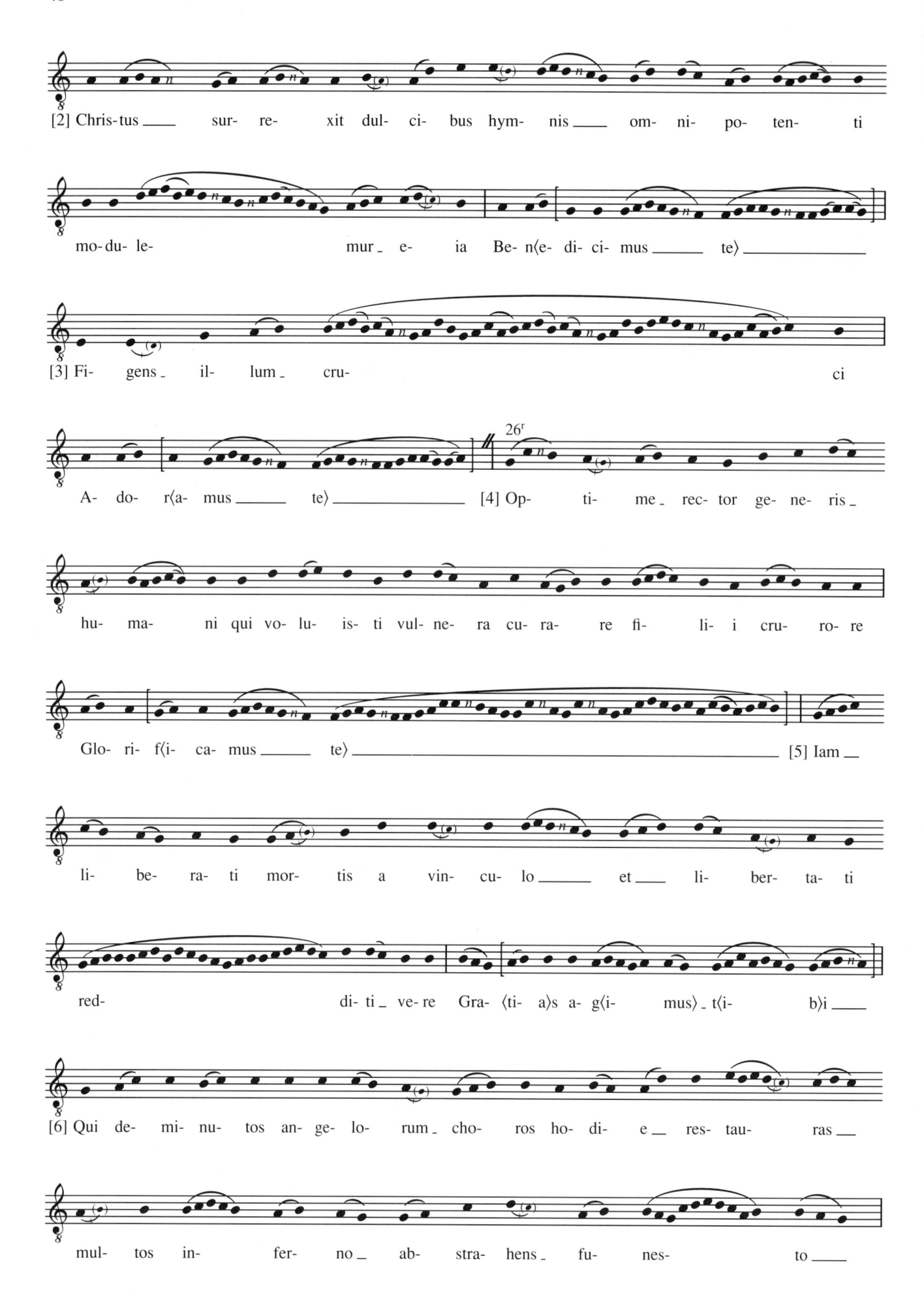

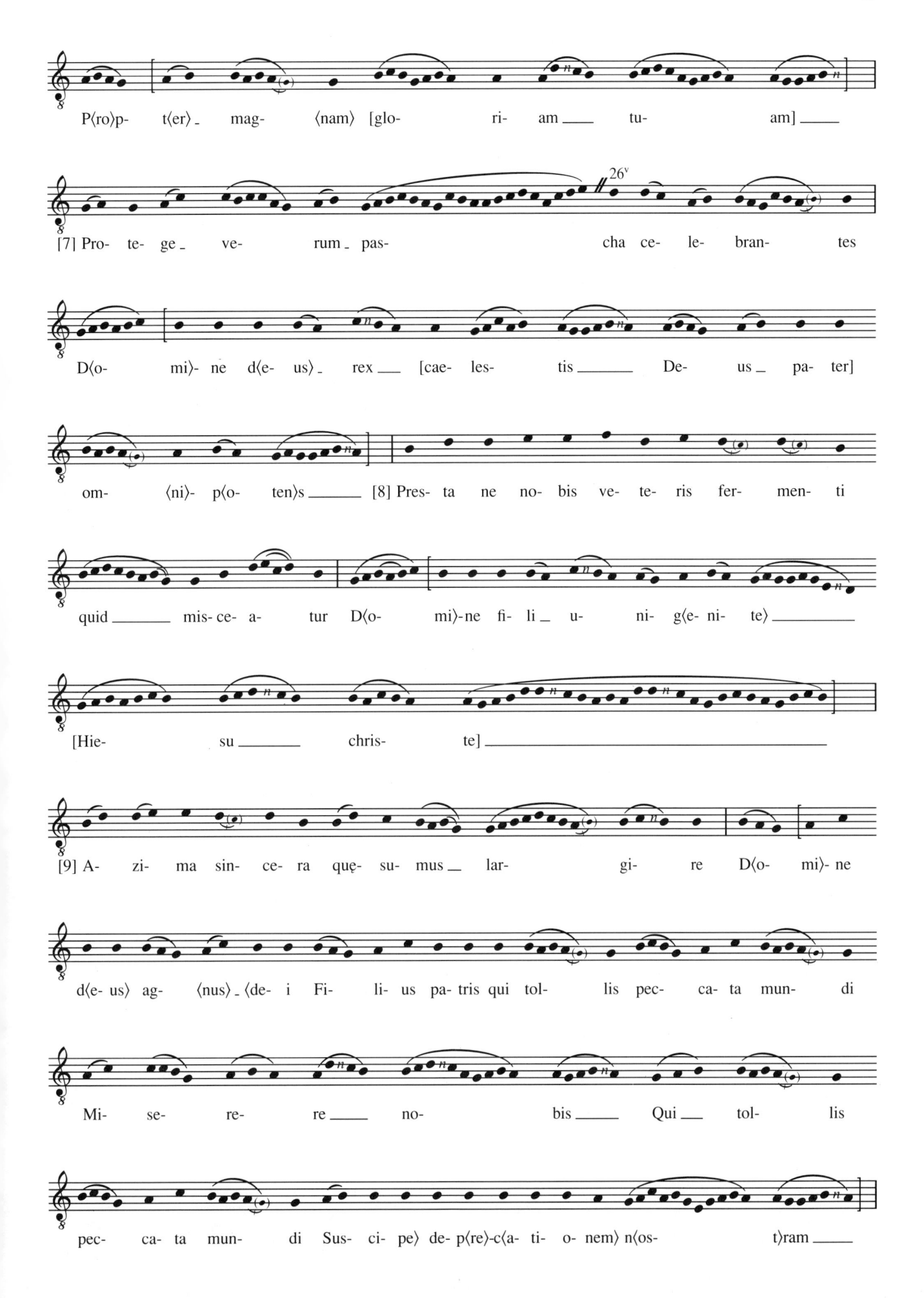

P⟨ro⟩p-t⟨er⟩ mag-⟨nam⟩ [glo- ri- am tu- am]

[7] Pro- te- ge ve- rum pas- cha ce- le- bran- tes

D⟨o- mi⟩- ne d⟨e- us⟩ rex [cae- les- tis De- us pa- ter]

om- ⟨ni⟩- p⟨o- ten⟩s [8] Pres- ta ne no- bis ve- te- ris fer- men- ti

quid mis- ce- a- tur D⟨o- mi⟩-ne fi- li u- ni- g⟨e- ni- te⟩

[Hie- su chris- te]

[9] A- zi- ma sin- ce- ra quę su- mus lar- gi- re D⟨o- mi⟩- ne

d⟨e- us⟩ ag- ⟨nus⟩ ⟨de- i Fi- li- us pa- tris qui tol- lis pec- ca- ta mun- di

Mi- se- re- re no- bis Qui tol- lis

pec- ca- ta mun- di Sus- ci- pe⟩ de- p⟨re⟩-c⟨a- ti- o- nem⟩ n⟨os- t⟩ram

48

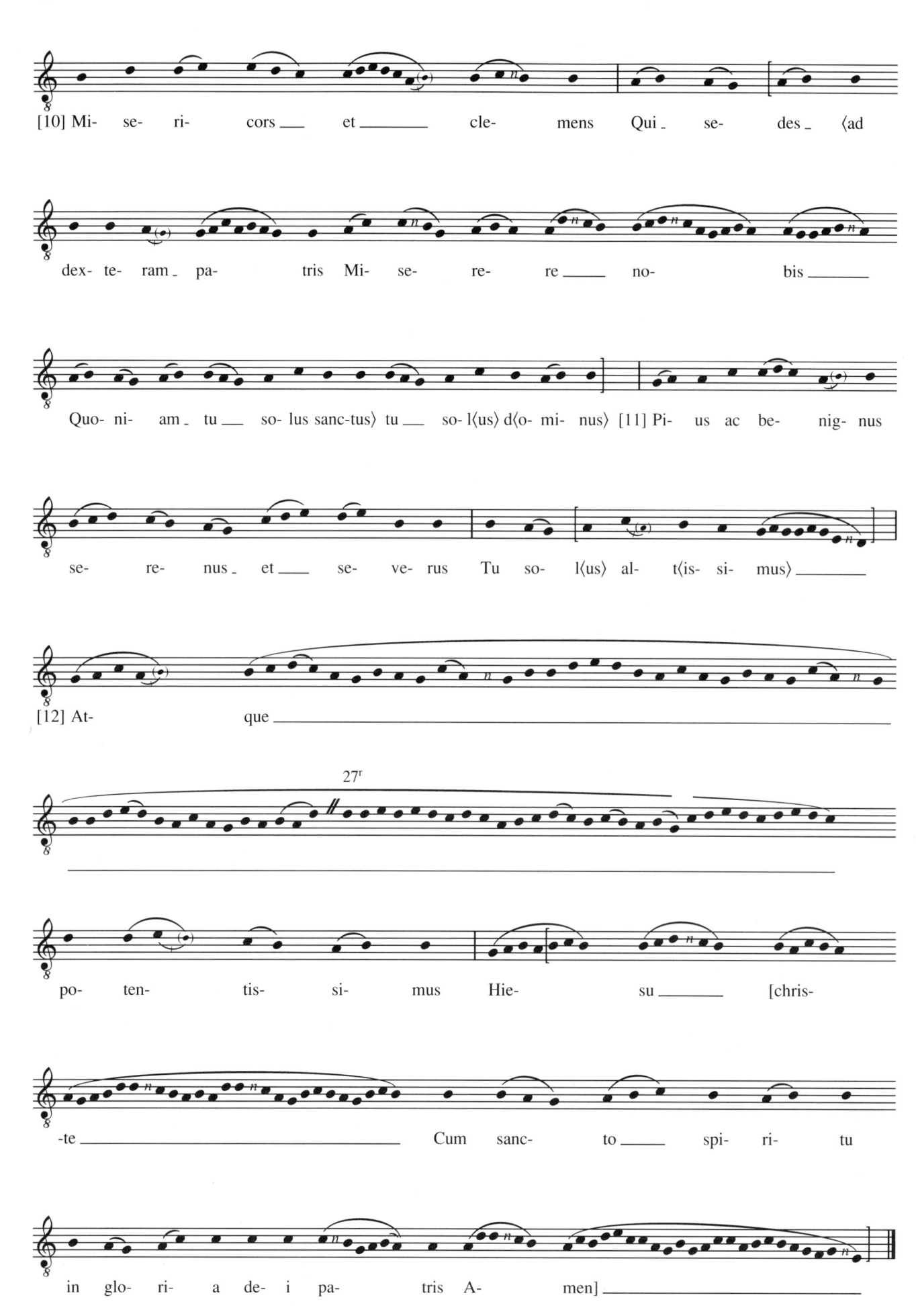

[10] Mi- se- ri- cors et cle- mens Qui se- des ⟨ad dex- te- ram pa- tris Mi- se- re- re no- bis Quo- ni- am tu so- lus sanc-tus⟩ tu so- l⟨us⟩ d⟨o- mi- nus⟩ [11] Pi- us ac be- nig- nus se- re- nus et se- ve- rus Tu so- l⟨us⟩ al- t⟨is- si- mus⟩ [12] At- que po- ten- ti- si- mus Hie- su [chris- -te Cum sanc- to spi- ri- tu in glo- ri- a de- i pa- tris A- men]

Gloria in excelsis 14
Bosse 11; Vatican XIV
Alme mundi hodie de morte

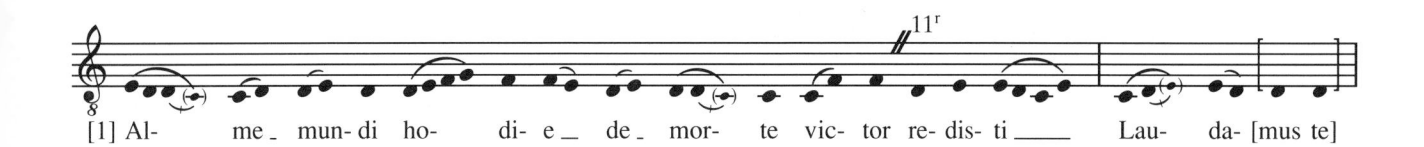

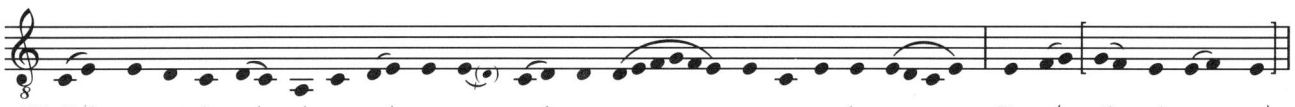

Rn 1343

Glo- ri- a in ex- cel- sis de- o [Et in ter- ra pax ho- mi- ni- bus bo- ne vo- lun- ta- tis]

[1] Al- me mun- di ho- di- e de mor- te vic- tor re- dis- ti Lau- da- [mus te]

[2] Qui nos re- de- mis- ti pro- pri- o san- gui- ne o rex an- ge- lo- rum Be- n⟨e- ci- mus te⟩

[3] Rex an- ge- lo- rum at- que arch- an- ge- lo- rum de- us A- do- r⟨a- mus te⟩

[4] Quem lau- dant sol at- que lu- na et u- ni- ver- sa cre- a- ta tu- a

Glo- ri- fi- c⟨a- mus te⟩ [5] Qui ge- nus hu- ma- num re- vo- cas- ti ad pris- ti- nam vi- tam

Gra- ⟨ti- a⟩s a- gi- m⟨us⟩ ⟨ti- bi⟩ prop- ter mag- nam glo- ri- am tu- am Do- mi- ne rex cae- les- tis

De- us pa- ter om- ni- po- tens Do- mi- ne fi- li u- ni- ge- ni- te hie- su chris- te et sanc- te spi- ri- tus

Do-mi-ne de- us Ag-nus de- i Fi- li- us pa- tris Qui tol-lis pec-ca- ta mun-di mi-se- re- re

no- bis Qui tol-lis pec-ca- ta mun-di Sus-ci- pe de-pre-ca- ti- o-nem nos-tram Qui se- des ad dex-te- ram

pa- tris mi- se- re- re no- bis Qui a) tu so- lus s⟨an⟩c- ⟨tu⟩s

[6] Hoc no- men est ti- bi in fi- ne et an- te om- ni- a se- cu-la

Tu so- l⟨us⟩ d⟨o- mi- nus⟩ [7] Et non est a- li- us in æ- ter- num

Tu so- lus al- tis- si- mus [8] Cu- i reg- num est si- ne

fi- ne In se- cu-la se- cu- lo- rum

Hie- su chris-te ⟨Cum sanc- to spi- ri- tu in glo- ri- a de- i pa- tris⟩ a- men

Gloria in excelsis 15
Bosse 11; Vatican XIV
Alme mundi hodie in caelum

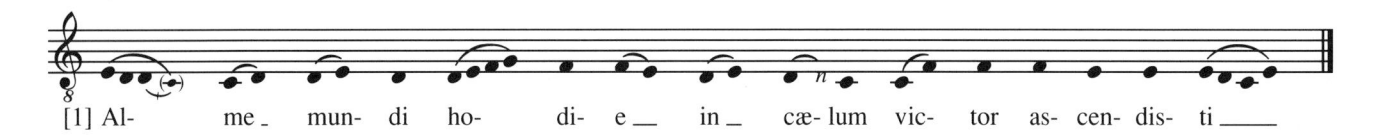

Rn 1343

Glo- ri- a in ex- cel- sis de- o ⟨Et in ter- ra pax ho- mi- ni- bus⟩ bo- ne vo- lun- ta- tis

[1] Al- me mun- di ho- di- e in cæ- lum vic- tor as- cen- dis- ti

Gloria in excelsis 16
Bosse 51; Vatican XI
O laudabilis rex

Rn 1343

Glo- ri- a in ex- cel- sis de- o ⟨Et in ter- ra pax ho- mi- ni- bus⟩ bo- n⟨e⟩ vo- l⟨un- ta- tis⟩

[1] O lau- da- bi- lis rex do- mi- ne de- us Lau- da- mus [te]

[2] A- do- na- y be- ne- dic- te de- us Be- n⟨e- di- ci- mus te⟩

[3] O a- do- ran- da et be- a- ta tri- ni- tas de- us A- do- r⟨a- mus te⟩

[4] Glo- ri- fi- can- de et me- tu- en- de de- us Glo- ri- fi- [ca- mus te]

[5] Rex se- cu- lo- rum do- mi- ne hie- su chris- te Gra- ⟨ti- a⟩s a- gi- m⟨us⟩

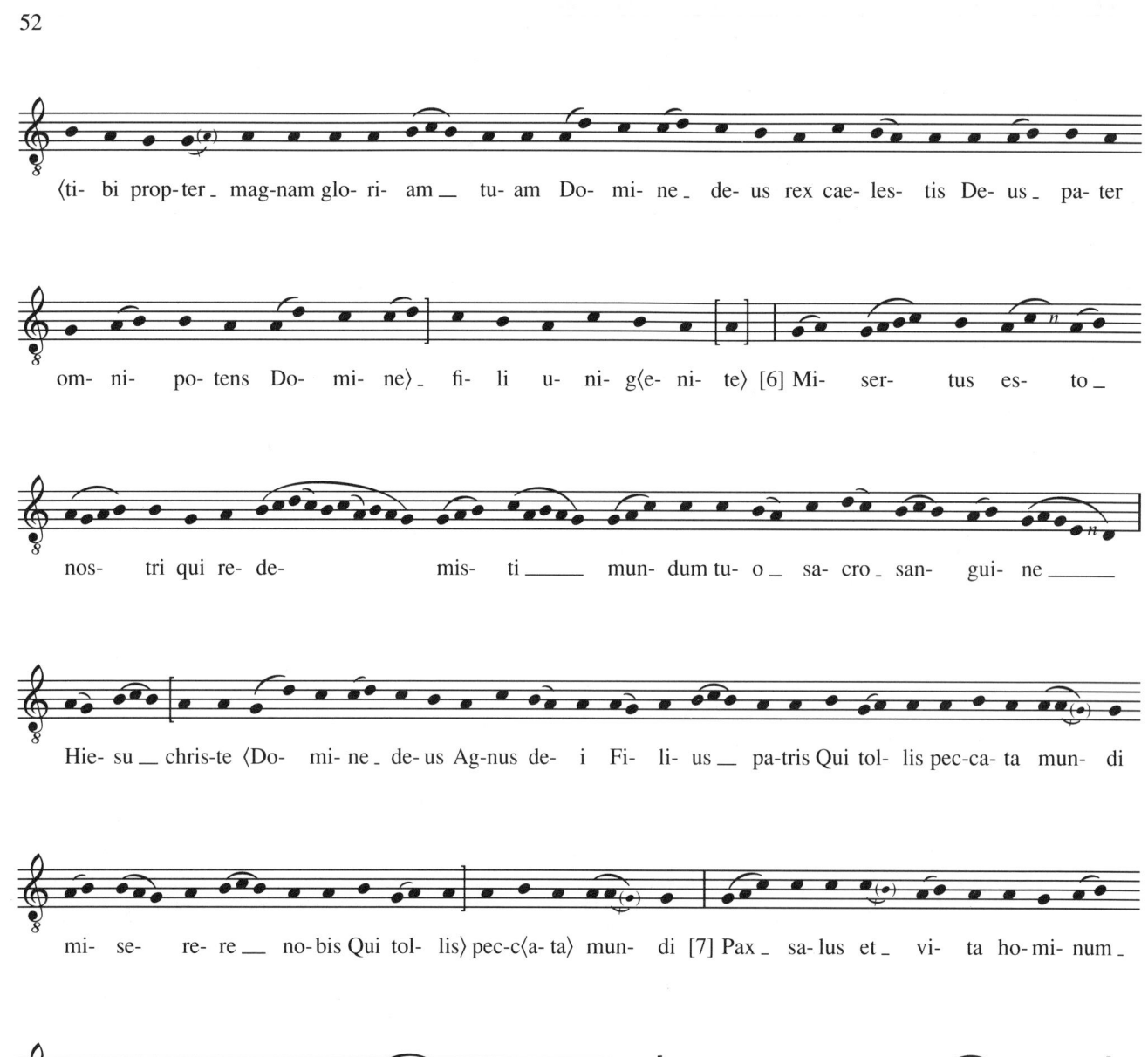

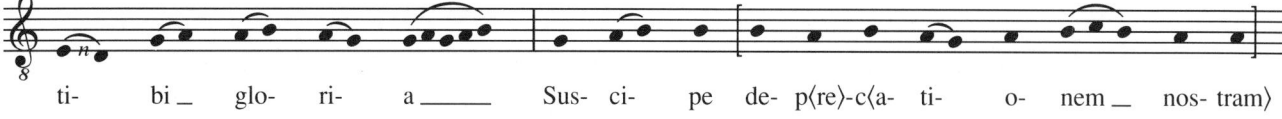

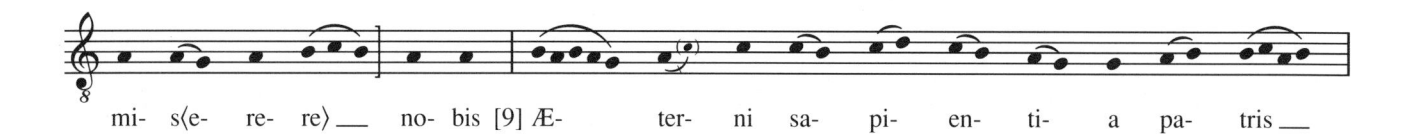

⟨ti- bi prop-ter⸱ mag-nam glo- ri- am⸱ tu- am Do- mi- ne⸱ de- us rex cae- les- tis De- us⸱ pa- ter om- ni- po- tens Do- mi- ne⟩⸱ fi- li u- ni- g⟨e- ni- te⟩ [6] Mi- ser- tus es- to⸱ nos- tri qui re- de- mis- ti⸱ mun- dum tu- o⸱ sa- cro⸱ san- gui- ne⸱ Hie- su⸱ chris- te ⟨Do- mi- ne⸱ de- us Ag- nus de- i Fi- li- us⸱ pa- tris Qui tol- lis pec- ca- ta mun- di mi- se- re- re⸱ no- bis Qui tol- lis⟩ pec-c⟨a- ta⟩ mun- di [7] Pax⸱ sa- lus et⸱ vi- ta ho- mi- num⸱ ti- bi⸱ glo- ri- a⸱ Sus- ci- pe de- p⟨re⟩-c⟨a- ti- o- nem⸱ nos- tram⟩ [8] No- bis in ter- ris mi- se- re- re de- us al- me⸱ Qui se- des ⟨ad dex- te- ram pa- tris⟩ mi- s⟨e- re- re⟩⸱ no- bis [9] Æ- ter- ni sa- pi- en- ti- a pa- tris⸱ Q⟨uo- ni- a⟩m tu so- lus s⟨an⟩c-⟨tu⟩s [10] Tu⸱ lux⸱ vi- a⸱ et⸱ spes nos- tra — Tu so- lus d⟨o- mi⟩- n⟨u⟩s [11] O — vir- tus ho- nor —

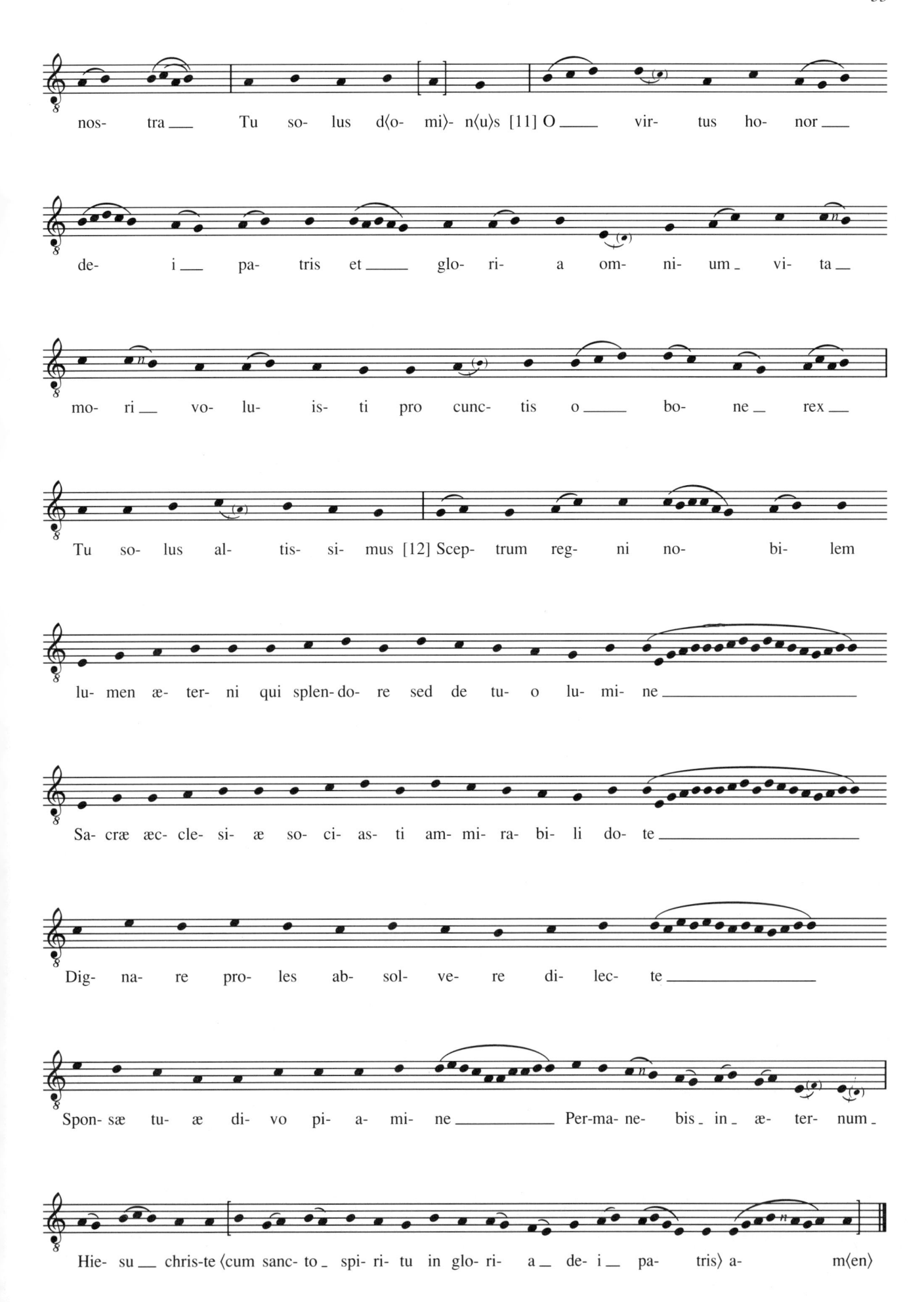

de- i — pa- tris et — glo- ri- a om- ni- um — vi- ta —

mo- ri — vo- lu- is- ti pro cunc- tis o — bo- ne — rex —

Tu so- lus al- tis- si- mus [12] Scep- trum reg- ni no- bi- lem

lu- men æ- ter- ni qui splen- do- re sed de tu- o lu- mi- ne ———

Sa- cræ æc- cle- si- æ so- ci- as- ti am- mi- ra- bi- li do- te ———

Dig- na- re pro- les ab- sol- ve- re di- lec- te ———

Spon- sæ tu- æ di- vo pi- a- mi- ne ——— Per- ma- ne- bis in æ- ter- num —

Hie- su — chris- te ⟨cum sanc- to — spi- ri- tu in glo- ri- a — de- i — pa- tris⟩ a- m⟨en⟩

Gloria in excelsis 17
Bosse 51; Vatican XI
Laudat in excelsis

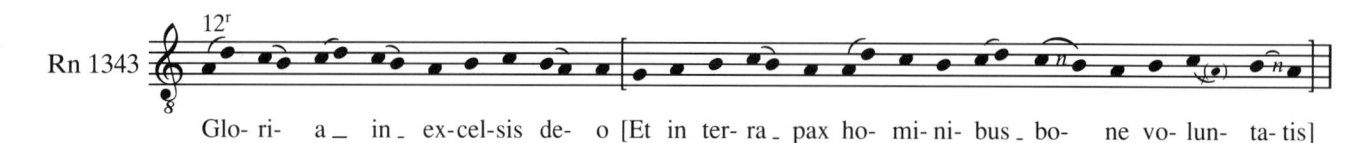

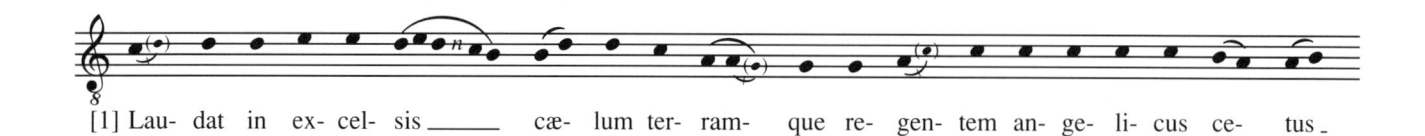

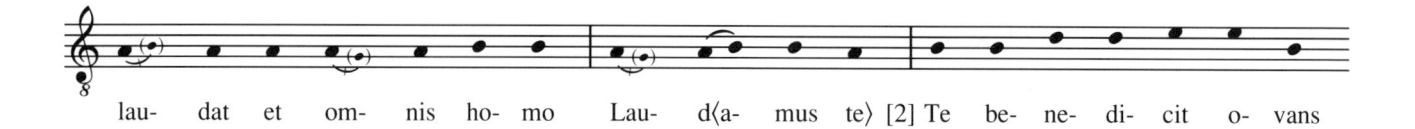

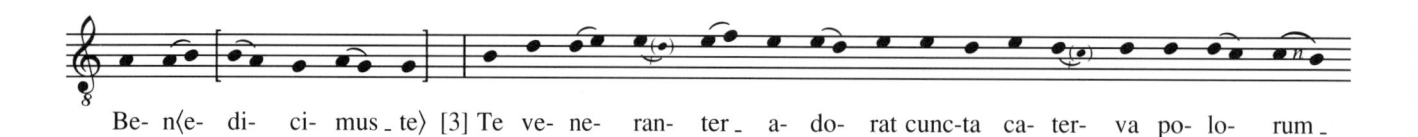

Rn 1343

Glo- ri- a in ex-cel-sis de- o [Et in ter- ra pax ho- mi- ni- bus bo- ne vo- lun- ta- tis]

[1] Lau- dat in ex- cel- sis cæ- lum ter- ram- que re- gen- tem an- ge- li- cus ce- tus

lau- dat et om- nis ho- mo Lau- d⟨a- mus te⟩ [2] Te be- ne- di- cit o- vans

an- ge- lo- rum cel- sa po- tes- tas et mor- ta- lis ho- mo te be- ne- di- cit o- vans

Ben⟨e- di- ci- mus te⟩ [3] Te ve- ne- ran- ter a- do- rat cunc-ta ca- ter- va po- lo- rum

te tel- lus pe- la- gus lau- dat a- do- rat a- mat. A- dor⟨a- mus te⟩

[4] Glo- ri- fi- cant do- mi- num ru- ti- lan- ci- a sy- de- ra cæ- li

glo- ri- fi- cant te rex cunc- ta cre- a- ta tu- a Glo- ri- f⟨i- ca- mus⟩ ⟨te⟩

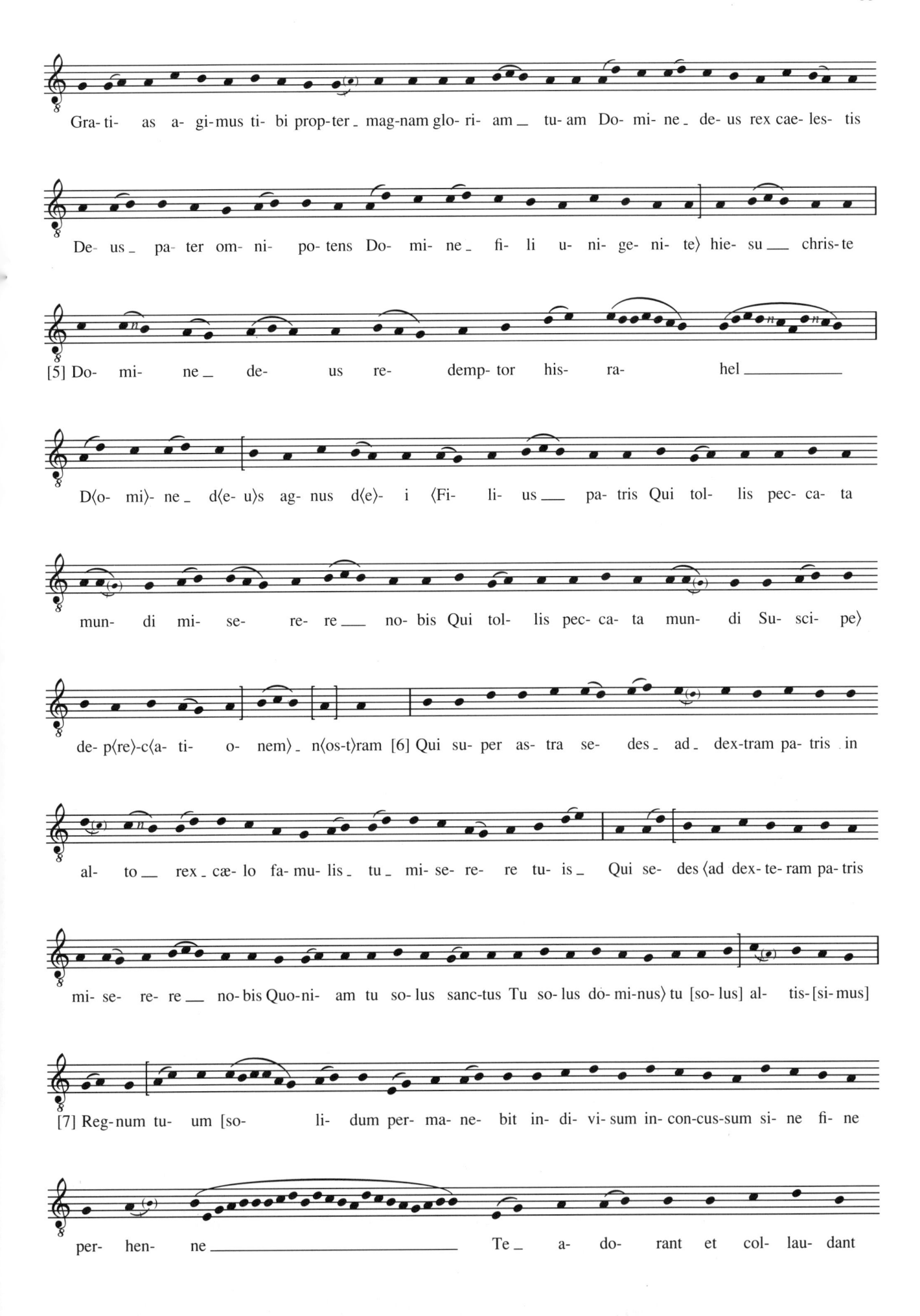

Gra-ti- as a- gi-mus ti- bi prop-ter mag-nam glo- ri- am tu- am Do- mi- ne de- us rex cae- les- tis

De- us pa- ter om- ni- po- tens Do- mi- ne fi- li u- ni- ge- ni- te⟩ hie- su chris- te

[5] Do- mi- ne de- us re- demp- tor his- ra- hel

D⟨o- mi⟩- ne d⟨e- u⟩s ag- nus d⟨e⟩- i ⟨Fi- li- us⟩ pa- tris Qui tol- lis pec- ca- ta

mun- di mi- se- re- re no- bis Qui tol- lis pec- ca- ta mun- di Su- sci- pe⟩

de- p⟨re⟩-c⟨a- ti- o- nem⟩ n⟨os-t⟩ram [6] Qui su- per as- tra se- des ad dex-tram pa- tris in

al- to rex cae- lo fa- mu- lis tu mi- se- re- re tu- is Qui se- des ⟨ad dex- te- ram pa- tris

mi- se- re- re no- bis Quo-ni- am tu so- lus sanc-tus Tu so- lus do- mi-nus⟩ tu [so- lus] al- tis-[si-mus]

[7] Reg-num tu- um [so- li- dum per- ma- ne- bit in- di- vi-sum in-con-cus-sum si- ne fi- ne

per- hen- ne Te a- do- rant et col- lau- dant

si- mul om- nes vir- tu- tes an- ge- li- cae ___ et nos sup- pli- ces col- lau- da- mus tu- um

no- men ___ Qui per- ma- ne- bit in ae- ter- num] Hie- su

[chris- te Cum sanc- to spi- ri- tu in glo- ri- a de- i pa- tris A- men]

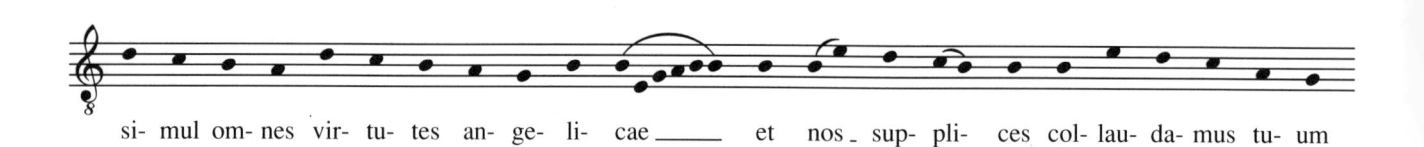

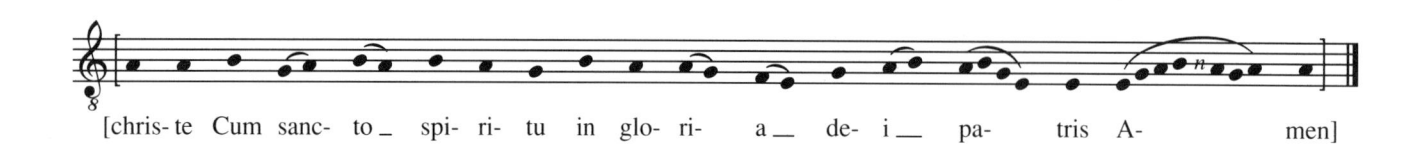

Gloria in excelsis 18
Bosse 12; Vatican I
Quando regis cunctos

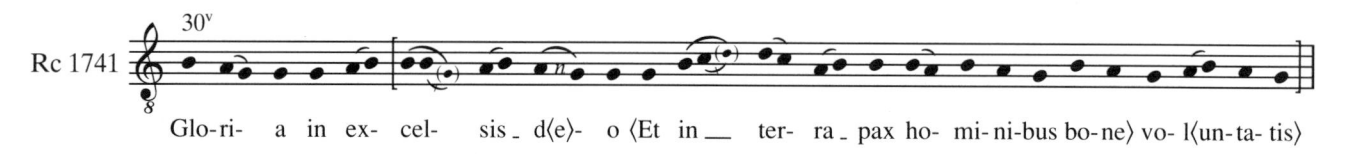

Rc 1741

Glo- ri- a in ex- cel- sis d⟨e⟩- o ⟨Et in ter- ra pax ho- mi- ni- bus bo- ne⟩ vo- l⟨un- ta- tis⟩

[1] Quan- do re- gis cunc- tos sem- per gra- tan- ter ho- mo- nes Lau- d⟨a- mus te⟩

[2] Com- pla- cu- it ti- bi met mor- tem rex iu- re sub- i- re Ben⟨e- di- ci- mus te⟩

[3] Ab- la- to loe- to vi- tam per- fun- dis ho- nes- tam A- do- r⟨a- mus te⟩

[4] Glo- ri- fi- cant te ment mi- tes in tem- po- re vo- ces Glor⟨i- fi- ca- mus te⟩ ___

[5] Tu no- bis a- pe- ris ce- les- ti- a reg- na po- lo- rum

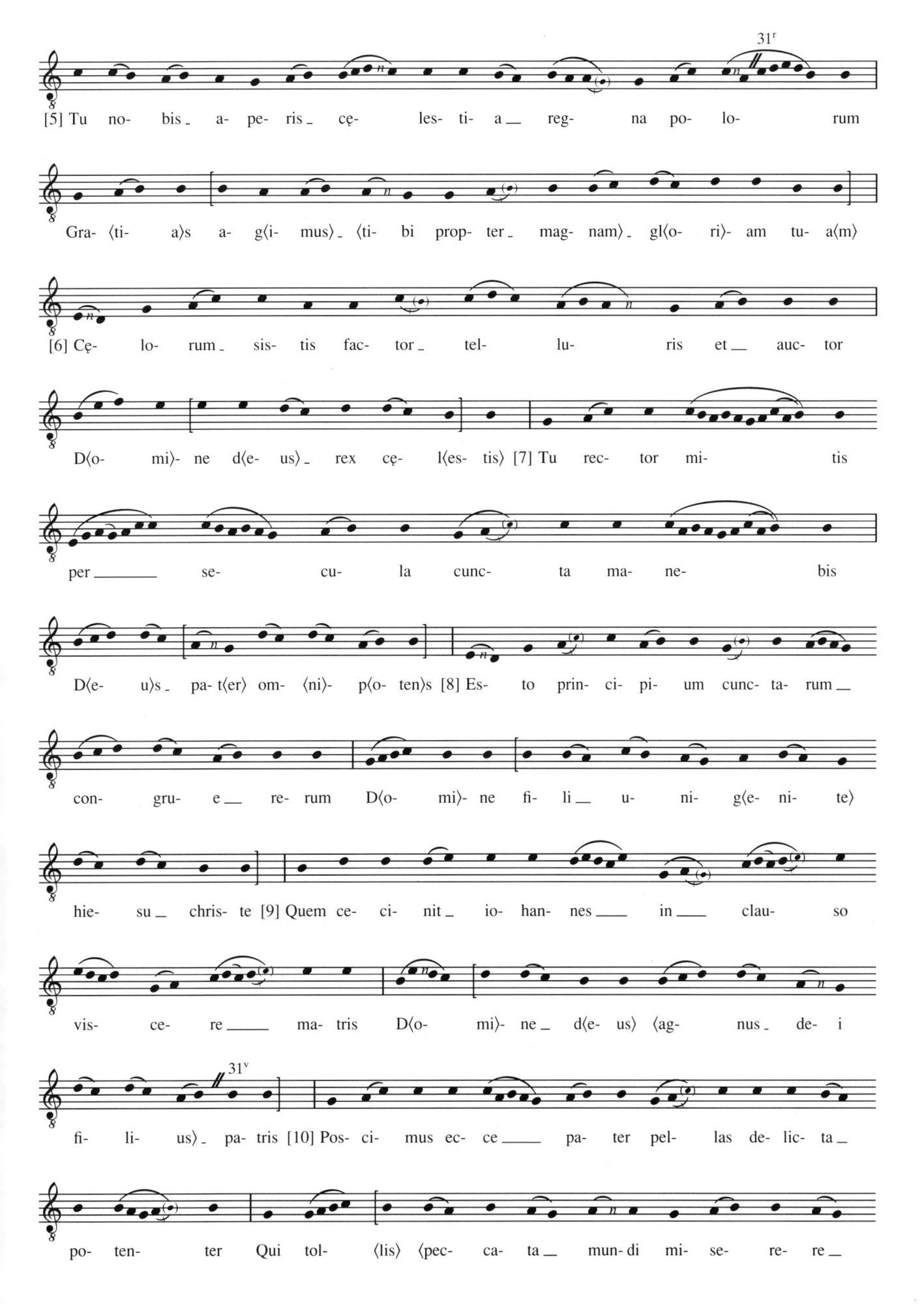

Gra- ⟨ti- a⟩s a- g⟨i- mus⟩ ⟨ti- bi prop- ter mag- nam⟩ gl⟨o- ri⟩- am tu- a⟨m⟩

[6] Ce- lo- rum sis- tis fac- tor tel- lu- ris et auc- tor

D⟨o- mi⟩- ne d⟨e- us⟩ rex ce- l⟨es- tis⟩ [7] Tu rec- tor mi- tis

per se- cu- la cunc- ta ma- ne- bis

D⟨e- u⟩s pa- t⟨er⟩ om- ⟨ni⟩- p⟨o- ten⟩s [8] Es- to prin- ci- pi- um cunc- ta- rum

con- gru- e re- rum D⟨o- mi⟩- ne fi- li u- ni- g⟨e- ni- te⟩

hie- su chris- te [9] Quem ce- ci- nit io- han- nes in clau- so

vis- ce- re ma- tris D⟨o- mi⟩- ne d⟨e- us⟩ ⟨ag- nus de- i

fi- li- us⟩ pa- tris [10] Pos- ci- mus ec- ce pa- ter pel- las de- lic- ta

po- ten- ter Qui tol- ⟨lis⟩ ⟨pec- ca- ta mun- di mi- se- re

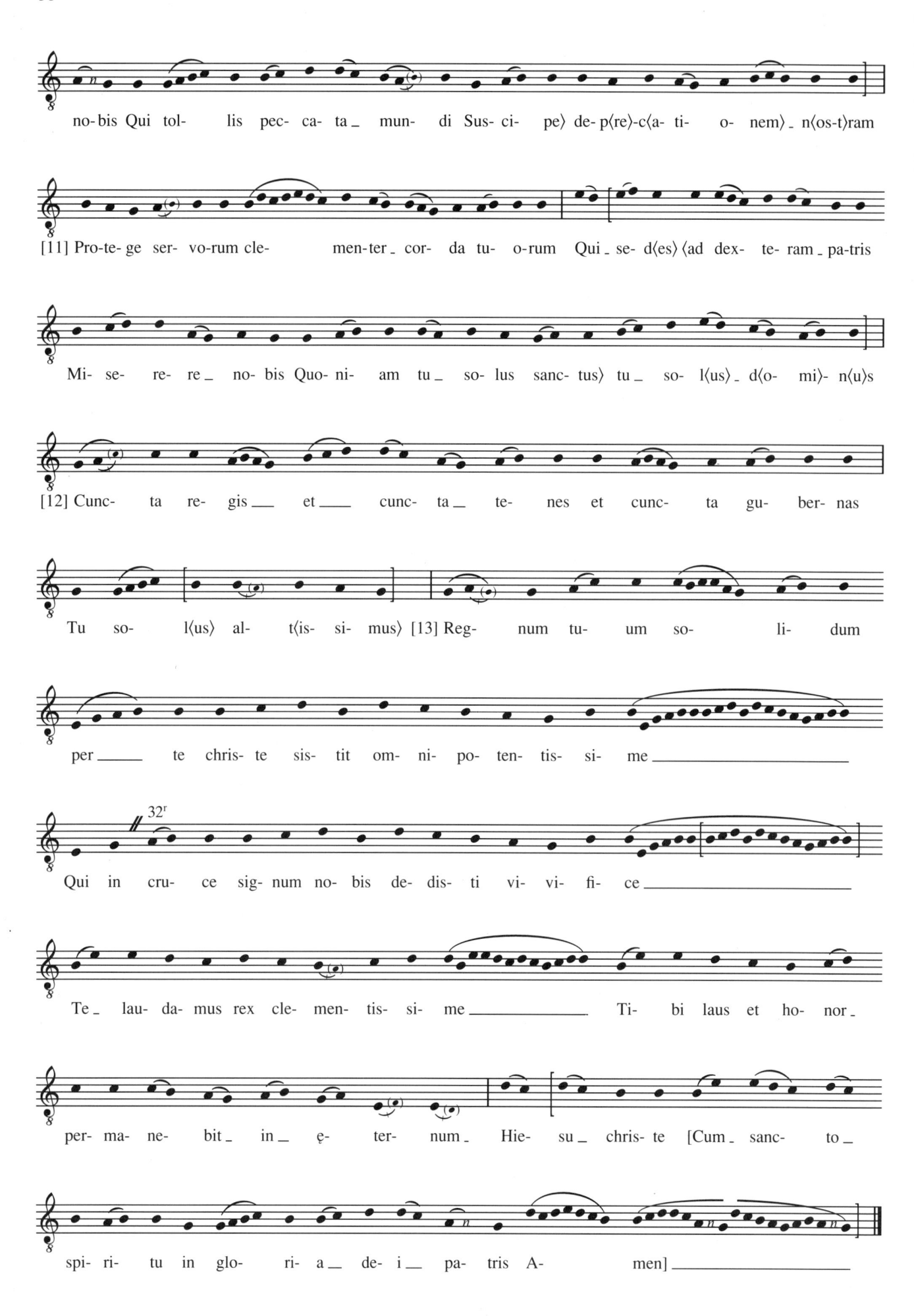

no-bis Qui tol- lis pec- ca- ta mun- di Sus- ci- pe de-p⟨re⟩-c⟨a-ti- o- nem⟩ n⟨os-t⟩ram

[11] Pro-te- ge ser- vo-rum cle- men-ter cor- da tu- o-rum Qui se- d⟨es⟩ ⟨ad dex- ter-am patris

Mi- se- re- re no- bis Quo-ni- am tu so- lus sanc-tus⟩ tu so-l⟨us⟩ d⟨o- mi⟩- n⟨u⟩s

[12] Cunc- ta re- gis et cunc- ta te- nes et cunc- ta gu- ber- nas

Tu so- l⟨us⟩ al- t⟨is- si- mus⟩ [13] Reg- num tu- um so- li- dum

per te chris- te sis- tit om- ni- po- ten- tis- si- me

32ʳ

Qui in cru- ce sig- num no- bis de- dis- ti vi- vi- fi- ce

Te lau- da- mus rex cle- men- tis- si- me Ti- bi laus et ho- nor

per- ma- ne- bit in e̜- ter- num Hie- su chris- te [Cum sanc- to

spi- ri- tu in glo- ri- a de- i pa- tris A- men]

Gloria in excelsis 19
Bosse 11; Vatican XIV
O gloria sanctorum

Rn 1343

Glo-ri- a in ex-cel-sis de- o [Et in ter- ra pax ho- mi- ni- bus bo- ne vo- lun- ta- tis]

[1] O glo- ri- a sanc-to- rum laus-que an- ge- lo- rum quam se- cu- tus est sanc-tus pe- trus

Lau- da-[mus te] [2] O de-cus et vir- tus laus-que be- a-ta sanc-to-rum quam lau- dat sanc-tus pe- trus

Be-ne-di-[ci-mus te] [3] An-ge-li-cus ti-bi a[d]-stat cla-ris-si-mus or- do cum quo te sem-per glo-ri-fi-cat sanc-tus

pe- trus A-do-r⟨a-mus te⟩ [4] Can-te-mus ti-bi lau-des de pec-to-re to- to te-que cum sanc-to be-ne-di-

-ca- mus pe- tro Glo-⟨ri⟩- fi- c⟨a-mus te⟩ [5] Glo-ri- fi- cant do- mi-num ru- ti- lan- ci- a sy-de-ra

cæ- li glo- ri- fi- cant te rex cunc-ta cre-a- ta tu- a Gra-⟨ti- a⟩s a- g⟨i-mus⟩ ⟨ti- bi prop-ter

mag-nam⟩ tu- am gl⟨o-ri⟩-am [6] Vi- ta sa-lus bo-ni- tas ka- ri- tas sa-pi- en- ti- a chris-te

D⟨o-mi⟩-ne rex ⟨cae- les- tis De- us pa- ter om- ni- po-tens Do- mi- ne fi- li u- ni-ge- ni- te

Hie- su christe et sanctæ spiritus [7] Bo- num om- ne pa- ri- ter cunc-ta per se- cu- la chris- te Do-mi-ne de- us ag- nus de- i Fi- li- us pa- tris Qui tol-lis pec-ca- ta mun-di mi- se- re- re no- bis Qui tol- lis pec-ca- ta mun-di Sus-ci- pe de-pre-ca- ti- o-nem nos- tram [8] An- ge- li- cis sor- te con-iunc-tus is- te ca- ter- vis as-sis-tit iu-gi- ter vul- ti- bus ec-ce tu- is Qui se- des ad dex-te- ram pa-tris mi-se- re- re no- bis Qui- a tu so- lus sanc- tus Tu so- lus do- mi- nus Tu so- lus al- tis- [si- mus] [9] Ti- bi laus im- pe- ri- um sa- lus vic- to- ri- a et gra- ci- a po- tes- tas glo- ri- a de- cus et ho- nor per- -ma- ne- bit in æ- ter- num Hie- su christe [Cum sanc- to spi- ri- tu in glo- ri- a de- i pa- tris A- men]

Gloria in excelsis 20
Bosse 12; Vatican I
Qui caelicolas

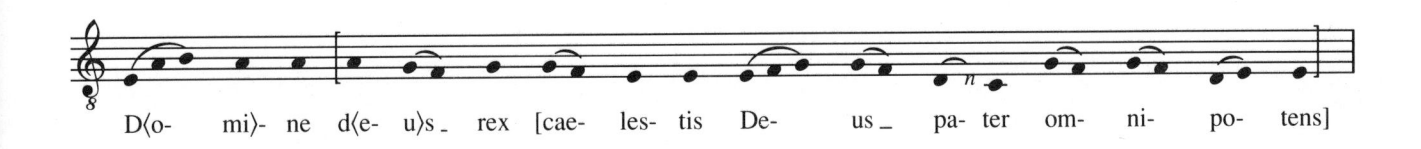

Rn 1343

Glo- ri- a in ex- cel- sis de- o ⟨Et in ter- ra pax ho- mi-ni-bus⟩ bo-n⟨e⟩ vo- l⟨un-ta-tis⟩

[1] Qui cæ- li- co- las et ter- ri- ge- nas fe- de- re sanc-to so- ci- as et ex- or- nas

Lau- d⟨a-mus te⟩ [Be- ne- di- ci- mus te A- do- ra- mus te] [2] Quem lau-dat cho-rus et

be- ne- di- cit su- pe- rus a- do- rant te cunc- ta sy- de- ra tur-me Glo- rif⟨i- ca- mus

te⟩ [Gra- ti- as a-gi-mus ti- bi prop-ter mag-nam glo-ri-am tu-am] [3] Qui-a tu nos re- di-me- ras

cum fi- nem se- cu- li im- po- su- e- ras ut an- te tem- po- ra de- cre- ve- ras

D⟨o- mi⟩- ne d⟨e- u⟩s rex [cae- les- tis De- us pa- ter om- ni- po- tens]

[4] Non mi- nus cle- men- ti- æ quam po- ten- ti- æ di- vi- ci- is lo- cu- ples

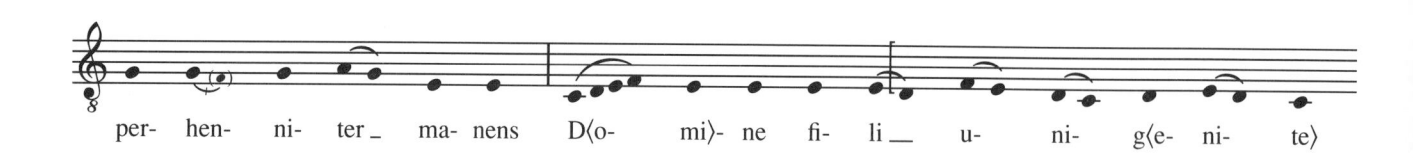

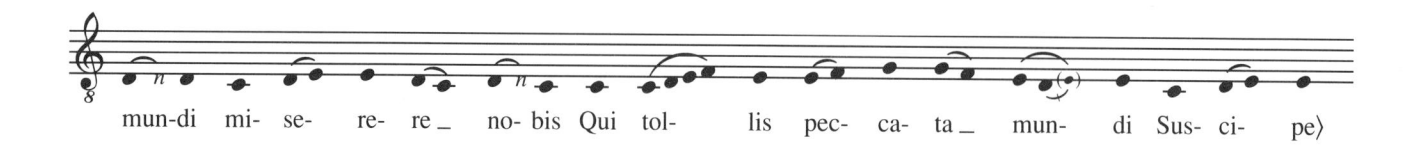

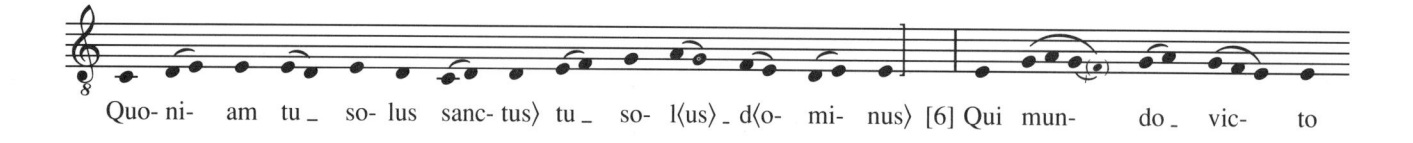

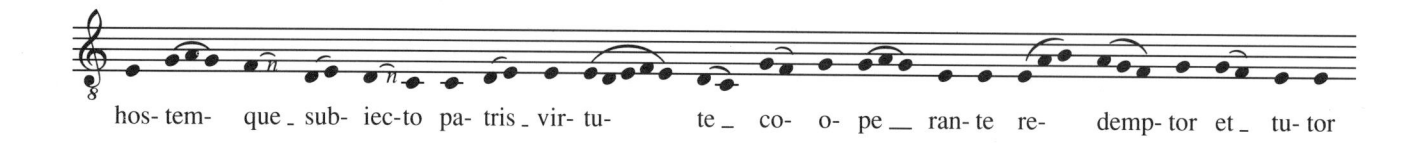

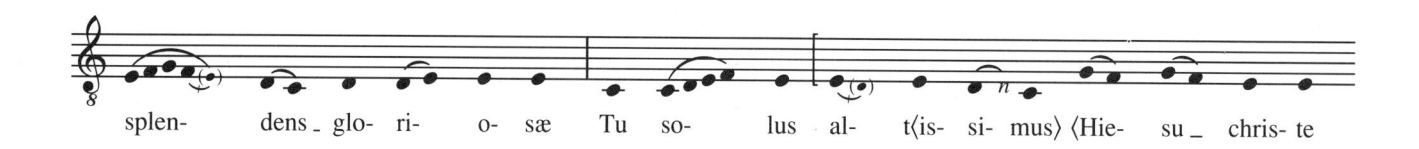

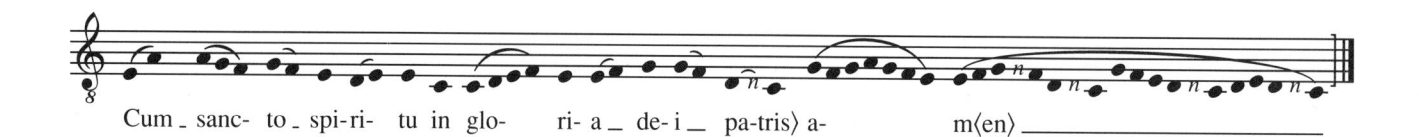

per- hen- ni- ter_ ma- nens D⟨o- mi⟩- ne fi- li_ u- ni- g⟨e- ni- te⟩ ⟨hie- su_ chris-te Do- mi- ne_ de- us Ag- nus_ de- i Fi- li- us_ pa-tris Qui tol- lis pec- ca- ta_ mun-di mi- se- re_ no- bis Qui tol- lis pec- ca- ta_ mun- di Sus- ci- pe⟩ de- p⟨re⟩-c⟨a- ti- o- nem⟩_ n⟨os-t⟩ram [5] Chris- te de_ pa- tre lu- men_ de_ lu- ce sum- me de_ sum-mo nos- tra_ fa- ve-to Qui_ se- d⟨es⟩ ⟨ad dex- te- ram_ pa-tris Mi- se- re_ no- bis Quo- ni- am tu_ so- lus sanc- tus⟩ tu_ so- l⟨us⟩_ d⟨o- mi- nus⟩ [6] Qui mun- do_ vic- to hos- tem_ que sub- iec-to pa- tris vir- tu- te_ co- o- pe_ ran- te re- demp- tor et_ tu- tor splen- dens_ glo- ri- o- sæ Tu so- lus al- t⟨is- si- mus⟩ ⟨Hie- su_ chris- te Cum_ sanc- to_ spi- ri- tu in glo- ri- a_ de- i_ pa-tris⟩ a- m⟨en⟩

Gloria in excelsis 21
Bosse 2 (var.); Milan IV
Hinc laudando patrem

Rc 1741

Glo- ri- a＿ in ex- cel- sis＿ d⟨e⟩-o Et in ter- ra pax ho- mi- ni- bus bo- ne vo- lun- t⟨a- tis⟩

[1] Hinc＿ lau- dan- do pa- trem hie- su＿ cum＿ neu- ma- te di- vo Lau- d⟨a- mus te⟩

[2] Cunc-ta cre- ans＿ ver- bo sal- vans- que et quod be- ne- di- cunt Be- n⟨e- di- ci- mus te⟩

[3] Quem ma- re ter- ra＿ po- lus sub＿ le- ge fa- ten- tur et o- rant

A- do- r⟨a- mus＿ te⟩ [4] Cel- sa ho- mi- nem i- ma de- um pi- um＿ a- man- do tre- men- do- que＿ius-tum

Glo- r⟨i- fi- ca- mus te⟩＿ [5] Gra- ci- a＿ lex＿ no- bis vir- tus＿

sa- pi- en- ti- a＿ pa- tris Gra- ⟨ti- a⟩s a- g⟨i- mus⟩ ⟨ti- bi prop- ter＿

mag- nam glo- ri- am＿ tu- am Do- mi- ne＿ de- us rex cae- les- tis Deus＿ pa- ter om- ni- po-tens

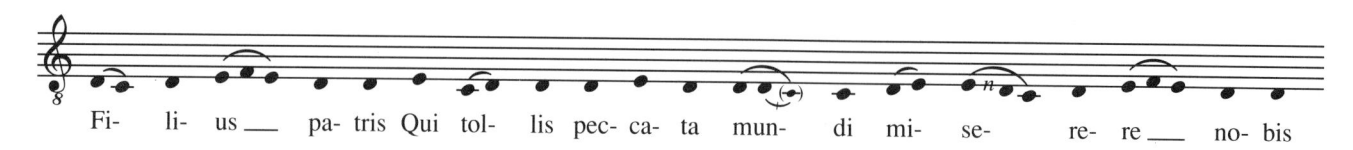

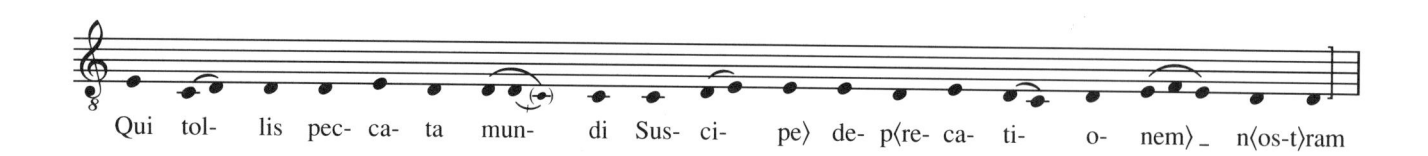

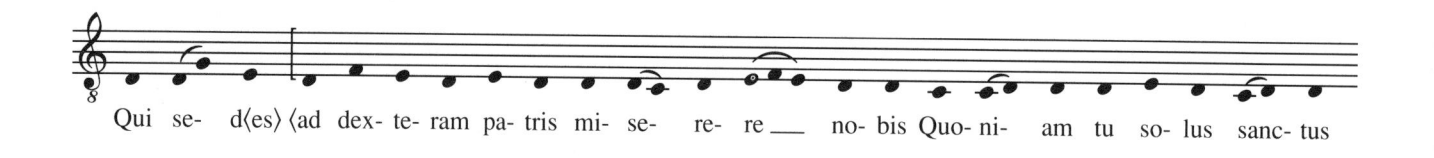

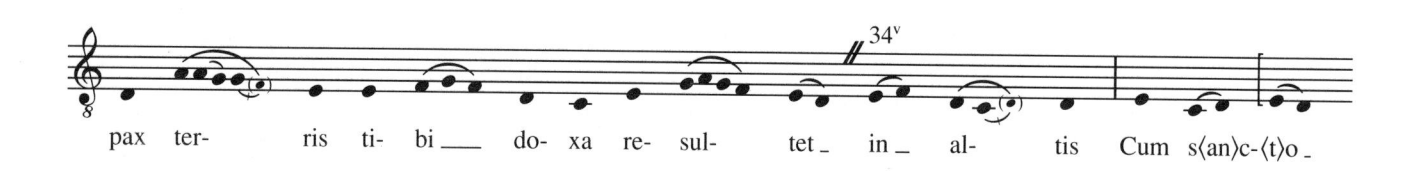

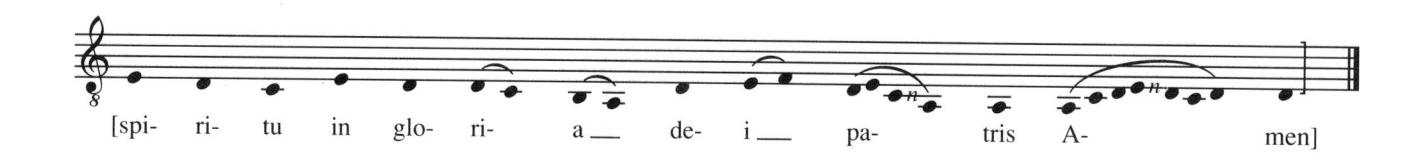

Do- mi- ne fi- li u- ni- ge- ni- te Hie- su chris- te Do- mi- ne de- us Ag- nus de- i

Fi- li- us pa- tris Qui tol- lis pec- ca- ta mun- di mi- se- re- re no- bis

Qui tol- lis pec- ca- ta mun- di Sus- ci- pe⟩ de- p⟨re- ca- ti- o- nem⟩ n⟨os-t⟩ram

[6] Es- to be- nig- ne pi- us mi- se- ris si- ne cri- mi- ne so- lus

Qui se- d⟨es⟩ ⟨ad dex- te- ram pa- tris mi- se- re no- bis Quo- ni- am tu so- lus sanc- tus

Tu so- lus do- mi- nus Tu so- lus al- tis- si- mus⟩ hie- su chris- te [7] Sit tu- a

paz ter- ris ti- bi do- xa re- sul- tet in al- tis Cum s⟨an⟩c-⟨t⟩o

[spi- ri- tu in glo- ri- a de- i pa- tris A- men]

Sanctus 1
Thannabaur 154; Vatican I
Deus fortis

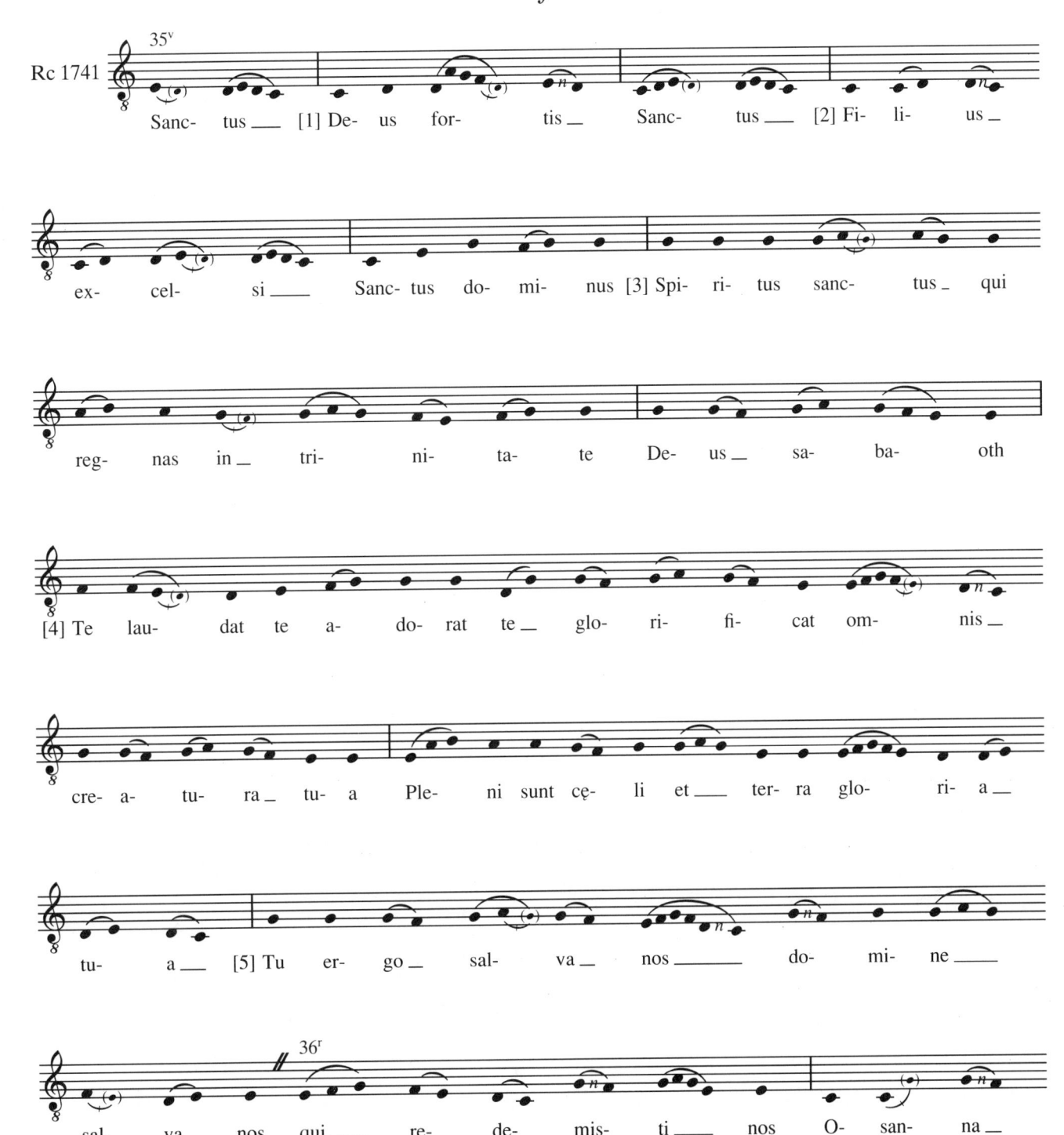

ti- bi om- nis tu- a sanc- ta proclamat ęc- cle- si- a

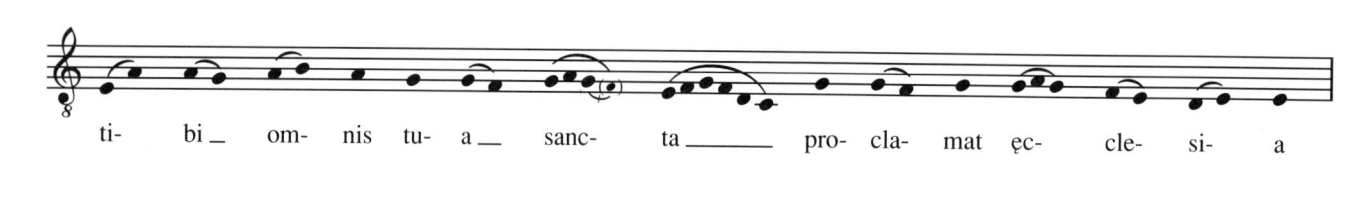

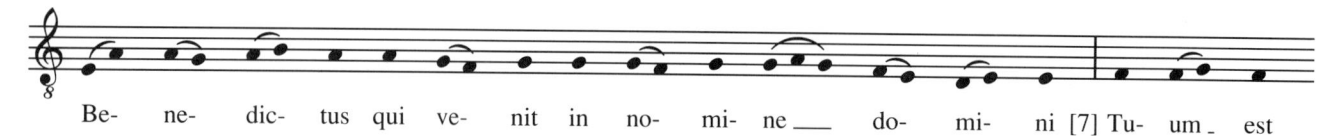

Be- ne- dic- tus qui ve- nit in no- mi- ne do- mi- ni [7] Tu- um est

do- mi- ne reg- num tu- a po- tes- tas ti- bi ho- nor

et im- pe- ri- um per cunc- ta se- cu- la O- san-

-na in ex- cel- sis

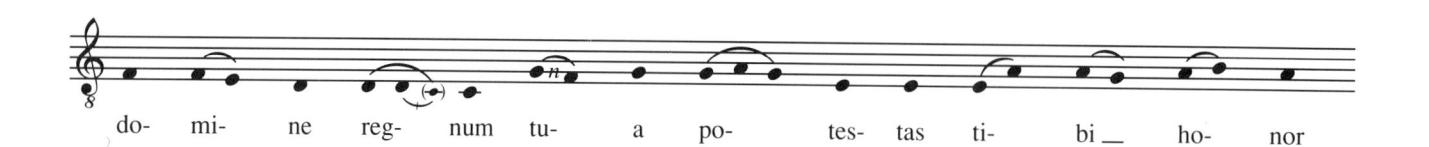

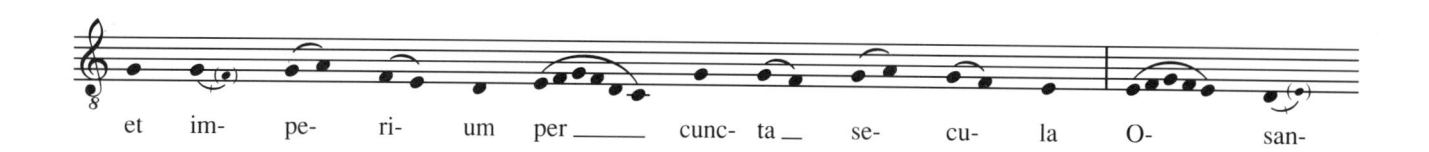

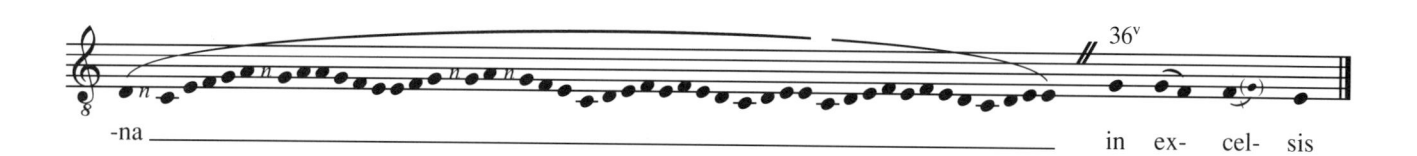

Sanctus 2
Thannabaur 154; Vatican I
Pater ingenitus

Rn 1343

Sanc- tus [1] pa- ter in- ge- ni- tus Sanc- tus [2] Or- bis re- demp- tor

fi- li- us Sanc- tus do- mi- nus [3] Vi- vi- fi- cans spi- ri- tus

pol- lens in tri- ni- ta- te Deus sa- ba- oth Ple- ni sunt cæ- li et ter- ra

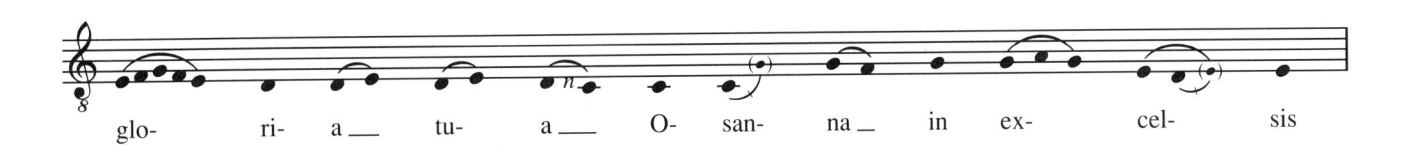

gloria tua O-sanna in excelsis

[4] Cuius in laude voces dabant pueri regem christum
conlaudantes in altissimis Benedictus qui
venit in nomine domini O-sanna in excelsis

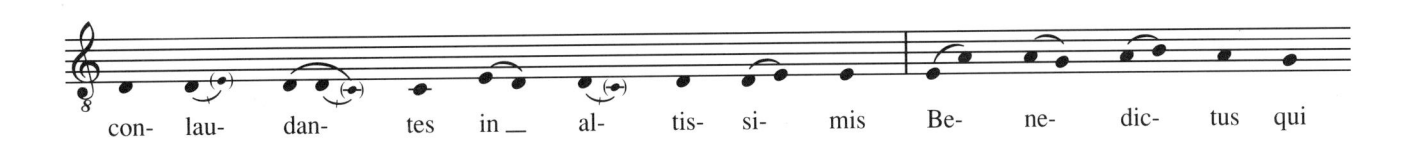

Sanctus 3
Thannabaur 216 (var.)
Pater lumen aeternum

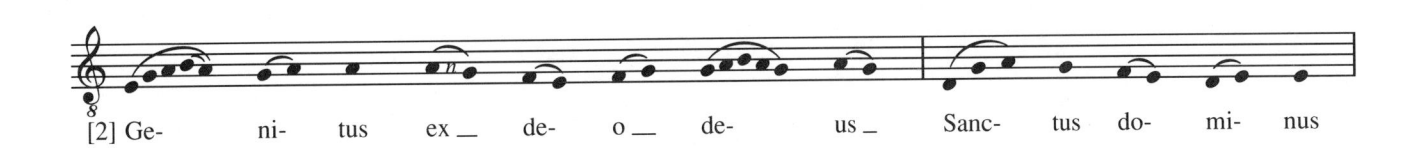

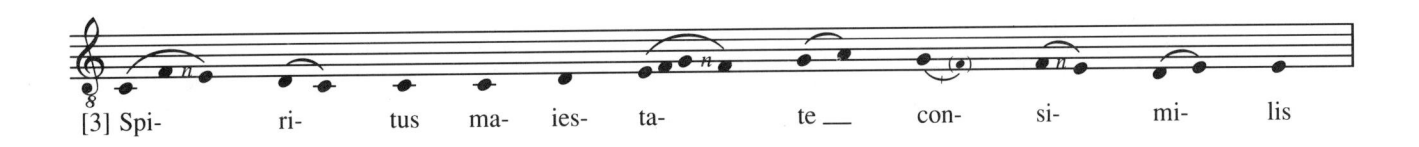

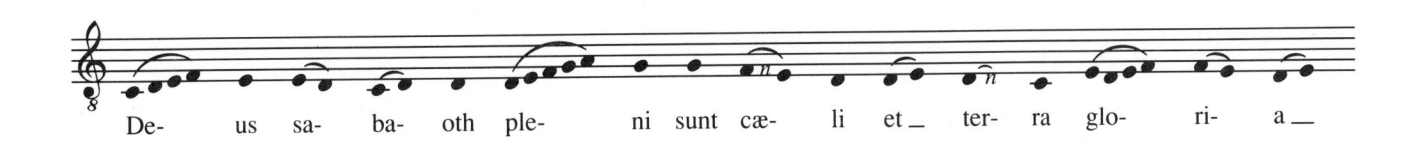

Rn 1343 Sanctus [1] Pater lumen æternum Sanctus

[2] Genitus ex deo deus Sanctus dominus

[3] Spiritus maiestate consimilis

Deus sabaoth pleni sunt cæli et terra gloria

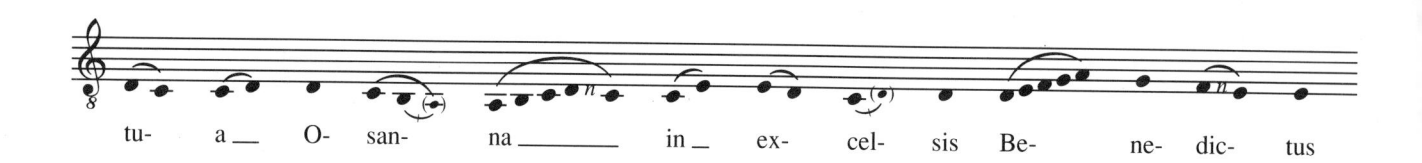

Sanctus 4
Thannabaur 154; Vatican I
Deus pater ingenite

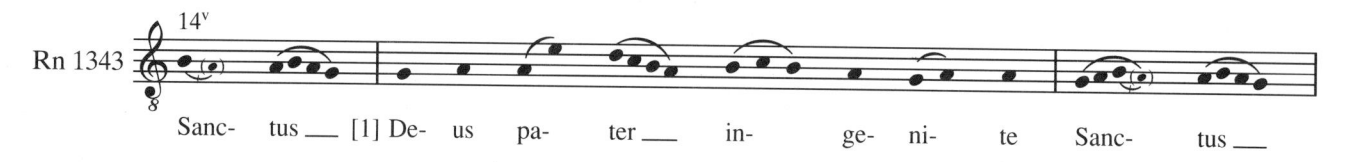

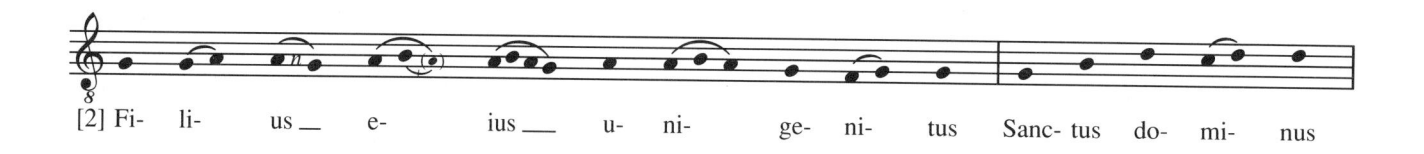

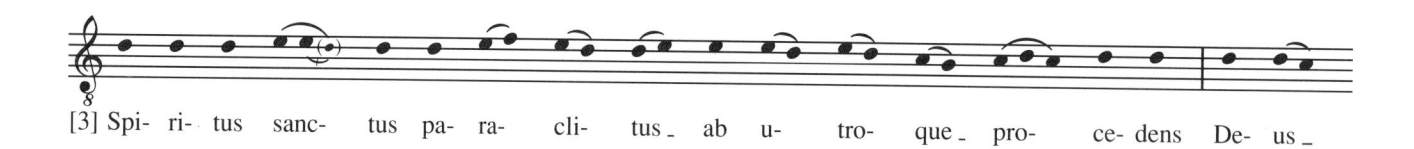

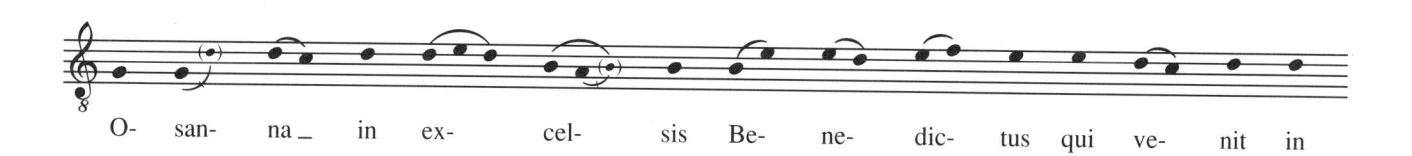

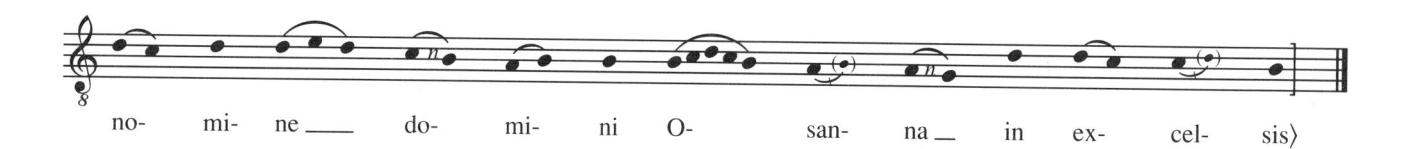

Rn 1343

Sanc- tus __ [1] De- us pa- ter __ in- ge- ni- te Sanc- tus __

[2] Fi- li- us __ e- ius __ u- ni- ge- ni- tus Sanc- tus do- mi- nus

[3] Spi- ri- tus sanc- tus pa- ra- cli- tus ab u- tro- que pro- ce- dens De- us __

sa- ba- oth ⟨Ple- ni sunt cæ- li et __ ter- ra glo- ri- a __ tu- a __

O- san- na __ in ex- cel- sis Be- ne- dic- tus qui ve- nit in

no- mi- ne __ do- mi- ni O- san- na in ex- cel- sis⟩

Sanctus 5
Thannabaur 223; Vatican XV
Mundi fabricator

Bu 2824

Sanc- tus [1] Mun- di fa- bri- ca- tor et rec- tor Sanc- tus

[2] U- ni- ce ip- si- us pa- tris et e- qua- lis

do- mi- nus Sanc- tus do- mi- nus de- us sa- ba- oth [3] Mun- di qui

cul- pas al- mis flam- mis mi- re de- ter- gis

Ple- ni sunt cæ- li et ter- ra glo- ri- a tu- a O- san- na

in ex- cel- sis [4] No- bis nunc fa- mu- lis mi- se- re- re

tu- is cu- ius in lau- de pu- e- ro- rum tur- ba de- vo- te

promp- sit Be- ne- dic- tus qui ve- nit in no- mi- ne

do- mi- ni O- san- na in ex- cel- sis

Sanctus 6
Thannabaur 74
Admirabilis splendor

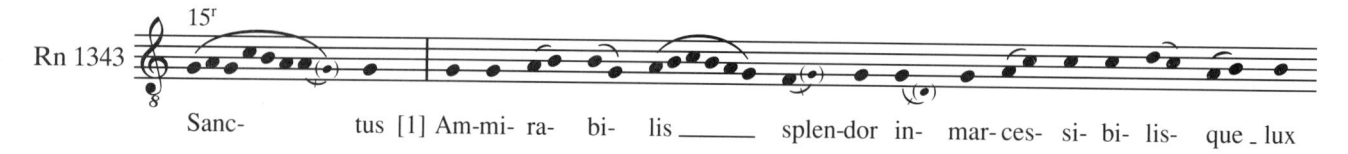

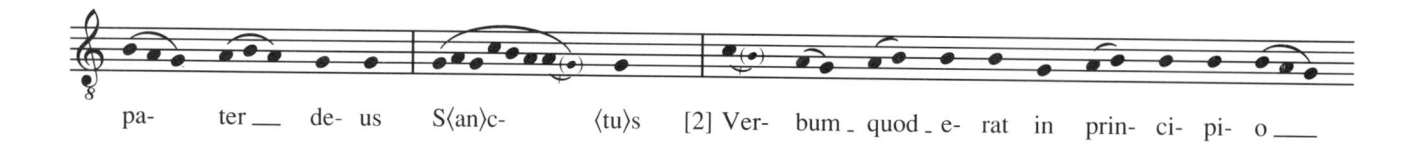

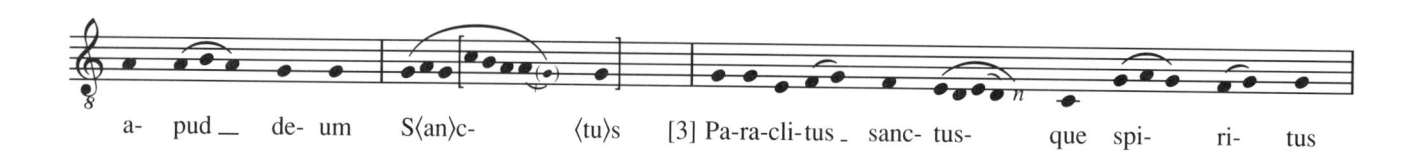

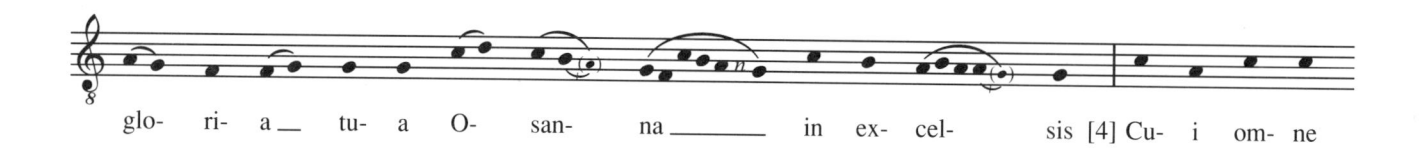

Sanctus 7

Thannabaur 63

Quem cherubim

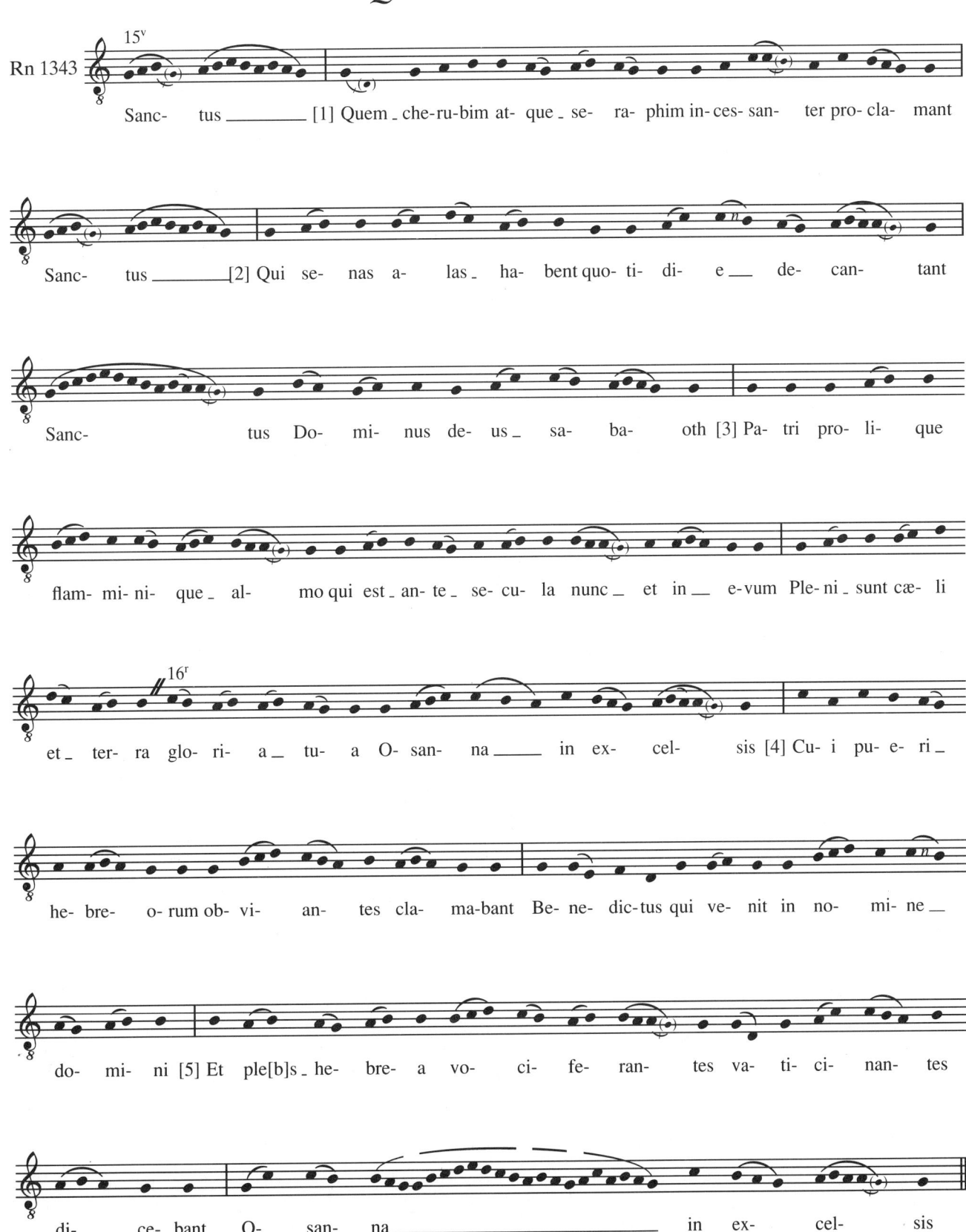

Sanc- tus [1] Quem che-ru-bim at-que se-ra-phim in-ces-san-ter pro-cla-mant

Sanc- tus [2] Qui se-nas a-las habent quo-ti-di-e de-can-tant

Sanc- tus Do-mi-nus de-us sa-ba-oth [3] Pa-tri pro-li-que

flam-mi-ni-que al-mo qui est an-te se-cu-la nunc et in e-vum Ple-ni sunt cæ-li

et ter-ra glo-ri-a tu-a O-san-na in ex-cel-sis [4] Cu-i pu-e-ri

he-bre-o-rum ob-vi-an-tes cla-mabant Be-ne-dic-tus qui ve-nit in no-mi-ne

do-mi-ni [5] Et ple[b]s he-bre-a vo-ci-fe-ran-tes va-ti-ci-nan-tes

di-ce-bant O-san-na in ex-cel-sis

Sanctus 8
Thannabaur 60

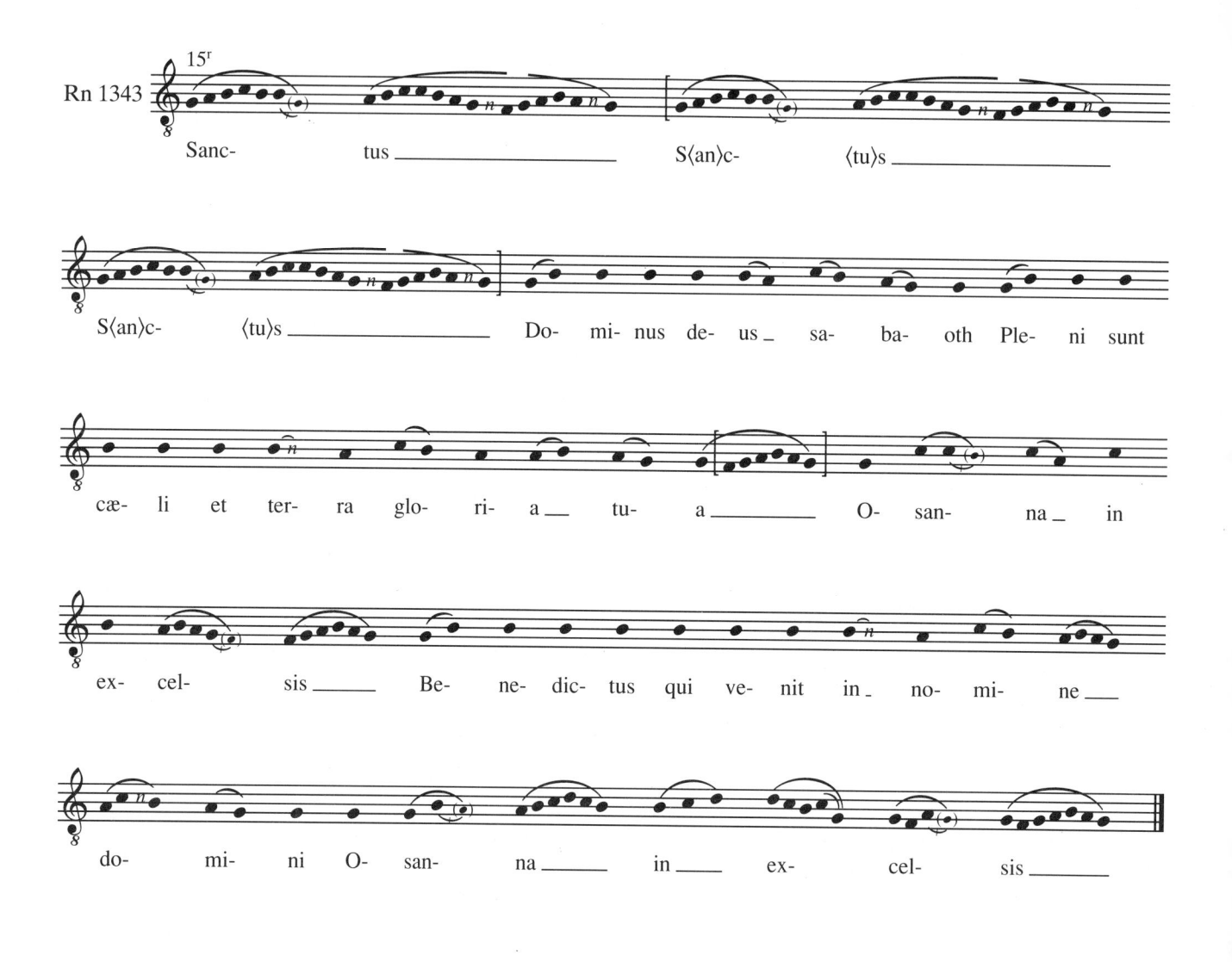

Sanctus 9
Thannabaur 111 (var.)

O- san- na _____ in ex- cel- sis

Be- ne- dic- tus qui ve- nit in no- mi- ne do- mi- ni

O- san- na _____ in ex- cel- sis

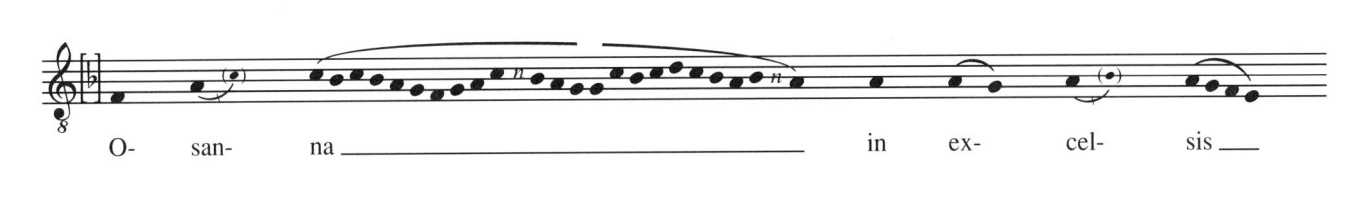

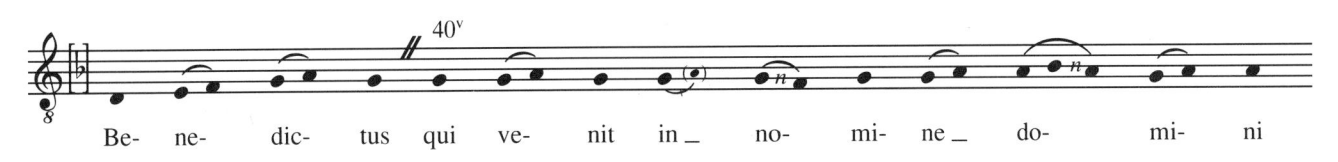

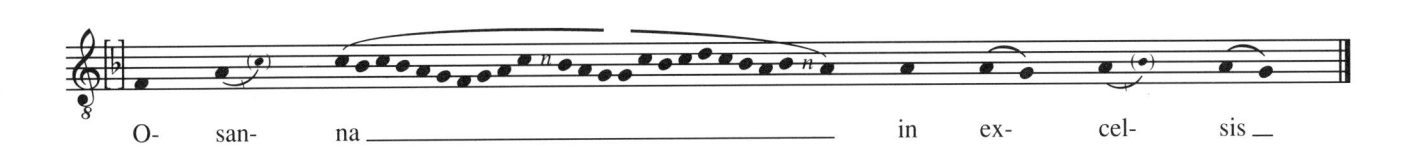

Sanctus 10
Thannabaur 9

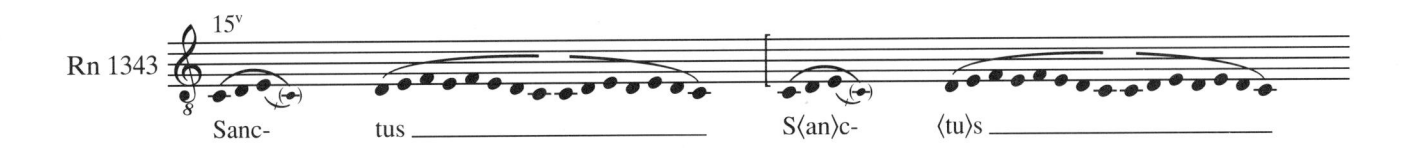

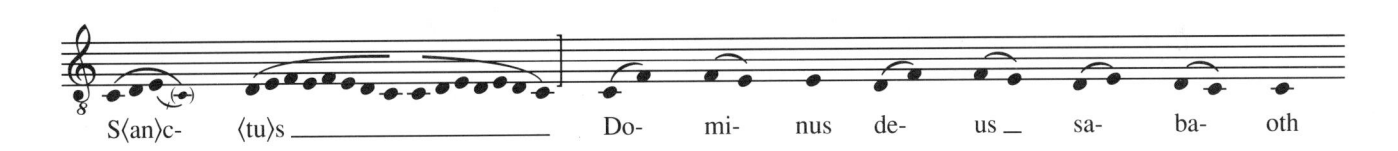

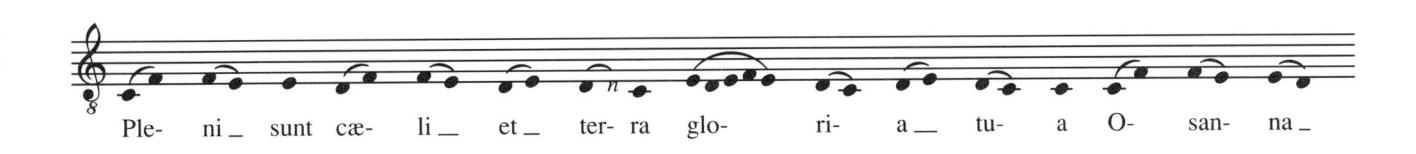

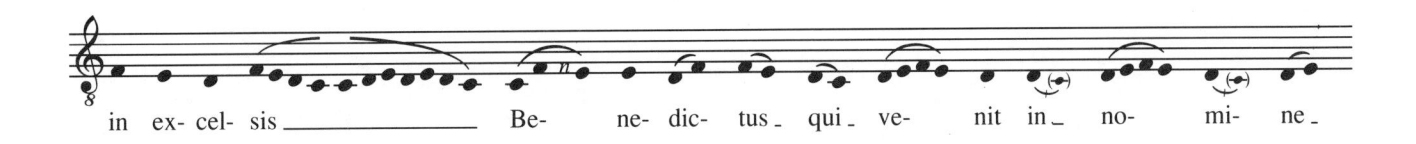

Rn 1343

Sanc- tus _____ S⟨an⟩c- ⟨tu⟩s _____

S⟨an⟩c- ⟨tu⟩s _____ Do- mi- nus de- us sa- ba- oth

Ple- ni sunt cæ- li et ter- ra glo- ri- a tu- a O- san- na

in ex- cel- sis _____ Be- ne- dic- tus qui ve- nit in no- mi- ne

do- mi- ni O- san- na in ex- cel- sis

Sanctus 11
Thannabaur 10

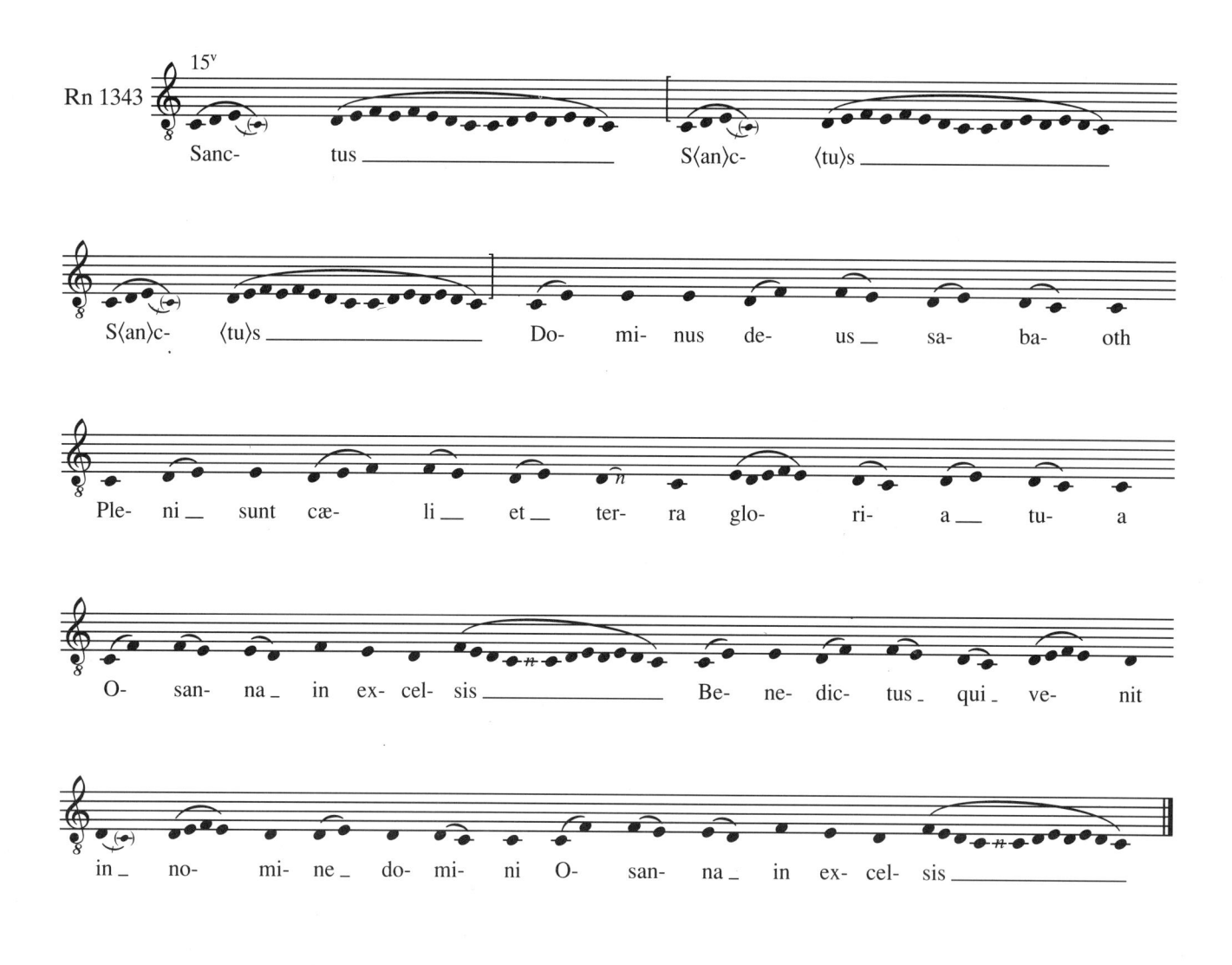

Rn 1343 — Sanc- tus S⟨an⟩c- ⟨tu⟩s S⟨an⟩c- ⟨tu⟩s Do- mi- nus de- us sa- ba- oth Ple- ni sunt cæ- li et terra glo- ri- a tu- a O- san- na in ex- cel- sis Be- ne- dic- tus qui ve- nit in no- mi- ne do- mi- ni O- san- na in ex- cel- sis

Sanctus 12
Thannabaur 32; Vatican XVII

Rn 1343 — Sanc- tus Sanc- tus Sanc- tus Do- mi- nus de- us sa- ba- oth Ple- ni sunt cæ- li et ter- ra glo- ri- a tu- a

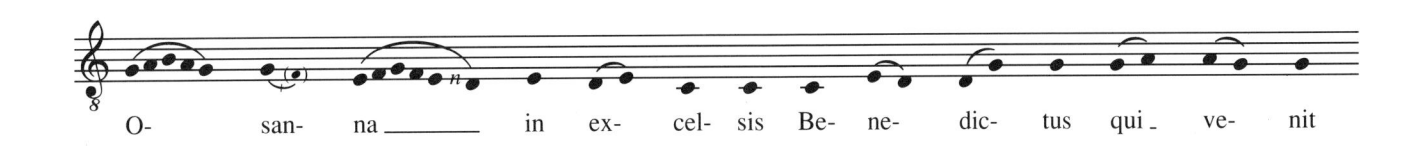

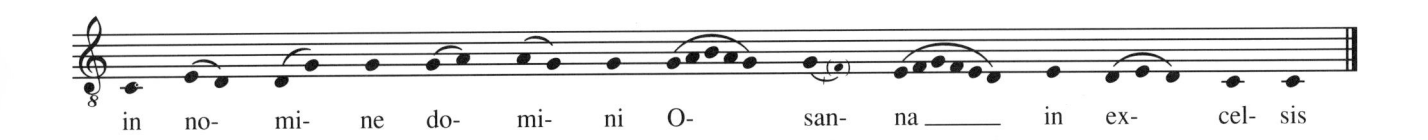

Sanctus 13a
Thannabaur 57

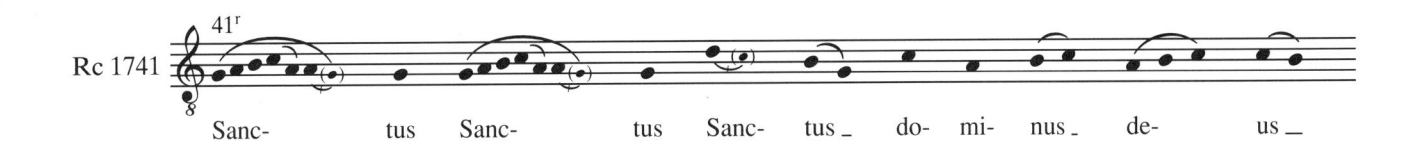

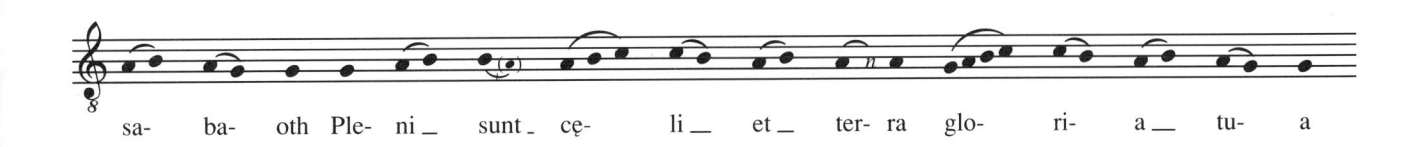

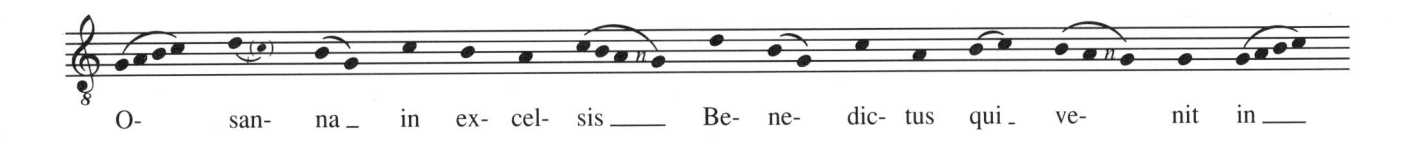

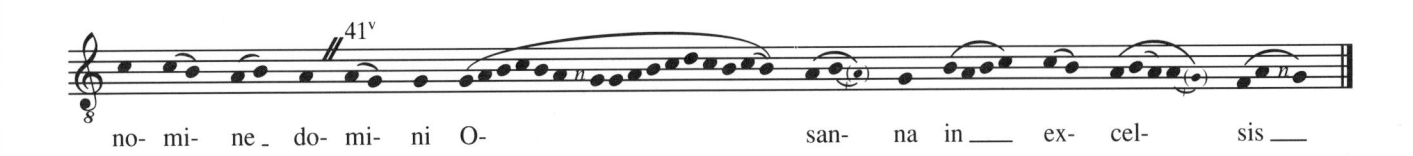

Rc 1741

Sanctus 13b
Thannabaur 57

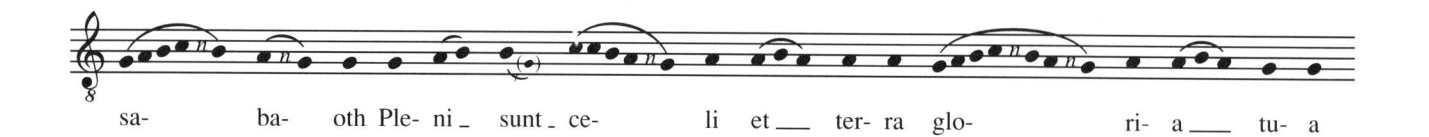

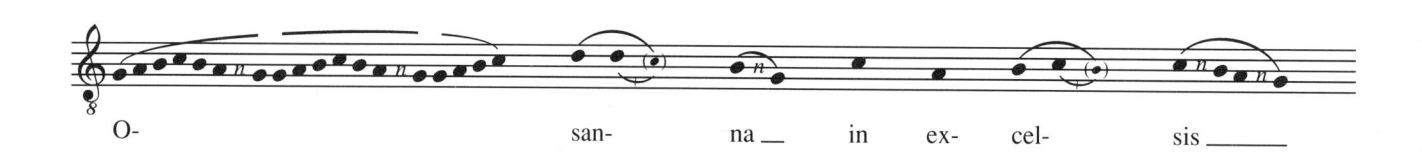

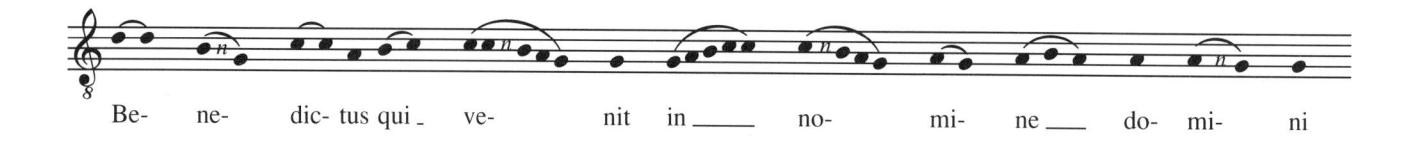

Agnus Dei 1

Schildbach 226; Vatican II

Qui sedes ad dexteram patris

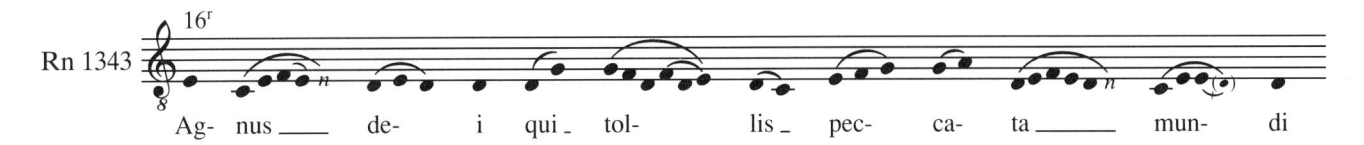

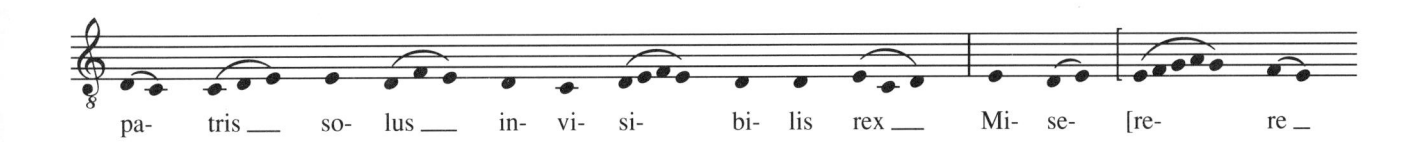

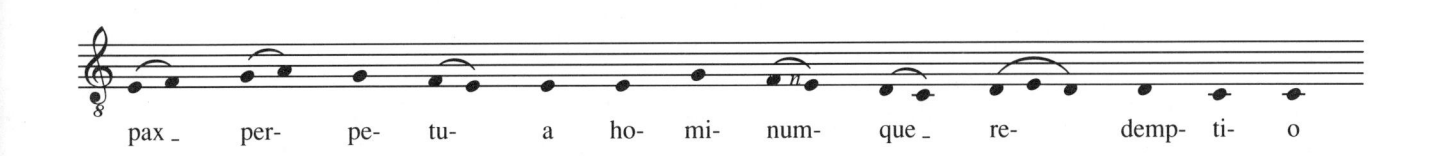

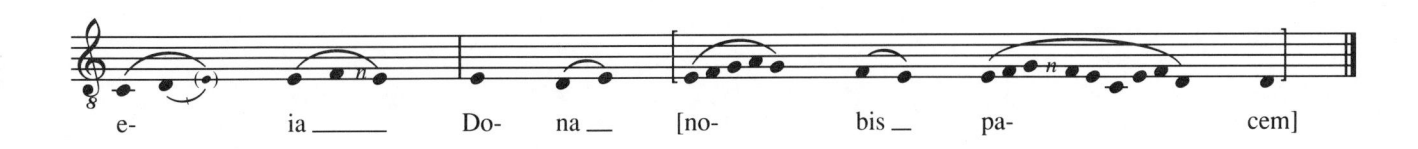

Agnus Dei 2
Schildbach 78
Omnipotens aeterna Dei

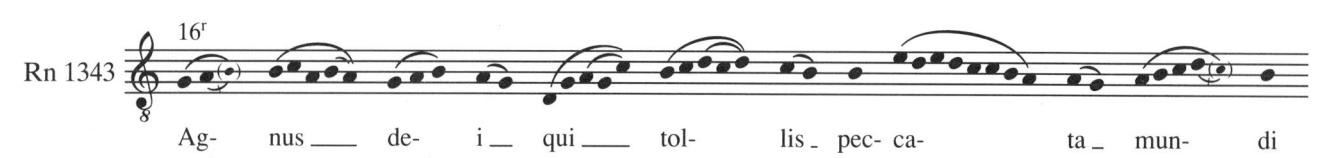

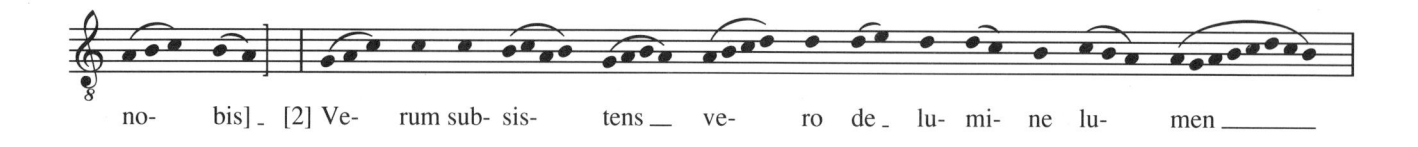

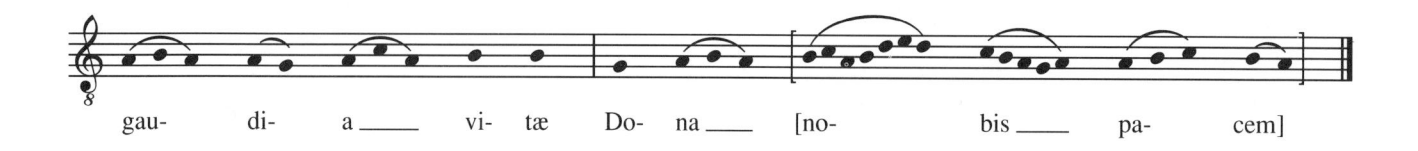

Ag- nus de- i qui tol- lis pec- ca- ta mun- di

Mi- se- re- re no- bis [1] Om- ni- po- tens æ- ter- na de- i

sa- pi- en- ti- a chris- te [M]i- se- re- [re

no- bis] [2] Ve- rum sub- sis- tens ve- ro de lu- mi- ne lu- men

Mi- se- [re- re no- bis] [3] [O]p- ti- ma per- pe- tu- e con- ce- dens

gau- di- a vi- tæ Do- na [no- bis pa- cem]

Agnus Dei 3
Schildbach 209 (var. 2)
Tu Deus et dominus

Rn 1343

Ag-nus de- i qui tol- lis pec- ca- ta mun- di Mi- se- re- re no- bis [1] Tu de- us et do- mi- nus cæ- lo- rum com-pos et or- bis chris- te Mi- se- [re- re no- bis] [2] In se- de e- the- re- a qui reg- nas cum pa- tre de- us Do- na [no- bis pa- cem]

Agnus Dei 4
Schildbach 236
Suscipe deprecationem . . . Dei patris

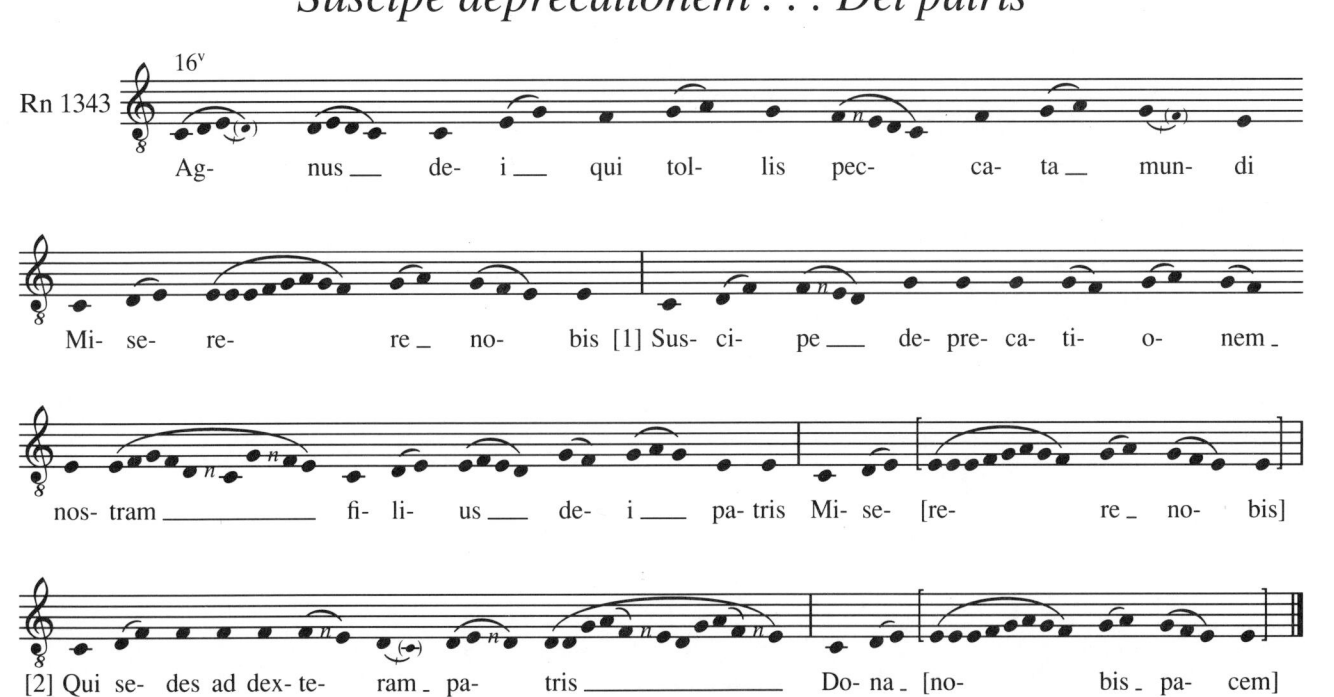

Rn 1343

Ag- nus de- i qui tol- lis pec- ca- ta mun- di Mi- se- re- no- bis [1] Sus- ci- pe de- pre- ca- ti- o- nem nos- tram fi- li- us de- i pa- tris Mi- se- [re- re no- bis] [2] Qui se- des ad dex- te- ram pa- tris Do- na [no- bis pa- cem]

Agnus Dei 5
Schildbach 236 (var. 3)
Ad dextram patris

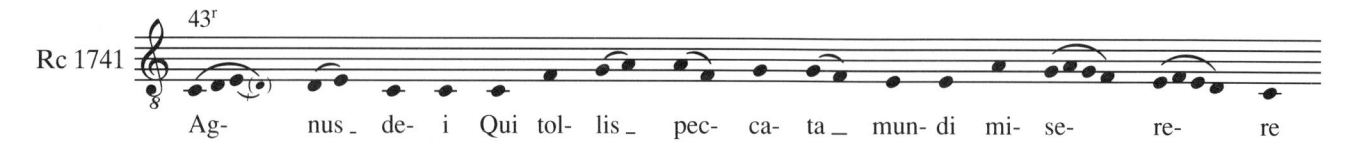

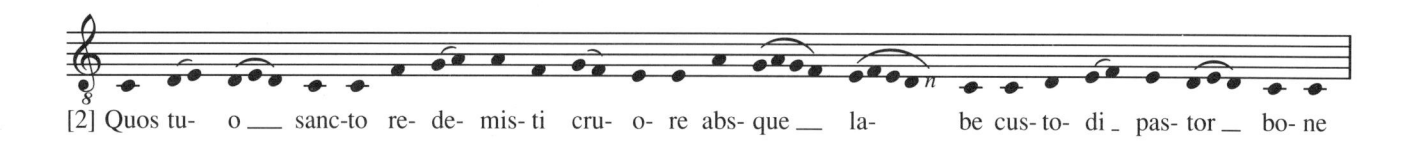

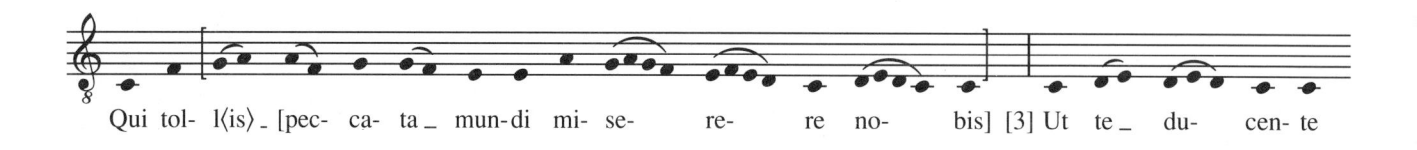

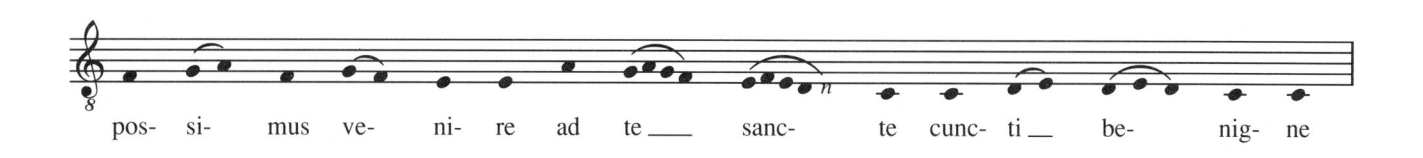

Ag- nus de- i Qui tol- lis pec- ca- ta mun- di mi- se- re- re no- bis [1] Ad dex- tram pa- tris re- si- des qui sem-per sal- va et par- ce tu- is al- me Qui tol- l⟨is⟩ [pec- ca- ta mun- di mi- se- re- re no- bis] [2] Quos tu- o sanc-to re- de- mis- ti cru- o- re abs- que la- be cus- to- di pas- tor bo- ne Qui tol- l⟨is⟩ [pec- ca- ta mun- di mi- se- re- re no- bis] [3] Ut te du- cen- te pos- si- mus ve- ni- re ad te sanc- te cunc- ti be- nig- ne Qui tol- lis [pec- ca- ta mun- di do- na no- bis pa- cem]

Agnus Dei 6
Schildbach 87
Exaudi domine

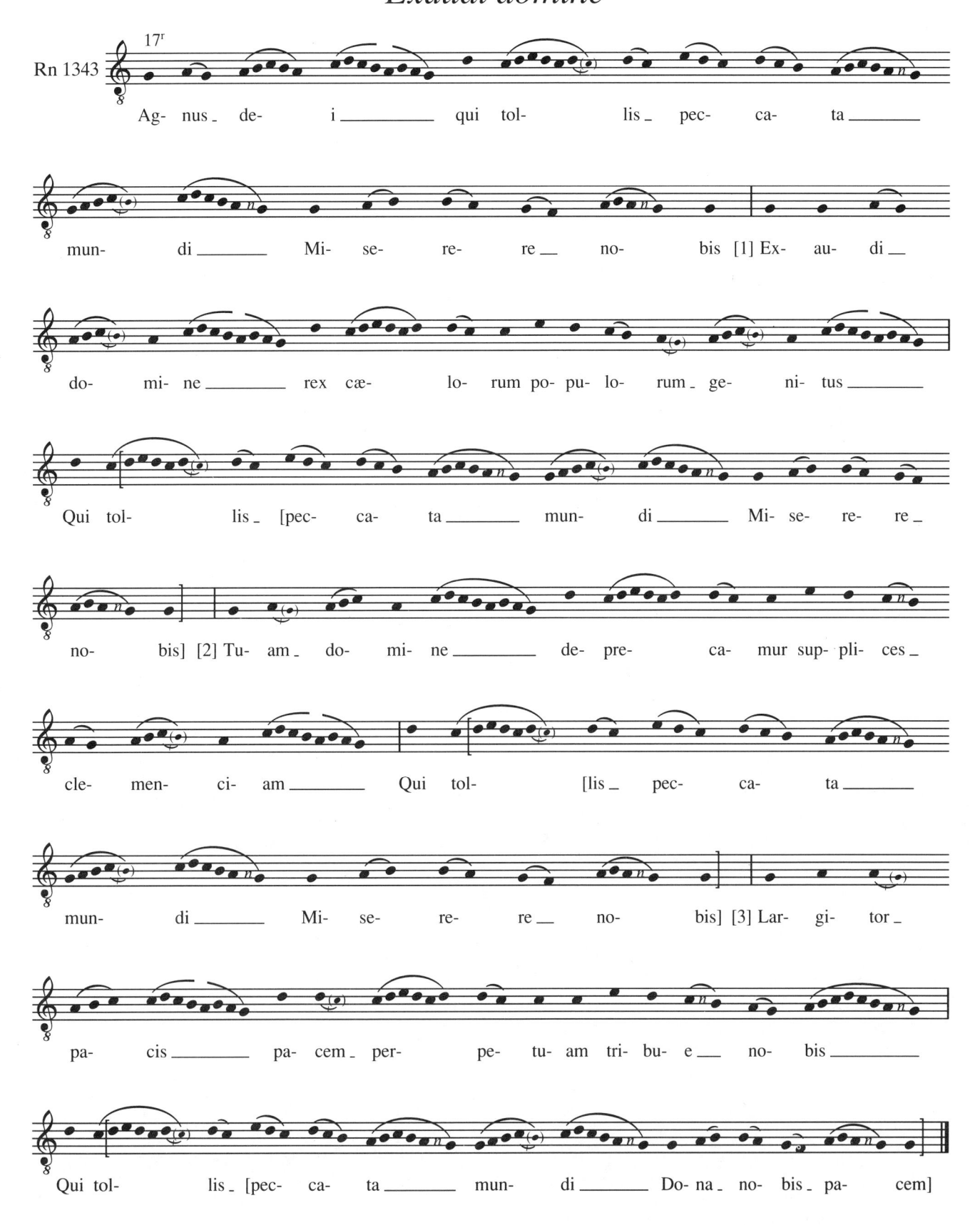

Agnus Dei 7
Schildbach 164; Vatican XVI
Suscipe deprecationem . . . Dei

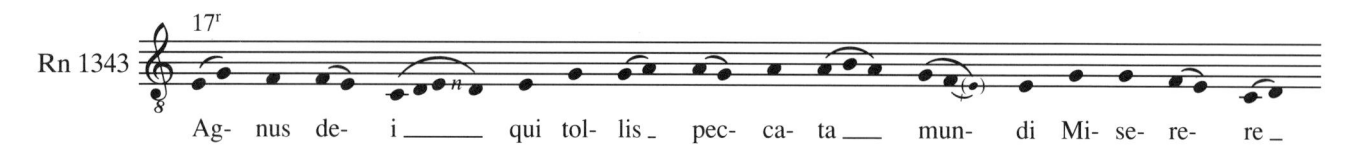

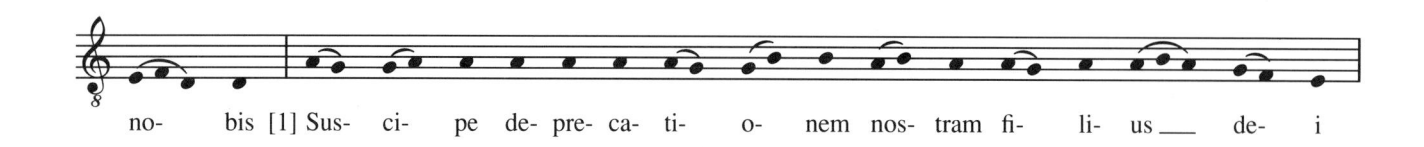

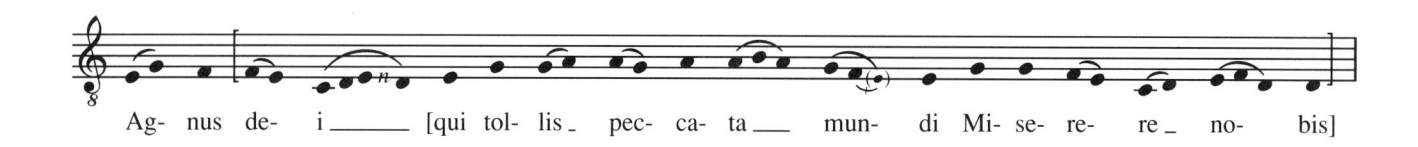

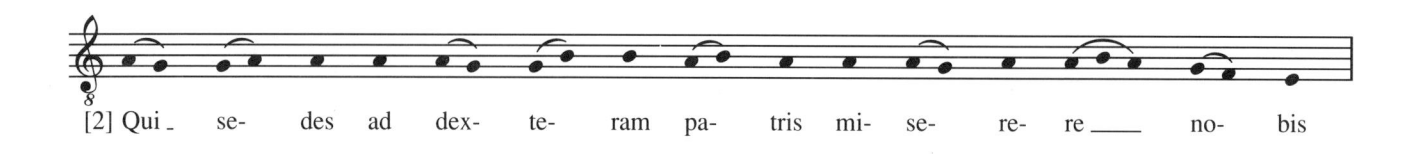

Agnus Dei 8
Schildbach 19
Agnus Dei . . . miserere nobis alleluia alleluia

Ag- nus de- i qui tol- lis pec- ca- ta mun- di Mi- se- re- re no- bis al- le- lu- ia al- le- lu- ia

Agnus Dei 9
Schildbach 81
Salus et vita

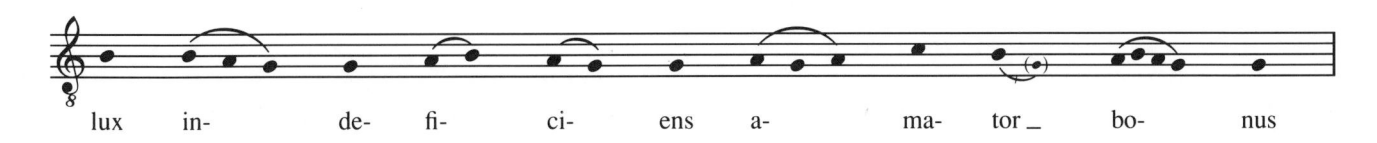

Ag- nus de- i qui tol- lis pec- ca- ta mun- di mi- se- re- re no- bis

[1] Sa- lus et vi- ta pax per- pe- tu- a lux in- de- fi- ci- ens a- ma- tor bo- nus

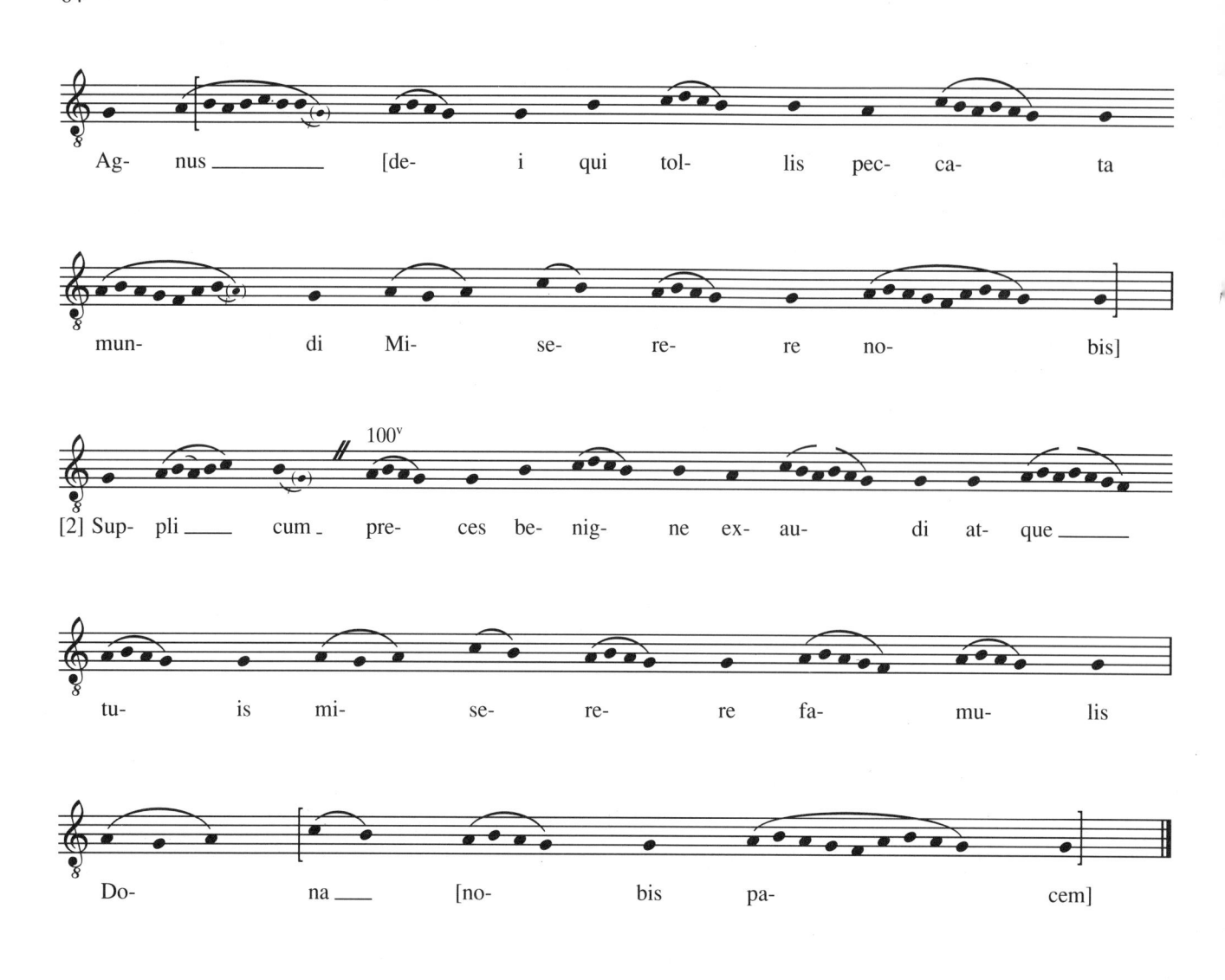

Agnus Dei 10
Schildbach 209 (var. 2)

Index of First Lines: Ordinary Tropes

The following abbreviations are used: K = Kyrie eleison; G = Gloria in excelsis; S = Sanctus; AD = Agnus Dei. Verse numbers are given in brackets.

Ab omni malo tu nos defende (K 6, [10])
Ablato loeto vitam perfundis (G 18, [3])
Ad caenum terrae missus genitoris (K 2, [4])
Ad dextram patris resides qui (AD 5, [1])
Adonay benedicte deus (G 16, [2])
Adonay domine deus iudex (K 4, [7])
Aequalis patri seu nato (K 2, [7])
Aeterni sapientia patris (G 16, [9])
Alleluia alleluia (AD 8)
Alme mundi hodie ad caelos (G 15, [1])
Alme mundi hodie de morte (G 14, [1])
Ammirabilis splendor inmarcessibilisque (S 6, [1])
Angelicis sorte coniunctus iste (G 19, [8])
Angelicus tibi astat clarissimus (G 19, [3])
Atque potentissimus (G 13, [12])
Auctor caelorum deus aeterne (K 6, [9])
Azima sincera quaesumus largire (G 13, [9])
Bonum omne pariter cuncta per (G 19, [7])
Caelestium terrestrium et infernorum (G 11, [9])
Caelorum sistis factor (G 18, [6])
Canentum ante te precibus annue (K 1, [5])
Cantemus tibi laudes de pectore (G 19, [4])
Carnis amictum teque subisse (G 12, [7])
Celsa hominem ima deum (G 21, [4])
Christe de patrem lumen (G 20, [5])
Christe deiforma humanae (K 7, [6])
Christe lux oriens per quem (K 7, [5])
Christe qui perfecta es (K 7, [4])
Christo melos et odas clamantes (K 3, [4])
Christus surrexit dulcibus hymnis (G 13, [2])
Cives superni hodie suam (G 13, [1])
Clamat incessanter nunc quoque (K 1, [7])
Complacuit tibimet mortem (G 18, [2])
Conditor generis humani (G 12, [8])
Consolator pie flamen (K 5, [7])
Consolator qui es alme (K 6, [7])
Cui magus offert poplite flexo (G 12, [3])
Cui omne flecitur genu et (S 6, [4])
Cui pueri hebreorum obviantes (S 11, [4])
Cui regnum est sine fine (G 14 & 15, [8])
Cuius a sede lux benedicta (G 8, [5])
Cuius in laude voces dabant (S 2, [4])
Culpas gestorum solvens (G 9, [6])

Cuncta creans verbo salvansque (G 21, [2])
Cuncta regis et cunta tenens (G 18, [12])
Cuncta tenens et cunta fovens (G 9, [8])
De nichilo iussu verbi (K 2, [2])
Deus fortis (S 1, [1])
Deus fortis et inmortalis (G 11, [7])
Deus pater ingenite (S 4, [1])
Dicamus incessanter omnes (K 1, [11])
Dominator deus piissime (K 5, [1])
Domine deus redemptor israhel (G 11, [6])
Domine deus redemptor israhel (G 17, [5])
Doxa patri ac pariter filio (K 3, [8])
Esto benigne pius miseris (G 21, [6])
Esto principium cunctarum (G 18, [8])
Et creatura creantem plasma (G 10, [6])
Et mundi culpam mundasti (K 2, [6])
Et non est alius (G 14 & 15, [7])
Et plebs hebrea vociferantes (S 11, [5])
Exaudi domine rex caelorum (AD 6, [1])
Fac nos tuis insistere (K 3, [7])
Figens illum cruci (G 13, [3])
Filius eius unigenitus (S 4, [2])
Filius excelsi (S 1, [2])
Fons et origo lucis perpetuae (K 6, [5])
Fons origo lucis perpetuae (K 5, [2])
Genitus ex deo deus (S 3, [2])
Gloria cuius prima colorem (G 12, [4])
Glorificande et metuende deus (G 16, [4])
Glorificant agnum cives (G 9, [4])
Glorificant dominum rutilancia (G 17, [4])
Glorificant dominum rutilancia (G 19, [5])
Glorificant tement mites (G 18, [4])
Gloriosus es rex israhel (G 11, [5])
Gracia lex nobis virtus (G 21, [5])
Gracia sanctorum splendor decus (G 9, [5])
Hiesu christe altissime quem (G 10, [8])
Hinc laudando patrem hiesu (G 21, [1])
Hoc nomen est tibi in fine (G 14 & 15, [6])
Humano generi peccati pondere (K 2, [3])
Hymnum canentes hodie quem terris (G 8, [2])
Hymnum maiestati gracias (G 10, [7])
Iam liberati mortis a vinculo (G 13, [5])
In cuius nutu constat (K 4, [3])
In excelsis deo magna (K 1, [9])
In sede etherea qui regnas (AD 3, [2])
In sede maiestatis tuae (G 11, [3])
Incarnate tu quoque (K 5, [4])

Insons omnipotens nostris (G 9, [7])
Kanamus cuncti laudes hymnificas (K 3, [1])
Kyrrie expurgator scelerum (K 7, [9])
Kyrrie luminis fons (K 7, [2])
Kyrrie qui nos tuae imaginis (K 7, [3])
Kyrrie rex genitor ingenite (K 7, [1])
Kyrrie spiritus vivifice (K 7, [7])
Kyrrie utriusque donum (K 7, [8])
Largitor pacis pacem perpetuam (AD 6, [3])
Laudat in excelsis caelum (G 17, [1])
Laudibus cuius astra matutina (G 10, [3])
Laus tua deus resonet (G 11, [1])
Lux de luce deus (K 5, [5])
Lux de luce deus de deo (K 6, [8])
Lux et origo lucis (K 4, [1])
Lux indeficiens pax perpetua (AD 1, [3])
Miserere fili dei vivi (K 1, [8])
Misericors et clemens (G 13, [10])
Misertus esto nostri qui (G 16, [6])
Mundi fabricator et rector (S 5, [1])
Mundi qui culpas almi flammis (S 5, [3])
Natus est nobis hodie salvator (G 8, [3])
Nobis in terris miserere (G 16, [8])
Nobis nunc famulis miserere (S 5, [4])
Non minus clementiae quam (G 20, [4])
Nos nostrasque preces caelo (G 9, [9])
O adoranda et beata trinitas deus (G 16, [3])
O agie infiniteque iudex noster (K 6, [4])
O bone rex qui super (K 1, [3])
O consolator dolentis animae (K 7, [11])
O decus et virtus lausque (G 19, [2])
O gloria sanctorum lausque (G 19, [1])
O ineffabilis rex et ammirabilis (G 8, [7])
O laudabilis rex domine deus (G 16, [1])
O mundi redemptor salus (K 4, [5])
O theos agie salvans vivifice (K 1, [4])
O virtus honor dei patris (G 16, [11])
Obediunt omnia illi quae (K 3, [5])
Omnia conformans illi (K 2, [8])
Omnia quem sanctum benedicunt (G 9, [2])
Omnipotens adorande colende (G 10, [5])
Omnipotens aeterna dei sapientia (AD 2, [1])
Omnipotens genitor lumenque (K 2, [1])
Optima perpetue concedens gaudia (AD 2, [3])
Optime rector generis humani (G 13, [4])
Orbis redemptor filius (S 2, [2])
Paraclitus sanctusque spiritus (S 6, [3])
Pater ingenitus (S 2, [1])
Pater lumen aeternum (S 3, [1])
Patri prolique flammanique almo (S 11, [3])
Patris natique qui es summus (K 5, [8])
Pax salus et vita hominum (G 16, [7])
Pax sempiterna christus illuxit (G 8, [1])
Per crucem redemptis a morte (K 4, [4])
Per quem omne sacrum (G 10, [4])
Pius ac benignus serenus et severus (G 13, [11])

Poscimus ecce pater pellas (G 18, [10])
Praesta ne nobis veteris fermenti (G 13, [8])
Protege servorum clementer (G 18, [11])
Protege verum pascha celebrantes (G 13, [7])
Quaesumus propter nostras offensas (K 7, [10])
Quam ministri domini verbo (G 10, [2])
Quando regis cunctos semper (G 18, [1])
Quem cecinit iohannes (G 18, [9])
Quem cherubim atque seraphim (S 11, [1])
Quem cives caelestes sanctum (G 10, [1])
Quem laudant sol atque luna (G 14 & 15, [4])
Quem laudat chorus et benedicit (G 20, [2])
Quem mare terra polus (G 21, [3])
Quem novitate sideris actus (G 12, [1])
Quem nunc adoramus glorificantes (K 3, [3])
Quem patris ad dextram collaudant (G 9, [1])
Quem solum laus et honor decet (K 4, [9])
Quem supera caelorum atque angelica (K 3, [6])
Quem terra pontus ethera (K 3, [9])
Quem vagientem inter angusti (G 8, [4])
Qui benedicis flumina fontis (G 12, [2])
Qui caelicolas et terrigenas foedere (G 20, [1])
Qui de supernis descendere (K 6, [6])
Qui deminutos angelorum choros (G 13, [6])
Qui es verbum patris (K 4, [6])
Qui genus humanum revocasti (G 14 & 15, [5])
Qui indueras carnem casta (K 2, [5])
Qui machinam gubernat rerum (K 4, [8])
Qui mundo victo hostemque (G 20, [6])
Qui nos redemisti proprio sanguine (G 14 & 15, [2])
Qui nos redemit proprio sanguine (K 1, [10])
Qui pius salvet semper et protegat (K 3, [2])
Qui sedes ad dexteram patris (AD 4, [2])
Qui sedes ad dexteram patris miserere nobis (AD 7, [2])
Qui sedes ad dexteram patris solus (AD 1, [1])
Qui senas alas habent (S 11, [2])
Qui solus potens miserere (K 4, [2])
Qui super astra sedes (G 17, [6])
Qui venisti hiesu christe et precioso (G 10, [9])
Qui venisti propter nos (G 11, [2])
Quia tu nos redimeras cum finem (G 20, [3])
Quos tuo sancto redemisti cruore (AD 5, [2])
Regnum tuum solidum permanebit indivisum (G 8, [8]; G 11, [9]; G 17, [7])
Regnum tuum solidum permanebit ineffabile (G 12, [9])
Regnum tuum solidum per te christe (G 18, [13])
Rex angelorum atque archangelorum deus (G 14 & 15, [3])
Rex magne domine quem sancti (K 6, [1])
Rex regum gaudium angelorum deus (AD 1, [2])
Rex s[a]eculorum domine hiesu (G 16, [5])
Salus et vita pax perpetua (AD 9, [1])
Salus vita via veritas (K 5, [6])
Sceptrum regni nobilem lumen aeterne (G 16, [12])

Servos tuos audi (K 6, [11])
Sine fine regnans nos guberna (K 5, [9])
Sit tua pax terris tibi (G 21, [7])
Spiritus maiestate consimilis (S 3, [3])
Spiritus sanctus paraclitus (S 4, [3])
Spiritus sanctus qui regnas (S 1, [3])
Supplicum preces benigne exaudi (AD 9, [2])
Suscipe deprecationem nostram filius (AD 4, [1])
Suscipe deprecationem nostram filius (AD 7, [1])
Te benedicit ovans angelorum (G 17, [2])
Te christe rex supplices (K 1, [1])
Te decet laus cum tripudio (K 1, [2])
Te deitatis nomine signant (G 12, [6])
Te fore verum aurea clamant (G 12, [5])
Te laudat te adorat (S 1, [4])
Te veneranter adorat cunta (G 17, [3])
Tellus atque polus mare (G 9, [3])
Temet devota plebs implorat (K 1, [6])
Tibi laus imperium salus (G 19, [9])
Tibi omnes angeli et archangeli (S 1, [6])

Trinus personis deus maiestate (K 2, [9])
Tu deus et dominus caelorum compos (AD 3, [1])
Tu ergo salva nos domine (S 1, [5])
Tu lux via et spes nostra (G 16, [10])
Tu nobis aperis caelestia (G 18, [5])
Tu rector mitis per s[a]ecula (G 18, [7])
Tuam domine deprecamur supplices (AD 6, [2])
Tuum est domine regnum tua potestas (S 1, [7])
Ultro mortali hodie indutus (G 8, [6])
Unice ipsius patris et aequalis (S 5, [2])
Ut te ducente possimus venire (AD 5, [3])
Veneranda trinitas (G 11, [4])
Verbi tui pater ingenite (K 5, [3])
Verbum quod erat in principio (S 6, [2])
Verum subsistens vero de lumine (AD 2, [2])
Vita salus bonitas karitas (G 19, [6])
Vivificandus est deus homo (K 6, [3])
Vivificans spiritus pollens (S 2, [3])
Voces nostras tu nobis (K 6, [2])

5474